OECD Trade Poli

Looking beyond Tariffs

THE ROLE OF NON-TARIFF BARRIERS IN WORLD TRADE

250601

**Library Commons
Georgian College
One Georgian Drive
Barrie, ON
L4M 3X9**

ORGANISATION FOR ECONOMIC CO-OPERATION AND DEVELOPMENT

ORGANISATION FOR ECONOMIC CO-OPERATION AND DEVELOPMENT

The OECD is a unique forum where the governments of 30 democracies work together to address the economic, social and environmental challenges of globalisation. The OECD is also at the forefront of efforts to understand and to help governments respond to new developments and concerns, such as corporate governance, the information economy and the challenges of an ageing population. The Organisation provides a setting where governments can compare policy experiences, seek answers to common problems, identify good practice and work to co-ordinate domestic and international policies.

The OECD member countries are: Australia, Austria, Belgium, Canada, the Czech Republic, Denmark, Finland, France, Germany, Greece, Hungary, Iceland, Ireland, Italy, Japan, Korea, Luxembourg, Mexico, the Netherlands, New Zealand, Norway, Poland, Portugal, the Slovak Republic, Spain, Sweden, Switzerland, Turkey, the United Kingdom and the United States. The Commission of the European Communities takes part in the work of the OECD.

OECD Publishing disseminates widely the results of the Organisation's statistics gathering and research on economic, social and environmental issues, as well as the conventions, guidelines and standards agreed by its members.

This work is published on the responsibility of the Secretary-General of the OECD. The opinions expressed and arguments employed herein do not necessarily reflect the official views of the Organisation or of the governments of its member countries.

Publié en français sous le titre :
Au-delà des tarifs
LE RÔLE DES OBSTACLES NON TARIFAIRES DANS LE COMMERCE MONDIAL

© OECD 2005

No reproduction, copy, transmission or translation of this publication may be made without written permission. Applications should be sent to OECD Publishing: rights@oecd.org or by fax (33 1) 45 24 13 91. Permission to photocopy a portion of this work should be addressed to the Centre français d'exploitation du droit de copie, 20, rue des Grands-Augustins, 75006 Paris, France (contact@cfcopies.com).

Foreword

Trade negotiations taking place within the Doha Development Agenda (DDA) of the World Trade Organisation (WTO) and in various regional or bilateral forums are presenting governments worldwide with new opportunities to increase consumption and welfare by reducing or limiting distortions of international trade.

At issue is a further reduction or removal not only of remaining import tariffs but also of non-tariff measures (NTMs) that distort international trade and from an economic viewpoint can be much more harmful than tariffs. In fact, as tariffs have been brought down substantially for trade in non-agricultural products and have become much less important, non-tariff barriers (NTBs) are receiving growing attention from traders and governments.

Assessing trends in the use of NTBs and their effect on international trade is among the most important, but analytically difficult, challenges confronting trade economists and policymakers. The reason is that the range of measures explicitly designed or inadvertently acting as obstacles to market access for goods is broad and that simply identifying the main NTMs is not a straightforward task. The availability of complete and accurate data is however is a prerequisite for effectively monitoring and making further progress in controlling the use of NTBs.

The OECD Trade Committee has traditionally played a key role in supporting multilateral trade negotiations in the GATT/WTO through rigorous analysis of issues under discussion. In 2001, WTO members embarked on a new round of multilateral trade negotiations, the so-called Doha Development Agenda. It is against the background of the DDA and the desire to support the work of the Negotiating Group on Non-Agricultural Market Access, that the Trade Committee decided to undertake a programme of research aimed at collecting and examining available data on NTBs and to see what conclusions could be drawn.

This volume draws on this programme of work with the objective of sharing the analysis and findings to date with a broader audience. The studies, presented in seven chapters, aim to expand our knowledge base by systematically compiling and reviewing available information on the use and incidence of NTBs and examining a set of specific types of measures in greater detail. They take stock of recent trade policy reforms and document issues that remain, including possible gaps in rules. The work has updated and added to existing data, for possible use by analysts and decision makers. Participation in trade negotiations typically involves reviewing national trade policies and setting negotiating goals and priorities that will create new market access opportunities abroad. It is hoped that the studies can provide background for setting an agenda of action on NTBs and help develop country positions for international negotiations.

ACKNOWLEDGEMENTS

The authors of the individual chapters of this volume are, or were at the time of writing, members of the OECD Trade Directorate. The overall project was co-ordinated by Barbara Fliess.

Many individuals and organisations provided data and other information for this project. The authors of the chapters in their individual capacity and collectively would like to particularly thank for their contributions and comments: the Andean Community Secretariat and the Ministry of Commerce of Peru (MINCETUR), the Association of Caribbean States, the European Commission (EU Card Programme for Western Balkans), the Ministry of Commerce of India, the Organization of American States (OAS), the South Centre in Geneva, the UN Conference on Trade and Development (UNCTAD), the UN Economic Commission for Latin America and the Caribbean (ECLAC), the UN Economic Commission for Asia and the Pacific (ESCAP), the World Trade Institute, many members of the staff of the Secretariat of the World Trade Organisation, the International Trade Centre (ITC), as well as Daniel Bokobza at the European Commission (now with the Commission on Finance of the French National Assembly), Werner Soontiens from Curtin University of Technology in Australia, and Arne Wiig from Chr. Michelsen Institute in Norway. The authors also gratefully acknowledge comments and suggestions from Anthony Kleitz, Didier Campion and other colleagues in the OECD and from individual OECD member countries.

Table of Contents

Acronyms 7

Executive Summary 11

Chapter 1: Overview of Non-tariff Barriers: Findings from Existing Business Surveys 19

Chapter 2. Import Prohibitions and Quotas 59

Chapter 3. Non-automatic Import Licensing 103

Chapter 4. Customs Fees and Charges on Imports 135

Chapter 5. Export Duties 177

Chapter 6. Export Restrictions 201

Chapter 7. Non-tariff Barriers of Concern to Developing Countries 227

Bibliography 297

Acronyms

ABAC	APEC Business Advisory Council
ABT	administrative barrier to trade
AC	Andean Community
ACWL	Advisory Centre on WTO Law
ALADI	Latin American Integration Association
ANCERTA	Australia-New Zealand Closer Economic Relations Trade Agreement
APEC	Asia-Pacific Economic Cooperation
ASEAN	Association of Southeast Asian Nations
BOP	Balance of payments
c.i.f.	cost, insurance and freight
CACEU	Central African Customs and Economic Union
CACM	Central American Common Market
CARICOM	Caribbean Community
CBI	Cross Border Initiative
CEPT	Common Effective Preferential Tariff Scheme
CET	common external tariff
CIS	Commonwealth of Independent States
CITES	Convention on International Trade in Endangered Species
CTG	Council on Trade in Goods (WTO)
DDA	Doha Development Agenda
DSU	Dispute Settlement Understanding (WTO)
ECLAC	Economic Commission of Latin America and the Caribbean
ECOWAS	Economic Community of West African States
EDI	Electronic data interchange
EFTA	European Free Trade Association
ESCAP	United Nations Economic and Social Commission for Asia and the Pacific
f.o.b.	free on board
FAO	Food and Agriculture Organization
GATT	General Agreement on Tariffs and Trade
GMO	genetically modified organism
IDB	Inter-American Development Bank
IDS	Import Diversification System (Korea)

ILP Agreement	Agreement on Import Licensing Procedures
IMF	International Monetary Fund
IPR	intellectual property rights
ITC	International Trade Centre
LAC	Latin America and the Caribbean
LDC	least developed country
MEA	multilateral environmental agreement
MENA	Middle East and North Africa
Mercosur	Southern Common Market
MFA	Multi-Fibre Arrangement
MFN	most favoured nation
MRA	mutual recognition agreement
n.e.s.	not elsewhere specified
NAFTA	North American Free Trade Agreement
NAL	non-automatic licensing
NAMA	Negotiating Group on Market Access for Non-agricultural Products
NTB	non-tariff barrier
NTM	non-tariff measure
OAS	Organization of American States
ODC	other duties and charges
OECS	Organization of Eastern Caribbean States
PBEC	Pacific Basin Economic Council
PIC	prior informed consent
PITC	Philippines' International Trade Corporation
QR	quantitative restrictions
RTA	regional trade arrangement
SAARC	South Asian Association for Regional Cooperation
SACU	Southern African Customs Union
SCM Agreement	Agreement on Subsides and Countervailing Measures
SDT	special and differential treatment
SIECA	Secretariat for Central American Economic Integration
SMEs	small and medium-sized enterprises
SPS Agreement	Agreement on Sanitary and Phytosanitary Measures
SSA	Sub-Saharan Africa
TBT Agreement	Agreement on Technical Barriers to Trade
TCM	trade control measures

TFB	trade facilitation barrier
TPR	trade policy review
TRAINS	Trade analysis and information system
TRQ	tariff rate quota
UDEAC	Customs and Economic Union of Central Africa
UNCTAD	United Nations Conference on Trade and Development
UNEP	United Nations Environment Programme
UR	Uruguay Round
USITC	US International Trade Commission
VER	voluntary export restraint
WAEMU	West African Economic and Monetary Union
WITS	World Integrated Trade Solution
WTO	World Trade Organization

EXECUTIVE SUMMARY

Addressing measures that restrict or distort trade in non-agricultural goods has been a central element of successive rounds of GATT negotiations since the 1960s. As a result, some policies or measures have been abolished while the use of others has been regulated under international trade rules so that they cannot be abused. The growth of market integration made possible by these achievements is most readily apparent in the growth of trade relative to world income. Yet we are far from a textbook situation in which trade of goods and services flows freely. There is considerable anecdotal evidence indicating that non-tariff measures (NTMs) remain significant impediments to trade in non-agricultural products, but systematically collected data are not available. Unlike tariffs, for which databases exist that enable changes to be readily measured and analysed, NTBs are not subject to comprehensive reporting requirements.

One reason for the data problem in the area of NTBs is that compared to tariffs, NTBs take many different forms and often are not transparent. Under the broadest definition, NTBs comprise all measures other than tariffs that restrict or otherwise distort trade flows. For example, UNCTAD maintains and periodically updates a Trade Analysis and Information System (TRAINS) database with data for over 100 different types of NTBs. Yet this is not a complete list (*e.g.* it includes only measures applied to imports). Moreover, in practice, the use of measures changes over time and new types of measures appear.

The studies included in this volume are not concerned with definitional issues. Nor do they seek to provide a typology, although the reviews of business surveys included in two of the studies (Chapters 1 and 7) document the diverse universe of procedural requirements, regulations and policies which impede, according to exporters, market access abroad, directly or indirectly. Attempts to build taxonomies and inventories of measures that adequately reflect the scope of trade issues arising in today's business environment may benefit from the results of these reviews.

It is a fact of life that any list of NTBs is bound to be long, and a classification of measures that enjoys broad consensus among trade specialists has yet to be developed. One way to simplify matters for analytical purposes is to distinguish border from behind-the-border measures. Although behind-the-border measures are of equal if not greater concern to many exporting companies, as is documented extensively in Chapters 1 and 7, the investigation of specific types of NTBs comprising Chapters 2 through 6 of this volume all concern measures undertaken at the border.

Are NTBs on the rise? Which NTBs have the biggest effect? Answers to these and other questions would be very helpful for policy makers and negotiators but are not straightforward.

One cannot say with certainty whether, overall, NTBs are decreasing or increasing in use. What seems clear is that the reduction or elimination of import tariffs resulting from past trade liberalisation has made NTBs relatively more conspicuous. For some sectors, the main form of government intervention in trade today consists of non-tariff barriers. Also, the observation that more disputes are brought for settlement to the Dispute Settlement Body of the WTO would seem to indicate that NTB issues are becoming more important.

Although only a limited set of NTBs are studied in depth, the analysis offers some interesting observations. For example, it draws the attention of governments to the fact that barriers to trade do not have to be confined to imports but can be restrictions and other measures affecting exports.

While reducing tariff and non-tariff restrictions on imports has been a primary goal in past market access negotiations, export-related measures have been addressed less systematically, with the result that multilateral rules for export duties and other restrictions are less developed than for import restrictions.

Furthermore, the analysis suggest that how border and behind-the-border policies are applied or administered can become a "procedural barrier to trade", which deserves attention in its own right. Trade can influenced by the specific ways in which customs classification, valuation and clearance procedures are being handled, by lengthy or duplicative product approval or certification procedures, or even private restrictive practices tolerated by governments. For example, import quotas, product standards and other policies that directly or indirectly affect trade can be designed, applied or enforced in a non-transparent or arbitrary manner that disadvantages foreign producers. These procedural aspects cause additional difficulties in export markets. WTO disciplines covering various types of NTBs consist of more or less detailed provisions designed to prevent or at least minimise adverse effects resulting from procedural factors. Yet exporters and policymakers continue to perceive procedural barriers as significant impediments to trade and look towards further improvements of existing rules.

The use of NTBs also has undergone changes. Prior to the Uruguay Round, import quotas and other quantitative restrictions on imports or exports were quite common in both developed and developing countries, covering such product s as steel, textiles and clothing, footwear, machinery and autos. As the studies in this volume show, countries have since discontinued many quotas and non-automatic import licensing, either as part of their unilateral liberalisation efforts or to honour their obligations resulting from the Uruguay Round. This trend is confirmed by other research, including earlier OECD work indicating that the incidence and importance of quantitative restrictions such as import quotas and voluntary restraint agreements and price control measures in OECD member countries has generally diminished over the last two decades (OECD, 1996).

With respect to other measures, the situation is less clear. It may well be that use of other types of measures mentioned in contributions to this volume but not investigated in detail, such as technical and sanitary standards, is spreading. This is at least the impression that one obtains from survey data reflecting business concerns. Today, exporters around the world are preoccupied less by traditional border measures, such as import or export licensing, quotas and prohibitions than by difficulties arising from product standards, conformity assessments and other behind-the-border policies in importing countries. Such concerns help explain the substantial efforts made by negotiators in the Uruguay Round to strengthen the rules governing the use of technical and sanitary and phytosanitary measures. In the OECD, work on market openness aspects of regulatory reform in member countries has identified principles that ensure that domestic regulation achieves its policy goals efficiently while at the same time contributing to and enhancing market access (OECD, 2003; Czaga, 2004).

Contributing to the difficulty of analysing NTBs is the fact that their effects on trade and economic welfare are not readily measurable. Not only do these measures take often non-transparent forms, analysis also has to take into account whether and how they are linked to non-trade policy objectives. Some NTBs serve important regulatory purposes and are legitimate under WTO rules under clearly defined conditions even though they restrict trade. For example, import licences may be used to control the importation of products carrying potential health risks. Countries may ban imports of farm products for food safety reasons or impose labelling requirements in response to consumer demands for information. The issue here is whether governments, in pursuing legitimate goals, are restricting imports more than is necessary to achieve those goals. Under multilateral rules, the objective is not to remove these measures but to ensure that they are set at an appropriate level to achieve legitimate objectives with minimum impact on trade. However, because legitimacy claims are typically associated with the introduction of these measures, they are hard to assess.

All this makes the issues that arise in connection with determining the economic impact of NTBs very different from those surrounding the use of tariffs. As far as trade and the economic impact of NTBs are concerned, much depends on the specific circumstances of their application. To understand the effect of a specific measure requires a case-by-case examination. This goes beyond the scope of the studies presented in this volume, however.

The reader is reminded that incidence does not serve as a good indicator of trade restrictiveness. It would be useful for policy makers to know which types of NTBs are the most harmful to trade and economic welfare. Such information would for example help negotiators to set priorities. However, this is a very difficult question in quantitative analysis and one that the present study does not address.

It should be understood, however, that the cost of protection caused by NTBs – in terms of trade flows, international resource allocation and productive efficiency – can be high. Moreover, economists tend to agree that NTBs usually are more trade-restrictive and distorting than tariffs, not least because they are much less transparent in their price effects.

In light of the data problems, the research underpinning the seven chapters of this volume has drawn on a range of sources. They include the WTO Trade Policy Reviews carried out since 1995, which generally permit identification, by broad product groups, of individual policies, measures or practices used in different countries based on economic rather than legal (consistency with WTO) criteria. They also include notifications by members to WTO bodies, the recent academic literature and findings from business surveys. At times, other sources have provided useful information. For example, the study on non-automatic import licensing takes account of the discussions in the WTO on trade facilitation. The study of NTBs of concern to developing countries compiles and analyses data from disputes brought under WTO and certain regional dispute settlement mechanisms.

Exploring the contribution that data collected by business surveys can make to NTB identification, Chapter 1 compiles and broadly analyses findings from survey-based research that seeks to identify barriers to foreign markets perceived by exporters in various countries and regions. These surveys typically ask companies to report obstacles that they encounter in foreign markets.

Exploring the extent to which different surveys report the same types of barriers, the chapter notes that technical measures, customs rules and procedures and, to a lesser extent, internal taxes or charges and competition-related restrictions on market access are measures of high concern to businesses reported in many surveys. More generally, there appears to be much greater concern among businesses about behind-the-border policy issues than about quantitative import restriction and other traditional types of NTBs. Moreover, perceived problems often are procedural or administrative, an observation that can inform trade negotiations and future work on refining existing taxonomies of non-tariff barriers.

In Chapter 2, analysis of two types of quantitative import restrictions, namely prohibitions and quotas, makes apparent that the level of transparency of measures controlling the quantity of imports is low compared to many other aspects of the trade regime that have come under multilateral disciplines. Therefore, it would be beneficial to find ways to strengthen rules and implementation with respect to the WTO's notification system in this area.

In general, among developing countries, there appears to be a declining trend in the application of quotas and prohibitions for economic reasons, such as balance-of-payment problems and industry protection. At the same time, prohibitions put in place for *non-economic reasons*, especially with the objective of protecting the environment and human safety and health, are present in virtually every country and their use seems to be on the rise. The incidence of these measures seems to be increasing faster in developed countries with stricter social regulatory frameworks.

Import prohibitions play an especially important role in the trade of certain used consumer and capital goods, such as automobiles, auto parts, apparel and machinery. The circumstances of these measures appear at times unclear and, by raising certain policy issues, point to an area that would merit further investigation and possibly consideration in the context of international trade negotiations.

When applied for non-economic reasons, import prohibitions are policy solutions used to ensure that different societal regulatory objectives are met. It is necessary to recognise countries' regulatory sovereignty. At the same time, governments should take into consideration existing principles of good regulatory practice. They should carefully consider whether import bans are the best regulatory solutions or whether more trade-friendly alternative tools for achieving the primary regulatory objective exist.

Chapter 3 examines the use in the non-agricultural sector of non-automatic import licensing schemes, which can be applied for a variety of economic and non-economic regulatory purposes. Their use has been evolving and, with the significant reforms that have been undertaken over the years, the pattern of perceived problems associated with these measures has changed.

Import licensing schemes implemented for economic reasons, *i.e.* with the primary intent of protecting domestic producers from international competition, have largely been discontinued. By contrast, import licensing to implement a wide variety of regulations related *inter alia* to national security and protection of health, safety and the environment is widely used across both OECD and non-OECD countries. Here, it is with respect to the procedural aspects of the measure that the question of the impact on trade of such licensing arises.

Although the WTO provides far-reaching disciplines in the area of licensing procedures, particularly through the Agreement on Import Licensing (ILP), business concerns suggest that traders still experience problems with the way in which licensing systems are implemented and applied. Besides the need to fully implement existing commitments, there appear to be areas in which further improvement of licensing-related disciplines might be warranted. Here, an important link exists between import licensing and the discussions about trade facilitation under way in the DDA and in other forums.

As Chapter 4 documents, when goods are imported, various customs fees and charges are frequently applied in addition to tariffs. This significantly adds to the costs of trading in many parts of the world. Low- and middle-income countries in particular levy high *ad valorem* fees that may negatively affect both South-South and North-South trade.

Upon closer examination, the use of customs fees and charges has evolved over time. The application of both customs surcharges and consular invoice fees has markedly declined over the last two decades, and more countries now charge importers fees for the use of various customs-related services. In practice, a great majority of these fees, like most other types of fees and charges, are applied *ad valorem* rather than with regard to the underlying cost of the services rendered. This is true for high-income and for lower-income countries alike.

Although GATT Article VIII requires customs fees and charges to be limited in amount to the approximate cost of services rendered, frequent application of high *ad valorem* fees and charges seems to signal that clearer guidelines on how customs fees and charges should be calculated would be useful and would remove some of the uncertainties regarding the legality of their application. In addition, a more precise definition of what constitutes the "services" whose costs are intended to be reflected in the fees would also remove some uncertainties in the interpretation of the article and potentially lead to a reduction in the costs of trading.

Two chapters of this volume call upon policymakers and negotiators to pay attention not only to border measures on the import side but also to trade-distorting measures on the export side. Export duties and export restrictions broadly defined, are analysed in depth in Chapters 5 and 6.

Chapter 5 points out that the issue of export duties has been raised in recent years in NAMA and various other trade negotiation contexts. To date, WTO disciplines on export duties are not clearly defined, and currently no member assumes obligations for scheduling and notification of export duties under the WTO. By contrast, more and more bilateral and regional trade agreements introduce disciplines to prohibit export duties, and the recent WTO accession process also has led to certain concessions by acceding countries in this regard.

Based on available data, the analysis of the use of export duties reveals certain trends. For example, export duties are introduced mainly by developing and least developed countries, and the products affected include forestry products, fishery products, mineral and metal products, leather and hide and skin products, and various agricultural products. The two main motives for imposing export duties are to gain revenue and to promote downstream processing industries. Another alleged reason is environmental protection or the preservation of natural resources or products. There is a growing tendency for governments to abolish export duties, notably in bilateral and regional contexts, which reflects recognition of their trade-distorting effects. The chapter explains these effects and offers observations on elements of possible rule making in regard to export duties.

Chapter 6 provides an overview of current disciplines governing export restrictions under the GATT/WTO, including the scope of exceptions. It also describes the current situation regarding the implementation of notification obligations concerning quantitative restrictions.

What justifications are provided for the exceptions? Are existing transparency disciplines sufficient in terms of predictability and is there room for strengthening disciplines in this area, on either a horizontal or a sectoral basis? These are some of the questions that this chapter addresses.

Key findings from a review of available data from the WTO Trade Policy Review process on minimum export price requirements, export quotas, export prohibitions, export licensing and other types of export restrictions indicate that one of the key objectives of export restrictions for economic reasons is the promotion of downstream industries. Hides and skins and leather, forestry products, certain mineral products and certain agricultural products are sectors in which such measures are being applied.

Possible orientations for future disciplines in the field of export restrictions include possibilities of scheduling, horizontal or sector-specific disciplines, and transparency measures. The WTO accession processes provide references for possible disciplines, such as the scheduling of certain products and notification requirements. In regional trade agreements, disciplines on export restrictions are mostly in line with the structure of GATT, allowing Article XX and XXI exceptions to general prohibition on quantitative restrictions. However, efforts have been undertaken to enhance transparency by specifying justifiable export regulations in the agreements and annexes or subsequent regulations.

Developing countries rely heavily on developed-country markets for their merchandise exports, although trade with other developing countries is becoming increasingly important and dynamic. Chapter 7 concludes this volume with a review and analysis of data that identify non-tariff barriers that are of interest to developing countries in their trade with developed countries and, at the regional level, among themselves.

Given that reduction or elimination of NTBs is included in the Doha Development Agenda and is under consideration in regional and other arenas discussing trade liberalisation, the chapter seeks to identify possible negotiating targets. Its findings can also contribute to discussions on how to make special and differential treatment more effective, and help raise general awareness among developing countries of NTBs which they themselves maintain but which interfere with their ability to trade with each other.

From a review of the literature, NAMA notifications, business surveys and other available data, certain broadly defined categories of NTBs appear consistently as a source of concern to developing countries. In their trade with developed countries, customs and administrative procedures and technical barriers to trade (TBTs) are the leading NTBs of concern to developing countries. For trade among developing countries, technical barriers are less prominently reported. However, customs and administrative procedures also rank high among reported concerns for all sets of data analysed. Issues identified under this category of measures include difficulties relating to import licensing procedures and rules of origin and generally appear to be more pervasive in trade with other developing countries than with developed countries. Para-tariff measures, such as fees and charges on imports, are also important barriers, in particular for intra-regional trade among developing countries.

In terms of product-specific issues, it appears that live animals and related products are a commodity category – and within that category, fisheries – that deserves particular attention for reported sanitary and phytosanitary measures and customs-related problems. Among the NTBs reported for items of machinery and electronics, TBT issues dominate. The same holds for pharmaceutical products. National export strategies and programmes reviewed in this chapter for a sample of countries confirm that these are sectors and products of key interest to developing countries in their pursuit of export growth and diversification over the longer term.

References

OECD (1996), *Indicators of Tariff and Non-tariff Trade Barriers*, OECD, Paris.

OECD (2003), "Integrating Market Openness into the Regulatory Process: Emerging Patterns in OECD Countries", TD/TC/WP(2002)25/FINAL, 17 February.

Czaga, Peter (2004),"Regulatory Reform and Market Openness: Understanding the Links to Enhance Economic Performance", OECD Trade Policy Working Paper No. 9, TD/TC/WP(2004)10/FINAL, 15 December.

Chapter 1

Overview of Non-tariff Barriers: Findings from Existing Business Surveys

by

Barbara Fliess

> *Our knowledge of NTBs, of how to assess their effects and the extent to which they may restrict trade is inadequate. Simply identifying the main non-tariff measures is a difficult task and data collected by business surveys can make a contribution. This chapter compiles and analyses findings from survey-based research that help identify barriers perceived by exporters from various countries and regions in foreign markets. It also explores the extent to which different surveys report the same types of barriers. Common areas of concern in many surveys are technical measures, customs rules and procedures and, to a lesser extent, internal taxes or charges and competition-related restrictions on market access.*

Introduction

Research aimed at obtaining a comprehensive and up-to-date picture of the post-Uruguay landscape of non-tariff barriers (NTBs) faces serious obstacles. Current knowledge of such barriers, both empirically and conceptually, is limited and hampered by a lack of data or the poor quality of available data on various trade barriers affecting products entering foreign markets.

Compared to tariffs, for which there are quantitative databases that make it possible to measure, analyse and monitor incidence, levels of protection and changes, it is quite difficult to identify NTBs, quantify their effects and obtain an up-to-date picture of the post-Uruguay landscape of NTBs. The most comprehensive available set of data on government trade measures is compiled by UNCTAD as part of the Trade Analysis and Information System (TRAINS); however, it is incomplete across countries and products, and the underlying typology of measures only partially captures today's complex NTB situation.

Alternative sources of information include reports on barriers to trade issued annually by the EU, Japan and the United States. Reflecting generally what EU, Japanese and US firms consider to be the main impediments to their access to foreign markets, these reports indicate a wide range of perceived NTBs encompassing a large variety of types of border and internal measures as well as associated procedural and administrative practices. These exercises, too, have methodological weaknesses. Nevertheless, the number of independent business surveys continues to grow, providing indications of what traders perceive as the most important impediments to trade. Although this information is often difficult to compare and is of questionable or inconsistent quality (see below), it gives a picture of real-world experience that in many respects is more telling than information based on government regulations (as in the case of TRAINS).

This chapter reviews what business surveys and related analysis reveal about NTBs. More specifically, it reports and broadly compares findings from a set of 23 survey-based studies or reports. The survey material focuses on NTBs, although the scope of the inquiries varies and at times includes tariffs or other obstacles to export performance rooted in the broader business environment (for methodology, see Annex 1.A1 and for details of the various surveys, see Annexes 1.A2-1.A4). No claims are made to the completeness of the compendium. Research that is industry-specific or addresses only a narrow set of NTBs is not reviewed but is referenced in the bibliography, along with some inventory-type materials that incorporate information from businesses.

After noting some of the limitations of the survey approach for NTB analysis and the survey findings presented here, the chapter takes a closer look at the survey results and assesses the extent to which similar non-tariff problems are reported in surveys covering different parts of the world. Surveys usually address various issues. The responses used in the analysis resulted from questions asking respondents to identify or report barriers that they encounter in foreign markets. Because comparability of survey information is limited, the results are tentative.

Nature and limitations of business surveys

Surveys provide a more systematic approach to the identification of NTBs than anecdotal evidence or inventories of trade barriers prepared from diverse sources of information. The research compiled for this chapter uses questionnaires and/or interviews to collect views from representatives of businesses, associations and occasionally other entities. A few studies (*e.g.* the Argentina survey) complement survey data with other sources of information, such as publications from international institutions and chambers of commerce.

Most of the research reviewed is carried out on the behalf of public authorities, often to provide input for the development of policy or negotiating priorities. At times, the surveys also collect the business community's recommendations for government action (*e.g.* Alberta survey) or opinions about the effectiveness of government initiatives to address barriers (*e.g.* PBEC survey).

In some of the surveys the export market is globally defined (Alberta and New Zealand surveys). Others survey regional export markets in Asia, Europe, the Americas and Africa (*e.g.* ALADI, EU and Brazil surveys). A few investigate barriers in specific countries (China/Japan/Korea and Finnish surveys).

The surveys ask respondents to identify in either an open-ended way or from a set of pre-specified items, the measures or policies that hinder their business's access to foreign markets. The responses are then used to rank barriers based on a measure of frequency. Surveys with data sets showing how often each barrier was reported are summarised in Annex 1.A2. Surveys using other types of parameters to describe barriers, such as the number of tariff lines affected by specific barriers (Argentina and ASEAN surveys) or mean scores of rated importance (*e.g.* MENA survey), are shown in Annex 1.A3. A third set of studies, grouped in Annex 1.A4, uses information collected from businesses to list and describe different types of barriers (*e.g.* China-Chinese Taipei, Indian and Zimbabwe surveys).

It must be kept in mind that surveys are crude analytical tools and their results are not necessarily reliable and accurate. The sophistication of the methodologies of the surveys reviewed here varies and not all inquiries are equally systematic. Sample size and selection of respondents do not always guarantee rigorous and significant results.

Also, the barriers identified reflect respondents' judgements and may be subject to various biases. For example, respondents may exaggerate claims if they know that the information will be used for policy purposes. Or they may be reluctant to report problems for certain export markets for fear that this may negatively affect their operations and business interests in those markets; this may be why they sometimes describe barriers without specifying the markets in which they occur. Also, firms are likely to judge any measure unjustified if it noticeably raises their costs. They usually do not distinguish between measures that are allowed under WTO rules and those that are not – both sorts, of course, may be trade-restrictive.

Other limitations inherent in survey-based NTB analysis concern the collection and interpretation of mainly frequency-of-response data. Counting the number of respondents who report a barrier or state that it represents a problem indicates how widely a barrier is experienced. It does not measure the barrier's importance in respect of trade impact. Therefore, the barriers identified by a large number of respondents are not necessarily the most trade-restrictive. Some surveys attempt to assess restrictiveness using other indicators.

Some observations about the survey findings

The general picture that emerges from the survey findings is that businesses feel constrained in their ability to access foreign markets by a broad set of non-tariff and other kinds of measures.

While the significant reduction of average tariffs in many countries over the past half-century has focused attention on NTBs, businesses sometimes still consider tariffs to be relevant in certain markets. This is indicated by the high ranking of tariffs in some of the surveys that include tariffs along with NTBs (*e.g.* ABAC/APEC, Swedish, MENA surveys).

With respect to non-tariff problems, surveys differ in their definition of NTBs and also in the scope of the barriers included in the questionnaires and other survey instruments. Responses indicate that quantitative import restrictions and other "core" non-tariff measures continue to cause some difficulty for exporters, but there appears to be much greater preoccupation with behind-the-border policy issues. This is to be expected, given the success of the multilateral trading system in disciplining the use of the most direct forms of intervention in trade. There remains significant scope for removing other kinds of obstacles to cross-border market access even in already highly integrated regional markets, as the results of the EU and Swedish surveys with respect to the EU single market indicate.

Another observation is that administrative, procedural and institutional factors figure prominently in business opinion. The survey material provides extensive evidence that exporters feel hampered by less direct and less obvious impediments that take the form of procedures for administering trade and domestic policies and regulations, attitudes and behaviour of regulatory authorities and public officials, poor administrative practices (corruption, discrimination) and weak domestic institutions (*e.g.* the legal and judicial systems). The PBEC survey focuses specifically on "administrative barriers to trade", but barriers of this kind are reported by many of the other surveys reviewed as well.

Some of the other reported factors influencing cross-border market access, such as infrastructure inadequacies or the high cost of domestic borrowing (*e.g.* ALADI and Zimbabwe surveys) are constraints on exports in the home country, rather than barriers originating in foreign markets.[i] In a few surveys, the scope of issues identified extends to cultural attitudes, language, distance from markets, production costs and other "natural" barriers affecting a firm's trading environment (*e.g.* China/Japan/Korea survey) that are normally not considered NTBs.

Analysis of the most reported barriers

Because the survey material is diverse, the scope for comparing the results of different surveys is limited. The cross-survey analysis undertaken here uses a subset of surveys and compares their most often reported barriers. Annex 1.A1 describes the methodology used.

After making certain modifications in the terminology to ensure consistent definitions, the five most reported categories of barriers are listed for each survey. These are shown in Table 1.1. Because many respondents identified these items, it can be assumed that they represent real problems for exporters.

Table 1.1. Concerns about NTBs: categories mentioned most frequently by businesses in selected surveys

EU survey (2000) focusing on the EU single market	Danish survey (1997) focusing on EU countries, Norway, Switzerland, Hungary, Czech Republic, Baltic countries, Poland	Swedish survey (2000) focusing on 10 EU countries; 3rd markets		Australian survey (2000)[1] focusing on Indian Ocean Rim region (18 IOR-ARC countries + Egypt)	New Zealand survey (2001) worldwide coverage
		Categories of non-tariff barriers, by order of importance			
		EU	3rd markets[1]		
Technical measures	Technical measures	Technical measures	Customs rules and procedures	Customs rules and procedures	Technical measures
Subsidies	Procedures and administration (general)	Restrictions on services	Technical measures	Competition-related restrictions on market access	Customs rules and procedures
Internal taxes or charges	Local marketing regulations	Competition-related restrictions on market access	Restrictions on services	Public procurement practices	Quantitative import restrictions
Inappropriate legal appeals mechanisms No legal security of cross-border contracts/transactions	Internal taxes or charges	Internal taxes or charges Public procurement practices	Investment restrictions Competition-related restrictions on market access	Investment restrictions Technical measures	Transport regulations or costs Internal taxes or charges

PBEC survey (1997) focusing on Asia-Pacific region	ABAC/APEC survey (2000)[1] focusing on 21 APEC countries	Brazilian survey (2001) focusing on Argentina, Paraguay, Uruguay	Chilean survey (2000) focusing on EU, Chinese Taipei, China, Korea, Japan, United States and 8 Latin American countries	ALADI survey (2001) focusing on ALADI countries (Argentina, Bolivia, Brazil, Chile, Columbia & others)	Zimbabwe survey (1995) focusing on Common Market of Eastern and Southern Africa (COMESA)
		Categories of non-tariff barriers, by order of importance			
Investment restrictions	Customs rules and procedures	Transport regulations or costs	Import policies (esp. import licensing and import quotas)	Technical measures	Economic policy environment
Procedures and administration (general)	Procedures and administration (general)	Customs rules and procedures	Technical measures	Customs rules and procedures	Lack of export incentive scheme
Restrictions on mobility of labour and business people	Competition-related restrictions on market access	Technical measures	Restrictions on services	Finance and payment mechanisms	Lack of knowledge of regional market
Competition-related restrictions on market access	Quantitative import restrictions	Quantitative import restrictions	Subsidies	Non-tariff barriers (not specified)	Customs rules and procedures
Internal taxes or charges	Technical measures	Internal taxes or charges	Trade defence instruments	Competition in costs and production	Transport regulations or costs

Note: Tariffs are omitted from the lists shown here. Moreover, where a survey breaks non-tariff measures down into two or more items that are related and belong to the same broad category and reports separate response frequencies for these individual items, the item with the highest response rate was retained for inclusion and related items reported less frequently were not counted. As a result, the items listed for each survey in this table and their rank may differ from the order of a survey's data set shown in the Annex.

1. The list takes into account responses for non-tariff and trade facilitation barriers.

Certain NTB categories appear more frequently in the surveys than others. However, by survey design or because firms are not concerned, many of the 12 surveys do not cover certain types of barriers. Therefore, in comparing the information relating to the NTB categories in Table 1.1 provided in the surveys, only those surveys that have collected responses for the item need to be examined. This is taken into account by the figures in Table 1.2, which show how many of the 12 surveys cover a specific category of NTBs and how many report a relatively high response rate (*i.e.* placing the category among the five most reported barriers).

Table 1.2. NTB categories most frequently reported by the surveys

NTB categories	No. of surveys (out of 12): that cover the category	No. of surveys (out of 12): that show the category among the 5 most reported
Technical measures	10	10
Internal taxes or charges	8	6
Customs rules and procedures	7	7
Competition-related restrictions on market access	7	5
Quantitative import restrictions	7[1]	3[1]
Procedures and administration (general)	7	3
Public procurement practices	7	2
Subsidies and related government supports	7	2
Investment restrictions or requirements	6	3
Transport regulations or costs	6	3
Restrictions of services (general)	5	3
Restrictions on mobility of business people or labour	4	1
Trade defence instruments (anti-dumping, countervailing-duty and safeguard measures)	4	1
Local marketing regulations	2	1

Note: The following high-ranking items are not shown in this table because they were reported by only one survey: Inappropriate legal appeal mechanism; lack of legal security of cross-border contracts/transactions; finance and payment mechanisms; economic policy environment; lack of export incentive scheme; lack of knowledge of regional market; competition in cost and production; and a general reference to non-tariff barriers.

1. The count of surveys includes the Chile survey, which uses the term "import policies" to describe mainly non-automatic import licensing and import quotas.

The ten and seven surveys that report *technical measures* and *customs rules and procedures*, respectively, rank these barriers high. They are always among the five most reported categories of barriers in Table 1.1. Where *internal taxes or charges* and *competition-related restrictions* on market access are reported, these are also often among the top five. Although less often mentioned, *restrictions for services in general* rank high in three out of the five surveys that report them.

The relatively consistent high ranking observed for these items does not hold in the case of other NTB categories, such as government procurement practices or subsidies, although they are reported by a substantial number of the surveys.

Table 1.3. **Reported concerns and issues relating to technical measures**

Markets (survey)	Specifications and standards	Conformity assessment procedures	Key sectors/industries mentioned
EU single market (EU)	•Additional costs to render products or services compatible with national specifications	Unusual testing, certification or approval procedures	No information provided
EU countries, Norway, Switzerland, Hungary, Czech Republic, Poland, Baltic countries Denmark)	•Problems relating to local standards •Problems relating to content and design requirements	Problems relating to testing and certification	No information provided
EU (Sweden)	Technical barriers		No information provided
Non-EU markets Sweden)	Technical barriers, especially binding technical rules taking the form of product requirements, testing, certification and labelling		For non-agricultural sector only: machinery and electrical material; transport industry; non-precious metals and goods of non-precious metals
Indian Ocean Rim region (18 IOR-RC countries + Egypt) (Australia) [1]	NTBs: •Labelling •Quality assurance requirements •Quarantine issues (not further defined) TFBs: •Aspects of business information needs: compliance with safety or technical standards; labelling requirements TFB: •Aspects of standards, (harmonisation of standards in export markets, transparency/consistency of requirements, costs and delays of testing procedures; multiple testing)	TFBs[2]: •Aspects of quarantine services (incl. lack of transparency/consistency of requirements in quarantine services, costs and delays	For primary and manufacturing industry only: *Labelling*: Textiles, clothing or footwear; processed food. *Quality assurance requirements*: agriculture; mining; processed food. *Aspects of standards*: mining; processed food; automotive; metals and metals products; automotive. *Aspects of quarantine services*: agriculture; mining; processed food; chemicals or related; automotive. *Aspects of business information needs*: mining; agriculture; processed food.
Global (New Zealand)	Main specific barriers identified: •Data certification and testing requirements •Labelling, marking or packaging problems •Food safety and health requirements •Arbitrary enforcement of requirements or procedures •Non-use of international standards	•Delays to obtain approval •Expenditure to attain approval •Non-recognition of foreign test results •Non-scientific basis to quarantine restrictions	*Standards and certification barriers*: food and beverage products. *Food safety and health requirements*: food and beverage products. *Non scientific basis to quarantine restrictions*: forest products; primary products; food and beverage products.
21 APEC economies (ABAC/APEC)	Standards issues for manufacturing sector (ranked by survey in descending order of rated seriousness): •Standards regulations too complex •Lack of transparency in standards •Differing national standards	•Delays in testing or authorisation •Costs of testing procedures •Lack of training programmes on standards issues •Need for multiple testing	No information provided

Table 1.3. **Reported concerns and issues relating to technical measures (cont.)**

Markets (survey)	Specifications and standards	Conformity assessment procedures	Key sectors/industries mentioned
Argentina, Paraguay, Uruguay (Brazil)	•Labelling requirements •Inspection and testing requirements •SPS requirements	•Technical certification •Pre-shipment inspection •Product registration •Exporter registration requirements	*Labelling requirements*: Footwear; clothing, meat. *Inspection and testing*: Textiles, footwear; electrical material; meat. *SPS requirements*: Meat; other food products. *Technical certification*: Footwear; electrical material; extractive minerals. *Pre-shipment inspection*: Plastic products; electrical material; textiles; meat; footwear; *Product registration*: Footwear; meat. *Exporter registration*: Meat; footwear
EU, Chinese Taipei, China, Korea, Japan, United States and 8 Latin American countries (Chile)	•Discrepancy in quality standards for domestic and imported products •Sanitary regulations, such as vaccination requirements •Costly regulations applying to fish and seafood		No information provided
Argentina, Bolivia, Brazil, Chile, Columbia, Cuba, Ecuador, Mexico, Paraguay, Peru, Uruguay (ALADI)	•Product standards: Lack of information about requirements •SPS and heterogeneous technical measures		No information provided

Note: Surveys that do not mention technical measures (PBEC, Zimbabwe) are not included in the table.
1. Based on incidence of dissatisfaction expressed by firms in the survey.
2. TFBs = trade facilitation barriers.

Finally, although respondents in almost half of the 12 surveys mention problems related to intellectual property protection and finance measures and a smaller number report price control measures, import charges and other para-tariff measures, these categories of barriers are not among the most reported.

Particular concerns among the most reported types of measures

The categories of barriers shown in Table 1.1 are broad and do not reveal the specific issues or problems of concern to firms. To learn more about the specific characteristics of barriers, all ten surveys that rank technical measures high were examined for what the responses said about technical measures. The results are described in Table 1.3. Similarly, the surveys that rank customs procedures high were researched for the type of concerns reported, which are shown in Table 1.4.

As the tables show, the level of descriptive detail varies significantly. For technical measures, survey responses show that firms are often concerned about technical specifications or standards as well as conformity assessment procedures. Also, references made to non-transparency, lack of information and delays suggest that for both technical measures and customs rules and procedures, procedural or administrative factors contribute to the difficulties reported. At times, specific sectors or industries are mentioned, but most surveys reveal very little about the products most affected by these two categories of NTBs and, by implication, the trade value.

Table 1.4. **Reported concerns and issues relating to customs rules and procedures**

Markets (survey)	Customs rules and procedures	Key sectors/industries mentioned
Non-EU markets (Sweden)	• Too much documentation required • Takes too long • Lack of predictability	Machinery and electrical material; non-precious metal and goods of non-precious metal; transport industry. These 3 categories of goods cover about 75% of all notifications in this area.

Indian Ocean Rim region (18 IOR-ARC countries + Egypt) (Australia)	• Slow customs clearance
	• Aspects of customs services:
	  – lack of harmonisation and simplification of clearance procedures; Requirements of paper documents and/or inability to use electronic communications in customs services;
	  – lack of consistency and transparency in decisions in customs services
		Slow customs clearance: Processed food; machinery, electrical or communications equipment; automotive; mining.
		Aspects of customs services: mining; processed food; chemicals or related; textiles, clothing or footwear; automotive.

Global (New Zealand)	• Major specific customs classifications and clearance procedures barriers are:
	  – arbitrary enforcement of rules;
	  – misclassification of goods or origin of goods;
	  – data or documentation requirements;
	  – delays due to lack of automation
	  – insufficient information about requirements
	  – irregular 'additional payments' expected to obtain customs clearance
		No information provided

21 APEC economies (ABAC/APEC)	Issues for the manufacturing sector (ranked by survey in descending order of rated seriousness): • Customs regulations too complex • Lack of information on customs laws, regulations, administrative guidelines and rulings • Problems with mechanism for appealing customs decisions • Customs procedures not harmonised with those of partner countries • Customs authorities failing to protect IPRs at border • Problems with valuation of goods • Problems with temporary importation of goods	No information provided
Argentina, Paraguay, Uruguay (Brazil)	• Customs clearance fees and charges • Customs clearance costs • Excessive customs procedures	*Customs clearance costs*: footwear; non-ferrous metals; electrical material; machinery and tractors. *Excessive customs procedures*: footwear; electrical material, meat.
Argentina, Bolivia, Brazil, Chile, Columbia, Cuba, Ecuador, Mexico, Paraguay, Peru, Uruguay (ALADI)	• Customs and bureaucratic procedures	No information provided
Common Market of Eastern and Southern Africa (COMESA) (Zimbabwe)	• Administrative blocking at the borders, caused by shorter working day, low efficiency, equipment breakdowns shortage of special forms for documentation, and by document requirements and transit charges.	No information provided

Note: Surveys that do not mention customs rules and procedures (EU, Denmark, Sweden [re. EU Single Market], Chile) are not included in the table.

No attempt is made here to investigate what business surveys tell about the trade impact of the non-tariff barriers identified. Some of the surveys attempt to collect data on impact or cost. Some ask respondents to rate on a scale the "significance" or "restrictiveness" of a barrier or the "costliness" or the "difficulty" of overcoming a barrier (*e.g.* China/Japan/Korea, MENA surveys and additional data not shown here for the New Zealand and ABAC/APEC surveys, respectively). Another indicator of the relative magnitude of obstacles, reported by the EU survey, sets the relative frequency ratings against business satisfaction ratings. Few of the surveys go further and ask firms to estimate in cost terms the impact of an NTB on the business of traders. The PBEC study asked respondents to quantify operating costs spent in dealing with the overall amount of so-called administrative barriers to trade and to estimate the change in profits if all administrative barriers to trade (ABTs) were removed. In the MENA survey, companies were also asked to quantify administrative costs in terms of numbers of working hours and days and informal constraints such as irregular payments to customs and tax officials.

These types of assessments often suffer from the problem that respondents do not always find it easy to make judgements in terms of degrees and seldom have the type of cost estimates requested readily at hand. Because the questions asked or ranking methods employed differ from survey to survey, the data cannot be compared directly.

Conclusions

The above review of survey-based research shows that businesses feel that numerous non-tariff barriers affect their access to foreign markets. The business surveys provide a rich account of the types of constraints experienced by the exporting firms of particular countries or regions. At the same time, the cross-survey analysis highlights the global dimension of obstacles; different surveys carried out in different parts of the world report similar kinds of obstacles as being relatively often mentioned by respondents. Indeed, some concerns from the business community appear to be widely shared across countries and regions.

Note

i. Surveys designed to collect information specifically about export barriers in the home country were excluded from this review. For a review of research that explores this category of barriers, see, for example, A.H. Moini, "Barriers inhibiting export performance of small and medium-sized manufacturing firms", *Journal of Global Marketing*, Vol. 10(4), 1997, pp. 67-94.

Annex 1.A1

NOTE ON METHODOLOGY

For the cross-survey analysis, only surveys that cover a range of barriers, examine regional or global export markets, and rank barriers on the basis of some frequency of response measure were included. The 12 surveys, taken together, cover a large number of export markets and most geographical regions of the world, were chosen from the material listed in Annex 1.A2. Research identifying barriers for individual export markets was excluded, which eliminated the Finnish survey included in Table 1.A1. The Alberta survey was also omitted because the set of barriers surveyed is small and the number of respondents varies across the survey questions. Excluded from the cross-survey analysis were all surveys included in Table 1.A2 because they use different parameters for ranking barriers, as well as the studies summarised in Table 1.A3, which do not use a ranking methodology.

No attempt was made to control for sample size or the sectors represented by the respondents (in some surveys, they are producers of goods and services and the survey results are not broken down by sector) because this would have reduced the usable set of surveys further.

Comparability of survey results is also made difficult by the fact that some surveys ask respondents to evaluate separately different measures or aspects of a measure belonging to a class of NTBs, whereas others investigate broadly defined policy areas. Consequently, the measures or issues reported by the 13 surveys are converted here, when necessary, into corresponding broader NTB categories. For example:

- Where a survey reported health and phytosanitary regulations, safety and industrial standards and regulations, packaging or labelling regulations, these items were redefined as technical measures.

- Where surveys mention issues or problems of customs valuation, classification and clearance and pre-shipment inspection, these items were classified as *customs rules and procedures*.

- Issues of sales, excise and other types of non-border taxes or fees were classified as *internal taxes or charges*.

- The category of *competition-related restrictions on market access* comprises monopolistic trade measures (such as state trading), distribution restrictions and restrictive business practices.

- *Quantitative import restrictions* refer to import quotas, import prohibitions, import licensing and voluntary export restraints.

- *Transport regulations or costs* groups requirements, procedures or costs involving cargo handling, port use, maritime insurance and logistics.

To the extent possible, the categories are defined and the barriers identified by the surveys converted using the classification underlying UNCTAD's TRAINS database. Some types of (mainly economic) barriers were left unchanged because it was not clear which aggregate label should be applied.

A simple rule was applied to rank categories based on the response frequencies reported by the individual surveys for different types of measures or issues. Where surveys list more than one item among the top five in the same category of NTBs, the item with the highest response rate was retained for the purpose of determining the five most reported categories. Lower-ranking items were not taken into account because no method was found to convert survey results for weighting by the number and relative ranking of individual items in the same category. As a result, the top five categories shown in Table 1.1 are not always identical to the top five (unconverted) items in a survey but sometimes pick up lower ranked survey items. Tariffs were also excluded from the ranking of the categories. The ranking of categories shown in Table 1.1 is therefore an approximation. Furthermore, the items and rankings in Table 1.1 are potentially affected by the fact that some surveys cover services, along with goods. This may increase the reporting and may inflate the relative ranking of items such as technical measures, competition-related restrictions on market access or investment restrictions.

Still, given that the surveys differ in many respects, the consistently high ranking of specific categories of barriers reflects a high degree of convergence of views among firms and is a good indicator that they are a serious problem for businesses around the world.

Annex 1.A2

SURVEYS USING FREQUENCY OF RESPONSES TO REPORT BARRIERS

EU Survey (2000)

I. General information	
Title of survey	Single Market Scoreboard
Survey producer	European Commission
Export market(s)	EU Single Market
Data set	Survey (interviews) of 3240 executives from companies in the services, distribution, manufacturing and construction sectors
Survey format	Specific questions
Types of NTBs/NTMs surveyed	Range of 16 behind-the-border measures
Measure/methodology of ranking	Number of interviewees (%) reporting a barrier; business satisfaction index or level of satisfaction of firms with internal market
Surveys definitions of NTBs/NTMs	Not specified
Product groups/industries most often mentioned as affected.	No information provided

II. Ranking by reported occurrence					
1	Additional costs to render products or services compatible with national specifications (33%)	7	Lack of legal security of cross-border contracts/transactions (23%)	13	Difficulties in the temporary posting of staff abroad (13%)
2	Unusual testing, certification or approval procedures (31%)	8	Restrictions on market access: existence of exclusive networks (20%)	14	Requirement to establish branch in another MS (13%)
3	State aids favouring competitors (subsidies or tax breaks) (27%)	9	Lack of protection against piracy and counterfeiting (18%)	15	Other legislative or regulatory obstacles (10%)
4	Difficulties related to the VAT systems and VAT procedures (26%)	10	Costly financing arrangements for cross-border transactions (18%)	16	Ban to market a product/service legally marketed in another MS (9%)
5	Inappropriate legal appeal mechanisms (breaches of contract) (24%)	11	Discriminatory practices of awarding authorities in public procurement markets (16%)		
6	Discriminatory tax treatment of operations (24%)	12	Requested rights or licences in hands of local competitors (13%)		

Danish Survey (1997)

I. General information	
Title of survey	Handelshindringer for Dansk Eksport
Survey producer	Gallup Research Institute, Oxford Research & Ronne & Lundgren
Export market(s)	EU countries and Norway, Switzerland, Hungary, Czech Republic, the Baltic countries, Poland
Data set	Survey (questionnaire) of 600 export companies (out of 2000 approached)
Survey format	Types of barriers specified by survey
Types of NTBs/NTMs surveyed	12 behind-the-border measures
Surveys definitions of NTBs/NTMs	Not specified
Measure/methodology of ranking	Number of companies (%) that report having encountered the barrier; also probability coefficient for likely occurrence within 1 year.
Product groups/industries most often mentioned as affected	Transport (including shipyards), building and construction, electronic equipment, foods, chemical products.

II. Ranking by reported occurrence

1. Product standards (56% of companies). Of these, 40% encountered problems relating to testing and certification, 35% problems relating to local standards, 25% problems to content and design requirements, and 1% other problems.

2. Administration and bureaucracy (19% of companies). Of these, 40% encountered unclear and complicated procedures, 20% slow procedures and delays, 20% problems with local representation, and 20% other problems.

3. Marketing (15% of companies). Of these, 50% encountered problems relating to local brands and declarations, 25% problems relating to translation and language requirements, and 25% problems relating to local constraints to the application/use of products.

4. Discrimination in VAT and taxes (10% of companies). Of these, 33% encountered higher taxes in foreign goods than domestic goods, 33% problems relating to payment and reimbursement of VAT, and 33% faced special taxes to get approval.

Swedish Surveys (2000)

I. General information

Title of survey	Trade Barriers Faced by Swedish Firms on the Single Market and in Third Countries
Survey producer	National Board of Trade (Kommerskollegium), on behalf of the Swedish Foreign Ministry
Export market(s)	(1) 10 EU countries and (2) rest of the world (third markets)
Data set	Survey (questionnaire) of 189 Swedish exporters of non-agricultural goods
Survey format	Pre-determined list of large number of barriers constructed in co-operation with a reference group of business representatives
Types of NTBs/NTMs surveyed	Broad range of tariff and non-tariff measures
Surveys definitions of NTBs/NTMs	Not specified
Measure/methodology of ranking	Number of firms reporting a barrier (cases where respondents describe a barrier as being of either medium or high importance); and degree of importance ("high" or "medium")
Product groups/industries most often mentioned as affected.	No information provided

II. Ranking by reported occurrence

	EU		3rd markets
1	Technical barriers (28 cases)	1	Customs procedures (111 cases). Of these, 64% were perceived to be of large importance. Most common type of problem: demands on too much documentation (47 cases or 42%); it takes too long (34 cases or 31%); and lack of predictability (30 cases or 27%).
2	Services restrictions (16 cases)	2	Technical barriers (99 cases). Of these, 41% were perceived to be of large importance. Most common type of problem: binding technical rules taking the form of product requirements, testing, certification and labelling (69 cases or 70%).
3	Competition problems (6 cases)	3	Services restrictions (84 cases). Of these, 70% were perceived to be of medium importance. Most common problems: domestic regulations (15 cases) and recognition of foreign standards/education/titles (13 cases), limits on market access (11 cases), anti-competitive behaviour (10 cases), and others.
4	Taxes and fees (5 cases)	4	High tariffs (48 cases). Of these, 73% were perceived to be of large importance. Half of the notifications concerning high tariffs involve machinery and electrical material; the second most common group is non-precious metals and goods of non-precious metals.
5	Government procurement (3 cases)	5	Investment restrictions (41 cases). Of these, 61% were perceived to be of large importance. Most common problems: requirement of national content in production (11 cases) and direct limitations to FDI (8 cases).
6	Government support (2 cases)	6	Competition problems (34 cases). Of these, 65% were perceived to be of medium importance. Most common problem: abuse of dominant position (11 cases) and collusion, cartels, etc. (8 cases).
7	Other barriers (4 cases)	7	Public procurement (23 cases). Of these, 65% were perceived to be of medium importance. Most common problem: lack of openness/information (9 cases), discrimination (7 cases) and local content requirements, etc. (5 cases).
		8	Taxes and fees (20 cases). Of these, 70% were perceived to be of large importance. Most common problem: discrimination (10 cases).
		9	Foreign exchange measures (18 cases). Of these, 44% were perceived to be of large importance. Most common problem: restrictions on inflow and outflow of capital.
		10	Rules of origin (16 cases). Of these, 50% were perceived to be of large importance.
		11	Government support to domestic enterprises (14 cases). Of these, 50% were perceived to be of large importance. Problems were characterised as being both discriminatory and trade-restrictive.
		12	Quantitative import restrictions (13 cases). Of these, 70% were perceived to be of large importance.
		13	Customs classification (13 cases).
		14	Antidumping (11 cases). Of these, 77% were perceived to be of large importance.
		15	Customs valuation (11 cases). Of these, 77% were perceived to be of large importance.
		16	Trade related intellectual property rights (10 cases). Of these, 60% were perceived to be of large importance.
		17	Export restrictions (8 cases).
		18	Tariff benefits in the form of tariff suspensions and tariff quotas (7 cases)
		19	State trading enterprises (5 cases)
		20	Environment rules (2 cases)
		21	Price and market arrangements (1 case)
		22	Sanitary and phytosanitary rules (1 case)

Finnish Survey (2001)

I. General information

Title of survey	Poland and Estonia on the Road to EU Membership – Finnish Companies' Experiences on the Applicant Country Markets
Survey producer	Central Chamber of Commerce of Finland
Export market(s)	Estonia and Poland
Data set	Survey of Finnish companies operating in Poland and Estonia: phone interviews with 168 firms, complemented by in-depth interviews with representatives of other firms. Firms represent mainly industry, some services and trade.
Survey format	Types of barriers specified by survey
Types of NTBs/NTMs surveyed	9 problem areas in the business environment and 7 administrative barriers (manners in which authorities operate)
Surveys definitions of NTBs/NTMs	Not specified
Measure/methodology of ranking	(1) % of firms reporting that a particular problem in the business environment has affected their operations "a lot" or "to some degree." (2) %of firms reporting that operations of authorities has slowed down firms' operations.
Product groups/industries most often mentioned as affected.	No information provided

II. Ranking

	Problems in the business environment		Problems in the operations of the authorities
	Estonia		
1	Level of infrastructure (34% of firms)	1	Customs and border control authorities (24% of firms)
2	Corruption (23%)	2	Inspection and certification authorities (21%)
3	Products approval, technical inspections and standardisation (23%)	3	Regional and local authorities (15%)
4	The economic policy environment (20%)	4	The police (9%)
5	Differing interpretations of the law (18%)	5	Competition authorities (7%)
6	Competition issues (15%): state enterprises, state subsidies, monopoly	6	Courts of law (5%)
7	Company law (15%)	7	Taxation authorities (4%)
8	Taxation issues (5%)		
9	Copyright issues (5%): patents, trademarks, etc.		
	Poland		
1	Level of infrastructure (41%)	1	Customs and border control (52%)
2	Product approval, technical inspections and standardisation (35%): perceived as an effort to safeguard national production; difficult and time-consuming.	2	Inspection and certification authorities (38%)
3	The economic policy environment (34%)	3	Regional and local authorities (19%)
4	Differing interpretations of the law (29%): problems with local and government authorities interpreting the same regulations differently.	4	Taxation authorities (14%)
5	Corruption (27%): appears in public procurement, or in the level of a priority given to a decision by the authorities, amongst other; government bodies perceived to have a large impact on business operations.	5	Courts of law (10%)
6	Taxation issues (23%): different procedures from those in the West	6	Competition authorities (10%)
7	Issues of competition (21%): state enterprises, state subsidies, monopoly	7	The police (9%)
8	Company law (16%)		
9	Copyright issues (3%): patents, trademarks, etc.		

//

Australian Survey (2000)

I. General information

Title of survey	Enhancing the Trade and Investment Environment in the Indian Ocean Rim Region
Survey producer	Australia South Asia Research Centre, RSPAS & the Australian National University
Export market(s)	Indian Ocean Rim region (18 IOR-ARC countries + Egypt)
Data set	Survey (questionnaire) of 146 Australian firms in primary, manufacturing & services industries (of 1 500 approached). Also uses published data from WTO, UNCTAD database and the Australian Department for Foreign Affairs and Trade (DFAT).
Survey format	Types of barriers specified by survey
Types of NTBs/NTMs surveyed	Broad range of border and other measures (19 NTBs, 4 Tariff Barriers and 9 Trade Facilitation Barriers). Among the trade facilitation barriers (TFBs) are those identified at the WTO Trade Facilitation Symposium in Singapore.
Surveys definitions of NTBs/NTMs	Trade facilitation defined as the simplification and harmonisation of international trade procedures, or cutting the red tape that exists in moving goods across borders. Survey includes under common Trade Facilitation Barriers customs delays, customs valuation procedures, TBTs, voluntary restraints and government procurement. NTBs are defined as instruments that interfere with trade and distort domestic production, generally operating as barriers at the border and acting as restraints to imports and/or exports. Survey includes under "core NTBs" exchange controls, tariff quotas, import licences and authorisations, anti-dumping investigations, technical standards and regulations, and bribes.
Measure/methodology of ranking	Proportion of firms that express dissatisfaction with a barrier (an expression of dissatisfaction is taken to represent an impediment); and intensity of dissatisfaction (calculated for each type of impediment by summing the number of questions or aspects of a single question in which dissatisfaction is reported)
Product groups/industries most often mentioned as affected.	Automotive, machinery and equipment, chemicals and related products, textiles, clothing and footwear.

II. Ranking (for NTBs and TFBs only) by proportions of firms expressing dissatisfaction

	NTBs		TFBs
1	Slow customs clearance (57% of relevant firms)	1	Inadequate laws, or enforcement of laws, dealing with anti-competitive conduct such as cartels, market sharing arrangements, boycotts, predatory pricing, and inadequate access to distribution channels (55% of firms)
2	Lack or recognition of intellectual property (49%)	2	Government procurement: Lack of access to adequate and timely information about requirements (53%)
3	Import/export levies (47%)	3	Foreign ownership restrictions (52%)
4	Domestic subsidies/production subsidies (45%)	4	Quarantine services: Lack of transparency/consistency of requirements (49%); Transport: Problems with access to, cost or efficiency of internal transport systems IOR-ARC (49%)
5	Import surcharges (45%)	5	Regulatory barriers to FDI (48%)
6	Discretionary import/export licensing (41%)	6	Government procurement: Lack of transparency of tendering procedures (47%)
7	Sales tax (39%)	7	Transport: High cost of regional international transport services (46%)
8	Tariff rate quota administration (39%)	8	Customs services: Lack of harmonisation and simplification of clearance procedures (44%)
9	Documentation requirements (38%)	9	Standards: Need for harmonising or more closely aligning standards in major markets (43%); Customs services: Requirements of paper documents and/or inability to use electronic communications in custom services (43%)
10	Quarantine issues (36%)	10	Transport: Lack of efficiency of regional and international transport services (42%)
11	Excise duties (35%)	11	Lack of access to up-to-date business information about import requirements (42%)
12	Investment restrictions (34%)	12	Licensing restrictions related to investment and competition (40%)
13	Export subsidies (34%)	13	Customs services: Lack of consistency and transparency of decisions in customs services (38%); Government procurement: requirements for localisation (38%)
14	Labelling (33%)	14	Government procurement: Lack of opportunities to tender for foreign government contracts (37%)
15	Import deposit requirements (31%)	15	Standards: Delays in testing procedures (36%); Quarantine services: costs of testing procedures (36%)
16	Quality assurance requirements (30%)	16	Standards: High costs of testing procedures (35%)
17	Quantitative import/export restrictions (29%)	17	Transport: requirements for firm localisation (35%)
18	Minimum import prices (27%)	18	High customs duties (35%)
19	Voluntary export restraints (20%)	19	Difficulties in identifying the barriers to entering export markets (34%); Need for information on customs duties (34%)
		20	Quarantine services: lack of harmonisation or alignment of standards in export markets (33%)
		21	Standards: Need for multiple testing (33%); Need for business information on compliance with safety and technical standards (32%), and on labelling requirements (32%)
		22	Quarantine services: harmonising regulatory procedures (31%); Limits to mobility of people due to inefficient procedures (31%)
		23	Quarantine services: Delays in testing procedures (30%); Need for business information on changes to regulations (general) (30%); Business mobility: onerous visa requirements (30%);
		24	Quarantine services: Delays in acceptance of certification in export markets (29%)
		25	Restrictions imposed by professional bodies, in such areas as education, legal, medical, financial and accounting services (27%)
		26+	Other

New Zealand Survey (2001)

I. General information

Title of survey	Assessing the Presence and Impact of Non-Tariff Trade Barriers on Exporters
Survey producer	ACNielsen, on behalf of Standards New Zealand (SNZ) in a partnership with the Min. of Foreign Affairs and Trade (MFAT), the Min. of Economic Development (MED), the Min. of Agriculture and Forestry (MAF), and Trade NZ
Export market(s)	Global
Data set	Survey (questionnaire) of 381 New Zealand companies that export goods and/or services related to goods (of 1591 approached)
Survey format	Types of barriers specified by survey
Types of NTBs/NTMs surveyed	19 broad border and other measures
Surveys definitions of NTBs/NTMs	Trade barriers comprise a range of obstacles, which are both tariff and non-tariff related. Tariff barriers can include tariff rates and import quotas. Non-tariff barriers comprise a range of obstacles, including technical, sanitary or phytosanitary regulations, product standards and conformance requirements, and other barriers such as customs procedures, government procurement procedures, and administrative procedures.
Measure/methodology of ranking	Number of firms (%) stating they have faced barrier in the last 3 years; and rating of degree of seriousness using a 4-point scale.
Product groups/industries most often mentioned as affected.	Foods and beverages (92% of all food and beverage exporters face any trade barriers), manufactures, forestry products

II. Ranking by reported occurrence

1. Standards and certification (50%): data certification and testing requirements; labelling, marking or packaging problems; delays in approval
2. Customs procedures (48%): arbitrary regulations; misclassification; excessive documentation requirements; delays due to lack of automation
3. Food safety and health requirements (30%)
4. Import quotas or import prohibitions (28%)
5. Cargo handling and port procedures and requirements (26%)
6. High internal taxes or charges (26%)
7. Subsidies or tax benefits given to competing domestic firms (22%)
8. Non-scientific basis to quarantine restrictions (22%)
9. Distribution constraints in importing countries (21%)
10. Import licensing (20%)
11. Irregular 'additional payments' (bribes) expected to effect imports (18%)
12. Lack of adequate intellectual property protection (17%)
13. Government procurement procedures (15%)
14. Restrictive foreign exchange allocations to importers (14%)
15. State trading or state monopoly control of import (13%)
16. Anti-import campaigns by importing countries (13%)
17. General lack of legal infrastructure (10%)
18. Domestic price controls or administered pricing (9%)
19. Domestic boycotts (8%)

PBEC Survey (1997)

I. General information	
Title of survey	Report on Administrative Barriers to Trade
Survey producer	City University of Hong Kong (Department of Economics and Finance & Faculty of Business) for the Pacific Basin Economic Council (PBEC), which is an association of senior business leaders from the Pacific Basin region
Export market(s)	PBEC countries (Hong Kong, Japan, Taiwan, Australia, New Zealand, China, Korea, Thailand, Malaysia, Philippines, Fiji, Indonesia, United States, Canada, Mexico, Columbia, Chile, Ecuador, Peru and Russia)
Data set	Survey (questionnaire) of 145 PBEC companies in the goods and services sectors (of 1 000 approached), supplemented by interviews with trade commissioners and chambers of commerce, and other research
Survey format	In part a questionnaire with specified barriers, divided into 3 categories: Type A: barrier imposed on companies by foreign government; Type B: barrier imposed by local government on companies' trading partners; and Type C: barrier imposed by local government on companies' business with other PBEC economies
Types of NTBs/NTMs surveyed	10 administrative barriers to trade, drawn from the list of impediments developed by institutions such as UNCTAD and WTO
Surveys definitions of NTBs/NTMs	Administrative barriers to trade (ABTs) are defined as practical problems arising from interpreting or applying trade and investment regulations which indirectly prohibit trade. The survey considers ABTs a form of non-tariff barrier and categorises these into (1) restrictions on market-access, (2) restrictions on personnel, and (3) transparency of regulatory information, all of which directly prohibit or restrict trade and foreign investment
Measure/methodology of ranking	% of firms reporting barrier; and degree of difficulty to overcome the barrier using a 5-point scale
Product groups/industries most often mentioned as affected.	Type A ABTs affect the services sector more than the manufacturing sector.

II. Ranking by reported occurrence (Type A barriers only)	
1	Restrictions on foreign ownership (42.1% of firms)
2	Inconsistency/confusion in regulations (40.7%)
3	Difficulty in obtaining visas (40.0%)
4	Inconsistency/confusion in implementation of regulations (37.2%)
5	Officially sanctioned monopoly/cartel (35.2 %)
6	Excessive documentation required (35.2%)
7	Lack of publicity of regulations (33.8%)
8	Restrictive property rights and commercial presence (32.4%)
9	Unfair tax treatment (31.7%)
10	Quota on number of foreign/local workers (25.5%)
11+	Other barriers (not specified by survey report)

ABAC/APEC Survey (2000)

I. General information	
Title of survey	Survey on Customs, Standards, and Business Mobility in the APEC Region
Survey producer	Asia Pacific Foundation of Canada, for the APEC Business Advisory Council (ABAC)
Export market(s)	21 APEC economies
Data set	Survey (questionnaire) of 461 APEC exporters (manufactures, services, primary and some other). Findings presented also separately for manufacturing sector respondents (198 respondents) only.
Survey format	Types of barriers specified by survey
Types of NTBs/NTMs surveyed	9 categories of border and other impediments, besides tariffs
Surveys definitions of NTBs/NTMs	Survey employs terminology of trade facilitation measures, broadly defined, and is particularly detailed for three major 'trade facilitation areas': customs procedures, standards and conformance, and mobility of business people
Measure/methodology of ranking	Number of respondents (%) considering a trade impediment "very serious" or "serious"; number of respondents considering a trade impediment "not very serious" or "not serious"
Product groups/industries most often mentioned as affected.	No information provided

II. Ranking by no. of respondents (manufacturing sector only) deeming a measure" very serious" or "serious"

1	Tariffs (56% of respondents)	6	Differing product standards (40%). High-ranked specific issues: Standards regulations too complex; lack of transparency in standards; problems with differing national product standards.
2	Customs procedures (55%) High-ranked specific issues: customs regulations too complex; lack of information on customs laws, regulations, administrative guidelines and rulings; and problems associated with classification of goods)	7	Government procurement (39%)
3	Restrictive administrative regulations (53%)	8	Impediments to mobility of business people (30%). High-ranked specific issues: applications process too complex and time consuming for business visas, work permits and temporary residency permits; overly stringent requirements for and/or restrictions on business visas, work permits and temporary residency permits.
4	Restrictive business practices (48%)	9	Anti-dumping measures (29%)
5	Quantitative restrictions (44%)	10	Foreign investment restrictions (26%)

Alberta Survey (2000)

I. General information

Title of survey	Alberta Non-Tariff Trade Barrier Study
Survey producer	Western Centre for Economic Research & University of Alberta (Faculty of Business), Canada
Export market(s)	Global
Data set	Survey (structured phone interview) of 197 Alberta exporters of manufactured goods
Survey format	Specific questions about specific types of barriers and open-ended "other barriers" question
Types of NTBs/NTMs surveyed	Mostly customs procedures, technical measures, import licensing.
Surveys definitions of NTBs/NTMs	NTBs are defined broadly: the term includes traditional non-tariff measures, such as standards, as well as 'invisible' trade barriers, such as procedural delays, excessive documentation requirements, and lack of transparency and predictability in the application of government rules and regulations
Measure/methodology of ranking	Number of companies reporting a barrier. Percentages calculated based on number of firms responding to specific questions, which varies
Product groups/industries most often mentioned as affected.	No information provided

II. Ranking by reported occurrence

1. Problems in determining necessary customs rules (paper work, fees, etc) (73 or 38% of 197 firms)
2. Problems with customs authorities (delays, corruption, ineptitude etc) (67 or 34% of 197 responding firms)
3. Customs fees too high (62 or 35.2% of 176 responding firms)
4. Import licences granted in discretionary manner (15 or 34.8% of 43 firms stating they require import licences)
5. Difficulty determining if there are technical regulations or standards (62 or 31% of 197 firms). Technical assistance was required by 57 (28.9% of firms)
6. Problems with conformity assessment procedures (37 or 18.8% of 197 firms)
7. Preferential or discriminatory treatment given to products of other countries (by customs authorities, preferential procurement, etc) (32 or 18.1% of 177 responding firms)
8. Discriminatory technical regulations or standards (26 or 13.2% of 197 firms)
9. Standards inconsistent with international standards (16 or 8.1% of 92 firms confirming existence of international standards for their product)
10. Import quotas (15 or 7.6% of 197 firms)
11. Private voluntary standards with negative effects on sales (11 or 5.6% of 32 firms stating they are affected by private standards)

Brazilian Survey (2001)

I. General information

Title of survey	Identificão das Barreiras ao Comércio no Mercosul: A Perceptcão das Empresas Exportadoras Brasileiras
Survey producer	Instituto de Pesquisa Econômica Aplicada (IPEA), Ministério do Planejamento, Orcamento e Gestão
Export market(s)	Argentina, Paraguay, Uruguay (3 Mercosur member countries)
Data set	Survey (questionnaire) of 412 Brazilian exporting companies (mainly from manufacturing sector)
Survey format	Types of barriers specified by survey
Types of NTBs/NTMs surveyed	16 NTBs, divided into 'visible' and 'non-visible' barriers
Surveys definitions of NTBs/NTMs	Not specified
Measure/methodology of ranking	Number of firms (%) reporting a barrier; and perceived importance of a barrier to the firm, using a scale from 1 to 6.
Product groups/industries most often mentioned as affected.	For 'visible' barriers (freight and insurance costs, customs clearance fees and charges): footwear, mining, non-ferrous metals, chemicals, electrical material. For 'non-visible' barriers: animal products, plastic articles, footwear, non-ferrous metals, electrical material, and textiles.

II. Ranking by reported occurrence

1. Freight and insurance costs (49% of companies)
2. Customs clearance fees and charges (48%)
3. Labelling requirements (48%)
4. Excessive customs procedures (35%)
5. Pre-shipment inspection (32%)
6. Inspection and testing requirements (31%)
7. Import licensing (23%)
8. Product registration (21%)
9. Technical certification (19%)
10. Indirect taxes (17%)
11. Exporters' registration requirements (16%)
12. Transportation regulations (15%)
13. Sanitary and phytosanitary measures (14%)
14. Regional content requirements (12%)
15. Patent requirements (9%)
16. Government procurement (8%)

Chile Survey (2000)

I. General information	
Title of survey	Catastro nacional sobre barreras externas al comercio (Segunda Versión)
Survey producer	Department of Trade, Ministries of Economics, Mining and Energy
Export market(s)	14 markets (EU, Chinese Taipei, China, Korea, Japan, United States and 8 Latin American countries)
Data set	Survey (questionnaire) completed by 220 Chile exporters of goods and services
Survey format	Types of barriers specified by survey
Types of NTBs/NTMs surveyed	7 broad border and other measures
Surveys definitions of NTBs/NTMs	Not specified
Measure/methodology of ranking	Number of firms (%) reporting a barrier (notifications)
Product groups/industries most often mentioned as affected.	Meats, fish and seafood, grapes, kiwi fruit; cosmetics and pharmaceuticals, fertilisers, copper.

II. Ranking by reported occurrence

1. Import policies (34% of firms). Particular problems mentioned: delays in automatic import licensing, partly due to centralisation of administration; wide coverage of non-automatic import licensing; too stringent import quotas.

2. Technical measures (30%). Specific problems mentioned: sanitary regulations such as vaccination requirements; costly regulations applying to fish and seafood; certain import prohibitions of products deemed dangerous; discrepancies in quality standards for domestic and imported products.

3. Restrictions on services (8%). Specific problem mentioned with respect to professional services: restrictions on the use of foreign workers.

4. Subsidies (6%). Specific problems mentioned: export subsidies that are not in accordance with the WTO.

5. Trade defence instruments (6%): antidumping, countervailing duty and safeguard measures, minimum import requirements.

6. Additional charges (4%). Specific problems mentioned: obligation to contract maritime insurance with importing country, which often is more expensive.

7. Intellectual property rights (1%). Specific problems mentioned: excessive time for registration of trademarks and patents.

ALADI (2001)

I. General information

Title of survey	Informe sobre los requerimentos de las PYMES para impulsar el comercio intrarregional que podría desarrollar la ALADI
Survey producer	Asociacion Latinoamericana de Integración (ALADI)
Export market(s)	ALADI countries (Argentina, Bolivia, Brazil, Chile, Columbia, Cuba, Ecuador, Mexico, Paraguay, Peru, Uruguay, Venezuela)
Data set	Survey (questionnaire) of 30 SMEs in ALADI (out of 220 approached)
Survey format	Information not yet available
Types of NTBs/NTMs surveyed	A broad range of tariff and non-tariff barriers
Surveys definitions of NTBs/NTMs	Not specified
Measure/methodology of ranking	Number of firms reporting a problem encountered by their exports (notifications)
Product groups/industries most often mentioned as affected.	No information provided

II. Ranking by reported occurrence

1	Product standards: lack of information re. requirements (17 notifications)	7	Lack of information re. marketing regulations and regional agreements (7 notifications)
2	Customs and bureaucratic procedures (12 notifications)	8	SPS and heterogeneous technical measures (5 notifications)
3	Finance and payment mechanisms (11 notifications)	9	Asymmetric physical and technological infrastructure of countries (5 notifications)
4	Non-tariff barriers – not specified (9 notifications)	10	Political and economic instability (1 notification)
5	Competition in costs and production (9 notifications)	11	Subsidies (1 notification)
6	Transportation: costs, frequency, and insecurity; inadequate logistics (9 notifications)		

Zimbabwean Survey (1995)

I. General information

Title of survey	Performance and Constraints to Zimbabwe's Manufacturing Sector in Intra-COMESA Trade; Export/Import Strategy and Technology Limitations
Survey producer	International Trade Centre
Export market(s)	Common Market of Eastern and Southern Africa (COMESA)
Data set	Survey (interviews) of 41 Zimbabwean manufacturing firms (of 60 approached)
Survey format	Types of barriers specified by survey
Types of NTBs/NTMs surveyed	12 border and other types of barriers
Surveys definitions of NTBs/NTMs	Survey divides barriers into i) direct trade barriers: import licences and quotas, and ii) indirect trade barriers: tariffs, transport costs, lack of knowledge of the regional market, dumping, inability to pay (foreign exchange requirements), late payments and bad debts, administrative procedures, lack of skills, lack of demand, high costs of finance, lack of trade finance and border delays.
Measure/methodology of ranking	Number of firms rating a barrier as "serious," "moderate" or "slight" obstacle to regional exports.
Product groups/industries most often mentioned as affected.	Textiles and clothing, metal works, staple food products

II. Ranking by no. of firms reporting barrier as "serious" or "moderate"

1	Inability to pay (95% of firms): mainly perceived to derive from lack of foreign currency and lack of trade finance throughout the region.	7	Tariffs (59%): despite the intention of moving on to a common market, the average level of tariff in individual exports was reported to be about 20%.
2	High domestic cost of borrowing (93%): was perceived to be eroding the cost advantages firms could otherwise enjoy.	8	Import licences (59%): import licensing was prevalent in the 1980s as a government means of rationing the scarce foreign currency but now affect mainly the export of staple food products.
3	Lack of export incentive scheme (88%): the removal of the export incentive as well as the export retention schemes was perceived to seriously affect most firms that had established export production lines, particularly to benefit from these schemes.	9	Lack of demand (56%)
4	Lack of knowledge of regional market (80%): unavailability of regional market information was singled out as a major difficulty (easier to get market information about Japan, Europe and America than about neighbouring regional markets).	10	Dumping (54%): dumping of some manufactured goods by the newly industrialized countries of Southeast Asia was perceived as a severe constraint; other cases of unfair competition stemmed from foreign based and local Zimbabwean firms.
5	Administrative blocking and border delays (80%): reasons given for delays were a shorter working day, low efficiency, equipment breakdowns and sometimes the shortage of special forms for documentation.	11	Late payments and bad debts (49%): payment problems and particularly bad debts were perceived to seriously affect the export determination of firms.
6	Transport costs, excluding those caused by border and administrative delays (68%): most firms perceived transport costs a moderate rather than a serious problem.	12	Overvaluation of NZD (20%)

Annex 1.A3

SURVEYS USING MEASURES OTHER THAN FREQUENCY OF RESPONSES TO REPORT EXISTENCE OR ESTIMATED MAGNITUDE OF BARRIERS

Morocco Survey (2001)

I. General information	
Title of survey	Les exportateurs marocains face aux barrières non-tarifaires dans le cadre inter-islamique
Survey producer	Association Marocaine des Exportateurs (ASMEX) & M. Ahmed Azirar
Export market(s)	56 countries from East Asia, Africa and Gulf Arab regions that are members of the Organization of the Islamic Conference (OIC)
Data set	Survey (questionnaire) of 3 Moroccan associations and 29 companies in goods sector (of all ASMEX members approached). Also analyses separately NTM data for certain ASMEX countries from the UNCTAD database.
Survey format	Types of barriers specified by survey
Types of NTBs/NTMs surveyed	A broad range of border and behind the border barriers
Surveys definitions of NTBs/NTMs	NTBs are composed of restrictive measures, imposed on imports and intended to compensate the removal of tariffs resulting from various trade agreements.
Measure/methodology of ranking	Number of countries cited as having the barrier
Product groups/industries most often mentioned as affected.	No information provided

II. Ranking (by no. of countries cited)				
1	Administrative Regulations: problems with certification of export documents in Morocco (12 countries). Complicated procedures that can generate fees of 3000 DHS per container; serious delays.	12	Country risk (3 countries)
2	Customs valuations (10 countries): perceived to be arbitrary, not based on invoice.	13	Requirements for additional documentation (3 countries)
3	Customs clearance procedures (9 countries): some countries do not have appropriate legislation on customs regulations and procedures, resulting in subjective interpretations and arbitrary decisions. This causes delays and damages to the merchandise.	14	Problems with customs procedures (3 countries)
4	Pre-shipment inspection (5 countries): even though the inspection is justified, in practice it is perceived to be similar to a para-tariff barrier in that it generates additional fees for the exporter. It also undermines the good faith of the economic agent and causes delays.	15	National regulations (3 countries)
5	Subsidies and government assistance to local products (4 countries)	16	Sample inspections (3 countries)
6	Additional charges for registration of products (4 countries): sometimes taxes are arbitrary and do not correspond to any service rendered.	17	Dumping (3 countries)
7	Exchange rate problems (4 countries)	18	Problems with visas (3 countries)
8	Import licensing and prior import declarations (3 countries)	19	Rules of origin (3 countries)
9	Sanitary and phytosanitary measures (3 countries)	20	Non-respect of agreements (2 countries)
10	Conformity assessment procedures (3 countries)	21	No insurance coverage for exports (2 countries)
11	Tariff barriers (3 countries): certain exporters have left the Islamic market when, for instance, a country suddenly imposed a tax of 250% on the product concerned to protect its domestic production.	22+	Other: Transportation and port entry, quotas, testing, investment barriers, negative lists in investment policy, customs classification, corruption.

ASEAN Survey (1995)

I. General information	
Title of survey	Non-Tariff Barriers
Survey producer	ASEAN Secretariat
Export market(s)	ASEAN countries
Data set	Submissions made by Member Countries, the ASEAN Chambers of Commerce & Industry (ASEAN-CCI), and information from GATT Trade Policy Reviews and UNCTAD's Trade Analysis and Information System (TRAINS) database. Sectors covered are minerals, electrical appliances, machinery, which are the key tradables in the region.
Survey format	Open
Types of NTBs/NTMs surveyed	A broad range of non-tariff barriers
Surveys definitions of NTBs/NTMs	Uses TRAINS working definitions for trade control measures
Measure/methodology of ranking	Number of tariff lines affected by an NTB
Product groups/industries most often mentioned as affected.	No information provided

II. Ranking (based on the number of tariff lines affected by an NTB)

1. Customs surcharges (applied to 2,683 tariff lines)
2. Technical measures (applied to 568 tariff lines)
3. Product characteristic requirements (applied to 407 tariff lines)
4. Additional charges (applied to 126 tariff lines)
5. Single channel for imports (applied to 65 tariff lines)
6. State-trading administration (applied to 10 tariff lines)
7. Marketing requirements (applied to 3 tariff lines)
8. Technical regulations (applied to 3 tariff lines)

Argentina Surveys (1999)

I. General information	
Title of survey	Survey I : Informe de barreras a las exportaciones argentinas en el NAFTA Survey II : Informe de barreras a las exportaciones argentinas en la Unión Europea
Survey producer	National Commission of Trade (Unit of Studies of Competition and International Trade), Argentina
Export market(s)	(I) 3 NAFTA markets and (II) EU
Data set	Survey (questionnaire) of 224 Argentinean firms (out of 2391 approached), supplemented by data from a permanent database in which Argentinian exporters register complaints; reports from national and international organisms, embassies and consulates. Database has 43 measures; typology is inspired from UNCTAD's database. Goods sector.
Survey format	Open-ended
Types of NTBs/NTMs surveyed	5 categories of measures classified by public policy objective.
Surveys definitions of NTBs/NTMs	NTBs are defined as governmental laws, regulations, policies or practices of a country that restrict the access of imported products to its market. Survey also uses UNCTAD's concept of 'core barriers,' which comprise antidumping and countervailing measures, prohibitions, quotas, non-automatic import licensing and seasonal high tariffs.
Measure/methodology of ranking	3 'Inventory Indicators': 'Global Indicator' (number of NTBs applied in the importing market); 'Frequency Indicator' (tariff lines affected by NTBs); 'Scope Indicator' (amount of imports relating to tariff lines affected by NTBs).
Product groups/industries most often mentioned as affected.	Meats, fish, cereals

II. Ranking (based on the number of tariff lines affected by an NTB and showing exports for 1992-96)

#	NAFTA	#	EU
1	Sanitary and phytosanitary measures (36.3%), of which 17% are 'core' barriers (i.e. from among antidumping and countervailing measures, prohibitions, quotas, non-automatic import licensing, seasonal high tariffs).	1	Sanitary and phytosanitary measures (49.5%), of which 1% are 'core' barriers.
2	Import policies (34.7%), of which 47% are 'core' barriers. Most restrictive import policies: non-automatic import licensing followed by quotas.	2	Import policies (45.5%), of which 60% are 'core' barriers. Most restrictive import policies: contingent protection followed by non-automatic import licensing.
3	Technical measures (15.6%), of which 1% are 'core' barriers.	3	Environmental measures (3.7%), of which 6% are 'core' barriers.
4	Environmental measures (7.2%), of which 47% are 'core' barriers.	4	Technical measures (1.2%), of which 0% are 'core barriers.
5	Discriminatory public policies (5.9%), of which 0% are 'core' barriers.		

Chinese, Japanese and Korean Joint Survey (2001)

I. General information	
Title of survey	Report and Policy Recommendations on Strengthening Trade Relations between China, Japan and Korea
Survey producer	Trilateral joint research by the Development Research Centre (DRC) of China, the National Institute for Research Advancement (NIRA) of Japan, and the Korean Institute for International Economic Policy (KIEP)
Export market(s)	China, Japan, and Korea
Data set	Survey (questionnaire) of 115 Chinese firms (of 2500 approached), 236 Japanese firms (of 1500 approached), and 331 Korean firms (of 1000 approached). Primary and industrial goods sectors.
Survey format	Types of barriers specified by survey
Types of NTBs/NTMs surveyed	Range of 15 non-tariff measures, with a focus on trade facilitation issues
Surveys definitions of NTBs/NTMs	Not specified
Measure/methodology of ranking	Score of importance of non-tariff barriers using weighted-average. Scale assigns 5 points to "Strongly agree," 4 points to "Agree," 3 points to "Neither agree or disagree," 2 points to "Disagree," and 1 point to "Strongly disagree."
Product groups/industries most often mentioned as affected.	No information provided

II. Ranking	China		Japan		Korea	
	Japan	Korea	China	Korea	China	Japan
Restrictions and quotas	3.00	3.16	3.27	2.59	2.90	2.80
Complexity of customs and trade administration	3.05	2.83	3.47	2.69	3.54	2.41
Sanitary and phytosanitary measures	3.05	3.30	3.51	2.80	2.77	2.65
Technical barriers to trade	3.00	3.09	2.93	2.56	2.61	2.64
Licences	2.63	2.85	3.18	2.63	3.09	2.64
Absence of policy	3.17	3.42	3.50	2.67	3.34	2.63
Protectionism	3.38	3.32	3.46	2.93	3.57	2.75
Complexity of government structure	3.03	2.94	3.60	2.65	3.66	2.59
Slow administrative measures	2.97	2.76	3.51	2.65	3.93	2.39
Unfairness and corruption	2.66	3.05	3.43	2.65	3.54	2.30
Cultural differences	2.82	3.37	3.36	2.82	3.21	2.66
Differences in business customs	2.89	3.24	3.88	3.11	3.53	2.93
Language difficulties	3.08	3.18	3.47	3.02	3.32	2.60
Lack of information	3.47	3.45	3.44	2.85	3.53	2.84
Exclusive culture	2.88	2.72	2.92	2.97	3.03	2.64

MENA Survey (2000)

I. General information	
Title of survey	Harnessing Trade for Development and Growth in the Middle East
Survey producer	Council on Foreign Relations Study Group on Middle East Trade Options (2002)
Export market(s)	9 markets in the Middle East and North Africa (MENA) region: Egypt, the West Bank and Gaza, Israel, Jordan, Lebanon, Saudi Arabia, Syria, Tunisia and the United Arab Emirates
Data set	Survey (questionnaire) of 250 companies in the manufacturing and services sectors, supplemented by interviews
Survey format	Structured questionnaire
Types of NTBs/NTMs surveyed	A set of trade policies and regulatory and administrative constraints that create additional burdens to trading within the MENA region
Surveys definitions of NTBs/NTMs	Not specified.
Measure/methodology of ranking	Companies' estimation of trading costs by type of constraint using a 4-point scale, where 1 means that the constraint is not costly and 4 means that the constraint is prohibitive. Constraints with an average score equal to or greater than 1.8 were retained in the final results of survey. Separately, companies were also asked to quantify administrative costs (in terms of no. of working hours and days) and informal constraints.
Product groups/industries most often mentioned as affected.	No information provided

II. Ranking

1. Customs duties (average score=3.0)
2. Domestic taxes (average score=2.6)
3. Customs clearance (average score=2.5)
4. Public sector corruption (average score=2.4)
5. Inspection, conformity certification (average score=2.2)
6. Trans-shipment regulatory measures (average score=2.1)
7. Entry visa restrictions for business (average score=1.8)

Annex 1.A4

INVENTORIES IDENTIFYING BUT NOT RANKING NTBs

Chinese Taipei Survey (2001)

I. General information	
Title of survey	2001: The Barriers to Trade Encountered by Chinese Exporters (China-Taipei)
Survey producer	Chinese National Federation of Industries (CNFI)
Export market(s)	East Asia, the Americas, Europe, Africa
Data set	Survey (questionnaire) of 125 Taiwanese exporters (mostly manufacturers)
Survey format	Open
Types of NTBs/NTMs surveyed	A broad range of tariff and non-tariff measures
Surveys definitions of NTBs/NTMs	Not specified
Measure/methodology of ranking	Specific exporter complaints about unreasonable trade barriers. No ranking applied.
Product groups/industries most often mentioned as affected.	Chemicals, steel, electronics, tires, and construction material

II. List of principal reported barriers

Non-membership in WTO: exporters complain their products are subject to higher tariff rates as a result of not being member of the WTO.

Customs rules and procedures: political discrimination in certain countries; arbitrary and non-transparent procedures.

Technical measures: non-recognition of local certification.

Quantitative restrictions: tariff quotas and import licensing.

Additional charges: excessive fees for obtaining visa and other required documents; excessive shipping and port fees.

Tariffs: high tariffs on specific products.

Indian Survey (1999)

I. General information

Title of survey	Non-Tariff Barriers (NTBs) Faced by India. Preliminary Report.
Survey producer	Ministry of Commerce, Economic Division, India
Export market(s)	United States, EU and Japan.
Data set	Meetings (common and individual) with Export Promotion Councils and exporters, and responses received from them regarding NTBs faced by their sector in the major destinations. Study also compiles separately data for these 3 trading partners from the TRAINS and the Indian Directorate General of Commercial Intelligence and Statistics (DGCI&S). Agricultural and manufactured products.
Survey format	Open
Types of NTBs/NTMs surveyed	A broad range of border and other measures
Surveys definitions of NTBs/NTMs	Not specified
Measure/methodology of ranking	A broad inventory. No ranking applied.
Product groups/industries most often mentioned as affected.	Agriculture, textiles, fish products, chemicals, electrical machinery

II. List of principal NTBs by destination

United States	EU	Japan
Tariff quotas (tobacco and dairy products): management of tariff quotas for tobacco are perceived to be more restrictive than necessary; in-built rigidities reported in the licensing arrangement for dairy products.	Restrictions on market access for fur products	Proposed reference pricing system results in market entry difficulties (especially for pharmaceuticals)
Unnecessary supplementary documents and information required by customs during clearance: overly-detailed; rule of origin problems.	Restrictions on production practices: only imported wines produced with the oenological practices of the EU authorised	Impediments in accessing distribution channels
Excessive fees (customs, harbour, arrival facilities, transport, etc)	Development of standards for certain product groups, based on minimum health and safety requirements: export of nutritional supplements affected due to strict SPS measures.	Lack of transparency in administrative practices and burdensome and unpredictable nature of application process; prevalence of informal directives
Import prohibitions on dairy products and on shrimp	Delays in exports due to delayed laboratory test reports: test reports face lengthy approval processes by European affiliates that are affected by political concerns; marketing bans on genetically modified organisms (GMOs) which run counter to EU regulations	Discriminatory excise tax system (imported distilled spirits)
Strict certification on industrial fasteners: strict International Standard; prevalence of third-party testing and certification instead of self-testing.	Labelling issues: labelling of all new processed foods and food ingredients; labelling to indicate recyclability or reusability causes problems for glass, plastic containers; eco-labelling	Burdensome on-site inspection requirements, fumigation policy, etc., for horticulture products: hence difficulty in market access for leafy vegetables, strawberries, some citrus and avocados
Labelling (esp. car parts, fur products, wine) and extensive product description requirements	Ban on the use of 'specified risk materials' in certain products	Labelling of foods produced using biotechnology
Strict sanitary and phytosanitary-sanitary requirements on fruits and vegetables Differences at state level in regulations	Strict sanitary measures: veterinary sanitary equivalency required to be at par with EU. Early phasing out of some hydrochlorofluorocarbons affects exports of refrigeration and air conditioning exports.	Import quotas (fish) Strict certification restricting competition
Other barriers: taxes (harbour maintenance, levy of luxury, penalty payments, gas guzzle and excise, ad valorem); unilateral sanctions; application of domestic legislation outside borders.	Reclassification by EU states raises tariff rates for certain goods	Other barriers: food sanitation laws (vitamins); poor market access and sales opportunities (automotive); standards and specifications (utilities); use of narrow technical standards rather than performance based standards; lack of equal access to procurement information for local and foreign firms

Brazilian Survey (2000)

I. General information

Title of survey	Obstáculos ao acesso das exportações do Brasil ao Mercado Comunitário
Survey producer	Missão do Brasil with the collaboration of European Communities
Export market(s)	EU Market (15 countries)
Data set	Information on barriers collected from Brazilian Embassies in Athens, Dublin, London and Paris. Agricultural and industrial goods sectors, surveyed separately.
Survey format	Open
Types of NTBs/NTMs surveyed	A broad range of tariff and non-tariff barriers. Uses UNCTAD's definition for certain barriers.
Surveys definitions of NTBs/NTMs	Not specified
Measure/methodology of ranking	List of identified tariff and non-tariff barriers. No ranking applied.
Product groups/industries most often mentioned as affected.	No information provided

II. List of principal barriers by sector

Agricultural sector		Industrial sector	
Tariff barriers	Non-tariff barriers	Tariff barriers	Non-tariff barriers
Tariff peaks (those ad valorem tariffs higher than 12%): these are concentrated in oranges and orange juices, tropical fruits, bananas, tuna, vegetable oils, meat, dairy products, tobacco.	Tariff quotas: particularly affects sugar, bananas, meats and fish.	High tariffs	Quantitative restrictions in specific products/sectors: textiles
Tariff escalations: identified in tuna, soya, sugar, coffee, cigars.	Sanitary and phytosanitary barriers: the authorisation process required by the European Commission to import any animal products is perceived to be slow and overly stringent (with requirements stricter that those of Codex Alimentarius).		Standards: eco-labelling program reflects the methods and procedures used in the EU, discriminating against other productive processes used in third countries.
SGP: loss of market share in certain products (coffee, melon, tobacco, mango) due to the lower tariffs the main competitors form LDCs enjoy within the WTO framework of the System of General Preferences.	Prices control measures: all fruits and vegetables that enter the EU with a price below the one stipulated by the Commission are penalised with an equivalent tariff, undermining the competitiveness of Mercosur exports.		Certification and other technical barriers: results in high costs and hinders exports. Examples provided are the following: need for special accessories to reduce the noise of machinery; labelling requirements of recyclable products; difficulties in the inspection and approval process of regulated products.
	Seasonal and product-specific tariffs: result mostly from the tarrification process of NTBs, and particularly affects cereals, sugar, milk, meat, and oil.		
	Export subsidies		

COMESA Survey (1999)

I. General information

Title of survey	Non Tariff Barriers in Common Market for Eastern and Southern Africa – Recent Developments (reviews the findings)
Survey producer	COMESA Secretariat
Export market(s)	COMESA regional market (Angola, Burundi, Comoros, Djibouti, Congo, Egypt, Eritrea, Ethiopia, Kenya, Madagascar, Malawi, Mauritius, Namibia, Rwanda, Seychelles, Sudan, Swaziland, Uganda, Zambia and Zimbabwe)
Data set	Studies conducted by COMESA in 1999 to identify and document information relating to non-tariff barriers and other restrictions to intra-COMESA trade
Survey format	Open
Types of NTBs/NTMs surveyed	Broad range of non-tariff barriers and other obstacles
Surveys definitions of NTBs/NTMs	Not specified
Measure/methodology of ranking	Non-exhaustive list of barriers. No ranking applied.
Product groups/industries most often mentioned as affected.	No information provided

II. List of barriers

Difficulties in issuance of passports and visa, especially for small and medium scale cross border traders	Inconsistent application of standards
Cumbersome and bureaucratic delays in the processing of documentation for the clearance of goods at border posts	Non-acceptance of certificates of origin
Pre-shipment inspection	Centralised clearing process for permits and licences
Insecurity of transit traffic including unauthorised examination of transit goods	Inconsistent application of sanitary and phytosanitary requirements
Cumbersome transit charges and procedures	Differentiated border opening hours
Inconsistent application of air cargo charges	Foreign exchange restrictions
Inadequate physical and communications infrastructure	High transit charges and toll fees
Unjustified import bans	No standardisation of customs documentation
Restrictive transit fees	Linguistic barriers
Unharmonised axle load limitations	

Bibliography (by export region)

I. Asia-Pacific

China's myriad customs regimes and their implications for openness (with reference to steel imports), *University of Adelaide, School of Economics, Chinese Economies Research Centre* (www.adelaide.edu.au/CIES/CERS/wrkpprs/97_18.pdf).

China's steel imports: An outline of recent trade barriers, *University of Adelaide Department of Economics*, July 1996 (www.adelaide.edu.au/CERU/wrkpprs/96_6.pdf).

Enhancing the trade and investment environment in the Indian Ocean Rim, *Australia South Asia Research Centre, RSPAS, the Australian National University*, December 2000 (www.dfat.gov.au/trade/iorarc/enhancing_trade.html).

Identification and analysis of trade barriers in Indonesia, Thailand, Malaysia and the Philippines: Final report, Prepared by *PricewaterhouseCoopers*, London, United Kingdom for Directorate General Trade, Commission of the European Communities, September 2001.

Market access analysis to identify barriers in China and Russia affecting the EU textiles industry, *Centre d'Etudes Economiques et Institutionnelles (CEEI), Brussels*, 10/04/2000 (europa.eu.int/comm/trade/pdf/mka_text_rus.pdf).

Non-tariff barriers, *AFTA Reader*, Volume 3, September 1996 (ASEAN Secretariat).

Report and policy recommendations on strengthening trade relations between China, Japan and Korea, *Development Research Center (DRC) of China, National Institute for Research Advancement (NIRA) of Japan, and Korea Institute for International Economic Policy (KIEP),* October 2001 (www.nira.go.jp/newse/paper/joint/english.htm).

Report on administrative barriers to trade, *Pacific Basin Economic Council (PBEC)*, 1997 (www.pbec.org/publications/policy.htm).

Selected non-tariff barriers (NTBs) to trade faced by the Philippines, *Bureau of International Trade Relations (BITR)*, Makati City, Philippines, 2001.

Survey on customs, standards and business mobility in the APEC region, *Asia Pacific Foundation of Canada for the APEC Business Advisory Council (ABAC)*, September 2000 (www.asiapacific.ca/analysis/pubs/listing.cfm?ID_Publication=111).

Vietnam's integration with ASEAN: Survey of non-tariff measures affecting trade, *United Nations Development Project*, January 1999 (www.undp.org.vn/projects/vie95015/).

II. South America

Audiovisual industry; trade and investment barriers in third country markets: Final report, Prepared by *Solon Consultants* for European Commission, DG1 Market Access Unit, November 1998 (www.obs.coe.int/online_publication/reports/00002413.pdf) [United States and Mexico are also covered].

Barreiras não-tarifárias às exportações brasileiras no Mercosul: O caso de calçados, *Patricia Anderson, Institute of Applied Economic Research (IPEA)*, Rio de Janeiro, IPEA Discussion Paper No. 791, May 2001 (in Portuguese) (www.ipea.gov.br/pub/td/td_2001/td0791.pdf).

Evaluation de restricciones al comercio interno del Mercosur, Su perspectiva desde Argentina, Brasil y Uruguya (Sintesis de tres documentos nacionales), Proyecto desarrollado en el marco de la Red-Mercosur (*ITDT, Argentina; IPEA, Brasil; De/FCS, Uruguay*) con el apoyo del IDRC-CIID, *Julio Berlinski*, Versión preliminar, Noviembre 2000 (in Spanish) (www.redmercosur.org.uy/espanol/proyectos/berlinski/comercio_interno.htm).

Identificacao das barreiras ao comercio no Mercosul, A percepcao das empresas exportadoras brasileiras, *Honorio Kume, Patrícia Anderson, & Márcio de Oliveira, Jr., Institute of Applied Economic Research (IPEA)*, Rio de Janeiro, IPEA Discussion Paper No. 789, May 2001 (in Portuguese). (www.ipea.gov.br/pub/td/td_2001/td0789.pdf).

Informe sobre los requerimentos de las PYMES para impulsar el comercio intrarregional que podría desarrollar la ALADI, *Asociación Latinoamericana de Integración (ALADI)*, June 2001 (in Spanish).

Medidas contrarias al libre comercio intrarregional aplicadas después de la resolución No. 41 – 99 (COMIECO XIII), *Ministerio de Comercio Exterior de Costa Rica*, December 2001 (www.comex.go.cr/acuerdos/comerciales/centroamerica/obstaculos/2001/noviembre.pdf) (in Spanish).

Restricões comerciais às exportações de produtos siderúrgios no Mercosul, *Marcio De Oliveira, Jr., Institute of Applied Economic Research (IPEA)*, Rio de Janeiro, IPEA Discussion Paper No. 792, May 2001 (in Portuguese) (http://papers.ssrn.com/sol3/papers.cfm?abstract_id=290269).

III. North America

Informe de barreras a las exportaciones argentinas en el NAFTA, *Unidad de Estudios de la Competencia y del Comercio Internacional (UECCI), Comisión Nacional de Comercio Exterior*, Buenos Aires, Argentina, May 1999 (in Spanish) (www.mecon.gov.ar/cnce/publicaciones/barreras/nafta_actual.pdf).

U.S. barriers to Brazilian goods and services, *Brazilian Embassy (Washington, D.C)*, October 2001. (www.brasilemb.org/barriers2001.pdf).

IV. Europe

Handelshindringer for Dansk Eksport, *Gallup Organization on behalf of the Danish Government*, Denmark, November1997 (in Danish) (www.efs.dk/publikationer/rapporter/handelsh/).

Informe de barreras a las exportaciones argentinas en la Unión Europea, *Unidad de Estudios de la Competencia y del Comercio Internacional (UECCI), Comisión Nacional de Comercio Exterior*, Buenos Aires, Argentina, October 1999 (in Spanish) (www.mecon.gov.ar/cnce/publicaciones/barrerasue/bar_default.htm).

Non-tariff barriers to trade in the core countries of the stability pact for South Eastern Europe, Study prepared by *Dr. Hanspeter Tschäni and Dr. Lawrence Wiedmer* for the Bureau Arthur Dunkel, Geneva (undated).

Obstáculos ao acceso das exportacoes do Brasil ao Mercado Comunitário, *Missao do Brasil*, Brussels, 2000, Doc.barreiras/Brasil/2000/rev.1 (in Portuguese).

Poland and Estonia on the road to EU membership, Finnish companies' experiences in the applicant country markets, *Central Chamber of Commerce of Finland*, Helsinki, August2001 (www.keskuskauppakamari.fi?kv-asiat/3_Poland_and_Estonia.pdf).

Single Market Scoreboard. Business survey headline results, *European Commission*, Brussels, Belgium, November 2000, No. 7, p.14-19 (http://europa.eu.int/comm/internal_market/en/update/score/score7en.pdf).

Trade and investment obstacles in the European Union, *Japan Business Council in Europe (JBCE)*, October 1999 (in Japanese).

Trade barriers faced by Swedish firms on the Single Market and in third countries, *Kerstin Berglöf, National Board of Trade (Kommerskollegium)*, Stockholm, April 2001 (www.snee.org/b1berg.pdf).

V. Africa and Middle East

Harnessing trade for development and growth in the Middle East. Report by the Council on Foreign Relations Study Group on Middle East Trade Option, *Council on Foreign Relations, Inc.*, New York, United States, 2002.

Les exportateurs marocains face aux barrières non-tarifaires dans le cadre interislamique, *Association Marrocain des Exportateurs (ASMEX)*, Casablanca, Marocco, June 2001.

Non tariff barriers in Common Market for Eastern and Southern Africa (COMESA), *COMESA Secretariat*, Lusaka, Zambia, December 2001.

Performance and constraints to Zimbabwe's manufacturing sector in intra-COMESA trade; export/import strategy and technology limitations, *Moses Tekere*, 1995. Report available through COMESA's electronic Regional Integration Research Project (www.comesa.int/finance/tekere.htm).

VI. Global Market

Alberta non-tariff trade barriers study, *Western Centre for Economic Research Faculty of Business, University of Alberta*, Canada, September 2000. (www.albertacanada.com/statpub/pdf/non_tariff.pdf).

Assessing the presence and impact of non-tariff trade barriers on exporters, *ACNielsen consultants on behalf of Standards New Zealand, the Ministry of Foreign Affairs and Trade, the Ministry of Economic Development, the Ministry of Agriculture and Forestry, and TradeNZ*, Wellington, New Zealand, June 2001 (www.standards.co.nz/exportsuccess/).

2001 – Barriers to Exports: A survey of Taiwanese investment overseas, *Chinese National Federation of Industries (Chinese Taipei)*, 2001 (in Taiwanese).

Comparative trade policy analysis to assess barriers to trade, *Federation of Indian Chambers of Commerce & Industry (FICCI)*, New Delhi, India, 1999 (www.ficci.com/ficci/trade-barriers.htm).

Global assessment of standards barriers to trade in the information technology industry, *Office of Industries, US International Trade Commission*, Washington, D.C., November 1998 (ftp://ftp.usitc.gov/pub/reports/studies/PUB3141.PDF).

Non-tariff barriers (NTBs) faced by India. Preliminary Report. *Ministry of Commerce, Economic Division*, New Delhi, India, November 1999.

Registro de barreras a las exportaciones argentinas, *Comisión Nacional de Comercio Exterior*, Buenos Aires, Argentina. Periodically updated – latest version 1999 (in Spanish) (www.mecon.gov.ar/cnce/default1.htm).

Segundo catastro nacional sobre barreras externas al comercio y la Inversión – 2000, *Gobierno de Chile, Ministerios de Economia, Mineria Y Energia*, 2000 (in Spanish). Updated in 2002 (www.economia.cl/minecon/decoex/catastro.htm).

VII. Other

An assessment of the costs for international trade in meeting regulatory requirements, TD/TC/WP(99)8/FINAL, OECD, Paris, 1999.

Impact of sanitary and phytosanitary measures on developing countries, *Department of Agricultural and Food Economics, University of Reading,* April 2000 [results from survey of country officials] (www.apd.rdg.ac.uk/AgEcon/research/workingpapers/SPS%20FINAL%20REPORT%20(2).pdf).

The impact of sanitary and phytosanitary measures on developing country exports of agricultural and food products, *Spencer Henson, Rupert Loader, Alan Swinbank and Maury Bredahl*, Draft for Discussion, presented at the Conference on Agriculture and the New Trade Agenda in the WTO 2000 Negotiations, Geneva, Switzerland, October 1-2,1999 (http://wbln0018.worldbank.org/trade/DECagridoc.nsf/cd1d51b0730b98388525657c007c9eb2/f9bf12819fa25cbf852568a300518455).

Chapter 2

Import Prohibitions and Quotas

by

Peter Czaga

This chapter investigates two specific types of quantitative restrictions, namely import prohibitions and quotas. It reviews information on these measures contained in the WTO Trade Policy Reviews, WTO notifications and in various other trade reports. The aim is to contribute to discussions, particularly on market access for non-agricultural goods, at the WTO or elsewhere. The research reveals that the use of quotas and prohibitions for economic reasons has declined, but most countries use prohibitions as part of their regulatory framework to protect human safety and health or the environment, and the tendency appears to be increasing. Traders would benefit if these measures were more transparent. Also, import bans hamper international trade in used goods; their circumstances and appropriateness in terms of regulatory efficiency merit scrutiny.

Introduction

The Uruguay Round re-emphasised the GATT objective of disciplining the use of quantitative trade restrictions and ended with some significant achievements. The rules that allow such restrictions in certain cases have been tightened, *e.g.* for balance of payment reasons. In addition, WTO members were required to phase out measures outside these new rules. In spite of these developments, a significant number of WTO members that notified non-tariff measures to the Negotiating Group on Market Access for Non-Agricultural Products (NAMA) under the DDA (Doha Development Agenda) mandate for negotiations to further reduce or eliminate tariffs and to address non-tariff barriers mention "quantitative restrictions". Similarly, various national and private-sector reports on trade barriers record complaints concerning measures that fall under the broad category of quantitative import restrictions. This indicates that quantitative restrictions, including prohibitions and quotas, remain a subject of concern to traders and governments and affect international trade relations. At the same time, it appears that neither the nature nor the pervasiveness of these measures is well documented. This chapter aims to contribute to a better understanding of the use of prohibitions and quotas and their trade and economic effects.

The chapter is divided into four major sections. The first defines the measures that are examined in detail and raises some methodological issues. Next, the study is situated in the context of the multilateral trading system by summarising existing GATT/WTO disciplines and rules that govern the application of quantitative import restrictions. Some illustrations of how prohibitions and quotas are dealt with by major regional and bilateral trade agreements are provided. The following section summarises findings from research conducted on the incidence of these two types of import restrictions as well as on their role and patterns of use. As it appears that prohibitions play an important role in the international trade of used consumer and capital goods, these cases are addressed in more detail. Finally, the trade and economic impact of prohibitions and quotas are analysed and quantitative data from research in this area are presented.

Definitions of measures and observations concerning methodology

According to WTO terminology, prohibitions and quotas, like other quantitative import restrictions, are measures that are applied at the border and have a direct effect on imports. Their explicit goal is either to limit the volume of specific imported products entering the domestic market or to prohibit their importation completely (Goode, 2003).

- Prohibitions are an unconditional interdiction to import. They may sometimes include further specifications-setting conditions under which the goods are allowed.

- Quotas involve restrictions of imports of specified products by setting a maximum quantity or value of goods authorised for import. Different types of quotas exist, such as global quotas, bilateral quotas, seasonal quotas, quotas linked to export performance, quotas linked to the purchase of local goods, quotas for sensitive product categories and quotas for political reasons.

The literature points out the difficulties of measuring the actual trade and economic impacts of quantitative restrictions (QRs). This chapter applies a methodology similar to one used in earlier investigations of non-tariff measures. To document the incidence of prohibitions and quotas, it relies on WTO notifications and on various trade reports. WTO notifications provide only a limited amount of information. Access to the detailed database on QRs is limited to WTO members, and reverse notifications are generally not very detailed. The primary data source reviewed for this study was the WTO's Trade Policy Reviews (TPRs), 85 of which, dating from 1998 to 2004, were examined. This information was supplemented by data collected by reviewing other material such as the EU's Market Access Database, the Report on WTO Consistency and Trading Policies by Major Trading Partners issued annually by the Japanese government, and the National Trade Estimate Report of Foreign Trade Barriers issued annually by the US government. For the section on used goods, some specialised reports were reviewed. The annexes to this chapter present selected data from these additional sources.

Although the above-mentioned sources provide a significant amount of data on prohibitions and quotas, they have important limitations. The information is not always clear and comprehensive. Also, the depth of treatment of different countries varies, and some of the data may be outdated. In view of these constraints, it was decided not to undertake a quantitative analysis. Nevertheless, the available data allow for identifying and analysing patterns of use of prohibitions and quotas in different countries, the nature and the range of affected products, the types of justifications invoked (economic and non-economic), and, on the basis of these examinations, make it possible to discern certain overall trends.

In the past, agricultural products were treated separately from industrial goods under the multilateral trading system, and they are currently negotiated separately under the DDA. For this reason, and in order to keep this study manageable, agricultural and food products have been largely excluded. Owing to the high incidence of prohibitions and quotas in this area, particularly tariff-rate quotas, agricultural and food products might merit a separate examination at a later stage.

This chapter also discusses briefly other types of quantitative restrictions, such as "quantitative restrictions made effective through state trading operations", "mixing regulations" and "minimum price triggering a quantitative restriction". A short summary of the findings at the end of the section on research findings indicates that these measures appear to be used significantly less often than prohibitions or quotas.

Overview of WTO disciplines on quantitative restrictions

As a fundamental rule, the GATT, through Article XI, prohibits quantitative restrictions on the importation or exportation of any product, by stating that "no prohibition or restrictions other than duties, taxes or other charges, whether made effective through quotas, import or export licences or other measures, shall be instituted or maintained" by any member. There are however a number of exceptions to this general rule. They permit the imposition of quantitative measures for specified objectives, given that such measures are not applied in a manner which would result in arbitrary or unjustifiable discrimination among countries or would represent a disguised restriction on international trade.

Exceptions provided for non-economic reasons:

- Article XI permits import and export prohibitions or restrictions necessary to the application of standards or regulations for the classification, grading or marketing of commodities in international trade.[1]

- Article XX authorises measures necessary for achieving certain public objectives such as protection of public morals and protection of human, animal or plant life or health.

- Article XXI allows a general deviation from WTO obligations in cases where the security interests of a country are concerned. Thus, quantitative restrictions are permissible in respect of trade in products that would negatively affect a country's security interests, *e.g.* arms and ammunition.

Exceptions for economic reasons:

- Articles XII and XVIII:B of the GATT 1994 permit the use of quantitative restrictions on imports by a member with the purpose of safeguarding its external financial position and its balance of payments. In order to reduce the potential for abuse, the GATT clarifies the conditions for invoking these provisions. Restrictive import measures may only be imposed to control the general level of imports and may not exceed the extent necessary to address the balance of payments difficulty. Countries using such measures must specify the products involved and the timetable for the elimination of the measures. Finally, the GATT states that wherever possible, price-based restrictions are to be preferred to quantitative restrictions, except in times of crisis.

- Article XVIII:C permits developing countries to deviate from the provisions when governmental assistance is required for the establishment of a particular industry. Under such conditions, quantitative restrictions are also permitted. The imposition of measures is subject to notification and prior consultations with the affected members or/and to the accord of the General Council.[2]

- Article XIX allows for measures that are necessary to prevent sudden increases in imports from causing serious injury to domestic producers or to relieve producers who have suffered an injury.

The WTO also permits import restrictions through a "waiver of obligations" granted in exceptional circumstances by the Ministerial Conference. Article XXV:5 of the GATT 1947 permits a partial waiver of obligations with the consent of the other contracting parties. When a waiver has been obtained, the contracting party is allowed to impose import restrictions. Waivers admitted under the GATT 1947 and still in effect when the WTO Agreement became effective could be extended under the WTO Agreement.

When in fact quotas or prohibitions are used, the GATT recommends ways to design them. Whenever feasible, such quotas are to be "global", *i.e.* fixed in terms of the total amount of permitted imports. These quotas can be allocated among supplying countries. In such an event, the quotas have to be allocated on the basis of proportions supplied by these countries during a previous representative period. In cases where quotas are not practical, the restrictions may be applied by means of import licences or permits.

Concerning the implementation of provisions, the current procedures for updating WTO documentation on non-tariff measures are based on two Decisions (G/L/59 and G/L/60), adopted in December 1995 by the Council for Trade in Goods. These decisions aim to strengthen the transparency of the application of quantitative restrictions, notably through an inventory of non-tariff measures that is available to members for consultation. All quantitative restrictions are to be notified under Decision G/L/59, which provides a list of such measures in an annex.[3] Members also have the right to make reverse notification. Under Decision G/L/60, measures not captured by the exhaustive list of G/L/59 can be notified by the party affected by the measure.[4]

Treatment of QRs in regional trade agreements

Regional trade agreements (RTAs)[5] usually address quantitative restrictions, including prohibitions and quotas, imposed on all or a subset of import goods. Among major RTAs worldwide, several agreements appear to have removed existing quantitative restrictions with respect to trade between the participating parties, either immediately or progressively over time.

The WTO has prepared an inventory of non-tariff provisions in RTAs based on information extracted from a total of 69 agreements notified to the GATT/WTO (Table 2.1). Provisions on quantitative restrictions in all these RTAs are examined, but the WTO report gives no information concerning specific types of QR measures. There is a definite trend in recent years towards broader as well as faster market access liberalisation in intra-RTA trade in relation to QRs on imports. RTAs signed in the 1990s provide for outright abolition of QRs on imports of all goods (*i.e.* both agricultural and industrial products) much more often than earlier RTAs. It was also found that, compared to free trade agreements (FTAs), customs unions tend to favour faster liberalisation of import QRs.

Table 2.1. Treatment of quantitative restrictions on imports in regional trade agreements

	QRs abolished at date of entry into force		Progressive elimination of QRs on industrial goods	Parties retain the right to impose new QRs on imports[1]
	On all goods	On industrial goods only		
RTAs	12	14	23	12
Customs unions	4	1	2	3
Pre-1990 customs unions	2	-	1	3
Post-1990 customs unions	2	1	1	-
FTAs	8	13	21	9
Pre-1990 FTAs	-	-	4	9
Post-1990 FTAs	8	13	17	-

1. Unless an agreement specifically states that parties may not impose new QRs, it is assumed that they retain this right.

Source: Inventory of Non-Tariff Provisions in Regional Trade Agreements, WT/REG/W/26.

Examples of the treatment of QRs in major RTAs:

- NAFTA (North American Free Trade Area) provides for complete prohibition of QRs (for new products), and for NAFTA partners existing quotas under the mutual recognition agreement (MRA) were eliminated (although safeguard provisions for the textiles and apparel sector permit QRs).

- The bilateral FTAs which the EC has concluded with Mexico and South Africa eliminate all existing QRs on bilateral imports and exports and prohibit the introduction of any new such measures.

- With the Closer Economic Relations (CER) Trade Agreement, Australia and New Zealand eliminated all tariffs as well as QRs on goods by 1 July 1990.

- Countries participating in the ASEAN (Association of South-East Asian Nations) Free Trade Agreement (AFTA) committed to the elimination of all QRs in respect of products under the Common Effective Preferential Tariff (CEPT) Scheme well ahead of the elimination of other types of non-tariff barriers. Special provisions apply to so-called "sensitive" and "very sensitive" products, for which the more developed members agreed to eliminate all QRs by 1 January 2010 while their less developed partners are given more time.

- Several bilateral FTAs (*e.g.* Singapore-Australia, Singapore-Japan, Chile-Canada) do not permit QRs except in accordance with GATT Article XI.

At times, however, the use of some types of QRs continues to be allowed for selected products, such as textiles and automobiles. For example, tariff rate quotas continue to restrict trade in automobiles among the member countries of Mercosur.[6] Similarly, the Chile-Korea FTA permits Chile to maintain or introduce QR measures related to the import of second-hand vehicles.

Occasionally, RTAs allow the use of QRs in circumstances that are defined so broadly that they are easily subject to abuse. The Southern African Customs Union (SACU) permits members to prohibit or restrict the import or export of any goods for "economic, social, cultural or other reasons as may be agreed upon by the Council" of Ministers, the supreme governing body of SACU (Article 25.1).

Finally, RTAs follow, and are consistent with, multilateral trade rules in that members reserve the right to take action and adopt measures that they judge necessary for non-economic regulatory goals related to the protection of human, animal or plant life and health, national security or public morals.

Research findings

This section analyses practices in the use of prohibitions and quotas based on information on these types of non-tariff barriers (NTBs) contained in existing studies on trade restrictions. As mentioned, the assessment is limited by the available data in three ways. First, the relevant trade reports treat different countries and different measures in various degrees of detail; therefore, the findings presented below are not comprehensive. Second, the reports indicate that in most countries prohibitions and quotas are subject to continuous and rapid change, so that some of the material may be outdated. Third, various studies repeatedly claim that it is difficult to obtain reliable information on the precise details of the import regime of certain countries. For this reason, it is likely that the data reflect concerns about access to world markets and about more readily identifiable policies. Quantitative restrictions in smaller markets and developing economies as well as less transparent measures may thus be under-represented.

Existing studies on the incidence of QRs

There is some research based on inventories of quantitative restrictions applied by particular countries with respect to different sectors or categories of trade. Many of these studies consider NTBs or quantitative restrictions as a single category, making it difficult to observe the specific use of prohibitions and quotas. Some findings from studies that treat different QRs as separate categories are as follows:

- A World Bank study carried out by Michalopoulus examined the evolution of non-tariff measures in developing countries over the period 1989-98 and found that non-automatic import licensing is the measure that affects by far the greatest number of imported products, with prohibitions ranking second.[7]

- Michalopoulos also found that resort to prohibitions and quotas, like other NTB measures, has declined for the large majority of countries examined.

- Finger and Schuknecht looked in detail at 33 notifications on quantitative restrictions submitted to the WTO in the period 1996-98. They found that the most often reported measures were prohibitions, followed by licensing and quotas.[8]

- According to research undertaken by the US International Trade Commission (USITC) to quantify NTBs and for which data are being collected from various trade reports, import prohibitions are the third most often cited non-tariff measures (NTMs) affecting imports, preceded by "import licensing" and "standards, testing, certification and labelling".[9]

This section aims to assess the validity of the trends identified in the existing literature with respect to the use and the relative incidence of different quantitative restrictions and to contribute additional information collected from various other data sources.

Findings from WTO notifications

As noted, WTO members are obliged to notify QRs, along with a statement on their trade effects, and the WTO Secretariat's Market Access Division maintains a central registry of such restrictions. Access to this registry is restricted to WTO members, but the Secretariat periodically publishes a document listing the WTO members that have made a notification. The latest list available was issued in March 2004 and reveals that, since 1996, 39 countries have submitted notifications of QRs and 16 have submitted notifications of changes to their QRs (see Annex 2.A1). In addition, 33 members notified the WTO that they do not maintain QRs. It seems that in these cases the countries interpreted the notification obligation as relating only to QRs that were not consistent with the WTO provisions, while other member countries may have notified details of existing QRs even if they can be justified under the exemptions provided by WTO provisions. The available WTO list of notifications does not specify the type of restriction reported by the members.

Information on prohibitions, quotas and other types of QRs can also be compiled from notifications to NAMA on non-tariff measures. The NTBs notified are not described in much detail; information is provided concerning the products affected by the barrier, the nature and trade effects of the barrier, and the WTO provision relevant to the notified measure. A closer examination of this material leads to the following observations:

- QRs have been reported predominantly by developed countries.

- When products are mentioned, textiles, vehicles and forestry products are the most notified categories. Electrical goods, steel products, chemical products, used goods, carpets and leather, and motor parts also feature in several instances.

- Concerning the type of QR, notifications mention most often import prohibitions, followed by quotas and state trading. In several cases, the notifications only indicate quantitative restrictions in general, and do not specify the exact type of the measure (whether prohibition, quota, or licensing) (Table 2.2).

Table 2.2. Notifications of quantitative restrictions made to the WTO Negotiating Group on Market Access for Non-agricultural Products under the DDA mandate

Nature of the barrier	Incidence
Unspecified quantitative restrictions	9
Prohibitions	17
Quotas	9
"Prohibitions or quotas"[1]	15
State trading	5
Total	55

As of May 2004, the countries that had made notifications were: Argentina, Bangladesh, China, Egypt, Japan, Korea, Mexico, Malaysia, New Zealand, Norway, Philippines, Switzerland, Chinese Taipei and Uruguay. The figure for the number of prohibitions reflects an unusually high number of measures notified by one member.

1. One country used the term "Prohibitions or quotas" to describe the measures notified.

Source: OECD, compiled from NTB notifications submitted to NAMA (TN/MA/A*).

As only around 39 WTO members have submitted notifications regarding quantitative (export and/or import) restrictions and the data provided are limited in detail, the WTO sources do not provide adequate information on the different QRs applied by members. The data indicate that, in practice, the notification obligation of the WTO is not fully achieving its aim of increasing transparency in this area.

QR issues in the context of the WTO dispute settlement process

Since 1995 a significant number of requests for consultations related to import restrictions have been submitted to the Dispute Settlement Body of the WTO. However, the large majority of these requests relate to agricultural products; non-agricultural products feature only in a few. The relatively few cases related to prohibitions and quotas are shown in Table 2.3.

Table 2.3. Overview of complaints at the WTO relating to prohibitions and quotas, excluding agriculture

Measure	Complaining party	Issue
Measures affecting asbestos and products containing asbestos (EC)	Canada	Measures taken by France to prohibit the importation of asbestos and products containing asbestos to protect human health and safety
Prohibition of imports of polyethylene and polypropylene (Malaysia)	Singapore	The imposition of import prohibitions on polyethylene and polypropylene to protect human health and safety
Quantitative restrictions on imports of agricultural, textile and industrial products (India)	Australia, Canada, EC, New Zealand, Switzerland, United States	QRs (including import prohibitions) maintained on more than 2 700 agricultural and industrial product tariff lines for balance-of-payment reasons
Import quotas introduced on certain textile and clothing products (Turkey)	Hong Kong, China; India; Thailand	Quotas on textiles and clothing products introduced by Turkey as part of implementing the customs union the between Turkey and the European Communities

Source: OECD, compiled from WTO documents WT/DS135/AB/R, WT/DS1/1, WT/DS91/3, WT/DS29/2.

The use of prohibitions and quotas for economic reasons

The use of prohibitions and quotas for economic reasons has declined substantially in recent years. It is much more common for governments to state health, safety, environmental and other concerns as reasons for applying these restrictions. Most of the countries that applied QR measures for economic reasons in the 1990s have subsequently abandoned or significantly limited their use. The tendency has been to transform prohibitions into import licensing, which can be automatic or non-automatic. However, a few exceptions still exist and are described below.

Balance of payment restrictions[10]

The records of the Balance of Payments (BOP) Committee of the WTO and the trade reviews show a considerable decline in the use of QRs for BOP reasons over the last decade. This development is largely due to the tightening of existing GATT rules as a result of the Uruguay Round and stricter enforcement relating to the use of these measures.

The Uruguay Round Understanding on Balance of Payments Provisions added a number of clarifications to Articles XII and XVIII dealing with balance of payments in the GATT 1947 and the GATT 1994: price-based measures, *i.e.* import surcharges, are preferred to quantitative restrictions, the use of quantitative restrictions is allowed only under exceptional circumstances, and measures taken for BOP reasons may only be allowed to protect the general level of imports (*i.e.* they must be applied across the board and should not protect specific sectors from competition). Additionally, the Understanding established strict notification deadlines and explicit documentation requirements and permitted reverse notification by members concerned by measures instituted, but not notified, by other members.

Pursuant to the GATT 1947 and the GATT 1994, any member imposing restrictions for balance of payments purposes is required to consult with the BOP Committee to determine whether the use of restrictive measures is necessary or desirable to address its balance of payments difficulties. In line with BOP provisions, the BOP Committee works closely with the International Monetary Fund (IMF) in conducting these consultations.[11]

These clarifications have played a significant part in ensuring that the BOP provisions are used as originally intended: to enable countries undergoing a balance of payments crisis to impose temporary measures until their situation improves. Previously, countries often applied quantitative restrictions or prohibitions selectively to specific sectors and maintained them for a long period of time. At present, fewer countries resort to quantitative restrictions to safeguard their BOP position, and they keep them in place for shorter periods of time.

The examination of the TPRs and of the annual reports of the Committee on Balance of Payments Restrictions reveals that in the last few years very few countries have applied import-restricting measures and that most of these countries have now discontinued these measures. Typically, countries have used either import surcharges or quantitative restrictions.[12] Since 1995, only eight countries (Burundi, Nigeria, Bangladesh, India, Pakistan, Egypt, the Philippines and Tunisia) have notified to the WTO their use of import prohibitions for BOP purposes. Most of these countries have focused their restrictive measures on a few goods, most often agricultural products, textiles and clothing, and, to a lesser extent, automobiles.[13]

Currently, Bangladesh is the only WTO member applying notified BOP measures. Bangladesh has long used import restrictions for BOP reasons. In 2000, about 2.2% of total HS 4-digit tariff lines were subject to trade-related prohibitions or restrictions,[14] but progress has since been made in reducing the size of the banned and restricted lists. Trade-related restrictions mainly applied or continue to apply to some agricultural products, packing materials and textile industry products, while import bans are in place on woven fabrics, and imports of grey cloth are restricted to the ready-made garment industry.

India presents an interesting case of the use of quantitative restrictions for BOP reasons. India's trade policy since the 1950s had featured QRs with economic aims. In 1991, India launched a market reform but maintained restrictions on imports of 1 429 items, citing BOP problems. Beginning in 1995, in the BOP Committee and continuing into dispute settlement in 1997, WTO members challenged India's need to maintain measures for BOP reasons. A 1999 WTO dispute settlement decision, responding to a complaint filed by the United States, ordered India to end curbs on all items by 1 April 2001, stating that the country's BOP situation had improved.[15] The curbs on the last 715 items were lifted by that date. Of these last 715 items, 342 were textile products, 147 were agricultural products, and the remaining 226 were manufactured products, including automobiles.

Industry protection

Like BOP measures, import restrictions (prohibitions and quotas) for industry protection reasons are rare.[16] A notable exception is textiles and clothing, which is discussed below. Article XVIII:C of GATT, which permits quantitative restrictions for industry protection purposes, has been invoked on only three occasions since the entry into force of the WTO Agreement.[17]

As reported in the TPRs, a limited number of other countries use prohibitions or quotas for the stated objective of protecting local industry. In most cases, however, reliance on these measures is diminishing. It is common for governments to switch from prohibitions and quotas to non-automatic import licensing or other types of measures that are usually less trade-disruptive.

For example, Papua New Guinea is a least developed country (LDC) which has used prohibitions to protect local producers from foreign competition. The government effectively granted monopoly status by initially applying import bans and quotas but more recently converted these to high, albeit often prohibitive, tariffs. Examples of industries protected in this manner in the past include the cement industry and certain food processing industries, such as sugar, fish and beef.

Nigeria still operates a long list of banned goods, predominantly agricultural goods, but also textiles, bicycles, toothpaste, pencils and ballpoint pens, etc. The government claims that these policies are in place for economic reasons. It is not clear whether they are consistent with WTO rules.[18]

The TPRs also indicate that Indonesia and Malaysia use several types of quantitative restrictions, including quotas, prohibitions and import licensing, to protect certain sectors of their domestic industry, but their QR regimes are subject to rapid changes and different trade reports often contain conflicting findings. The product coverage of import restrictions and the exact types of QR used are often unclear. Indonesia has maintained an import ban and quantitative restrictions on a variety of items in order to protect domestic industries; for example, it has a template import ban on automobiles and motorbikes and import quotas on commercial vehicles. Recent deregulation has caused a year-by-year decrease in the number of covered items. The authorities indicated to the WTO Secretariat that by December 2002, the importation of 179 9-digit HS items was restricted and 41 9-digit HS items were prohibited. Malaysia also uses a combination of import licensing and quota measures on a discretionary basis to regulate import flows with a view to developing certain important infant and strategic industries and to promoting greater forward and backward linkages.[19] For example, import quotas and licensing systems are applied to imported automobile parts.

The use of quotas and prohibitions is also observed in the motor vehicles sector. For example, according to the TPRs, Venezuela and Brazil both used QRs to protect their automotive industries. Venezuela bans the import of automobiles with used engines and chassis (except for public transport vehicles or taxis), with the stated intent of laying the regulatory foundations for the functioning and development of its national automotive industry. Brazil eliminated its import quotas on automotive goods in 1999, when the existing automotive regime ended. Table 2.4 shows examples of other countries where quotas and prohibitions apply on the imports of motor vehicles and spare parts.

Table 2.4. Quotas and prohibitions affecting imports of new motor vehicles

Country	Description
Argentina	Foreign vehicles that do not have a domestic equivalent are subject to import quotas. This quota system limits imports to a percentage of total domestic production.
Brazil	Ban on diesel passenger car imports.
China	Quotas on autos will be phased out by 2005 with an initial level of USD 6.0 billion, which exceeds the actual level of trade prior to implementation of the 1994 Auto Industrial Policy. Quotas will rise 15% annually until eliminated.
Chinese Taipei	Import of diesel vehicles (except jeeps) and two-stroke engine cars is prohibited.
Colombia	Import prohibition on new vehicles from previous years.
Ecuador	Import prohibition on new vehicles from previous years.
Malaysia	Import ban on motor vehicles from Israel.
Mexico	Vehicles that comply with the Mexico-EU FTA are subject to quota restrictions until 2007. Imports in excess of the quota (15% of the previous year's total market for similar vehicles) are subject to a 10% duty. Up to 50 000 new vehicles per year manufactured in Brazil enter at an 8% tariff rate; and additional units are subject to a rate of 20%.
Singapore	The Vehicle Quota System pre-determines the number of cars that will be registered for the year. This number is based on the number from the previous year plus 3%, added to the number of cars that are expected to be scrapped.
Thailand	Ban on buses with 30 seats and over.
Venezuela	Import prohibition on new vehicles from previous years.

Source: US Department of Commerce, International Trade Administration, Office of Automotive Affairs, Compilation of Foreign Motor Vehicle Import Requirements, December 2003.

Quantitative restrictions for industry protection purposes have been used by more developed countries as well. Korea once operated a system of import restrictions for economic purposes that was abandoned only at the end of the 1990s. The so-called Import Diversification System (IDS) ban, put in place in 1978, was conceived as a way to relieve Korea's excessive trade imbalance with Japan and promote a geographically balanced import structure. In compliance with WTO commitments and the IMF stabilisation package, Korea advanced the elimination of import prohibitions from 31 December 1999 to 30 June 1999. The IDS was removed in three stages. The last 10-digit HS items (all taken off the IDS list at the end of June 1999) covered certain types of motorcars (including jeeps), radial tyres for cars, engine parts, excavators, machining centres, colour television sets (above 25 inch), video cassette recorders, portable radio-telephony apparatus, electric rice cookers, and cameras for 35 mm roll film.[20]

Many countries have turned their quotas and prohibitions into non-automatic licensing procedures. However, data from the TPRs indicate that several of these import licensing procedures are *de facto* prohibitions as it is considered impossible to receive a positive answer to applications for a licence. For example, the TPR of Thailand mentions that it is virtually impossible to receive licences for the import of certain vehicles and worked monumental and building stone.

China's WTO accession agreement obliges it to reduce import quotas and prohibitions that had historically been used to restrict trade. On this basis, China has been gradually eliminating many of its import prohibitions and quotas over a multi-year phase-in period. However, some trade reports indicate that for some products, such as automobiles, China's implementation of the required quota system was characterised by delays, lack of transparency and inappropriate allocations in both 2002 and 2003.

The case of textiles and clothing

Textiles and clothing is the only product group (apart from agricultural goods) where QRs taking the form of import quotas have been frequently used for industry protection purposes. However, most of these restrictions are abolished as of 2005, when the Agreement on Textiles and Clothing (ATC) is fully implemented.

For several decades, international trade in textiles has been subject to a complex system of bilateral QRs that certain developed countries have introduced and maintained in order to shield their domestic textile and clothing industries from growing competition from developing-country producers. These quotas fall under the Multi-Fibre Arrangement (MFA). While some nations with strong political ties to developed countries benefited from preference agreements that raised or eliminated their quota levels, many developing countries suffered from severely restricted market access. Concluded in 1995, the ATC resulting from the Uruguay Round negotiations subjects trade in textiles and clothing to the fundamental WTO principles of non-discrimination and national treatment. The agreement mandated that WTO members implement the ATC over a period of ten years, from 1 January 1995 to 1 January 2005, from which point quotas on textile and clothing products can only be used for BOP (*e.g.* by Bangladesh) but not for industry protection reasons.

There exists a considerable body of analysis on the economic and trade effects of quotas on textiles and clothing products. An earlier study of the OECD Trade Directorate provided a survey of quantitative studies of market liberalisation in this sector (OECD, 2003). It concluded that all the reviewed studies foresaw increases in global welfare as a result of ATC reform, but their conclusions differed with respect to the distribution of welfare effects. Some analysts see developing countries as the main beneficiaries of the ATC, while others point out that the effects are likely to differ from country to country. Canada, the European Union and the United States are expected to experience substantial increases in welfare from the reform owing to lower consumer prices and more efficient resource allocation.

Import prohibitions for non-economic reasons

Countries tend to place a substantial number of products on prohibition lists for a variety of non-economic reasons – such as health (hygiene and sanitation), safety, environment (to protect animal and plant life), moral, cultural and religious and security reasons. The general picture emerging from this investigation is that the number of products whose importation is prohibited on non-economic grounds has been rising somewhat in recent years. However, it is not possible to quantify developments in this area. Products whose importation is prohibited on non-economic grounds in a large number of countries are:

- Counterfeit goods and related production equipment (including coins and notes).
- Articles infringing on patents and other intellectual property rights (IPR).
- Narcotic drugs.
- Items banned for security reasons, such as weapons, ammunitions, explosives.
- Products that contain substances that are banned on the basis of environmental protection, and/or public health and safety considerations.
- Materials that might offend public morals, culture or religion.
- Certain protected animals and plants.
- Certain used goods.

The first three categories of goods (counterfeit and IPR-infringing products, as well as narcotics) are mentioned as banned items by almost all of the 85 countries reviewed by the WTO between 1998 and 2004. Concerning weapons, ammunitions and explosives, they are in many cases listed as banned items and in other cases are subject to import licences or can be imported only by state trading enterprises.

The largest number of prohibitions has been introduced on the grounds of environmental protection and public health and safety considerations, or both. Such products broadly fall into two categories. First, countries most commonly ban products that contain substances they consider dangerous to the environment and to human and animal health. The incidence of such bans seems to be on the rise, especially in the developed countries, which apply more stringent environmental and health and safety regulations than the developing world. Different countries often use export licensing or prohibitions for the same types of substances or products. Among other products, the trade reports indicated a high incidence of prohibitions for different types of asbestos, and for human, animal and industrial waste.[21]

Other potential sources of information on quantitative restrictions introduced for environmental reasons are the WTO environmental databases that were published annually between 1997 and 2001. These documents compile all environment-related notifications to the WTO, grouped according to the Agreements under which they were issued. The documents indicate that the number of environment-related measures notified under the Agreement on Quantitative Restrictions is much lower than that of measures that fall under other agreements, such as the Agreement on Technical Barriers to Trade (TBT Agreement), the Agreement on Sanitary and Phytosanitary Measures (SPS Agreement), the Agreement on Subsidies and Countervailing Measures (SCM Agreement) or the Agreement on Agriculture.[22] Only the 2000 and 2001 edition of the database contained enough information to identify the exact type of QR measures in question. Measures notified under the TBT Agreement also occasionally refer to prohibitions or quotas. Annex 2.A2 contains the environment-related prohibitions and quota measures reported in 2000 and 2002. The second-largest category is made up of used goods, which some countries consider damaging to the environment and to human health and safety. Such prohibitions occur mostly in developing countries, which might otherwise represent a large market for the export of used goods from developed countries. Trade policies affecting used goods raise many issues. International trade in used goods is frequently restricted by QRs and other trade measures, and the justifications given by governments when they ban or otherwise intervene in the trade of such goods are varied and often not clear. QRs affecting used goods are examined separately below.

The TPR reports reveal that several developed countries operate a complex system that regulates the importation of dangerous substances by introducing bans or licensing requirements. For example, the European Union has a system in place that aims to protect the public by regulating the placement and use of dangerous substances on the Community market, including by importation. The list of substances covered is regularly updated to take account of technical progress.[23] The European Union also applies the international notification and prior informed consent (PIC) procedure established by the United Nations Environment Programme (UNEP) and the Food and Agriculture Organization (FAO).

Box 2.1. The WTO consistency of MEAs

The relationship between the WTO agreements and trade measures pursuant to multilateral environmental agreements (MEAs) is an issue that is currently debated in the WTO. According to the WTO, out of over 200 MEAs in existence, only 20 contain provisions concerning trade. Some of these MEA-related trade measures are quantitative import restrictions.

As described by the WTO, "WTO Members have basically agreed to clarify the legal relationship between WTO rules and MEAs, rather than leaving the matter to the WTO's dispute settlement body to resolve in individual cases (in the event of the lodging of a formal dispute). However, they have explicitly stated that the negotiations should be limited to defining how WTO rules apply to WTO Members that are party to an MEA. In other words, they should not venture into their applicability between a party and a non-party to an MEA. The reason for this limitation is that while WTO Members were willing to let the negotiations define the relationship between WTO rules and MEAs they have joined, they were not ready to let them alter their WTO rights and obligations *vis-à-vis* MEAs they were not part of. Moreover, paragraph 32 of the Doha Ministerial Declaration carefully circumscribed the negotiations under paragraph 31(i) and (ii): The outcome of the negotiations carried out under paragraph 31(i) and (ii) shall be compatible with the open and non-discriminatory nature of the multilateral trading system, shall not add to or diminish the rights and obligations of Members under existing WTO agreements, in particular the SPS Agreement, nor alter the balance of these rights and obligations, and will take into account the needs of developing and least-developed countries."

Source: WTO, *Environment Backgrounder: the Relationship between MEAs and the WTO, The Doha Negotiating Mandate on MEAs*
(www.wto.org/english/tratop_e/envir_e/envir_backgrnd_e/c5s3_e.htm).

Prohibitions for environmental and health and safety reason are made unilaterally but also often under multilateral agreements or conventions. Box 2.1 discusses the relationship between WTO agreements and multilateral agreements, an issue that is under debate at the WTO. The following multilateral agreements are most often cited as justifications for import prohibitions (see also Table 2.5):

- Convention on International Trade in Endangered Species of Wild Fauna and Flora.

- Basel Convention on the Control of Transboundary Movements of Hazardous Wastes and their Disposal.

- Stockholm Convention on Persistent Organic Pollutants.

- Rotterdam Convention on the Prior Informed Consent Procedure for Certain Hazardous Chemicals and Pesticides in International Trade.

- Montreal Protocol on Substances that Deplete the Ozone Layer, CFCs and other ozone-depleting substances.

Table 2.5. References to import prohibitions in important MEAs

Name of the MEA	References to prohibitions
International Plant Protection Convention	Parties might prohibit the importation of particular plants or plant products with the aim of avoiding the spread and introduction of pests in plants and plant products
International Convention for the Conservation of Atlantic Tunas	Recommendations can call for the introduction of non-discriminatory trade-restrictive measures, consistent with their international obligations, with respect to subject species
Convention on International Trade in Endangered Species of Wild Fauna and Flora	Can prohibit commercial international trade in selected specimens
Montreal Protocol on Substances that Deplete the Ozone Layer	Ban on the importation of certain controlled substances
Basel Convention on the Control of Transboundary Movements of Hazardous Wastes and their Disposal	Parties can exercise the right to prohibit the importation of hazardous wastes or other wastes
Stockholm Convention on Persistent Organic Pollutants	Parties prohibit the imports of listed chemicals

Source: WTO, Matrix on Trade Measures Pursuant to Selected Multilateral Environmental Agreements, WT/CTE/W/160/Rev.2TN/TE/S/5, 25 April 2003.

Prohibitions are also sometimes applied to achieve foreign policy objectives. This may be done unilaterally or pursuant to multilateral agreements such as the United Nations Security Council Resolutions. Mostly developed countries also apply bans on goods for humanitarian reasons. For example, goods manufactured by prison labour, forced labour or child labour are prohibited to be imported to the United States. Another example is recent EU legislation that bans both the sale and import of cosmetic products containing ingredients that have been tested on animals. The ban on most categories will take effect in 2009. A transitional period is needed to allow companies to develop alternative testing procedures.

A fairly large number of countries also ban goods in order to safeguard public morality. The trade reviews reveal some variations among countries concerning which goods are prohibited on the grounds of safeguarding public morality. For example many Muslim countries impose bans on cultural or religious grounds on a wider variety of goods than other countries (*e.g.* Indonesia, Malaysia, Bahrain, Mauritania, Maldives,

Algeria, etc.) They prohibit the importation of materials offensive to Islam, and ban or very severely restrict the import of alcohol and spirits and pigs and pork meat. There is also a small group of countries (Turkey, Thailand, El Salvador, Pakistan and China) that ban imports of gambling instruments in order to protect public morals.

The trade policy reports examined for this study indicate that the number of products affected by prohibitions applied on non-economic grounds, especially environmental and health and safety reasons, has been on the rise in recent years. However, to date, it appears that these products do not represent a large share in international trade and the WTO conformity of these measures is usually not questioned. The import prohibitions placed on used goods appear to be an exception and are discussed below. A more detailed examination of whether the same prohibitions apply to domestic products would reveal information about the legitimacy of such prohibitions. However, the data available for this study do not permit such an assessment.

Import prohibitions affecting used goods

On closer examination, quantitative restrictions, especially prohibitions, play an important role in the international trade of used consumer or capital goods (such as used clothing, equipment and vehicles), as many countries design their trade policies to discriminate against importation of second-hand goods. It is a potentially interesting market with opportunities for trade. However, these are not well documented and the import restrictions tend to vary by product and by country of destination.

For approximately one-third of the countries that were reviewed, the TPRs report some kind of prohibition of imports of certain types of used products. The frequency of these and other types of trade restrictions in this area is further underlined by the fact that the EU Market Access Database, which is assembled from input from the business community, reports a very high number of instances in which the importation of used goods, primarily automobiles, is prohibited. A similar picture emerges from a review of other sources of information. In fact, it has been noted that used goods are an overlooked exception to the widespread liberalisation of trade that has occurred in recent times (Pelletiere and Reinert, 2003).

Products affected by restrictions

Based on the review of TPRs and other reports, it appears that the used goods most commonly affected by QRs are motor vehicles and automotive parts, machinery, clothes and medical devices. The measures applied are very often import prohibitions. They may be absolute bans or prohibitions under defined conditions. With respect to motor vehicles, for example, relevant criteria include age, environmental standards, etc. As mentioned in the reports, some countries also use strict non-automatic licensing (NAL) that amount to *de facto* prohibitions.

These trade restrictions are most common in developing countries; however, developed countries at times also discriminate against used products. A large number of countries in Latin America, Africa, and Asia do not allow importation of certain used goods. Among them are several countries with large markets, such as Brazil, China and India, which operate strict import regimes involving prohibitions of a wide variety of products with respect to the used-goods market (Table 2.6).

Justifications for the measures

The justifications governments give for the bans relate predominantly to health, safety and protection of the environment. However, the available literature suggests that economic motivations also play a role. The reason for these policies is a combination of a desire to protect domestic producers (or distributors) of new goods from competition from low-priced second-hand or remanufactured goods, an attempt to avoid becoming a "dumping ground" for cast-offs from high-income countries, and an attempt to push industries towards the "technological frontier" and avoid the use of "obsolete" technologies.[24]

Table 2.6. Incidence of import prohibitions on used products

	Motor vehicles	Tyres	Clothes	Machinery	Electrical appliances	Medical equipment
Argentina		x	x			x
Bolivia	x					
Brazil	x		x	x		
Brunei	x					
Canada	x					
Chile	x					
Dominican Rep.	x		x		x	
Ecuador	x	x	x			
Egypt	x					
Ghana	x					
India	x					
Israel			x			
Maldives	x					
Mozambique		x	x			
Nicaragua	x					
Nigeria	x				x[1]	
Pakistan				x		
Peru	x	x	x			
Salvador	x					
Sri Lanka				x		
Tanzania			x			
Thailand	x					
Venezuela	x	x	x			

1. Refrigerators, air conditioners, compressors.

Source: Compiled from WTO Trade Policy Reviews, 1999-2004; EU MAD database (as of 2004); and USTR reports (2003).

Anecdotal evidence and local press reports, for example, shed some light on how demands from the local textile industry have led to export bans on used clothes in several African countries. Furthermore, empirical research on Latin American trade policies finds that quantitative restrictions on used automobiles are largely the result of pressure from domestic carmakers and distributors of new cars (Pelletiere and Reinert, 2002).

The case of motor vehicles and parts

Statistical data on the size of the global market and on trade flows for used motor vehicles are scarce. Assuming that the average car has four owners over its lifespan, the used car market clearly is much bigger than the new car market. Dominating used car exports, Japan was expected to have shipped abroad a record USD 1 million worth of used vehicles in 2003. The data in Table 2.7 are from various news and other reports and are only intended to give, for some countries, a rough idea of the volume of used cars imported and the significance of the used car market. Because growth in increasingly saturated developed-country markets is slowing, there is growing interest in market access abroad (*The Wall Street Journal*, 2004).

Table 2.7. Imports of used cars in selected countries

	Year	Cars imported	% of total market
Australia	1999	25 000	-
Bulgaria	2001	120 000	90
Czech Republic	1999	145 000	42
Cyprus	2000	10 000	60
Estonia	2000	12 000	35
Kenya	1999	30 000	-
New Zealand	2000	116 000	70
Philippines	2001	50 000	39
Poland	1999	2000 000	20
Russia	2001	360 000	80
United Kingdom	1998	60 000	-

Source: Adapted from Sofronis K. Clerides, "The Welfare Effects of Trade Liberalisation: Evidence from Used Automobiles", University of Cyprus & Yale University, April 2003.

The data sources reviewed for this study indicate that international trade in used motor vehicles is very often subject to QRs. The types of measures used are most commonly prohibitions with narrowly defined exceptions under certain conditions. In addition, some countries use NAL or heavy tariffs to discourage imports, but the level of prohibitions is high compared to other methods. Where conditions are used to define whether motor vehicles can be imported or not, they often relate to maximum age restrictions, which usually vary from three to five years. Many countries apply restrictions only for certain types of vehicles, such as passenger cars, motorcycles, trucks, minivan and buses above or below certain size.

One-third of the countries that had TPRs in the last five years placed some kind of prohibition on imports of second-hand vehicles. These are not sales bans but bans discriminating against imported vehicles. Domestic used vehicles can be sold in the local market.

Prohibitions are most widely used in Latin American (Pelletiere and Reinert, 2002) and African countries. They are used by some Asian countries as well. Several central European countries (*e.g.* Czech Republic, Hungary) also prohibited importation of cars above a certain age in the 1990s. However, these bans have most often been replaced by a duty system based on environmental and safety attributes. Environmental and health and safety reasons are the explanations most commonly given for the prohibitions.

Many predominantly developing countries also restrict the import of used or remanufactured or rebuilt vehicle parts.[25] Countries in Latin America especially prohibit the importation of these goods outright. Box 2.2 gives some illustrative examples of the import restrictions affecting these products.

In many developing countries, there is a large market for used automotive spare parts because there is a tendency to overextend the useful life of a vehicle to avoid purchasing a new one. An increasing population in the major cities and low incomes are factors that boost the demand for used vehicles as well as remanufactured, rebuilt and/or used motor vehicle parts. On the other hand, a high percentage of new vehicles and an ample supply of low-cost new parts tend to slow the development of a used parts market.

Trade liberalisation is also boosting demand for used goods. This is illustrated by Jamaica, which liberalised its automobile sector in 1993. Since then, imports of used cars have grown rapidly. Whereas in 1993, approximately 12 000 of the 19 000 vehicles imported were new, one year later, in 1994, only 6 000 of the 26 000 motor vehicles imported were new. This trend continued to 1998, when the market for imported automobiles began to show signs of saturation (US Department of Commerce, Office of Automotive Affairs, 1999, p. 43).

Box 2.2. Import restrictions affecting remanufactured/rebuilt vehicle parts

In *Brazil*, imports of remanufactured parts are only authorised when the remanufacturing is performed by the original manufacturer. Remanufactured and rebuilt parts are considered used parts.

In *Chile*, importation of used vehicles is prohibited but importation of remanufactured, rebuilt and used motor vehicle parts is allowed. However, customs authorities are concerned that imported parts may be used to assemble used cars, or significant portions of used cars, and these types of goods are generally closely scrutinised.

In *China*, importation of used car parts is banned. In rare cases, *e.g.* parts for antique cars, special import permissions may be given. The importer must submit a petition describing the proposed use and reason for importation.

In *Israel*, imports of remanufactured, rebuilt and used motor vehicle parts are limited and authorised by the Ministry of Transport on a case-by-case basis. For critical automotive systems components such as steering and braking systems, the ministry only authorises imports of new parts and these parts must be imported from a pre-authorised manufacturer.

In *South Africa*, the importation of remanufactured, rebuilt or used motor vehicle parts is limited to gasoline engines > 3 000 cc, diesel engines > 3 500 cc, transmissions for motor vehicles and micro-buses, and any other motor vehicle part not originally manufactured in South Africa. All these parts are assessed on a case-by-case basis by the Department of Trade and Industry.

In the *United Arab Emirates*, importation of reconditioned and used auto parts is prohibited unless they are reconditioned by the original manufacturer. The reseller is prohibited from claiming that the part is the same as an original part. There is no difference in the treatment of remanufactured and used auto parts.

Source: US Department of Commerce, Office of Automotive Affairs, International Trade Administration. *Compilation of Foreign Remanufacturing Parts Import Restrictions*, October 1999.

Exporters of these goods face bans or other QRs predominantly in developing countries. Restrictions were reported only for two of 20 OECD countries that were included in a 1999 survey of trade restrictions affecting market access for motor vehicle parts, and only in one case was this an import ban (Pelletiere et Reinert, 2002).

Tyres also belong to the category of motor vehicle and parts goods that fall under import bans in relatively many countries, again mostly in the Latin American region and in Africa. In most cases the ban is unconditional and justified by safety and environmental reasons.

Other sectors

Prohibitions on the importation of used clothing are also common. World exports of worn clothing amounted to USD 990 million in 2001, a small fraction of the exports of new clothing, valued at USD 146 billion, but the comparison is somewhat misleading because the value of worn clothing is very small (about USD 0.73 per kilogram) (United Nations COMTRADE database). In this area, import prohibitions exist mostly in African countries and in some low-income Asian (and also in China) and Latin American countries. Bans are usually unconditional and are justified by health and sanitary reasons. Some countries (*e.g.* South Africa) permit the entry of used clothing only if these are humanitarian donations.

Several countries impose conditional bans on the importation of used machinery, for safety and environmental reasons. This is mainly the case in some Asian and Latin American countries. Unconditional bans are rare; instead, most countries impose requirements mandating strict technical standards for the goods in question.

Finally, reports document that some countries adopt a policy of barring the importation of certain other categories of products, such as used medical devices (China, Egypt, Kuwait, Syria and Thailand reportedly employ total bans),[26] electronic appliances (Dominican Republic), refrigerators, air conditioners and compressors (Nigeria).

It appears that there is some momentum and progress towards abandoning outright bans and prohibitions, at least where bilateral agreements or RTAs are concerned. A brief review of some of the major RTAs reveals that some of these agreements address the issue of trade of used goods.

For example, under NAFTA, Mexico agreed that in 2009 it will begin a ten-year phase-out of the embargo on used vehicles (light vehicles, buses and heavy trucks) that meet the NAFTA rules of origin. This means that the ban will be fully abolished by 2019 (US Department of Commerce, Free Trade Area of the Americas, 2002b, p. 55). As a result of the EU-Mexico FTA, the European Union will have the same benefits in terms of market access for used vehicles as the United States and Canada have under NAFTA, provided the vehicles meet the Mexico-EU rules of origin (US Department of Commerce, Free Trade Area of the Americas, 2002b, p. 56). However, there are also cases where RTAs do not provide for any liberalisation of this market. For example, Mercosur and the US-Chile FTA include indefinite bans on used cars (Automotive Provisions Report, Office of Automotive Affairs, ITA, US Department of Commerce, www/ita.doc.gov/auto).

The extensive import restrictions affecting international trade in used goods raise a number of questions that are of potential interest to policy makers and negotiators. Why, for example, are used goods treated differently from new goods in situations where risks relating to safety, health or environmental protection arise from new and used goods alike? In many circumstances where domestic regulatory goals are at issue, used items should probably be treated like new ones in terms of policy, and regulations should be the same for both. Where safety is an issue, importation of new and used goods could be obliged to meet the same standards.

Even if there are valid reasons for distinguishing between new and used goods (for example, because used goods usually carry no warranty, or a reduced one), it may be asked whether a prohibition on the importation of used goods is warranted if the policy goal can be reached by other, less trade-restrictive means. Used or remanufactured items could simply be carefully scrutinised to determine whether they conform to environmental, safety and other standards. Inspection and certification against standards, and, if necessary, use of import permits, are less trade-restrictive options which are available and have already been adopted by some countries.

The environmental protection rationale for banning used goods may deserve greater scrutiny. The recycling of products and the long life cycle of certain products, such as clothing and auto parts, appear to be in the interest of good environmental policy. In Japan, for example, the government and environmental groups are reported to emphasise to Japanese consumers and the public their responsibility in saving natural resources and to make them aware of the advantages of using remanufactured or used parts.

An argument used for restricting the importation of used goods is that trade in such goods is more susceptible to fraud. However, import bans and other QRs have similar disadvantages. For example, they encourage the operation of a parallel market that escapes regulatory oversight.

Other types of quantitative restrictions

As part of this study, the incidence of references to three other types of measures that are listed as quantitative restrictions by the WTO, namely "quantitative restrictions made effective through state trading operations", "mixing regulations" and "minimum price triggering a quantitative restriction" was also examined. It was found that references to these measures are significantly less common than to other types of QR, such as automatic and non-automatic licensing, prohibitions and quotas.

Minimum price triggering a quantitative restriction was not mentioned in the trade reports and databases that were examined.

State trading enterprises, as defined by the WTO, are "governmental and non-governmental enterprises, including marketing boards, which deal with goods for export and/or import".[27] Article XVII of the GATT 1994 is the principal provision dealing with state trading enterprises and their operations. It instructs that members are to notify their state trading enterprises to the WTO annually.[28]

State trading operations raise a wide range of issues, and the use of quantitative restrictions is only one of them. The WTO rules intend to ensure that state trading enterprises are not used to implement WTO-inconsistent measures. Members' substantive obligations under the rules governing state trading are: non-discrimination, commonly referred to as "most favoured nation" or "MFN" treatment; no quantitative restrictions; preservation of the value of tariff concessions; and transparency.[29]

The examination of TPRs and other sources reveals that competition issues (monopoly situations), transparency issues, rent-seeking and discrimination are the concerns most often mentioned regarding state trading regimes. The overview of data sources showed very rare references to the existence of QRs as part of state trading operations. The few exceptions are:

- In Gabon, the company with the sugar monopoly applies prohibition on importation of sugar in all its forms.

- In Brunei sugar and rice are subject to import restrictions and licensing and are imported directly by the government.

- In Bangladesh, the importation of sugar and salt is usually banned except in cases of shortage, when two state corporations are the exclusive importers.

Mixing regulations specify an amount of domestically produced goods that must be bought by an importer for given quantities of imports. Such arrangements exist in a few developing countries mainly in relation to government procurement contracts. Some examples are:

- In Thailand, all procurement contracts by government agencies and state enterprises that involve imports above a certain value must have a related counter-trade transaction of at least one-half of the procurement value.

- The Philippines' International Trade Corporation (PITC) encourages the inclusion of counter-purchase or offset obligations in government procurement projects worth at least USD 1 million.

- The TPR review of Israel revealed that during the review period (1994-99), under Israeli law, every public procurement contract worth more than ILS 1.5 million must include an "industrial co-operation" clause, obliging foreign suppliers to purchase Israeli goods or services of a value equivalent to 35% of the value of the contract. Alternatively, foreign suppliers can invest in local industries.

Economic and trade implications of QRs

This section provides a short conceptual overview of the trade and economic impacts of QRs, based on quantitative data derived from research conducted in this area. Economic research indicates that when QRs are motivated by the desire to protect particular domestic products from competition with foreign goods, they impose costs that clearly outweigh the benefits for both the importing and the exporting countries. It is widely accepted that QRs undermine trade and economic efficiency more than tariffs because with tariffs, resources are allocated through the price mechanisms, while, under quotas, they are allocated administratively by the state. In spite of these negative effects, however, governments still apply QRs, although less often than in the past. From the viewpoint of importing countries, quotas may be more attractive than tariffs, since the effect of a given tariff on import volumes is uncertain, as it depends on the domestic elasticities of demand for and supply of the product.

Concerning their economic effects, the first observation is that prohibitions and quotas exacerbate the terms of trade for exporting countries and reduce their economic welfare. At the same time, quotas help a few selected exporters realise a "quota rent" or higher profit owing to the higher prices they can obtain for their products. As described in Box 2.3, the way in which a government administers the quota determines who obtains the quota rents.

Second, quantitative restrictions create an import substitution effect that harms consumers in the importing countries. The policy-induced scarcity of imports inevitably raises the price of the good on the domestic market to the maximum amount consumers are willing to pay. Consumers, including downstream industries, bear the economic cost of losing access to lower-priced competitive products and facing less product choice and higher product prices. A further loss of welfare comes from the fact that, unlike tariffs, prohibitions and, at times, quotas generate no revenues for the government.[30]

Box 2.3. The effects of different types of quota allocations

The method of administering a quota can make a great deal of difference as to its effects. The method of administration that most economists would prefer, but which governments only occasionally use, involves the auctioning of quotas. This method of administering the quota comes close to replicating a tariff equal to the price of the licence, since it not only raises the domestic price above the world price, but also allows the government to acquire the price difference (quota rent) as revenue.

A second way of administering a quota is to allocate the right to import fixed amounts free of charge among importing firms. Once the allocation is made, the firms receive the price difference between the domestic and world market price as a pure rent. If the allocation is made among a sufficiently large number of firms, they will still compete among themselves on the domestic market and will end up charging a single competitive price. But that price will be enough above the world price to clear the domestic market. The situation is again analogous to a tariff, though here the "revenues" from the NTB, or quota rents, accrue to the firms that were allocated the right to import.

If the allocation is made on a political basis, potential importing firms will have an incentive to spend resources in competing for these rents, for example, by bidding for licences in the political market, by lobbying or whatever other mechanism is acceptable in the country. If the allocation is made on economic grounds, there is an incentive for firms to distort the behaviour to be used as an indicator. For example, if allocations are to be based on firm size, as measured by the book value of capital stocks, the quota rents become part of their return to capital, and firms have an incentive to over-invest. Or if allocations are made on the basis of domestic sales, and if firms have access to a domestic source of supply, they will expand their domestic supplies beyond even what would be indicated by the elevated domestic price in order to capture more of the quota rents.

Source: Alan V. Deardorff and Robert M. Stern, "Measurement of Non-tariff Barriers", Economics Department Working Paper, No. 179, OECD, 1997, pp. 21-25.

Third, in the short run, domestic industries whose products are protected may benefit from the restrictions, as they can avoid foreign competition and secure market share, increase their profits and secure employment. However over the middle and long term, QRs have a detrimental impact on industry: they discourage companies from working to enhance productivity, as they would be required to do if exposed to market competition. Domestic industries shielded from foreign competition by way of QRs are likely to become or remain inefficient and fail to achieve or maintain export competitiveness in the long run. Unless QRs are clearly designated as temporary measures contingent upon efforts to modernise or adjust and make sufficient productivity gains while the QRs are in place, they are very likely to hinder the industry's development and to harm the economic interests of the country imposing the restrictions.[31]

Finally, from a global perspective, quotas also distort resource allocation. They are invariably discriminatory, as they are imposed on imports from a particular source, which is very often the world's lowest-cost supplier of the product. Therefore, not only do they reduce the volume of trade, they also divert trade and hence production from a low-cost to a high-cost source.

Concluding remarks

Because of he limited availability and inconsistent quality of the data only tentative conclusions can be drawn. The difficulty of obtaining comprehensive and detailed information is partly due to the fact that the WTO notification system does not appear to perform well in this area. First, only a few countries have submitted notifications and the details provided by notifying countries and access to this information are limited. Second, the TPRs themselves draw attention to the difficulties of obtaining reliable data from national authorities. Third, any investigation of QRs is made difficult by the tendency of such measures to change rapidly, probably more so than other types of NTBs.

It is apparent that the level of transparency of quantitative restriction measures is low compared to many other aspects of the trade regime that have come under multilateral disciplines. For this reason, it would be beneficial to explore ways of strengthening rules and implementation with respect to the WTO's notification system in this area.

In general, the application of quotas and prohibitions for economic reasons is declining. The use of such measures for BOP as well as for industry protection reasons has diminished. Most importantly, several large developing countries, notably China, India, Bangladesh and Indonesia, have been progressively reducing the scope of such measures in recent years. Motor vehicles, textiles and electrical equipment are the most commonly affected by these restrictions. International agreement on textiles and clothing will also lead to the abolition of trade restrictions in this sector, which is the last remaining industry to be significantly affected by quota restrictions.

At the same time, prohibitions for non-economic reasons, especially on grounds of protecting the environment and human safety and health, are present in virtually every country and seem to be on the rise. The incidence of such measures seems to be increasing faster in developed countries with well-developed regimes of social regulations. Prohibitions play an especially important role in the trade of used consumer and capital goods. Bans restrict particularly the importation of used cars, car parts, clothes and machinery from developed to developing countries. The circumstances of these bans appear at times unclear and, by raising certain policy issues, mark an area that may merit further investigation and possibly consideration in the context of the NAMA negotiations.

When applied for non-economic reasons, an import prohibition is a policy solution that is used to ensure that different societal regulatory objectives are met. It is important to recognise countries' regulatory sovereignty and their right to set and pursue regulatory objectives of their choice. At the same time, countries should take under consideration the principles of good regulatory practice that have been developed and promoted by the OECD. The principles provide recommendations for governments on how to create regulations that meet their policy objectives efficiently but are also supportive of market openness. In the case of prohibitions, governments should carefully consider whether import bans are the best regulatory solution or whether there are policy alternatives that can deliver the primary regulatory objective with a less distorting effect on the economy or other societal goals.

Annex 2.A1

Notifications of Quantitative Restrictions

Note by the WTO Secretariat[32] G/MA/NTM/QR/325 March 2004

The Decision on Notification Procedures for Quantitative Restrictions, adopted by the Council for Trade in Goods (G/L/59) provides that "Members shall make complete notifications of the quantitative restrictions which they maintain by 31 January 1996 and at two-yearly intervals thereafter,[33] and shall notify changes to their quantitative restrictions as and when these changes occur." Members that have made, under other WTO provisions, notifications of quantitative restrictions that fulfil the requirements for quantitative restriction notifications under the 1984 and 1985 decisions and that are up to date, shall notify the fact to the Secretariat. These notifications will be stored in the new database of quantitative restrictions.

This document has been prepared by the Secretariat pursuant to this Decision according to which "the Secretariat shall publish periodically a document listing the WTO Members having made a notification". Such a list is provided hereunder along with the years in which the notifications were made.

Since 1996, notifications of quantitative restrictions have been received from the following Members: Argentina (1997); Australia (1996); Bahrain Kingdom of (1997, 2000); Bulgaria (2003); Chile (1996); China (2002, 2003); Cyprus (1996); European Communities (1996, 1998, 2000, 2002); Fiji (1997); Germany-European Communities (2000); Georgia (2003); Hong Kong, China (1996, 1998, 2000, 2002); Hungary (1996, 1998, 2000, 2002); India (1996, 1997, 1998); Jamaica (1996, 1998, 2002); Japan (1998, 2000, 2002); Korea, Republic of (1997); Liechtenstein (1997, 2002); Macao, China (1996, 1999, 2001, 2003); Maldives (1999); Malta (1996, 2000); Morocco (1997, 1999, 2001, 2002); New Zealand (1996); Nigeria (2002); Norway (1996, 2000); Oman (2001, 2004); Pakistan (1997); Peru (1996, 1997); Philippines (1996); South Africa (1996); Switzerland (1997, 2001); Chinese Taipei (2002); Tunisia (1999, 2001) Turkey (1996, 1998, 2000); United States (1999); Venezuela (1996, 1999); Zambia (1996, 2002).

Notifications of changes to their quantitative restrictions were received by the following Members: Argentina (2002); Bahrain Kingdom of (2000); China (2003); European Communities (1998, 2000); Hong Kong, China (1996); India (1996, 1998); Jamaica (2002); Macao, China (2001, 2004); Maldives (1999); Malta (2000); Morocco (1999, 2002); Norway (2000); Peru (1997); Tunisia (2001); Turkey (1998, 2000); Zambia (1997).

The following members have notified that they do not maintain quantitative restrictions: Argentina (2002); Bolivia (1997); Brunei Darussalam (1996); Burundi (2001); Costa Rica (1998); Dominica (2001); Dominican Republic (1996); Estonia (2002); Gabon (2001); The Gambia (1997); Guatemala 1999, 2000); Guyana (2003); Haiti (1999); Honduras (1997); Iceland (1996, 2000); Jordan (2002); Kyrgyz Republic (2000); Latvia (1999); Madagascar (2001); Moldova (2002); Mongolia (2000); Myanmar (2001); Namibia (1999); Paraguay (1998); Qatar (1999); Singapore (1996); Sri Lanka (2003); Trinidad and Tobago (1998); Uganda (1996, 2000); United Arab Emirates (1996,1997, 2000); Uruguay (1996, 1999); Zambia (2002); Zimbabwe (2000, 2003).

Annex 2.A.2

Environment-related Import Prohibition and Quota Measures Reported to the WTO in 2000 and 2001

Measures notified under the Agreement on Quantitative Restrictions

Member	Measure or product	Objective
Macao, China	Prohibition for used motor cars and other motor vehicles, tractors, motorcycles, and parts and accessories	To protect the environment (among others)
	Global quota for CFCs, halons, other fully halogenated CFCs, carbon tetrachloride, methyl chloroform, bromomethane	To fulfil obligations under the Montreal Protocol
Bahrain	Prohibitions for Pakistani "Bulbul"	To preserve the local environment and birds
	Prohibitions for worked ivory	To preserve the environment
Hong Kong, China[1]	Prohibitions for endangered species of animals and plants listed in Appendix I of CITES	To fulfil obligations under CITES
	Prohibitions for chlorofluorocarbons whether existing alone or in a mixture	To fulfil obligations under the Montreal Protocol
	Global quota and non-automatic licensing for HCFCs and halogenated derivatives of acyclic hydrocarbons containing two or more different halogens	To fulfil obligations under the Montreal Protocol
Japan	Import quotas for animals and plants, and their derivatives of CITES, and controlled substances listed in the Montreal Protocol	To fulfil obligations under CITES and the Montreal Protocol
	Prohibition for used motor cars and other motor vehicles, tractors, motorcycles, and parts and accessories thereof	To protect the environment (among others)
	Global quota for CFCs, halons, other fully halogenated CFCs, carbon tetrachloride, methyl chloroform, bromomethane	To fulfil obligations under the Montreal Protocol

Measures notified under the TBT Agreement

Member	Measure or product	Objective
Chile	Ban on mixing kerosene with other fuels and establishment of requirements for kerosene for domestic and industrial use stored, distributed and marketed	To control air pollution
Netherlands	Regulation banning the manufacture or, whether or not processed in a preparation or product, import into the Netherlands, use or the having available of 1,1 (isopropylidene)bis [3,5-dibromine-4 (2,3-dibromine propoxy) benzene]	To protect the environment
	Decree concerning exemptions from the trade ban on the preparation of certain species	To prevent the capture of game for the illegal preparation of the animals
United States	Restrictions or prohibitions on substitutes for ozone-depleting substances under the Environmental Protection Agency's Significant New Alternatives Policy Programme	To expedite movement away from ozone-depleting compounds while avoiding a shift into substitutes posing other environmental problems

1. This notification is issued also under the Agreement on Import Licensing (G/LIC/N/3/HKG/4).

Sources: WT/CTE/W/195; WT/CTE/EDB/1.

Annex 2.A.3

Information on Quantitative Restrictions (Prohibitions, Quotas and State Trading) from the EU Market Access Database

Country	Sector/product type	Details
Bangladesh (2003)	Textiles and leather	Bangladesh maintains a restriction on export of raw hides and wet blue leather on the basis of its Export Policy (1997-2002). Only exports of finished leather and leather goods are permitted. According to Bangladeshi authorities, the ban is in place in order to maintain adequate domestic supply and to facilitate the development of the domestic leather industry. However, the ban appears to be a clear infringement of Article XI of GATT.
Brazil (2003)	Used goods and tyres	In 2000, Brazil extended the blanket ban on the importation of used tyres to cover retreated or recycled tyres as well. According to the Brazilian authorities, the ban was introduced for environmental reasons. However, this does not seem to be a valid argument, since retreated tyres, as a new product, are not covered by the waste definition of the Basel Convention or the Community Regulation on the shipment of green waste to non-OECD countries. In addition, the import ban creates a discriminatory situation between Brazilian and imported goods, because there is domestic production of retreated tyres in Brazil, which can be legitimately marketed.
Brazil (2003)	Used vehicles	Imports of used cars and motorcycles are prohibited.
Canada (2001)	Used vehicles	Under the Canadian Customs Tariff (tariff item No. 9897.00.00, Memorandum D9-1-11) a prohibition on imports of used or second-hand vehicles of all kinds remains in place, except on those imported from the United States; imports of used vehicles from Mexico are to be progressively liberalised, with unlimited access planned for 2019.
Canada (2002)	Textiles	Canada maintains quotas on some textiles and clothing products.
China (2002)	Electronics	According to China's accession agreement to the WTO, import quotas for some electronic products (colour televisions, electronic calculators, household satellite television receivers, printers, cassette and radio recorders, clock radios, laser disk players, household video camera recorders) should be phased out by 2004 as scheduled.
China (2002)	Textiles	China applies import quotas to textiles. According to WTO accession commitments, China should phase out import quotas upon accession.
China (2002)	Automobiles	Until WTO accession, China applied import quotas and import licences on automobiles. According to WTO accession obligations, China should phase out quotas on automobiles by 2005. Initial quota value should amount to USD 6 billion in 2001 with an early increase of 15%. In the first year, 25% of the quota will be allocated to new importers (*i.e.* USD 1.5 billion).
China (2003)	Cosmetics	China published a new regulation in March 2002 which prohibited cosmetic product imports containing certain ingredients of animal origin from 18 countries which have officially declared cases of BSE. The justification of this measure is to protect human health.
Egypt (2002)	Used vehicles	Imports of passenger cars witnessed severe restrictions in 1999. New measures limit imports to cars manufactured in the year of importation.
Egypt (2002)	Textiles	Egypt ended its import ban on fabrics on 1 January 1998 but introduced on the same date extremely burdensome labelling requirements.

Country	Sector/product type	Details
India (2002)	General	Import restrictions have been maintained in India under various categories, such as those subject to non-automatic licensing, prohibited items and items importable only by government trading monopolies. Most of these take the form of non-automatic licences. There were approximately 582 items on the restricted list in 2001. The list included agricultural products, chemicals, fertilisers, pharmaceuticals, metal, stones, jewellery, transmission apparatus, helicopters and aircraft, to mention a few. Often, non-automatic licensing effectively bans or prevents competing imports of certain items from entering the domestic market at commercial levels.
		In the EXIM policy for 2002-07 introduced in March 2002, there was some forward movement due to the removal of 63 items from the restricted list. The major products, which were freed, belong to pharmaceutical products, antibiotics, chemicals (with certain conditions), organic and inorganic compounds and gems and jewellery. Certain insecticides and pesticides (32 products falling under heading 3808) were freed provided that they were registered and not prohibited for import under the Insecticides Act.
Japan (2003)	Phthalates in toys and food contact packages	The Japanese authorities notified the WTO in October 2001 their intention to restrict the use of two plasticisers – diisononyl phthalate (DINP) and di(2-ethylhexyl) phthalate (DEHP) – in certain food-contact apparatus and synthetic resin toys.
Mexico (2001)	Used vehicles	Currently Mexico requires an import permit for most used vehicles made in the United States, Canada or the European Union. Permits are granted only for special purpose vehicles for which there is no relevant production in Mexico, such as ambulances and vehicles adapted for handicapped people. In practice, imports of used vehicles are prohibited in Mexico.
		The EU-Mexico FTA eliminates all import prohibitions or restrictions other than customs duties and taxes, whether made effective through quotas, import licences or other measures (Art. 12). However, FTA Annex IV.6 allows Mexico to maintain import prohibitions or restrictions on nearly all used vehicles.
Mexico (2001)	Used machinery	Import licences are required for imports of certain used machinery. The list of used machinery subject to a compulsory import permit includes automatic data processing machines, magnetic or optical readers, and machines for transcribing data onto data media in coded form. In practice, imports of used machinery are prohibited. The Free trade agreement between Mexico and the European Union allows Mexico to maintain prohibitions or restrictions on the importation of aforementioned used products until 31 December 2003.
Nigeria (2002)	Used products	Vehicles over five years old from the date of manufacturing.
		Used refrigerators, air conditioners, compressors.
Nigeria (2002)	Textiles	Textiles containing hazardous chemicals such as chloride.
Nigeria (2002)	Different goods	The Federal Executive Council on 7 January 2004 approved the following list of banned import goods: corrugated boards and curtains, textiles, men's footwear and bags (leather and plastics), soap and detergents, furniture, bicycles (assembled), flowers (fresh and plastic), fresh food, cutlasses and associated products, toothpaste, pencils and ball point pens, plastic products, barite and bentonite, vegetable oil, meat products.
Singapore (2001)	Chewing gum	The importation of chewing gum is prohibited for public safety reasons.
Chinese Taipei (2003)	Automobiles	Historically Chinese Taipei has maintained import bans on passenger cars equipped with diesel engines, motorcycles of 150 cc or above, and vehicles equipped with two-cycle engines. These restrictions will continue for two years after Chinese Taipei's accession to the WTO. The government lifted the restrictions on the importation of motorcycles over 150 cc on 1 July 2002. However, regulatory or possibly market factors have resulted in few motorcycles over 150 cc in circulation.
Thailand (2001)	Automotives	The importation of six-wheeled buses seating over 30 persons and of motorcycles is prohibited in order to protect the (infant) domestic industry. These prohibitions were turned into non-automatic licensing. Moreover, imports of used automotive products are prohibited on public health grounds. Imports are allowed by the public sector only, or for temporary entry for re-export.
United States (2002)	Textiles and clothing	Quantitative restrictions are in place for commercial reasons in a few sectors, notably textiles and clothing.

Source: http://mkaccdb.eu.int.

Annex 2.A4

Information on Prohibitions and Quotas Derived from WTO Trade Policy Reviews Completed between 1998 and 2004

Australia (2002)
Prohibitions for reasons of human health, hygiene and sanitation, protection of animal and plant life, environmental conservation, and essential security, in compliance with domestic legislative/policy requirements (including revenue objectives) as well as international commitments.

Bangladesh (2000)
Prohibitions for social, religious, health, environmental, security or trade reasons. Major categories: *i)* products that require a certificate, prior permission or clearance from the relevant authorities; *ii)* products that can be imported only by registered industrial consumers, including export-oriented ready-made garment, hosiery and specified textile industries operating under the bonded warehouse system, the pharmaceutical (allopathic) industries, and foreign exchange hotels, *iii)* state trading products, including arms and ammunition, which can be imported only by government-designated firms, and *iv)* products required to meet certain conditions.

Barbados (2002)
Prohibitions to ensure national security, safeguard consumer health and morality, or to preserve domestic plant and animal life and the environment.

Bolivia (1999)
Bolivia does not use import prohibitions except for products deemed by the authorities to cause prejudice to public health, environment or morality. Prohibited items are pharmaceuticals and drugs not registered in the country; spoiled or adulterated beverages and food products; diseased animals; plants that contain parasites and germs or are declared harmful by the Ministry of Agriculture; foreign lottery bills; used string and rope; toxic and radioactive materials; advertisements imitating money or bank certificates; and postage stamps. The import of used right-hand drive vehicles transformed to left-hand drive is prohibited. Refrigerating equipment and air conditioning equipment containing CFC-12 are banned.

Botswana (2003)
Prohibitions to protect health, safety, and morality. The import of environmentally hazardous products, such as toxic or radioactive waste, is banned.

Brazil (2000)
Prohibitions to safeguard consumer health and well being, or to preserve domestic plant and animal life and the environment. As at May 2000, no imports seemed to be subject to import quotas. Goods imported into the Manaus Free Trade Zone were subject to quotas until 1998. Import quotas on automotive goods were eliminated on 31 December 1999. Import quotas also applied to rubber. Importation of used machinery, automobiles, clothing, and many other used consumer goods is banned.

Brunei (2001)
Import prohibitions are maintained on a small number of products, including opium, firecrackers, vaccines from Chinese Taipei, and arms and ammunition. The prohibitions are maintained for security, health, and moral reasons. In addition, the import and manufacture of alcohol and alcohol products are restricted for religious reasons under the Customs Prohibitions and Restriction of Imports and Exports Amended Order 1990. The order, which became effective on 1 December 1990, allows imports through a licence issued by the Controller. There appears to be a "temporary" import ban on cement, while a similar "temporary" ban on roofing material was lifted recently. Import of used motor vehicles older than five years is banned with the aim to improve road safety.

Burundi (2003)
Over the period 1993-2000, Burundi had gradually expanded its negative list of prohibited or controlled imports, citing a foreign currency shortfall to justify the measure. In order to address the problem, a licensing system was applied until August 2002. As the peace process advanced, prohibitions were progressively lifted. Bans currently apply on items such as narcotic drugs, ivory, weapons and ammunition.

Cameroon (2001)
Prohibitions for security, public order, health, environmental, and emergency reasons.

Canada (2003, 2000)
Prohibitions to ensure national security, safeguard consumer health and morality, to implement inter-governmental arrangements, or to preserve domestic plant and animal life and the environment. The import of reprints of Canadian and British works copyrighted in Canada is banned. Since the 1960s, tariffs on textiles and clothing have been complemented by import quotas; these were progressively dismantled over a ten-year period to January 2005 under the WTO Agreement on Textiles and Clothing. In late 2002, about one half of the value of clothing imports entered the Canadian market under quota. Prohibition on the import of second-hand motor vehicles less than 15 years old, except if manufactured in the United States; used or second-hand aircraft, except if imported from the United States.

Chile (2004)
Prohibitions for the protection of human health, animal and plant life, and the environment, in compliance with domestic legislation or international commitments. Prohibition of used vehicles; according to the authorities, this is for environmental reasons. Prohibition on the import of hazardous waste (Basle Convention) and of products containing CFC (Montreal Protocol).

Costa Rica (2001)
Banned items: ozone depleters, asbestos, arms and explosives, natural products in pharmaceutical form and tisanes, narcotics, psychotropic substances and unauthorised drugs, cosmetics, hazardous products and medications.

Dominican Republic (2002)
Prohibitions for the protection of human health, animal and plant life, the environment, and essential security interests and military reasons, in compliance with domestic legislation or international commitments. To protect the environment, national legislation prohibits the import of vehicles over five years old, motorcycles within five years of manufacture, used electrical household appliances, vehicles over five tons within 15 years of manufacture, and used clothes.

Egypt (1999)
Egypt disinvoked GATT Article XVIII:B (on trade measures taken for balance-of-payments reasons) on 30 June 1995, and made a commitment to remove its remaining conditional import prohibitions on fabrics and on apparel and made-ups, no later than 1 January 1998 and 1 January 2002, respectively. Conditional prohibitions on the import of fabrics were lifted in 1998 and tariffed at 54%. Non-tariff barriers on all textile and clothing items were to be phased out by 2002, in line with Egypt's Uruguay Round commitments. Imports of second-hand goods are allowed for certain products, although in most cases permission is required from the designated Ministries. The import of air conditioners, refrigerators and aerosol products using ozone-damaging substances is prohibited as part of Egypt's participation in the Montreal Protocol on Substances that Deplete the Ozone Layer.

El Salvador (2003)
Prohibition on the importation of light passenger and cargo motor vehicles in use for more than eight years and heavy passengers and cargo motor vehicles in use for more than 15 years.

European Community (2002, 2000, 1997)
A general safety requirement applies to the placement of consumable products on the Community market, except for those for which specific product regulations or standards have been established at Community or member state level such as food products. Member states may invoke this requirement to take action in emergency situations, and Community-wide measures may be taken, at the initiative of the Commission, under the RAPEX system for non-food products. In 2000, the Commission decided to ban the placement on the market of toys and childcare articles, intended to be placed in the mouths of children under three years of age, made of soft PVC containing certain phthalates; this Decision was extended during the period under the last TPR review, until 20 February 2002. For food products, the EU adopted a new instrument for food safety in February 2002 which was first used on 27 March 2002 to suspend the placing on the Community market and import of jelly confectionary containing the food additive E 425 konjac.

The placement and use of dangerous substances on the Community market, including by importation, is strictly regulated to protect the public; the list of covered substances is regularly updated owing to technical progress. Bans affecting creosote and hexachloroethane were announced, to be effective on 30 June 2003. The ban on remaining uses of chrysotile asbestos, to be effective by 2005, was unsuccessfully challenged by Canada under the WTO dispute settlement procedures.

Through a common system of notification and information for imports from and exports to third countries, the EU controls the trade of certain chemicals that are banned or severely restricted on account of their effects on human health and the environment; the Community applies the international notification and prior informed consent (PIC) procedure established by the United Nations Environment Programme (UNEP) and the Food and Agriculture Organization (FAO).

The EU applies regulations to trade in relation to the following MEAs: Convention on International Trade in Endangered Species of Wild Fauna and Flora (CITES), International Commission for the Conservation of Atlantic Tunas (ICCAT), Basel Convention, Montreal Protocol.

As of 1 January 2002, the EU continues to maintain quotas carried over into the WTO from the longstanding Multi-Fibre Arrangement (MFA) on imports from Argentina; Brazil; Hong Kong, China; India; Indonesia; Korea; Macao; Malaysia; Pakistan; Peru; the Philippines; Singapore; Sri Lanka (suspended); and Thailand.

With respect to China, the EU maintains quotas under the ATC carried over from the MFA, as well as other quotas (linen, silk and ramie). With respect to the former, the timetable for the elimination of quotas by 1 January 2005 is presumed to apply. The EU also maintains quotas on imports from Belarus, Uzbekistan and Vietnam under bilateral agreements. The EU applies quantitative restrictions on an autonomous basis on imports from the Federal Republic of Yugoslavia (Serbia and Montenegro) and the Democratic People's Republic of Korea.

Quotas are applied on imports from China of footwear, tableware and kitchenware (ceramic, porcelain and china), as well as surveillance on certain products. Upon the accession of China to the WTO, the EU made the commitment to progressively liberalise the quotas and remove them by 2005.

The EU maintains quotas on certain steel products imported from Kazakhstan, the Russian Federation, and the Ukraine, and maintains surveillance on imports of certain steel products from these countries.

Gabon (2001)

Control measures applied to pesticides and industrial chemicals in accordance with the PIC schedule (prior information and consent principle) of the United Nations Environment Programme (UNEP) and the United Nations Food and Agriculture Organization (FAO).

Gambia (2004)

Prohibitions of counterfeit or non-standard coins or currency notes, indecent articles and pornography, firearms that are not properly licensed, narcotic drugs, handcuffs, rough or uncut diamonds, certain types of noxious gases, and books, newspapers or any other matter whatsoever that is seditious, scandalising or demoralising. Participation in CITES has led to the prohibition of imports of ivory and articles of ivory, wild animal skins, including snake skins, and articles made from these skins, and shells.

Ghana (2001)

Prohibitions to protect human health and national security, such as restrictions on imports of obscene articles, dangerous weapons, contaminated food or infected animal carcasses. Importation of motor vehicles, including lorries and buses over ten years old was banned in 2000. Previously, imported over-age motor vehicles were subject to a penalty tariff.

Guatemala (2002)

Prohibitions for the protection of human health, animal and plant life, the environment, or essential security interests and military reasons, in compliance with domestic legislation or international commitments. Guatemala's import prohibitions apply equally to all its trading partners. Human or animal wastes, treated or untreated, are prohibited. Products containing CFC products not freely and legally marketed in their country of origin are prohibited.

Guyana (2003)

Prohibitions on the import of counterfeit or substandard coins; food unfit for consumption; indecent articles; and matches containing white and yellow phosphorus.

Haiti (2003)

Prohibitions for reasons of health, security or morality. The product list includes brochures, printed matter or films of a pornographic nature, military tanks and armoured vehicles and parts thereof, boats, arms and ammunition not intended for the government, narcotics, and equipment to be used to manufacture or print counterfeit currency or securities. Haiti is not party to the Convention on International Trade in Endangered Species of Wild Fauna and Flora (CITES) but according to the authorities, it applies the CITES directives.

Honduras (2003)

Prohibitions on grounds of health, safety, public morality or environmental protection. Banned products include *e.g.* drugs, narcotics, psychotropics and pornography.

Hong Kong, China (2002)
Prohibitions to ensure security, protect the environment and public heath, and comply with international obligations, including the United Nations Security Council's resolutions and international conventions, such as the Basel Convention, the Montreal Protocol and CITES. In general, imports of all ozone-depleting substances (ODS) are prohibited. However, as of 1 January 1995 and 1 January 1996, respectively, imports of methyl bromide and hydrochloro-fluorocarbons (HCFCs) originating in a country that is party to the Montreal Protocol are allowed, for local consumption only (*i.e.* not for re-export).

Iceland (2000)
Prohibitions of narcotics and dangerous drugs, various weapons, and imports of ozone-depleting substances other than hydrochloro-fluorocarbons (HCFCs).

India (2002)
While most products previously restricted for balance-of-payment reasons have been derestricted, restrictions are maintained on some products for reasons of health, security and public morals. These include firearms, explosives and ammunition, certain medicines and drugs, and jewellery, notified by India under Articles XX and XXI of the GATT 1947. Imported second-hand motor vehicles must not be older than three years from the date of manufacture. In addition, they must meet several technical conditions. The authorities claim that the restrictions are maintained for consumer protection and road safety reasons. In addition, the prohibition on waste, parings and scrap plastics, was relaxed by allowing imports of these products by export-processing zones. The importation of products protected under the Wildlife Protection Act 1972, the Convention on International Trade in Endangered Species (CITES), and the Montreal Protocol on Substances that Deplete the Ozone Layer is also prohibited.

Indonesia (2003)
Prohibitions for reasons of public morality, public order, public security, to protect human or animal health or life, to conserve plants, to protect the environment, to protect national treasures of artistic, historical or archaeological value, to protect industrial or commercial property, to protect consumers, for reasons of product packaging, customs inspections or control of financial transactions with other countries. Importation of luxury cars (from February to 1 June 2000) has been banned.

Israel (1999)
Prohibitions relate to public morals, health or safety considerations.

Japan (2002, 2000)
Prohibitions apply under five categories: narcotics; revolvers and pistols; imitation currencies; books and other articles considered contrary to public security or morality; and articles infringing patents or other intellectual property rights. Some commodities, including fish and silk yarn and certain silk fabrics, are subject to import quotas or restraints under bilateral trade agreements and arrangements, for instance with China and Korea.

Kenya (2000)
Prohibitions for moral, health, security, and environmental reasons, and under international conventions.

Korea (2000)
Prohibitions for the protection of public morals, human health, hygiene and sanitation, animal and plant life, environmental conservation or essential security interests in compliance with domestic legislation requirements or international commitments. Law No. 218 of 22 May 1984 prohibits the importation of human, animal and industrial waste.

Madagascar (2001)

Prohibitions for reasons of health, security or morals, and products such as arms, explosives and radioactive products. Import restrictions also apply to products considered by the government to be strategic (*e.g.* vanillin and precious stones).

Malaysia (2001)

Prohibitions for moral and national security reasons. No major changes in the list of prohibited items since the last TPR review. Prohibited goods are articles bearing the imprint or reproduction of any currency note, banknote or emblems and devices for which there might be a reasonable presumption that they will be used in a manner prejudicial to or incompatible with peace, welfare or good order in Malaysia; indecent or obscene articles; cloth bearing the imprint or reproduction of any verses of the Koran; daggers and flick knives; certain broadcast receivers; certain liquors containing lead; sodium arsenite; all genus of Piranha fish; turtle eggs; cocoa pods, rambutan, pulasan, longan and namam fruits produced in the Philippines and Indonesia; pens, pencils and other articles resembling syringes; and certain poisonous chemicals.

Maldives (2003)

Prohibitions for health, safety, security, environmental and religious reasons. Banned products include arms and ammunition, alcohol and spirits, pork and its by-products, dogs and dangerous animals, religious materials offensive to Islam, worship idols, pornographic material, narcotics, and live pigs. Imports of used motor vehicles and cycles over five years and three years old, respectively, are banned for environmental reasons.

Mauritania (2002)

Prohibitions for reasons such as safety, public order and health. Prohibited items: alcohol (without government authorisation); arms and ammunition; gold and rough diamonds; military equipment; warfare equipment; drugs; explosives; counterfeit goods. Distilling equipment, seeds, rough diamonds, obscene publications or films, saccharin, narcotic drugs and explosives may be authorised by an official, a ministry or a competent government office. According to the authorities, Mauritania does not currently apply quantitative restrictions on imports in order to protect domestic production.

Mexico (2002)

Prohibitions exist on 17 tariff items for reasons of public safety, health, morality or child protection. Prohibited imports are classified under the following headings: 0301.9901, 1211.9002, 1302.1102, 1302.1902, 2833.2903, 2903.5903, 2903.5905, 2910.9001, 2925.1901, 2931.0005, 2939.1002, 3003.4001, 3003.4002, 3004.4001, 3004.4002, 4908.9005, 4911.9105. Mexico also applies import prohibitions on a number of countries as provided for in United Nations Security Council resolutions.

Morocco (2003)

Import bans or restrictions may be imposed under special legislation on the following products: narcotic drugs and psychotropic substances; weapons, parts of weapon, and ammunition, with the exception of those for the army; written or printed matter, drawings, posters, engravings, paintings, photographs, slides, or reproductions of a pornographic nature and any articles contrary to morality or likely to cause a breach of the peace.

Mozambique (2001)

Prohibitions for reasons of health, morals or counterfeiting, including products such as pornography, narcotic drugs, and certain used automobiles over five years old. Certain products may only be imported temporarily. Other specific products that are subject to special import regulations and licensing include certain medications, arms and explosives, certain used clothes, gold, silver and platinum, certain foreign and domestic currency. Import of certain used clothes and certain used tyres is banned.

Namibia (2003)
The importation of certain products is prohibited as a result of Namibia's participation in the following multilateral agreements: the Montreal Convention on the Emission of Ozone Depleting Substances, the Vienna Convention and the London Amendment; the Basel Convention on Trade in Toxic or Hazardous Waste and the Cartagena Protocol on Biosafety.

New Zealand (2003)
A number of imports are prohibited or restricted for health and safety reasons or in compliance with international conventions to which New Zealand is party.

Nicaragua (1999)
Prohibitions for the protection of human health, animal and plant life, the environment, or essential security interests and military reasons in compliance with domestic legislation or international commitments. Since 1995 prohibitions have been ordered against imports of alcoholic beverages, spare parts, medicinal and pharmaceutical products, paints, chemicals, kitchenware, Land Rover vehicles, and cloth fabric made by specific firms. In July 1999, 12 cases of import prohibition against parallel imports remained in force.

Norway (2000)
Prohibitions for safety or health reasons include asbestos and products containing asbestos; and products containing CFCs, halons, carbon tetrachloride, methyl chloroform and other ozone-depleting substances in accordance with Regulation for CFCs and halons of 21 January 1991 and Regulation for carbon tetrachloride and methyl chloroform of 28 March 1995. Import prohibitions apply to some live plants and plants that host certain diseases.

Pakistan (2002)
The number of prohibited items seems to have been reduced. In September 2000, the list contained 71 items (excluding those of general nature) under around 121 HS headings, compared with 75 in 1994 (GATT, 1995). Other changes to the negative list include the withdrawal of a number of products prohibited on commercial grounds (potatoes, certain textiles and clothing items). The main prohibitions on commercial grounds affecting numerous textiles and clothing articles and chassis for trucks were phased-out between July 2000 and January 2001; these prohibitions were introduced for balance-of-payments reasons in 1997. Although imports of second-hand machinery, reconditioned goods or any kind of factory rejects are prohibited, some second-hand or used goods not manufactured locally are importable subject to certain conditions. Other exceptions include used books, magazines, journals, clothing (including footwear, travelling rugs, and blankets), certain waste, seconds and cuttings of iron and steel, stainless steel, tin sheets and plates and rerollable scrap. Imports of permissible second-hand machinery are subject to preshipment inspection, however, to ensure that the machinery has a reasonable useful life. Two items were placed on the prohibition list on environmental grounds (waste plastics, pressure horns).

Papua New Guinea (1999)
According to authorities, the country no longer operates any prohibitions or import quotas. Import bans and quotas were previously used to encourage domestic manufacturing industries, such as canned beef, sugar, cement, vegetables, flour, batteries and canned mackerel. These import bans and quotas were removed, mainly by 1996, and converted to protective and prohibitive tariff rates, ranging mostly from 30% to 80%, with some higher rates. The authorities ban the importation of certain pesticides for agricultural use, namely DDT, chlordane, dieldrin and endrin, because of environmental concerns. As a party to the Montreal Protocol on Substances that Deplete the Ozone Layer, it also bans imports of CFCs and other ozone-depleting substances. It also belongs to the Basel Convention on Control of Transboundary Movement of Hazardous Wastes and their Disposal. Import restrictions apply on wild fauna and flora under the Convention on International Trade in Endangered Species of

Fauna and Flora (CITES). These are contained in the International Trade (Fauna and Flora) Act of 1979.

Peru (2000)
Prohibitions are motivated by health and environmental protection considerations. The only exceptions are the prohibition on geographical texts or mappings that mutilate national territory (national identity) and on foreign alcoholic beverages bearing the name Pisco (protected denomination of origin).

Philippines (1999)
The authorities noted that the Import Liberalisation Programme has eliminated most non-tariff measures other than those maintained for reasons of health, safety and national security. Since 1993, various restrictions have been removed: balance-of-payments restrictions on coal and coal products in force in early 1999 appear to have been eliminated; their liberalisation had been foreshadowed for end 1997. The Philippines disinvoked Article XVIII:B subject to the liberalisation of remaining balance-of-payments restrictions by 31 December 1997. In 1995 restrictions were lifted on importation of new motor vehicles and some used trucks and buses.

Romania (1999)
Prohibitions for reasons of public morality, health, protection of human life, environmental protection and national security. The import control system currently applies to weapons and ammunition, military equipment, spare parts and any technical documentation or material used to manufacture such products, scrap metal and other waste products that are dangerous to human health, including drugs and narcotics, or for the environment, goods under control of the final destination, for reasons related to non-proliferation of weapons of mass destruction and missile carriers, as well as radioactive materials, nuclear installations and nuclear-related products.

Senegal (2003)
Prohibitions on the import of weapons and ammunition, explosives, raw diamonds not cleaved or cut, drugs and narcotics, and obscene publications. Prohibition on the import of certain second-hand vehicles has been abolished in 1996.

Singapore (2000)
Prohibitions for reasons of public health and safety, environmental protection, national security, and in accordance with international agreements and the United Nations Security Council regulations. New prohibitions were introduced on controlled telecommunications equipment, including scanning receivers and military communications equipment, and cosmetics containing prohibited substances or additives above the stipulated limit.

South Africa (2003)
The import of certain used goods is prohibited. The import of waste and hazardous materials is prohibited. Imports of pesticides such as aldrin, dieldrin, mercury compounds and certain mixtures of isomers are banned, and imports of other pesticides (*e.g.* inorganic arsenic compounds, chlordane, DDT) are severely restricted.

Sri Lanka (2004)
Prohibitions maintained for health, safety, security, environment, and moral reasons. In 2004 the maximum age limit for import of used construction machinery was reduced from ten to seven years.

Switzerland (2000)
Prohibitions apply under international conventions and for public health and safety reasons (toxic chemical substances, "ABC" weapons and antipersonnel mines). Under the Ordinance relating to Environmentally Hazardous Substances, the manufacture, supply, import and use of certain chemical substances are also banned on the basis of environmental protection, and/or public health and safety considerations. These include hexachlorocyclohexane, aldrin, dieldrin, endrin, heptachlor and heptachlorepoxid, isodrin, kelevan, chlodecone, telodrin, stroban, toxaphene, hexachlorobenzene, PCBs, PCTs, halogenated naphtalenes, halogenated diarylalkanes, DDT, 2,4,5-T, and PCP.

Tanzania (2000)
The restrictions currently in force are retained for reasons of health, security or morals and concern products such as arms and ammunition, explosives, military equipment and narcotic drugs.

Thailand (2003, 1999)
Import bans are in place to protect public morals, national security, human, animal or plant life, and health. They also include counterfeit goods and the equipment for their manufacture and marble. The import of worked monumental or building stone is prohibited for industry protection reason; sacks and bags of jute or other textile to secure farmers' income; used motorcycles and their engines for public health and safety reasons. Household refrigerators utilising CFC in the production process and glazed ceramic ware are banned. New cars and engines are under licensing, but are banned *de facto*.

Togo (1999)
The dismantling of quantitative restrictions on, licences for and prohibitions of imports, begun in 1989 within the framework of the structural adjustment programmes, was completed in 1995 by the abolition of the last of these measures on wheat flour, cement, concrete-reinforcing bars and galvanized sheet. The restrictions currently in force are retained for reasons of health, security or morals and concern products such as arms and ammunition, explosives and military equipment, narcotic drugs and certain pharmaceutical products such as psychotropic drugs.

United States (2004, 2001, 1999)
Prohibitions to ensure national security, safeguard consumer health, protect public morals or for environmental purposes. Restraints on imports of uranium, ammonium nitrate, and steel products have been negotiated with Russia and on imports of silicon-manganese and steel products with Ukraine. QRs are in place on imports of a number of steel products pursuant to suspension agreement following anti dumping investigations with Russia, China and Brazil. Trade in textiles and clothing continues to be affected by import quotas applied to imports of certain products from over 40 countries. Merchandise that can be proven to have been mined, produced or manufactured wholly or in part in any foreign country by bonded, industrialised, slave or forced labour may not enter the United States

Any wild animal or bird if captured or exported contrary to the law of the foreign country; feathers or skins of any wild bird, except for scientific and educational purposes; immoral articles; cattle, sheep, swine and meats from any country for which the Secretary of Agriculture has determined the existence of rinderpest or foot-and-mouth disease. In order to implement the International Convention on the Conservation of Atlantic Tunas (ICCAT), imports of Atlantic Bluefin Tuna and its products in any form harvested by vessels of Panama, Honduras and Belize are prohibited.

Venezuela (2002)
Prohibitions to protect the life and health of people and animals, to preserve plant life and to protect public morals, the environment or the country's essential security interests. Matches may not be imported, except from certain Andean countries. Used vehicles or obsolete models for private use, along with worn clothing and second-hand tyres are also under import prohibition. The prohibition on used vehicles is intended to lay regulatory foundations for the functioning and development of the national automotive industry. An exception is made in the case of tyres imported from Andean countries.

Zambia (2002)
Prohibitions for environmental, moral, health and security reasons, and under international conventions: *i)* false or counterfeit coins or banknotes, and any coins or banknotes that are intended for circulation in Zambia but are not legal tender in Zambia; *ii)* any goods that are indecent, obscene or objectionable; *iii)* goods manufactured or produced wholly or in part by prison labour or within or in connection with any prison, jail or penitentiary excluding *bona fide* gifts made by a prisoner for the personal use of a private individual; *iv)* pirated and counterfeit goods and any goods bearing false or misleading marks or descriptions as to their origin, purpose and use.

Notes

1. Article XIII of GATT 1994 extends the most favoured nation (MFN) principle to the administration of quantitative restrictions when they are used as an exception to Article XI. As a general rule, in the application of prohibitions or restrictions on imports and exports, a member should treat all other members equally.

2. In urgent cases, the Tokyo Round Decision on Safeguard Action for Development Purposes waives the requirement of time limits after consultation with affected members or prior agreement of the General Council.

3. For QRs that were already notified under other WTO agreements, members are to state that a previous notification was made and to report the document reference of this notification. For those QRs justified under Articles XX, XXI or XVIII, a full description of the product, HS number and WTO justification are required. The Decision provides for a central registry of QRs in the WTO Secretariat's Market Access Division. The notification has to describe the tariff lines affected by the measure, indicate the type of restriction and give the grounds and the WTO justification for its maintenance. A statement on the trade effects of the measures should also be included.

4. The reverse notification contains the same elements as the notification by a member applying a quantitative restriction. If the content of the reverse notification is challenged, the comments made are to be included in the inventory of quantitative restrictions, and further information is to be sought from the notifying member. Consultations may be held to verify the existence and scope of the measure.

5. The term "RTA" is used here to cover the range of free trade areas and customs unions.

6. Exports in excess of a set amount of imports are subject to a tariff which is scheduled to decrease gradually over time and reach 6.9% by 2006 (Automotive Provisions Report, Office of Automotive Affairs, ITA, US Department of Commerce, www/ita.doc.gov/auto).

7. Michalopoulos (1999). The analysis relies on frequency ratios as indicators of the existence and scope of application of various protective measures. The data also show that machinery and electrical equipment, vehicles, plastics and textiles were the groups most subject to prohibitions. At the same time, vehicles, arms, textiles and plastics were the product groups most restricted by quotas. Over the period examined, the number of countries imposing prohibitions on textiles and machinery and electrical equipment declined but remained relatively unchanged for vehicles.

8. Finger and Schuknecht (1999). The study also found that Articles XX (General Exceptions) and XXI (Security Exceptions) are most frequently used as a justification for QR measures. In Article XX, the paragraph allowing restrictions for the protection of human, animal and plant life or health was used the most often. Finger and Schuknecht also commented on the overall progress in reducing NTBs, including quantitative restrictions. They noted a significant decline in the use of NTBs among both developing and developed countries.

9. The Office of Economics of the US International Trade Commission (USITC) is currently conducting research to improve the quantification of the effects of NTMs on trade flows and other economic variables. A central element of this effort is the preparation of a database of NTMs that includes information on 53 economies. It provides information on the goods and services products and on the sectors that are affected by NTMs as well as reference sources. An overview of this research and some preliminary findings were presented at the APEC Capacity-building Workshop on Quantitative Methods for Assessing NTMs and Trade Facilitation, held on 8-10 October 2003 in Bangkok, Thailand.

10. This section deals only with measures involving quantitative restrictions evoked for balance of payment reasons, although several other measures also exist, such as import surcharges, etc.

11. The IMF provides documentation, normally a paper on recent economic developments, including statistics covering the balance of payments, and makes a formal statement to the Committee. Under simplified consultations, the IMF provides documentation, but does not address the Committee.

12. A number of countries applied import surcharges for BOP reasons in the 1990s. The countries that used these measures were mostly transition economies, such as Poland, Hungary, the Slovak Republic, the Czech Republic, Bulgaria and Romania, and also Sri Lanka and South Africa. These measures were abandoned in the second part of the 1990s, with Romania and the Slovak Republic being the last to lift the restrictions in 2001.

13. The following are examples of measures invoked and disinvoked for BOP reasons: Israel disinvoked the BOP provisions in 1995. It had used restrictions under these provisions at various times since 1961. The most recent import restrictions applied to agricultural products and were converted into tariffs and tariff quotas. The Philippines placed restrictions on coal and coal products and on agricultural products which were eliminated by 1999. Further, Nigeria in 1999 and Tunisia in 2001 discontinued the use of import prohibitions on automobiles. Over the period 1993-2000, Burundi had gradually expanded its negative list of prohibited or controlled imports, the government arguing a foreign currency shortfall to justify the measure. After 2000, as the peace process advanced, prohibitions were progressively lifted. Finally, Pakistan has been prohibiting the importation of several products for BOP reasons since 1997, although the number of items has been gradually reduced. The main prohibitions on commercial grounds affecting numerous textiles and clothing articles and chassis for trucks were phased out between July 2000 and January 2001.

14. TPR report of Bangladesh, 2000.

15. India – Quantitative Restrictions on Imports of Agricultural, Textile and Industrial Products, Report of the Panel, WT/DS90/R, April 1999.

16. There is no designated body to which such notifications should be sent. The Council for Trade in Goods (CTG), which operates "under the general guidance of the General Council", is responsible for "oversee(ing) the functioning of the Multilateral Trade Agreements in Annex 1A". This includes GATT 1994, of which Article XVIII:C is a part. The CTG, on the other hand, is competent, under its terms of reference, to "consider any questions which may arise with regard to either the application or the use of special provisions in the Multilateral Trade Agreements and related Ministerial Decisions in favor of developing country Members and report to the General Council for action".

17. Malaysia: polypropylene and polyethylene (1995);.Colombia: imports of salt (1998); and Bangladesh: chicks, eggs, cartons and salt (2002). Source: WTO.

18. EU MAD database.

19. APEC and WTO document G/LIC/N/3/MYS/1, 19 December 1997.

20. By mid-1999, the market shares of several popular Japanese products for which IDS prohibitions were lifted at the end of 1998 had expanded to up to 92%. These included numerically controlled milling machines, camcorders, ceramics and china products, and analog watches (*Digital ChosunIlbo* [Online], 3 June 1999, www.chosun.com/w21data/html/news/199906/ 199906030454.html.

21. See Annex 2.A3 for a list of products affected by prohibitions in different countries derived from the TPR reviews.

22. The number of environmental measures notified between 1997 and 2001: TBT Agreement: 435; SPS Agreement: 95; SCM Agreement: 133; Agreement on Agriculture: 150; Agreement on Import Licensing Procedures: 79; Quantitative Restrictions: 12. WT/CTE/EDB/1 Annex 3, p. 73.

23. Council Directive 76/769/EEC, as amended.

24. Navaretti *et al.* (1998). Pelletiere and Reinert (2003) analysed data on used car import restrictions in a large number of countries and found that the existence of a domestic industry is an important predictor of a restrictive policy.

25. Used parts are usually parts that have been removed from a vehicle and no additional value added except cleaning has been performed. By comparison, remanufactured or rebuilt parts are motor vehicle parts that have been fully reconditioned to original factory specifications. However, in practical terms, countries often treat remanufactured or rebuilt parts as "used". The market for remanufactured automotive parts has been estimated to represent USD 60-70 billion in sales worldwide (US Department of Commerce, Office of Automotive Affairs, 1999, p. 88).

26. According to a report on Global Import Regulations for Pre-owned (Used and Refurbished) Medical Devices, by the US Department of Commerce (2002a). The research reviewed the available information on import regulations for pre-owned medical devices for 99 markets. Of these, 78 appeared to permit the unrestricted importation of used or refurbished medical equipment. However, for several of these markets, the study notes that it may be safer to say that there are no reported restrictions, since available reports either do not mention restrictions, or simply indicate that authorities permit the importation of used equipment generally without a specific reference to medical devices. The countries that impose restrictions of various severity are Argentina, Brazil, Canada, Columbia, Croatia, India, Japan, Korea, Moldova, Pakistan, Peru, South Africa, Turkey, Uzbekistan, and Vietnam. The five countries that impose ban are China, Syria, Egypt, Thailand and Kuwait.

27. WTO, "The Regulation of State Trading under the WTO System", www.wto.org/english/tratop_e/statra_e/statrad.htm.

28. The examination of the overview of WTO and national reviews revealed that several, mostly developing, countries, have state trading systems in place that cover a wide range of products. Among large WTO members, for example, the state participates in a wide range of trading activities in China, India, Pakistan and Indonesia. The products involved are most often basic agricultural goods, such as rice, grain, sugar, salt and cotton. Some countries also only import industrial goods and raw materials (most commonly fuels, fertilisers, steel products, military equipment) through state enterprises. For example, in Indonesia, the state maintains exclusive import rights for a great number of products, *e.g.* alcoholic beverages, sugar, textile cloth

certain steel products, etc. In many developed countries as well, certain sectors or product categories fall under state trading operations. For example, in Japan, state trading involves several agricultural products. In Korea different agricultural and steel products and also some services fall under state trading operations. However, several countries have made efforts to liberalise their state trading enterprises. For example, linked to its accession to the WTO, China has been implementing the required liberalisation of trading rights of Chinese enterprises.

29. WTO, "The Regulation of State Trading under the WTO System", www.wto.org/english/tratop_e/statra_e/statrad.htm.

30. It is also common to have both a tariff and a quota on a given good, so that a tariff is paid on units of the good that are admitted under the quota.

31. On the limitations of the use of QRs for infant industry protection and the rent-seeking effects, see, for example, Krueger (1974). Furthermore, Bhagwati (1978) argues that the use of fiscal and monetary instruments is superior to trade restrictions and exchange control measures in addressing BOP difficulties.

32. This document has been prepared under the Secretariat's responsibility and without prejudice to the positions of members and to their rights and obligations under the WTO.

33. By 31 January 1998, by 31 January 2000, by 31 January 2002, by 31 January 2004.

References

Bhagwati, J.N. (1978), *The New International Economic Order: The North-South Debate*, Cambridge, Mass.: MIT Press, 1978.

Clerides, S.K. (2003), "The Welfare Effects of Trade Liberalization: Evidence from Used Automobiles", www.econ.yale.edu/seminars/trade/tdw03/clerides-030512.pdf.

European Commission, DG Trade, EC's Market Access Database, http://mkaccdb.eu.int/.

Finger, J.M. and L. Schuknecht (1999), "Market Access Advances and Retreats: the Uruguay Round and Beyond", http://econ.worldbank.org/docs/959.pdf.

Goode, W. (2003), *Dictionary of Trade Policy Terms*, WTO and Cambridge University Press.

Krueger, A.O. (1974), "The political economy of the rent seeking society", *American Economic Review*, Vol. 64, No. 3, pp. 291-303.

METI, Japan (2004), "Report on the WTO Consistency and Trading Policies by Major Trading Partners", www.meti.go.jp/english/report.

Michalopoulos, C. (1999), "Trade Policy and Market Access Issues for Developing Countries", World Bank, Washington, www.econ.worldbank.org/docs/940.pdf.

Navaretti, G.B., I. Soloaga and W. Takacs (1998), "When Vintage Technology Makes Sense: Matching Imports to Skills", World Bank, Washington, http://econ.worldbank.org/docs/750.pdf.

OECD (2003), *Liberalising Trade in Textiles and Clothing: A Survey of Quantitative Studies*, OECD, Paris.

Pelletiere, D. and K.A. Reinert (2002), "The Political Economy of Used Automobile Protection in Latin America", *The World Economy*, Vol. 25, No. 7, pp. 1019-1037.

Pelletiere, D. and K.A. Reinert (2003), "Used Automobile Protection and Trade: Gravity and Ordered Probit Analysis", School of Public Policy, George Mason University, Fairfax, Virginia, http://mason.gmu.edu/~kreinert/paperspdf/usedwe.pdf

The Wall Street Journal (2004), "How Japan's Second-Hand Cars Make Their Way to Third World", 8 January.

US Department of Commerce, Office of Automotive Affairs (1999), International Trade Administration, Compilation of Foreign Remanufacturing Parts Import Restrictions, Washington, DC.

US Department of Commerce (2002a), Global Import Regulations for Pre-Owned (Used and Refurbished) Medical Devices, Washington, DC.

US Department of Commerce: Free Trade Area of the Americas (FTAA) (2002b), "Key automotive markets and issues", 9 May versionwww.ita.doc.gov/td/auto/FTAAAuto.pdf.

US Department of Commerce (2003), "Automotive Provisions Report, Office of Automotive Affairs", ITA, www/ita.doc.gov/auto.

USTR: US Trade Representative (2003), "National Trade Estimate Report of Foreign Trade Barriers", www.ustr.gov/reports/nte/2003/.

WTO (1999), "India – Quantitative Restrictions on Imports of Agricultural, Textile and Industrial Products", Report of the Panel, WT/DS90/R.

WTO (2003), "Matrix on Trade Measures Pursuant to Selected Multilateral Environmental Agreements", WT/CTE/W/160/Rev.2TN/TE/S/5.

WTO (2003) and WTO (2004), "Non-Tariff Barrier Notifications", TN/MA/W/*.

WTO, "Environment Backgrounder: The Relationship between MEAs and the WTO, The Doha Negotiating Mandate on MEAs", www.wto.org/english/tratop_e/envir_e/envir_backgrnd_e/c5s3_e.htm

WTO, "The Regulation of State Trading System under the WTO System", available at www.wto.org/english/tratop_e/statra_e/statrad.htm

Chapter 3

Non-automatic Import Licensing

by

Massimo Geloso Grosso

This chapter looks at the nature and scope of non-tariff measures, specifically non-automatic import licensing, which is a means of controlling imports linked to compliance with specific criteria. These schemes can be applied for a variety of purposes relating to both economic and non-economic regulatory goals. The use of these measures has been evolving, and significant reforms that have been undertaken over the years have changed the pattern of perceived problems associated with them. This chapter reviews and summarises on a country basis the information contained in the WTO trade policy reviews, which generally permit identification of licensing measures used in different countries and the broad product groups covered. It also looks at ongoing discussions at the WTO on trade facilitation, highlighting the important link with import licensing.

Introduction

As part of a broad effort to learn more about the nature and scope of non-tariff measures, this chapter presents a detailed analysis of non-automatic import licensing. The purpose is twofold. First, to enhance understanding of the characteristics of today's import licensing regimes. Second, to identify which aspects of licensing may still act as significant barriers to trade and suggest options for addressing them. This may contribute to post-Doha WTO discussions, particularly in the areas of market access for non-agricultural goods and trade facilitation.

The chapter presents a systematic review of detailed information on licensing systems contained in the trade policy reviews (TPRs) of 78 countries that were prepared for GATT/WTO over the period 1989-2002.[1] These countries represent all regions of the world.

The TPRs contain a significant body of consistent and detailed information on licensing regimes over time, which has been reviewed and discussed on a country-by-country basis and can be considered relatively accurate and authoritative. The description provided, however, is not always clear[2] and there are some differences in the depth of treatment of various countries.[3] A quantitative analysis was ruled out, as the results would have been affected by these differences in the data and other methodological shortcomings, which would diminish the usefulness of the analysis for policy makers and negotiators. Moreover, Michalopoulos (1999) has already undertaken a quantitative analysis based on a systematic review of trade policies contained in TPRs, including import licensing.[4]

Nevertheless, the TPRs generally make it possible to identify the use of licensing measures in different countries and for broad product groups, including licensing intended for economic and non-economic purposes. In an effort to support and complement the information contained in the TPRs, the available WTO notifications and replies to the questionnaire of the Committee on Import Licensing were reviewed for each country examined in the TPRs.

Following an overview of the history and characteristics of licensing, two sections present the findings of the present study, together with a description of the characteristics and the effects of the different measures on trade and on the economy in general. Next, the procedural aspects of licensing implementation are considered in the context of on-going discussions at the WTO on trade facilitation. A summary of the main findings and their implications for action by nations and the international community on steps that would further deepen the reform process concludes the chapter.

Overview

Non-automatic licensing refers to the practice of requiring, as a prior condition for the importation of goods, an import licence that is not granted automatically. The basic difference with automatic licensing is that the latter is mainly used for compiling trade statistics and approval is granted in all cases, almost immediately upon application. Non-automatic licensing systems, instead, are a means of controlling imports, by making them comply with specific criteria. These schemes can be applied for a variety of both economic and non-economic (social) regulatory goals. Such systems typically operate on the basis of product lists of various types, usually lists of banned products or of restricted products that require licences.

Import licensing schemes implemented for economic purposes are a means to control import flows and thus have an effect similar to that of import quotas. These schemes were typically used in the past to control balance of payments (BOP) problems. Most developing countries[5] maintained relatively rigid exchange controls to offset chronic balance of payments problems resulting from strong demand for imports at an overvalued exchange rate. Nations systematically linked controls to import restrictions by adopting procedures that tied the rationing of foreign exchange to a system of import licensing.

Import licensing – often as a consequence of the inefficiencies created by foreign exchange controls – has also been employed as an "industrial policy" tool to channel resources into sectors that are viewed as important for future economic growth. Industrial policy packages usually involve government support or protection of domestic industries that are deemed to have potential comparative advantages but not yet to be internationally competitive on their own. The most common justification for active industrial policy is the "infant industry" argument, which implies that countries should be able to speed up the development of new industries by the use of protective measures at early stages of development. However, the distortions created by such measures may undercut the initial objectives (see below).

Since the mid-1980s, with some variations in dates, developing countries have undertaken to reform their licensing regimes. These reforms have been aided significantly by three factors. First, nations embarked on unilateral trade reforms – often associated with IMF/World Bank stabilisation and structural adjustment lending operations – as much of the developing world, including a majority of countries in Latin America and Africa, became engulfed in a debt and macroeconomic crisis of major proportions. Second, WTO rules that allow exceptions to the GATT prohibition to the use of quantitative restrictions, such as the provisions of the BOP exception, were considerably tightened under the Uruguay Round Agreement. Third, countries adopted reforms of their licensing schemes under preferential agreements.[6]

As a result, licensing restrictions intended for economic purposes only remain in use in a few countries or regions. In addition, although licensing is still an important instrument in some countries, those that continue to make use of this type of licensing have also undertaken substantial reforms (see below). The one exception is the worldwide increase since the Uruguay Round in the use of tariff rate quotas (TRQs) in the agricultural sector, which are often implemented through non-automatic licensing systems. Though TRQs have in some cases opened up markets formerly closed or restricted, it is recognised that these measures have also led to a new wave of governmental interference in trade and made possible new opportunities for rent-seeking behaviour among potential beneficiaries of the licences.[7]

For their part, schemes relating to import licensing for non-economic purposes are used to implement a wide variety of regulations related to national security, protection of health, safety, the environment, morality, religion, intellectual property and compliance with international obligations. In contrast to licensing for economic reasons, these schemes are widespread in both OECD and non-OECD countries (see below).

Market access problems arising from licensing can result not only from the measure taken, but also from the way in which the measure is implemented and administered (Figure 3.1). Evidence from business reports suggests that the procedural aspects of licensing continue to act as an impediment to trade. This explains why improvement of the administration and implementation of licensing has received attention in recent discussions concerning trade facilitation.

Figure 3.1. Import licensing viewed as a subset of regulations

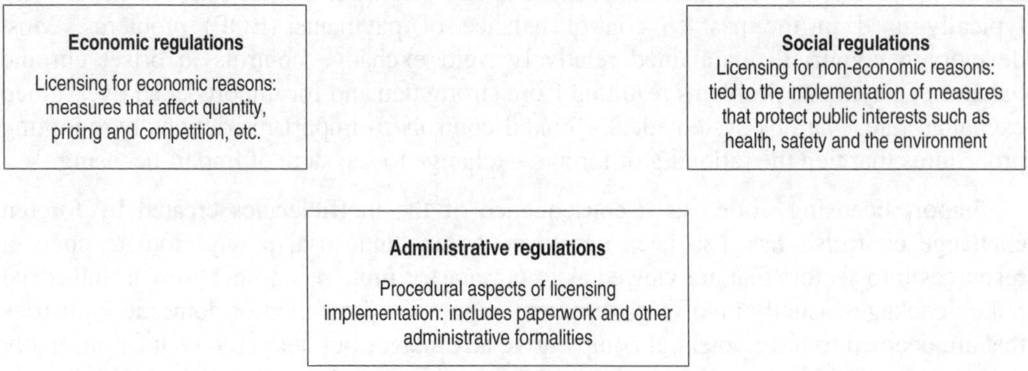

Economic regulations	Social regulations
Licensing for economic reasons: measures that affect quantity, pricing and competition, etc.	Licensing for non-economic reasons: tied to the implementation of measures that protect public interests such as health, safety and the environment

Administrative regulations
Procedural aspects of licensing implementation: includes paperwork and other administrative formalities

Source: Adapted from Roberts *et al.* (1999).

Licensing for economic reasons

Nature of licensing imposed for economic reasons

Non-automatic licensing for economic reasons has typically been used to implement quotas, with allocations reflecting historical trends or other factors. However, this type of licensing is not the focus here, as the basic barrier to trade is the quota rather than the licence. It is important to recognise, nevertheless, that administration of quotas (or of TRQs) through licensing may operate as an additional impediment to trade, as the type of administration used determines who gets the licence, and under what conditions, and thus may distort market access opportunities.

The focus here is on instances in which licensing for economic reasons acts as a quantitative restriction by reducing the volume of imports without *a priori* setting explicit quotas. This situation arises under a variety of schemes with different purposes and types of allocation. Goods may encounter so-called origin or agency restrictions. Origin restrictions concern instances in which imports from some countries are allowed but not from others. Agency restrictions concern situations in which only the end user, not dealers or distributors, can import.

In other cases, private traders obtain import licences only if they exported more than a certain amount in the previous year, or they must buy a certain proportion of their needs from domestic producers in return for licences to import the rest. This tying of import licences to exports or to local content requirements is designed in part to ensure that those who get the rents from importing scarce commodities also contribute to sustaining and expanding the level of national output and exports. Similarly, end-user restrictions that exclude traders from importing are designed to ensure that rents go to producers, on the assumption that they will use them more productively than traders.

Licensing criteria may also vary according to "domestic availability". This form of import licensing imposes import restrictions to the extent that the goods imported are "similar" in type and quality to products made locally. Such restrictions aim to promote the development of a local manufacturing base through import substitution, while at the same time not unduly restricting firms from obtaining needed products which are not available locally.

In these schemes, an importer of an item requiring a licence is asked to provide evidence that domestic suppliers cannot meet his terms on price/quality or delivery. The importer may be asked to furnish a letter from the relevant association of producers. Wade (1990) termed this the "approval mechanism" of import control, in the sense that reference must be made to domestic producers of import substitutes to determine whether they might meet the request.

In still other cases, the relevant authorities may require special import authorisation from a body other than the main licensing body, either in addition to or as a substitute for the licence. One such case is the requirement that imports of equipment for a new plant receive prior approval. Before granting the licence to import, the relevant authorities take into account the feasibility of the project, whether the industry is already overcrowded, and its priority in the national plan.

Economic cost for the importing country

The primary intent of quantitative restrictions such as non-automatic import licensing for economic purposes is to limit imports to protect domestic producers and these can result in potentially substantial barriers to trade for producers in exporting countries. However, the negative effects of licensing are most significant in the importing country, as the distortions created by these systems often undercut the initial objectives. In other words, most of the benefits of liberalising or dismantling licensing systems accrue to the importing country.

To be more explicit, the artificial scarcity created by the restriction of trade flows drives the domestic price above the world price, domestic supply expands and demand contracts, generally reducing social welfare. The welfare effects are in many ways similar to those of a tariff. However, the distributional consequences are different, as governments do not receive tariff-related revenue from licensing.[8] Moreover, in contrast to tariffs, licensing grants particular traders a privileged position, thus limiting the competitive effect of trade and further contributing to higher prices for the goods concerned in the domestic market. Limiting trade's competitive effect also reduces its ability to contribute to increased efficiency in the use of national resources.

It has also been recognised that there are other costs associated with licensing, including paperwork and the cost of the administrative apparatus necessary to issue licences. Moreover, further costs to society arise from what Krueger (1974) termed "rent-seeking" behaviour, which arises from the desire of traders to benefit from the economic activities allowed to possessors of import licences. A limited supply of licences encourages economic actors to make efforts to receive them. The resources allocated to this end are unproductive expenditures.

A typical example of rent seeking occurs with the application of the principle of domestic availability. For instance, the licensing rules associated with this principle can sometimes give local firms wishing to import an incentive to demand excessively high quality that is unavailable locally, so as to increase their chances of obtaining an import licence, yet this undermines the goal of the policy (Spencer, 1996). Some empirical support is provided by a 1996 World Bank study directed by Pursell and Wogart, in which clothing and garment producers in Brazil and India were surveyed concerning the effects of import licensing requirements for imports of capital goods. The survey results indicate that in Brazil the licensing scheme put into motion a complex game in which Brazilian textile firms adjusted the kinds of machinery they ordered so as to obtain an import licence on the grounds that no similar local machinery was available, and Brazilian machinery manufacturers expanded the range of machines they produced to block import licence applications.

Another example of rent-seeking behaviour occurs when licensing is tied to an export promotion scheme under which exporters receive entitlements to import licences. In this type of scheme, firms commit to undertake future exports of specified fractions of their output in return for "normal treatment" in obtaining their import licences. The implied penalty for failing to honour the export commitment is licence denial. In general, this leads to a situation in which firms, in effect, pay for their monopoly positions in the sheltered domestic market by exporting at a loss.

Furthermore, since import licences are an essential document for getting specific goods cleared by customs, firms may allocate resources to influence the probability and expected size of licence allocations. Their efforts to influence allocation may involve trips to the capital city or locating their offices in the capital. It can also involve bribery, the hiring of relatives of officials or the employment of the officials themselves upon retirement, in which case government officials receive part of the rents themselves.

During the 1970s and 1980s, a considerable body of empirical literature attempted to quantify the economic effects of the licensing described above, including rent-seeking behaviour, applying increasingly sophisticated techniques in a partial or general equilibrium setting (for a review of some of these studies, see Greenaway and Milner, 1993). Up-to-date relevant empirical research, though, is lacking.

Patterns of use and reform of licensing for economic purposes

The economic costs of import licensing for economic reasons have been widely recognised. With some limited exceptions, *e.g.* for balance of payments purposes, the WTO has prohibited the use of such licensing, and nations have undertaken significant reforms of their licensing regimes over the years.

This section takes stock of relevant reforms in major regions of the world and explores whether licensing for economic reasons remains an important trade policy instrument in WTO member countries. As mentioned earlier, the analysis is based on a systematic review of detailed information on licensing systems contained in the TPRs of 78 countries (both the European Community and the OECS-WTO members[9] count as one) prepared for GATT/WTO over the period 1989-2002. The countries reviewed are all of the OECD countries, 15 developing or emerging economies from Asia-Pacific, 17 from Latin America and the Caribbean, 27 from Africa and the Middle East, and three southeast European countries.

The focus of the analysis is on licensing intended for economic purposes. The discussion excludes, to the extent possible, licensing used to implement TRQs or quotas, *e.g.* those for the textiles and clothing sector under the Agreement on Textiles and Clothing (ATC). However, information on commitments that countries have made to liberalise their licensing regimes in the future is often unavailable, and the discussion does not capture changes in licensing regimes that may have occurred since the last TPRs reviewed here took place.

With these limitations in mind, Table 3.1 shows the use of import licensing in the countries reviewed, and Annex 3.A1 summarises the licensing-related information contained in the TPRs of countries that still make use of licensing for economic reasons (including all reviews of each country over the period). It is clear that most of the 78 countries reviewed have either abandoned or significantly reduced their use of licensing for economic reasons. (For nine countries, some of the information contained in the reports is unclear.)

Table 3.1. Non-automatic import licensing: country coverage

Country	Licensing for economic reasons	Licensing for non-economic reasons	Country	Licensing for economic reasons	Licensing for non-economic reasons
OECD countries			*Non-OECD Africa and Middle East*		
Australia		x	Bahrain	...	x
Canada		x	Benin		x
Czech Republic	x	x	Botswana		...
EU		x	Burkina Faso		x
Hungary		x	Cameroon		x
Iceland		x	Côte d'Ivoire	...	x
Japan		x	Egypt	...	x
Korea		x	Gabon		x
Mexico	x	x	Ghana		x
New Zealand		x	Guinea		x
Norway		x	Israel		x
Poland		x	Kenya		x
Slovakia		x	Lesotho		...
Switzerland		x	Madagascar		x
Turkey		x	Malawi		x
United States		x	Mali		x
Non-OECD Asia and Pacific			Morocco	x	x
Bangladesh	x	x	Mauritius	...	x
Brunei Darussalam		x	Mozambique		x
Fiji	...	x	Namibia	...	x
Hong Kong, China		x	Nigeria	x	x
India		x	South Africa		x
Indonesia	x	x	Swaziland	x	x
Macao, China		x	Tanzania		x
Malaysia	x	x	Togo		x
Papua New Guinea		x	Uganda		x
Pakistan	...	x	Zambia		x
Philippines		x	*Non-OECD Southeast Europe*		
Singapore		x	Cyprus	x	x
Solomon Islands		x	Romania		x
Sri Lanka		x	Slovenia		x
Thailand	x	x			
Non-OECD Latin America and Caribbean					
Argentina		x			
Brazil	x	x			
Bolivia		x			
Chile		x			
Colombia	x	x			
Costa Rica		x			
Dominican Republic	x	x			
El Salvador	...	x			
Guatemala		x			
Haiti		x			
Jamaica	x	x			
Nicaragua		x			
OECS-WTO members	x	x			
Paraguay		x			
Peru		x			
Uruguay		...			
Venezuela	...	x			

x = Licensing system in place.

Blank = No licensing system in place.

... = Not clear.

Source: GATT, TPR; WTO, TPR; and WTO Notifications/Replies to the Questionnaire on Import Licensing Procedures.

OECD countries

As Table 3.1 shows, only two OECD countries (the Czech Republic and Mexico) still appear to make use of non-automatic import licensing for economic purposes. However, Annex 3.A1 shows that these countries have undertaken significant reforms and currently apply licensing restrictions only to a few products.

In the Czech Republic, non-automatic import licensing is still used to protect the domestic industry for some sugar items (from Slovakia) and some fuels made from coal (from Poland and Ukraine). In Mexico, after the balance-of-payments crisis of 1982, import licensing applied to 100% of Mexico's tariff lines; today it covers slightly more than 1%. In particular, licensing requirements still appear to protect the automotive industry from imports significantly.

Non-OECD Asia-Pacific

In the Asia-Pacific region, while there are substantial differences across countries, broadly speaking all have undertaken significant reforms of their licensing systems in recent years. As shown in Table 3.1, most of the 15 countries reviewed in this region have freed all products from licensing requirements for economic reasons, with Bangladesh, Indonesia, Malaysia and Thailand the only ones that still make use of this type of licensing.

These countries have for the most part significantly reduced the use of such licensing (see Annex 3.A1). Indonesia's reform process is a case in point. A complex and non-transparent licensing system was identified by the 1994 TPR as one of Indonesia's main impediments to trade. The number of tariff lines subject to restrictive licensing fell gradually from 1 122 in 1990 to 261 in 1994, and then to 160 after 1994. The remaining items were agro-food products, motor vehicles, chemicals and basic metals. The authorities have subsequently liberalised a further 26 items relating to agricultural products and have made commitments to further liberalise another 43 tariff lines relating to vehicles, effectively reducing the total tariff items subject to licensing from 160 to 119. The 1998 TPR indicates that the authorities intend to completely dismantle the licensing system except when it concerns non-economic purposes.

Bangladesh has also largely removed licensing restrictions except for 2% of the tariff lines (this includes absolute bans) relating mostly to textiles. Thailand has largely reformed its licensing system as well, although it continues to protect the domestic industry through licensing, particularly in the agricultural and agro-food sector and in textiles. Malaysia is the only country in the region in which the number of tariff lines subject to non-automatic import licensing requirements has increased in recent years; the 2001 TPR indicates that some 27% of Malaysia's tariff lines are subject to such requirements, up from 17% in 1997. However, although the promotion of selected strategic industries is among the stated reasons for the restrictions, the rationale is not clear for all products. Licensing requirements are most pervasive in forestry and logging, agricultural products, chemical products, machinery and electrical products, transport equipment (notably automobiles) and arms and ammunition.

Although India (the largest country in the sample) is not included in Annex 3.A1, its removal of the licensing system for economic reasons should be noted, as it is perhaps the most important accomplishment in the region. The government progressively liberalised imports by removing licensing restrictions maintained under BOP cover. At the time of the 1998 TPR, some 32% of the tariff lines were still subject to a complex system of licensing restrictions for economic reasons, but the 2002 TPR indicates that the remaining licensing restrictions are for non-economic purposes.[10]

As Table 3.1 indicates, the information for Fiji and Pakistan is not clear. Although the respective TPRs indicate that both countries operate licensing restrictions mainly for non-economic reasons, the rationale behind certain restrictions is not clear.

Non-OECD Latin America and the Caribbean

Countries in the Latin American region have also undertaken substantial reforms of their licensing systems. Table 3.1 shows that outside the Caribbean region (see below), the only two countries that still make use of licensing for economic reasons are Brazil and Colombia.

Data from the 2000 TPR of Brazil show that non-automatic licensing applies to some 30% of all imported products (see Annex 3.A1). However, except for used machines, which are licensed to protect the domestic industry, the rationale behind licensing restrictions for the other product groups is not clear. The TPR also indicates that the authorities are reviewing the entire licensing system, including the feasibility of drawing up a list indicating the type of licensing for each product. Colombia has undertaken substantial reforms of its licensing system; in 1984, licensing restrictions applied to 83% of all tariff lines, but as of 1995 the share of items subject to licensing was 6.7%. The remaining restrictions relate mostly to agricultural products.

On the other hand, licensing for economic reasons is still widespread in the Caribbean region, particularly among OECS-WTO members. Their licensing regimes are similar to those of other Latin American countries (and of other developing countries) before the reforms of the 1980s and 1990s. Indeed, all these countries, except Dominica, apply extensive systems of import licensing. Licensing restrictions apply mostly to food products and beverages, and to textiles. Dominica reformed its licensing system by tariffying the products in its negative list in 1998. The resulting tariffs are high, up to 200%, but they are to be progressively reduced over a period of time until the Caribbean Community (CARICOM) common external tariff (CET) is reached. The phasing out is intended to give domestic producers time to become more competitive.

The information relating to El Salvador and Venezuela is not clear (see Table 3.1). The respective TPRs indicate that over the years both countries have eliminated licensing restrictions for a wide range of products. Nevertheless, the rationale for certain licensing requirements is not clear.

Non-OECD Africa and the Middle East

Import licensing for economic purposes has been substantially reformed in Africa and the Middle East. Table 3.1 shows that most of the 27 countries reviewed have dismantled their licensing systems, with Morocco, Nigeria and Swaziland the only countries still making use of these measures.

These countries have either undertaken significant reforms of their licensing systems or are in the process of doing so (see Annex 3.A1). Morocco has substantially reduced licensing and only applies licensing restrictions provisionally for some agricultural products, with a view to completely abolishing the regime. Nigeria has abolished its general import licensing system, although a number of banned products, mainly food and mineral products, *de facto* require a licence from the head of state if imported. Protection of the domestic industry is among the stated reasons for the restrictions.

The 1998 Swaziland TPR indicates that its licensing system covers all imports, although the country is currently in the process of reforming its regime and working on a negative list of the remaining items under control. This list comprises drugs, arms, used vehicles, wild animal products, and gold and other precious metals. The rationale for the licensing requirement for these remaining products is not clear.

As Table 3.1 indicates, the information for Bahrain, Côte d'Ivoire, Egypt, Mauritius and Namibia is not clear. For all these countries, except Bahrain, the information in the respective TPRs relating to whether certain products are still restricted for economic reasons is not clear. The 2000 TPR of Bahrain indicates that most of its licensing restrictions are for non-economic reasons. At the same time, it indicates that licences for imports (presumably all sectors) for the purpose of trading (*i.e.* not including raw materials and capital goods imported for manufacturing in the country) may only be granted to companies established locally with at least 51% ownership by nationals of Bahrain and/or other Golf Cooperation Council (GCC) countries.

Non-OECD southeast Europe

Among the three southeast European countries, Cyprus is the only one still making use of this type of licensing (Table 3.1) Cyprus applies such licensing to only one agricultural product, groundnuts, and ties it to a domestic content requirement (see Annex 3.A1).

Licensing for non-economic reasons

Nature of licensing imposed for non-economic reasons

Import licensing for non-economic reasons is used to achieve a wide variety of social goals, *e.g.* protecting health, safety, quality, the environment, security, morality, religion and intellectual property rights and ensuring compliance with international obligations. Licensing can help realise these policy objectives by restricting entry of foreign products that undermine their achievement.

Licensing of this kind may entail prior approval for importation, in the sense that to carry out the import transaction requires approval by the competent agency. One example is the use of non-automatic import licensing systems to implement sanitary and phytosanitary (SPS) measures. In such a scheme, importation of products subject to the requirement of an import licence may be obliged to undergo inspection before they are cleared by the customs authority, which then finalises the process for obtaining the licence.

Similar licensing requirements may be used for chemical and pharmaceutical products. For example, prior authorisation by the competent agencies can be required for controlled or restricted drugs in order to ensure that the imported substances meet domestic medical and scientific requirements and that the drugs remain in the legitimate distribution channels. Figure 3.2 provides a schematic description of the steps that may be involved in operating such a system for pharmaceutical products.

In other instances, licensing for non-economic reasons can be used to regulate the import of vehicles for environmental reasons (*e.g.* to combat air pollution in major cities), road safety or consumer protection. A country may require imported second-hand motor vehicles to meet certain conditions, such as a requirement that motor vehicles must not be more than three years old from the date of manufacture or that they show a certificate declaring a minimum roadworthiness of five years from the date of import. In yet other cases, licensing can be used to allow only imports of textile products that have undergone fumigation or it can require telecommunications equipment to be compatible with established standards (*e.g.* electromagnetic compatibility).

Licensing can also be used to comply with international obligations such as the Convention on International Trade in Endangered Species (CITES) or the Montreal Protocol on Substances that Deplete the Ozone Layer. With respect to CITES, for example, a licensing requirement may be imposed to ensure that only exempted wildlife is imported or that the importer falls within one of the categories exempted from the requirement (e.g. for research purposes).

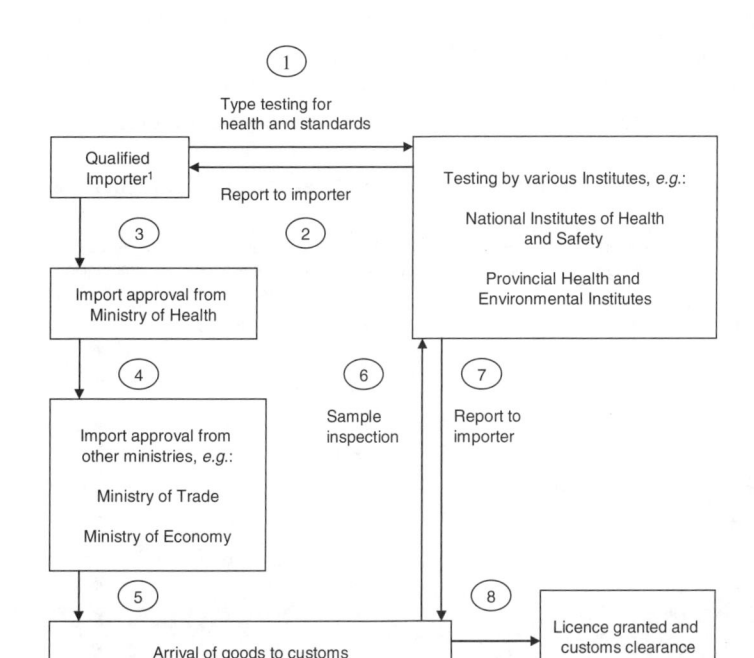

Figure 3.2. Example of an import licensing scheme for pharmaceutical products

1. It is a common requirement for an activity licence to qualify to receive import licences.
Source: Adapted from GATT (1992).

With respect to the effect of these measures on trade and the overall economy, an important distinction should be made. This type of licensing serves as a tool to implement other measures, *e.g.* regulations on technical barriers to trade (TBT). In this case, it is a TBT issue and not a licensing issue if, as a precondition for receiving a licence, specific foreign goods are systematically checked for conformity with TBT regulations prior to customs clearance. It may be questioned, for example, whether such systematic control is unjustified or unnecessarily trade-restrictive. On the other hand, the way in which the procedures for granting the licence are designed, implemented and applied – which may also involve elements that deliberately impose an additional burden on foreign suppliers –

is indeed a licensing issue. It is with respect to the procedural aspects that the question of the trade impact of licensing for non-economic reasons arises.[11]

Patterns of use of licensing for non-economic reasons

In contrast to licensing for economic purposes, the use of licensing for non-economic purposes is widespread in both OECD and non-OECD countries. As Table 3.1 shows, 75 of the 78 countries reviewed make use of these instruments. For the remaining three countries, it is not possible to determine use from the information contained in the TPRs.

Tables 3.2 and 3.3 show the use of these systems for selected product categories and for different rationales in OECD and non-OECD countries, respectively. Some product categories are not shown, as licensing is not or is seldom used. The TPR data on this type of licensing only make it possible to identify the use of these measures at the aggregate level of groupings of Harmonised System (HS) sections. It is therefore not possible to distinguish between instances in which licensing covers one or a few products from situations in which licensing is used for a large number of products. It should also be kept in mind that the data reflect the situation at the time of the most recent TPR.

Table 3.2. Non-economic licensing in OECD countries: product categories and rationales

	Agro-food products	Textiles and clothing	Mineral products	Chemicals & pharmaceuticals	Machinery & electircal equipment	Arms & ammunition	Vehicles	Misc. mfg. articles
Australia	+ ●	+		+	+ ■	X	+	+
Canada	+		■	+ X ●		X		
Czech Republic	+ ●			+ X		X		
EU				+				
Iceland	+		+	+ ●	+ ■	X	+ ●	
Japan	●			+ X	X	X		
Korea	+ ●		+	+ X ●	+	X	●	
New Zealand				●	●			
Norway	+ ●		+	+ X		X		+
Poland	+		X	X		X	+	
Slovak Republic				X		X		
Switzerland	+			+		X		
Turkey			+	+ X	■	X	+	
United States	+		+	+		X		

+ = Health and safety. X = Security. ● = Environment. ■ = Other.

Note: The symbols indicate that licensing covers at least one product in the respective product categories (for a full methodological explanation, see below. Hungary and Mexico have been excluded because the relevant information is not clear. "Other" comprises morality, religion, prevention of illegal activities, protection of consumers' rights, protection of national identity, protection of intellectual property rights, and for reasons of compatibility with established standards.

Source: GATT, TPR; WTO, TPR; WTO Notifications Replies to the Questionnaire on Import licensing Procedures.

Table 3.3. Non-economic licensing in non-OECD countries: product categories and rationales

	Agro-food products	Textiles and clothing	Mineral products	Chemicals & pharma-ceuticals	Machinery and electrical equipment	Arms and ammunition	Vehicles	Misc. manufactured articles
Argentina	+			+ X		X		
Bahrain	+			+		X		
Bangladesh	+ ■	+ ■	X ■	+ X	X	X	+ X ●	
Brunei Darussalam	+ ■			+	X	X	+	■
Bolivia			X	+ X	+ X	X		
Burkina Faso				X		X		
Cameroon	+		+	+ ●		X		
Cyprus		●	+ X	+	+	+	+	
Chile								
Colombia	+			+ X		X		
Costa Rica	+ ●	+		+ X ●	X	X	●	+
Dom.Republic	+			+	+	X		
El Salvador	+	+		+		X		
Fiji	+			+		X		
Gabon	+			+ X	X	X		
Ghana	+			+ X ●	■	X		X
Guatemala	+		+	+ X ●	●	X		
Haiti	+ ●			+				
Hong Kong, China	+ ●			+ X ●	X	X		
India	+			+ X		X	+ ■ ●	
Israel	+		+ X	+ X	+ X	X	+ X	X
Jamaica	+			+ X		X	X	X
Kenya	+ ●			+ X ●	X	X	X	
Macao, China	+ ■			+ ■ ●	X	X	■	
Madagascar		■		+	■	X		
Malaysia	+ ●			+ ●		X		X
Malawi	+ ●	X ●	+	+ ●		X		
Mali	+	●				X	+	
Morocco	+ ●	+		X		X		
Mozambique	+			+ X		X	+	
Namibia	+			+		X		
Nicaragua	+			+ X		X		
Nigeria	+			+ X		X		■
OECS-WTO members	+			+ X		X		
Pakistan	+		+	+ X	+	+ X		
Paraguay	+			+ X		X		

Table 3.3. Non-economic licensing in non-OECD countries: product categories and rationales (cont.)

	Agro-food products	Textiles and clothing	Mineral products	Chemicals & pharmaceuticals	Machinery and electrical equipment	Arms and ammunition	Vehicles	Misc. manufactured articles
Papua New Guinea	●			+ ●		X		
Peru	+			+ X	X	X		
Philippines			X	+ X ●	X	X	+ X	
Romania				+ X ●		X		
Singapore	+ ●			+ X ●	X	X		
Slovenia	+		+ ●	+ X ●	X ●	X	X	
Solomon Islands	+	+		+		X		
South Africa	+		■	+ ●		X		■
Tanzania	+			+ X	X	X		
Thailand	●			+	■			+
Togo				+ X	X	X		
Uganda	+	+		+X		X		
Venezuela	+			+X ●		X		

+ = Health and safety.   **X** = Security.   **●** = Environment.   **■** = Other.

Note: The symbols indicate that licensing covers at least one product in the respective product categories (for a full methodological explanation, see below. Hungary and Mexico have been excluded because the relevant information is not clear. "Other" comprises morality, religion, prevention of illegal activities, protection of consumers' rights, protection of national identity, protection of intellectual property rights, and for reasons of compatibility with established standards.

Source: GATT, TPR; WTO, TPR; WTO Notifications Replies to the Questionnaire on Import licensing Procedures.

In addition, the TPRs do not always specify the rationale for the use of licensing, so that the data included in the tables may underestimate the incidence of non-economic licensing for certain countries. Furthermore, given that international obligations usually entail licensing for several product categories (e.g. CITES or the Basel Convention on the Control of Transboundary Movements of Hazardous Wastes), and that these products are often not mentioned in the reviews, such schemes are not reflected in the tables. This underestimates the use of licensing by most countries.[12]

Even so, the tables show that this type of licensing usually covers several product categories in OECD as well as non-OECD countries. Chemicals and pharmaceuticals, agro-food products and arms and ammunitions are most frequently subject to these measures, followed by machinery and electrical machinery and vehicles. With respect to the rationales, the protection of health and safety, security and the environment are the policy goals most often evoked. It thus appears that, with the significant reduction or elimination of the traditional use of licensing as an instrument to limit the quantity of imports for economic reasons, today's licensing systems are largely employed to implement TBT and SPS measures.

Procedural aspects: the link between licensing and trade facilitation

As noted above, market access problems arising from licensing can be the result of the specific measure taken or the way the measure is implemented and administered. This section aims to identify these licensing-related procedural problems and suggest options to address them in the context of ongoing WTO discussions on trade facilitation. However, it first provides a broad overview of the economic benefits that can accrue to nations through the adoption of more efficient licensing procedures and then describes existing procedure-related licensing disciplines.

Economic benefits of efficient licensing procedures[13]

The adoption of simplified and more efficient licensing procedures can lead to identifiable economic benefits through several channels, as it does for other import or export measures. First, enhanced procedures can increase participation in international trade by allowing previously excluded traders to access international markets. Firms may be excluded or their sales may be inhibited, for example, by non-transparent licensing procedures, overhead costs of exporting or of importing inputs, or overly complicated/bureaucratic licensing procedures in overseas markets.

These problems can be particularly acute for SMEs and firms in developing countries that suffer from economy-of-scale weaknesses or are unaware of information on public-sector opportunities. SMEs are the engine of economic growth in most countries, accounting for over 65% of turnover generated by the private sector in the EU (EC, 1996) and for nearly 50% of APEC economies' total GDP and 35% of their exports (APEC, 1999). Obstacles to growth of SMEs cause economies to stagnate, especially in developing and transition economies.

Second, more efficient licensing procedures can help lower the costs of trade transactions. Business estimates put the cost of a two-month delay in licensing (and related warehousing expenses) at the equivalent of an additional 4% to 6% import duty, while additional costs such as penalties imposed by customers for failure to meet delivery deadlines can reach up to 10% of the price paid for the good (Pruzin, 2001). Simplifying and improving licensing procedures results in increased profits where exports already take place and makes exports possible where firms have been discouraged from trading owing to complicated procedures.

More efficient licensing procedures can also improve the climate for investment, particularly in developing and emerging economies. Flows of foreign direct investment (FDI) remain largely confined to developed countries. When asked to identify the reasons for investing in specific countries, businesses often point to the administration of trade as a key component in any successful investment regime. In an era of outsourcing and just-in-time production techniques, the rapid passage of inputs and finished goods through customs and other administrative controls and the establishment of streamlined transaction procedures are crucial. Their absence is a disincentive to investment.

Simplification of licensing operations (and automation where feasible) by customs and other agencies can also result in significant reductions in administrative costs. Introduction of simplified and harmonised data requirements for documentation requirements, co-ordination with other agencies and streamlined customs procedures (see below for explanations) all reduce time, running/administrative costs (which are borne by taxpayers), allow for a more efficient allocation of human resources (with a motivating effect on staff) and reduce levels of error. Greater efficiency also benefits traders through more rapid release and more predictable procedures around which they can fashion their transport and logistical planning.

Modern and simplified licensing procedures can enable governments to enforce more effectively the regulations and policies that the licensing systems implement through more efficient management of goods moving across borders. This can help control illegal movement of restricted goods, the proper protection of intellectual property rights and achieve other public welfare goals.

Improved import licensing procedures, together with other import and export-related procedures, can also help reduce corruption. Some customs authorities are currently underfunded or lack strategic management, with implications for efficiency and integrity. Simplification and modernisation, though not in themselves enough, contribute to solving corruption and related problems.

Lastly, more efficient licensing procedures can foster a culture of co-operation between government and business. Traders have more confidence in their dealings with customs and other governmental agencies if they find authorities efficient and trade-friendly.

Notwithstanding these benefits, it should be stressed that some of the reforms needed cannot be implemented overnight or at no cost; resources are needed to build capacity and initiate long-term change. However, resources are often limited in developing countries for achieving comprehensive technical progress, which includes modification of administrative procedures, training, software development and installation for risk assessment, among others. For this reason a concerted effort in technical assistance and capacity building is needed to support national reform efforts and to tackle the main problems of delays and administrative inefficiencies.

The Agreement on Import Licensing Procedures (ILP) and other relevant multilateral disciplines

The WTO provides far-reaching disciplines in the area of import licensing procedures, particularly in the ILP. The main objectives of the ILP are to simplify and bring transparency to import licensing procedures, to ensure their fair and equitable application and administration, and to prevent procedures used for granting import licences from having in themselves restrictive or distortive effects on imports (*i.e.* additional to those caused by the measure). To achieve these objectives, the ILP stipulates several conditions and measures with which WTO members have to comply.

With respect to transparency, the ILP requires prior publication of rules and all information concerning procedures for the submission of applications for licences, including the eligibility of persons, firms or institutions to make such applications, the administrative bodies to be approached, and the list of products subject to the licensing requirement, in such a manner as to enable governments and traders to become acquainted with them. This information should be published in the sources notified to the Committee on Import Licensing (see below), and the publication shall occur whenever possible 21 days before the effective date of the requirement but in any case no later than such effective date. In addition, licensing applications must be processed within a reasonable time period, and the validity of licences is to be of reasonable duration.

The ILP also contains provisions aimed at decreasing and simplifying import formalities and documentation requirements. It stipulates that application and renewal forms should be as simple as possible and requires that, on application, only those documents considered strictly necessary for the proper functioning of the licensing system may be required. The ILP also explicitly requires that application and renewal procedures shall be as simple as possible. Furthermore, a limit of three is placed on the number of agencies to consult in order to obtain a licence.

With respect to due process, the agreement states that no application will be refused for minor documentation errors, and that excessive penalties should not be imposed in respect of documentation or procedural errors.

Similar to other agreements developed during the Uruguay Round, the ILP established a committee to oversee the implementation of and review the agreement. Members are required to notify the Committee on Import Licensing of new licensing procedures or changes in the existing procedures within 60 days of publication. The Committee also requires members to provide replies to a questionnaire on import licensing procedures on an annual basis.

Licensing-related disciplines are also contained in other WTO agreements, as well as in GATT articles. Relevant especially to procedural aspects are Articles VIII and X of the GATT. Article VIII (Fees and Formalities Connected with Importation and Exportation) deals with import licensing procedures in a non-specific manner. It stipulates that fees charged in connection with importation and exportation should be limited to the appropriate cost of the service rendered (intended as the government regulatory activities performed in connection with importation and customs entry processes) and should not be used for other purposes. It also contains specific legal obligations prohibiting members from imposing substantial penalties for minor breaches of customs regulations or procedural requirements. Furthermore, it contains hortatory statements recognising the need to reduce the number and complexity of import- and export-related fees and formalities.[14]

Article X (Publications and Administration of Trade Regulations) requires members to publish promptly laws, regulations, judicial decisions and administrative rulings of general application, including those pertaining to requirements on imports or exports and to administer them in a uniform, impartial and reasonable manner. It also requires members to establish independent administrative agencies to ensure that administrative actions related to customs matters are reviewed and appropriately corrected.[15]

Possible areas for strengthening

Notwithstanding the fact that the WTO provides far-reaching disciplines in the area of licensing procedures, evidence from business reports, *e.g.* at the WTO Trade Facilitation Symposium held in 1998, suggests that further improvements may be warranted. In the broader context of trade facilitation, the business community has voiced concerns with respect to the administration and implementation of import and export rules and regulations, to which import licensing belongs.[16] Concerns have been expressed in the following areas:

- *Transparency*: Traders still lack full knowledge of other members' trade rules and practices.

- *Formalities and requirements*:
    - Unnecessary or excessive data or documentation requirements and lack of harmonisation, both within individual countries and internationally, in terms of both form and content of data supplied.

- Multiple requests for documents from different agencies, with little attempt to rationalise or co-ordinate those requirements.

- Outdated customs administrations and methods.

- Lack of due process, particularly with respect to lengthy and inefficient judicial and administrative review of determinations, and excessive penalties imposed by customs for breaches of procedural requirements.

Considerable exploratory and analytical work has been undertaken at the WTO in recent years in the area of trade facilitation, in order to assess how the main problems in terms of delays and administrative inefficiencies mentioned above could be addressed through new WTO rules. While the natural focus of simplification is on customs procedures, some WTO members have argued that it is essential for the scope of any WTO commitments to extend beyond customs to other agency interventions. This would ensure that any efficiency gained through simplification and harmonisation of customs procedures is not diminished by other border procedures that may be inefficient or unnecessary. In this connection, the inclusion of import licensing in the scope of commitments seems highly desirable.

At Doha, in preparation for the envisaged negotiations, which were formally launched in July 2004, the WTO Council for Trade in Goods (CTG) was instructed to "review and, as appropriate, clarify and improve relevant aspects of Articles V, VIII and X of the GATT 1994". CTG meetings in May and July 2002 were devoted to the review of GATT Articles VIII and X, which are of particular relevance here. In the context of these reviews, several WTO members submitted communications relating to the GATT articles under scrutiny, identifying elements that might be clarified or improved. The remainder of this section describes some aspects of these proposals as they relate to the business complaints described above, including how suggested improvements would apply to the specific area of licensing.

Transparency in border procedures

As of 7 June 2002, communications relating to GATT Article X had been submitted by five WTO members (Canada, the European Communities, Japan, Korea and the United States).[17] The core issue raised in this area relates to the publication and availability of information, including the identification of the elements of information that should be made publicly available and the appropriate means to publicise the information. Other issues raised include:

- Provision of advance rulings on the main elements of import requirements.

- Establishment of consultation/feedback mechanisms for affected parties prior to the finalisation of customs regulations.

- Establishment of appeal procedures allowing for accessible, non-discriminatory and efficient review of rulings related to importation and exportation, including the provision of a standard time set for resolution of minor appeals at administrative level and the possibility of interim measures (such as release subject to the provision of a security).[18]

With respect to the specific area of licensing, it can be noted that the ILP already contains detailed provisions related to publication and availability of information (see above). However, the implementation of the ILP is at present incomplete. According to the 2001 report of the Committee on Import Licensing, since the entry into force of the agreement, 72 and 74 members (the European Community counting as one) have notified and submitted replies to the questionnaire, respectively. In addition, while some notifications and replies to the questionnaire are completed in a comprehensive and detailed manner, others appear less comprehensive and fairly general.

This is regrettable given that both notifications and replies to the questionnaire provide the foundation for enhancing transparency and for reducing the potentially trade-distorting effect of non-automatic import licensing. The adoption of advance rulings (the Canadian communication specifically mentions import licensing requirements as one of the main elements to be covered by such rulings) and of consultation/feedback mechanisms would no doubt bring identifiable benefits in the area of licensing, but the proper implementation of existing commitments is crucial to achieving the objective of transparency of licensing rules and practices.

With respect to appeal procedures, the introduction of measures such as standard times for resolution of minor appeals at administrative level and of interim measures for the release of goods would logically also apply to licensing-related administrative requirements, act effectively as a disincentive to drawn-out appeal procedures, and ensure that trade is not unduly affected pending the outcome of such procedures.

Formalities and requirements

As of 22 July 2002, proposals relating to GATT Article VIII had been submitted by six WTO members (Canada; the European Communities; Hong Kong, China; Japan; Korea; and the United States).[19] Issues raised include:

- Reduction and harmonisation of documentation requirements, including the use of agreed international standards as a basis for documentation and data requirements (both format and content of the documents and data), as well as acceptance of relevant commercially available information as the norm.

- Co-operation and co-ordination among different authorities in charge of border controls at entry and exit point, *e.g.* introduction of a "single window" through which a trader can submit, once and for all, the required data to a single agency in question. This could also include the co-ordination of procedures and formalities.

- Introduction of simplified and modern customs procedures based on international standards and instruments, including also streamlined special procedures for authorised persons. This can be made possible through a risk management system which screens for high- and low-risk factors by using information such as client demographics, customs examinations, audits, client profiles, pre-arrival data analysis, etc.

- Automation of customs and other agency procedures related to importation and exportation, including the possibility to present customs and other declarations electronically, and to the payment of duties or other fees and charges.

These areas logically apply to import licensing or can only fully achieve their aims if they do.[20] As for other documents relating to importation, it would be desirable to base data requirements for licences on international standards, to align them to data required for other control purposes, and to base them as far as possible on commercially available information. Similarly, it would be desirable for licences to be processed in a way that does not require applications or submission of data to multiple agencies (single window).

The agency processing the application would carry out any co-ordination with other agencies. Such a system has been put in place by a number of countries and is described in more detail for Costa Rica (see Box 3.1).

Simplified customs controls, including modern methods based on risk assessment, pre-arrival processing of data, etc., would normally apply also to controls of licensing documentation, and could be administered by one and the same agency, normally customs (principle of concentrating controls in the hands of one agency). Lastly, while automating licensing operations would no doubt increase the speed and efficiency of processing (and improve control and reduce errors inherent in manual paper-based processes), simplification and improvement of procedures should be applicable in either a non-automated or technology-based environment, given the significant technology gap that currently exists in the trading environment. These can serve in either case to promote efficiency and minimise procedural delays, the main difference being the degree of change.[21]

Box 3.1. Single window: the case of Costa Rica

The early 1990s marked the launch of a comprehensive project in Costa Rica to overhaul and modernise the country's National Customs System.

Among the mechanisms that have simplified trade transactions both qualitatively and quantitatively is the so-called Single Window for Foreign Trade (VUCE) system. This window has, for example, centralised procedures for obtaining permits and prior authorisation for importing goods that are subject to phytosanitary and zoosanitary requirements.

The facilities offered by this mechanism include centralisation of officials from a range of institutions in charge of issuing prior import and export licences, such as the Ministry of Health, the Ministry of Agriculture and Livestock and the Council for Textile Quotas. Response time per formality is 30 minutes or less.

The head offices are located in the Costa Rican capital of San José, in the buildings of the Foreign Trade Promotion Agency (PROCOMER), and there are branches in all of the customs offices throughout the country. It has an Executive Board made up of private- and public-sector officials who work together to suggest constant improvements to the system.

Source: "Trade Facilitation Experience Paper by Costa Rica", WTO, G/C/W/265 of 17 May 2001.

Conclusion

This chapter has attempted to describe the different aspects of today's import licensing systems as well as their linkages with other policy areas. The use of these measures has been evolving, and the significant reforms that have been undertaken has changed the pattern of perceived problems associated with them.

The main findings and recommendations are presented below. It is important to keep in mind that these conclusions do not take into account, and therefore do not extend to, TRQs in the agricultural sector.

- The traditional use of licensing as a quantitative restriction for economic reasons – once among the most important barriers to trade in developing countries' markets – has largely been abandoned by WTO member countries. It is currently in use only in a few countries or regions where, in certain cases, it still represents an important trade policy instrument. Given the damaging effects to their economies, for reasons that include higher prices, economic inefficiencies and the stimulation of wasteful rent seeking, the full elimination of these measures in countries still applying them should continue to be pursued.

- The use of non-automatic import licensing for non-economic purposes, particularly to implement TBT and SPS rules, is widespread in both OECD and non-OECD countries. With respect to the possible effects of these measures on trade and on the overall economy, it may be noted that this type of licensing is used to implement other rules so that potential impediments to trade related specifically to licensing in this area would arise mainly from procedural aspects (see below). Clearly, where such procedural issues arise, they may also include the possibility of deliberate use for protectionist purposes.

- Concerns voiced by business suggest that traders still experience problems relating to the implementation and administration of licensing measures. Besides the need to fully implement existing commitments, there appear to be areas in which further improvement of licensing-related disciplines may be warranted. Considerable licensing-related work has been undertaken since 1996 in the WTO in the context of its work on trade facilitation, in an attempt to develop a set of rules to tackle the main problems of delays and administrative inefficiencies. In July 2004, WTO members formally launched negotiations as part of the Doha Round to clarify and improve, among other things, Articles VIII and X of the GATT. These articles could include licensing, which could bring identifiable benefits taking the form of enhanced transparency and reduced delays and costs. If licensing is not included in possible WTO commitments in this area, with commitments not extended beyond customs to other agencies, efficiency gained through simpler customs procedures could be diminished by unnecessary procedures applied by other agencies. Such efforts need to be undertaken in parallel with adequate capacity building and support for technical assistance.

- Besides its possible inclusion in the negotiations on trade facilitation, import licensing might also be dealt with in the Doha Round in discussions relating to market access for non-agricultural goods. Regardless of the decisions taken in this respect, this chapter suggests that today's perceived problems associated with licensing are mostly of a procedural and administrative nature.

Annex 3.A1

Remaining Non-automatic Licensing Regimes Used for Economic Reasons

OECD countries

Czech Republic 1996/2000[22]
Import licences are required only for goods contained in the negative lists, as published in the Decree on Import Licensing (Decree No. 560 of 199, last amended by the Decree of the Ministry of Industry and Trade No. 175/1994). Non-automatic import licensing requirements apply to certain sugar (from Slovakia), isoglucose (Slovakia), coal, briquettes and similar solid fuels made from coal (Poland and Ukraine). These licences result from safeguard measures or are in place to protect the domestic industry.

Mexico 1993/1997/2002
In the past, import licensing was one of the most restrictive elements of Mexico's import regime and was used effectively to curtail imports during unstable periods, such as after the 1982 balance-of-payments crisis, when import licensing was extended to cover all imports. Since then Mexico has considerably reduced the coverage of import licensing requirements, and in 2001 the list of products subject to import licensing represented slightly more than 1% of Mexico's tariff lines (this includes also arms, which are restricted for non-economic reasons). Imports from MFN sources subject to licensing include: petrochemical products, automotive products; used machines and office machines; and used clothing. Import permits are issued by the Department of Economy; petrochemicals are reserved to the state. For used vehicles and machines, the Department of Economy issues import licences only when the foreign product has no domestically produced substitutes.

Import licences for automotive products (notably new vehicles) are granted only to final assemblers complying with the requirements and conditions established in the Decree for the Development and Modernisation of the Automotive Industry (Auto Decree),[23] which include minimum national value added and trade balance requirements.[24] In addition, licences are granted provided that the imported product has no domestically produced substitute.

Non-OECD Asia and Pacific

Bangladesh 1992/2000
Until 1985, Bangladesh issued a positive list of importable items annually. The Import Policy Order (IPO) of 1985-86 introduced a shift to negative lists detailing banned and restricted items, so that all items not on the lists became freely importable. In the IPO of 1989-91, the two lists of banned and restricted products were combined into a single control list.

Bangladesh has undertaken substantial reforms of its import regime during the last decade and progress has been made in reducing the size of the banned and restricted lists. The number of items has been reduced from 193 at the HS 4-digit under the IPO 1991-93, to 110 under the IPO 1993-95, and 120 items under the IPO 1995-97. There are 122 items under the IPO 1997-2002, comprising 48 in the banned list and 97 in the restricted list. In total, these items represent approximately 2% of total tariff lines, and are related mainly to agricultural products (chicks, eggs, tendu leaves, sugar and salt), packing materials and textile products. The textile sector enjoys the heaviest protection, accounting for 38.7% of all tariff lines with import prohibitions or restrictions. Import bans are in place on all woven fabrics, and imports of grey cloth are restricted to the ready-made garment industry.[25]

Indonesia 1991/1995/1998
During the past decade, Indonesia has substantially reduced the scope of non-automatic import licensing. Inherently complex and non-transparent, the licensing system was described in the 1994 TPR as one of Indonesia's main impediments to trade. The system classifies licences according to the type of operator: importer-producer (IP licences), registered importer (IT) and agent or sole importer (AT licences). IP holders are licensed to import goods that compete with their own output. These licences basically control the degree to which domestic producers are exposed to competition. IT licences restrict to six state trading firms imports of a wide range of products, and AT licences are granted to national distributors appointed by the Indonesian government. A fourth category, importer-producer (PI), was abolished in 1993. PI allowed domestic producers to import inputs only if they could demonstrate that domestic production was not available.

The number of tariff lines subject to restrictive import licences fell gradually from 1 122 in 1990 to 261 in 1994. While this represented only 3% of tariff lines, its economic incidence was much greater. Import licences covered 13% of total imports, 35% of agricultural production and about 30% of manufacturing production. The large share of production protected by such licensing was explained by the inclusion of major food commodities controlled by the state-owned BULOG (such as rice, wheat and wheat flour, sugar, and soybeans) and several key "strategic" industrial products (processed food and beverages, certain chemicals, iron and steel, cars not assembled in Indonesia).

In the period following 1994, Indonesia continued to reduce the number of products subject to licensing. The number of tariff lines covered fell by nearly half, from 261 to 160, as a result both of the implementation of Indonesia's commitments under the Uruguay Round[26] and unilateral reform. Nevertheless, the most "sensitive" products, which accounted for the bulk of remaining licences (agricultural commodities, alcoholic beverages, motor vehicles, certain chemicals, iron and steel products, and scrap material) remained unreformed. The economic significance of licensing thus remained strong.

Indonesia has subsequently undertaken to remove other products from licences in the context of the IMF programme, particularly those that were not covered by WTO commitments. A first step was taken in late 1997 with the removal of import licensing requirements on commodities controlled by BULOG (except rice). This involved 26 tariff lines (seven lines for milk and milk products, seven for sugar and sugar products, eight for soybeans, two for cloves, and two for wheat flour and meslin). These products can now be imported freely under the general importers' licence (UI). According to the government, licensing requirements for completely assembled cars, covering a total of 43 tariff lines, will be removed in the near future, effectively reducing the total number of tariff items subject to licensing from 160 to 119. The Indonesian authorities have further committed to completely dismantle the licensing regime, except for licensing used for non-economic purposes.

Malaysia 1993/1997/2001
Malaysia continues to apply import licensing on various industrial and agricultural products. Imports of conditionally prohibited items (which require a licence) are listed in several schedules of the Customs Order 1988. In most cases, non-automatic licensing on a discretionary basis is used to regulate the flow of imports in order to promote selected strategic industries.

Malaysia is the only country reviewed in this region in which the use of licensing has increased in recent years. Indeed, since 1997, a number of heavy and construction equipment, hot and cold rolled flat products of iron or non-alloy steel, ephedrine and its salts, pseudoeohedrine (INN) and its salts, machines for making master compact discs and parts thereof, coin- and machine-making machines, and certain electrical household goods have been brought under the import licensing regime; however, import licensing has been removed on button and button blacks of artificial plastic materials, polyethylene, diamonds, shotgun cartridges, coin- or disc-operated amusement machines.

Thus, the overall number of tariff lines subject to non-automatic import licensing requirements would appear to have increased since 1997; some 27% of Malaysia's tariff lines are subject to such requirements, compared with 17% in 1997. Licensing requirements are most pervasive in forestry and logging, agricultural products, chemical products, machinery and electrical products, and transport equipment (notably automobiles).

Thailand 1991/1995/1999

Thailand's Export and Import Act provides for licensing under the authority of the Department of Foreign Trade at the Ministry of Commerce. At the time of the 1991 TPR, import licensing affected about 8% of the total tariff lines (at the HS 4-digit). Since then, Thailand has progressively liberalised its licensing system, although a number of restrictions remain for economic reasons. Non-automatic licensing is used to prevent the importation of a number of products in order to protect farmers' income or the domestic industry. State enterprises or government institutions may apply for import licences for these products. The items include certain silk products, certain buses, motorcycles, and building stones, as well as 23 agricultural and agri-food products.

Non-OECD Latin America and the Caribbean

Brazil 1992/1996/2000

All goods imported into Brazil are subject to an import licence. Licensing can be automatic or non-automatic. Automatic licences are in place for statistical purposes and as a tool to monitor trade flows. Non-automatic licences may be obtained before or after shipment of goods from abroad, but always before customs clearance. Effective 18 December 1997, the *Departamento de Operaçoes de Comercio Exterior* (DECEX) issued a list of products subject to non-automatic licensing. Goods subject to this requirement included agricultural products, food and wine; hide, textiles, clothing, and footwear; pharmaceuticals, chemicals, petroleum and energy products; metals and paper; tapes and compact discs; certain vehicles; and radioactive materials. In August 1998, Brazil apparently introduced other modifications of its non-automatic licensing system.

It is estimated that non-automatic licences apply currently to some 30% of all products imported into Brazil. However, the rationale behind the licensing restrictions for each product category is not clear. The only licensing scheme which appears clearly intended for economic reasons is related to used machines, where authorisation is granted only if the machine is not produced in Brazil or cannot be replaced by locally produced equipment. The *Secretaria de Comercio Exterior* (SECEX, within the Ministry of Industry, Trade and Tourism) publishes the request to import such used items in the *Official Journal;* thereafter manufacturers have 30 days to prove local production or the import authorisation is granted.

Nevertheless, it is noted in the 2000 TPR that the Brazilian authorities are reviewing the entire licensing system, including the viability of drawing up a list indicating the licensing type for each product. At that time, no list had yet been consolidated.

Colombia 1990/1996

Colombia has undertaken substantial reforms of its licensing system in the last 20 years. In 1984, the number of items under licensing restrictions was 4 160, or 83% of all tariff lines. As trade deficits began to decline in 1985, Colombia began to liberalise its import licensing regime and, in October 1989, 3 090 items, or 60% of the total, remained under the licensing system. Between 1991 and 1995 the share of items subject to licensing restrictions dropped by 47% to 6.7% of total imports.

The remaining items subject to licensing are mostly agricultural products. The Ministry of Agriculture is required to approve (*visto bueno*) the granting of prior import licences for 64 10-digit NADINA agricultural items, including poultry meat, wheat, malting barley, maize, rice, sorghum, wheat flour, starches, oilseeds, soybeans, soybean meal and oil, stearic acid, other animal and vegetable oils and fats, and certain types of foods for animals. These are maintained on domestic absorption/self sufficiency grounds.

Licensing in the form of prior authorisation is also required for certain types of goods (*e.g.* used, defective, waste) by the Imports Committee. This procedure, which takes an average of three days, consists of determining whether there is a specific need to import in light of the situation in the domestic market (*i.e.* adequate and competitive supplies from domestic producers) and the economic "feasibility" (including all import costs) of the import. This also covers imports of raw materials and inputs of used machinery and equipment (including transport and communication materials).

The Dominican Republic 1996

The coverage of import licensing requirements was greatly reduced under the reforms which the Dominican Republic undertook during the 1990s. Nevertheless some commodity-specific licences are still required for a few agricultural products. Import licences are still applicable to beans, chicken meat, garlic, onions, pork, potatoes, rice, sugar, tomatoes and tomato paste, and wheat flour.

Import licences are granted by the relevant government authorities who have wide discretionary powers. There are no clearly established procedures for the granting of import licences; depending on supply conditions in the domestic market, the authorities can authorise or prohibit imports.

There is no general legislation on import licences or on licensing procedures; they vary according to the product. For example, import licences for rice are granted by the Ministry of Agriculture, INESPRE, and the Agricultural Bank, which is also responsible for buying, selling and distributing husked rice. Wheat flour can be imported only by a state mill company (*Molinos Dominicanos*). Licences for tomato imports are granted exclusively to firms belonging to a domestic producers association (*Asociación de Fábricas de Conservas de Frutas y Vegetales*, AFCONAGRO). For garlic, onions and potatoes, INESPRE grants import licences to registered importers when there is a shortage of domestic supply. Licences for imports of poultry are exclusively granted to domestic producers. A bidding procedure is used for the allocation of import licences for beans.

Jamaica 1998

The coverage of import licensing was greatly reduced during the 1980s and 1990s. Before 1981, over 90% of non-bauxite imports required a licence. Licensing requirements were subsequently reduced between 1981 and 1984, when they applied to around half of Jamaica's imports. Since 1985, the scope of the import licensing system has been significantly reduced. Some products, however, remain subject to licensing, including motor vehicles and parts and agricultural products such as refined sugar and milk powder.

The licensing system is administered by the Trade Board, under the Ministry of Commerce and Technology. Licences are normally granted on request by the importer, if all conditions are fulfilled. For example, in the case of motor vehicles, dealers must be approved and certified by the Ministry of Commerce and Technology before being granted a licence by the Trade Board. They must be registered under the Company Act, offer guarantees to clients, maintain spare parts facilities and stocks. Inspections are made annually by the Ministry of Commerce and Technology, for a fee of JOD 60 000.

OECS-WTO members 2001

The licensing regimes of countries in this region can be characterised as similar to those of other Latin American countries (and of other developing countries) before the reforms of the 1980s and 1990s. All OECS members, except Dominica, have an extensive system of import licensing. The import licensing regime is generally administered by the Ministry of Commerce or Trade in each country. The list of products subject to licensing is contained in a negative list, or in an external trade (restricted imports) order, and generally comprises three or four schedules containing products subject to licensing. Generally, goods are divided between products that require an import licence when imported from any country that is not an OECS member and goods that require a licence when imported from any country that is not an OECS or CARICOM member. In some countries licences are also required for goods from other OECS members, as for example when a domestic marketing board has, in principle, an import monopoly of the good.

Licensing is required for the importation of soaps and for margarine, shortening and oils when the source is a more developed CARICOM country (CARICOM MDC) or a third country, under Schedule IX of the CARICOM Treaty. These and some other goods are subject to priority sourcing from CARICOM, although, according to the authorities in various countries, this rule is seldom enforced. In some countries, licences are required for imports of certain clothing products from non-CARICOM sources and there is priority sourcing if these products are from other CARICOM states.

Non-automatic import licensing is also applied on products under Article 56 of the CARICOM Treaty. To promote the development of an industry, OECS countries and other less developed CARICOM members may impose non-automatic import licensing on imports from CARICOM MDCs. Although these restrictions refer in principle only to other CARICOM members, in practice they are applied to all trading partners. The following products are subject to import licensing: curry powder, wheat flour, uncooked pasta, aerated beverages, beer, candles, oxygen, carbon dioxide, acetylene, paper bags, solar water heaters, chairs and other seats of wood and upholstered fabric.

Other restrictions besides those mentioned above are also applied in some countries. These include restrictions on textiles under the Importation of Textile Act in Grenada and restrictions on beer and malt in Grenada, St. Vincent and the Grenadines from third countries and from the CARICOM MDCs. In addition, Antigua and Barbuda reserves 75% of its domestic market for locally produced brewery products.

Dominica is the only OECS country to have tariffied the products in its negative list in 1998. The rates were calculated based on the c.i.f. value of imports, plus the CET tariff, plus a number of other costs and a margin of preference of 25% for CARICOM products. Tariffication has resulted in an increase in the number of tariff rates, compared with their previous CET levels, but were calculated taking into account WTO bindings. These higher tariffied rates are to be reduced over a period of time until the prevailing CARICOM CET is reached. The authorities envisaged a period of seven years for agricultural items (until 2006), and five years (until 2004) for all other products. The delay was intended to allow domestic producers to become more competitive during the period. The authorities noted that the first reduction in rates was intended to take place in 2001.

Non-OECD Africa and the Middle East

Morocco 1996

At the beginning of the 1980s, under the General Import Programme (PGI) the products that could be imported into Morocco were allocated every year to several lists: List A for products that could be freely imported, List B for those subject to licensing requirements or List C for those that were prohibited. The transfer of products from Lists B and C to List A since 1983 and the abolition of List C in 1986 helped to narrow the range of import licensing restrictions. In September 1990, 436 products were transferred from List B to List A and, in 1992, the PGI comprising Lists A and B was abolished. The Notice to Importers 01/92 of 13 February 1992 notified the liberalisation of 456 products.

The remaining import licensing requirements are applied provisionally to basic agricultural products (oils, sugar, cereals and their derivatives). The Moroccan authorities are waiting for accompanying measures to be introduced before proceeding to liberalise the remaining products subject to licensing.

Nigeria 1998

Nigeria's customs legislation establishes an Import Prohibition List, covering a number of food items, minerals and used tyres for commercial purposes. Among the stated reasons for the prohibition are to protect domestic industries and the balance of payments. The authorities have indicated that importation of products on the Import Prohibition List may be allowed as part of FDI contracts. Also the head of state may grant licences for imports of prohibited goods.

Thus, although Nigeria has notified the WTO that general import licensing was abolished in 1986, in practice all items under import prohibition may be imported with a licence if permitted by the head of state on the recommendation of the Tariff Review Board. In addition, other specific requirements remain in place for a number of restricted products. Among these are petroleum products, subject to import licences issued by the Ministry of Petroleum Resources exclusively to the Nigerian National Petroleum Company. Petroleum products were the largest single imported item in 1996, valued at nearly USD 2 billion. Also, imports of unmanufactured tobacco require a Tobacco Importer's Licence, issued by the Customs.

Swaziland 1998

All imports still require an import permit. However, it is expected that the import permit requirement will be abolished and that Swaziland will work on a negative list of items that will still be subject to import control. This list, which has already been prepared and is awaiting approval by the authorities, comprises drugs, arms, used vehicles, wild animal products and gold and other precious metals in any form. The list will be updated on a continuous basis depending on economic and non-economic considerations. In addition, Swaziland maintains restrictions in respect of regional trade in fresh agricultural products, such as vegetables and milk, which may be restricted at certain times of the year to protect local producers.

Non-OECD southeast Europe

Cyprus 1997

Cyprus has completely dismantled its licensing system for economic reasons with the exception of one agricultural product, groundnuts. Notified as a trade-related investment measure to the WTO, since 1992 importers have to purchase predetermined quantities of locally grown groundnuts before they are allowed to import groundnuts.

Source: GATT, TPR; WTO, TPR.

Notes

1. The third TPR of India, which dates from May 2002, was the last examined. Countries that were reviewed for the last time before 1995 were not included.

2. For example, it is not clear whether certain products require a licence for economic or non-economic purposes.

3. For example, the reviews of some countries indicate all products subject to licensing requirements at the 8-digit HS level, while for others they only mention the broad product categories affected by the measure.

4. Besides traditional sources of information such as UNCTAD's Database on Trade Control Measures and national reports on trade barriers of the EU, Japan and the United States, information on non-tariff measures can be found in WTO members' non-agricultural market access (NAMA) notifications, in which a few licensing issues are brought up. Yet another source of information worth mentioning with respect to licensing is a database developed by the Tuck School of Business of Dartmouth College, which contains information on licensing, among other non-tariff measures, derived from several sources. Scores are available for a selected group of developing and emerging economies based on evaluations by a panel of international experts drawn from government and business. The database, however, does not provide data on sectors or distinguish between types of licensing, and information is not available for every country. Information on the database is available at www.dartmouth.edu/tuck/fac_research/centers/caee_emai.html.

5. As regards developed countries, "...trade and payments regimes have generally been less complex, and reliance upon quantitative restrictions for purposes of managing the balance of payments was gradually reduced, if not eliminated, in the 1950s and early 1960s..." (Krueger, 1978).

6. Examples of these are the two bilateral agreements between India and the United States, and India and the European Union, in which India has undertaken to liberalise its textiles and clothing sector.

7. Given the particular conditions of the use of TRQs, they are not analysed here.

8. When licensing is used to administer quotas (or TRQs), governments may receive revenue if auctioning is the method used for allocation of licensing. However, analysis of this type of licensing is beyond the scope of this chapter.

9. Organisation of Eastern Caribbean States. OECS-WTO members comprise Antigua and Barbuda, Dominica, Grenada, Saint Kitts and Nevis, Saint Lucia and Saint Vincent and the Grenadines.

10. The 2002 TPR indicated that, according to the authorities, the paperwork to remove the remaining restrictions for economic reasons (on palm stearin, other than crude [HS Ex 382311.01], and other parts of watches [HS 911490.01] was proceeding.

11. Efforts to minimise trade-distorting effects of specific TBTs, for example, often need to be supported by complementary action, such as the removal of correlated procedural and administrative inefficiencies resulting from non-automatic licensing schemes. Otherwise, the benefits of a reduction of TBTs may be neutralised by continuing complicated procedures for the application and granting of import licences (see below for the procedural aspects of licensing).

12. In general, however, these schemes are applied by the vast majority of countries and cover several economic sectors. The rationales relate mainly to protection of health, safety, environment and national security.

13. This section draws primarily on European Communities, "Trade Facilitation in Relation to Development", G/C/W/143 of 10 March 1999.

14. A more comprehensive description of Article VIII from a legal perspective can be found in "Article VIII of GATT 1994 – Scope and Application", WTO, G/C/W/391 of 9 July 2002, Geneva.

15. A more comprehensive description of Article X from a legal perspective can be found in "Article X of GATT 1994 – Scope and Application", WTO, G/C/W/374 of 14 May 2002, Geneva.

16. As Switzerland pointed out in a proposal submitted in 1998 to the WTO for work on trade facilitation (G/C/W/114), "the tenor of most interventions at the Symposium addressed onerous and cumbersome procedural requirements for the import and export of goods, be they set up and/or implemented at the border or domestically, by customs authorities or other governmental bodies. For many of the queries made, the Agreement on Import Licensing Procedures would therefore seem to be a useful starting point for examining the link between traders' requests and governmental commitments in the WTO." For business complaints related specifically to administrative requirements in the licensing area, see PricewaterhouseCoopers (2001); Pruzin (2001); and Nortel Networks (1999).

17. WTO Documents G/C/W/379 of 30 May, G/C/W/363 of 12 April, G/C/W/376 of 22 May, G/C/W/377 of 22 May, and G/C/W/384 of 7 June.

18. Appeal procedures, particularly penalties resulting from breaches of customs regulations or procedural requirements, are also to be discussed in the context of Article VIII. However, the lack of sufficient relevant information (owing to the preliminary nature of the discussions) has not allowed any meaningful coverage of this aspect here.

19. WTO Documents G/C/W/397 of 17 July, G/C/W/394 of 12 July, G/C/W/398 of 18 July, G/C/W/401 of 22 July, and G/C/W/400 of 19 July. No code is available for the Korean submission.

20. See the European Communities communication "Trade Facilitation in Relation to Existing WTO Agreements", WTO, G/C/W/136 of 10 March 1999, Geneva.

21. See the Canadian communication "Trade Facilitation: Article VIII of GATT 1994 on Fees and Formalities connected with importation and Exportation" WTO, G/C/W/397 of 17 July 2002.

22. The years indicated refer to the years of the TPRs.

23. Of 11 December 1989 and amended on 8 June 1990, 31 May 1995 and 12 February 1998.

24. However, the Department of Economy may authorise the importation of new vehicles when the prices, before taxes, set by final assemblers exceeds the corresponding international prices for equivalent vehicles. The authorities noted that this mechanism is applied only in exceptional circumstances; it was used once in 2001. The other exception established in the Auto Decree refers to new-vehicle dealers established in Mexico's northern border strip and free-trade zones in Baja California and parts of Sonora, which may import new vehicles for use in these regions provided they meet a local-content requirement (*i.e.* they may import up to an amount not in excess of the difference between the value of sales of new vehicles manufactured in Mexico and the value of imports incorporated into such vehicles).

25. Some of the banned textile goods are: woven fabrics of silk; cotton-synthetic blended suiting fabrics above 60 inches wide; shirting and suiting fabrics of synthetic or man-made fibres; all knitted or

crocheted fabrics, etc. The restricted textile products include drill and cellular dyed fabrics, "khaki" fabrics, combat fabrics, grey fabrics, etc.

26. As described in the 1994 TPR, Indonesia committed itself in the Uruguay Round to remove all non-tariff barriers on bound items. This concerned 179 tariff items, of which 98 are manufactured products and 81 agricultural products. This commitment did not apply to the agricultural commodities controlled by BULOG, which were covered by the WTO provisions on state trading.

References

APEC (1999), "APEC Releases Study on Electronic Commerce Adoption by Small and Medium Enterprises in APEC Member Economies", APEC Secretariat Press Release.

European Commission (1996), "Public Procurement in the European Union: Exploring the Way Forward".

European Commission (1998), "TBR Proceedings Concerning Brazilian Practices Affecting Exports of Textile Products to Brazil". Report to the EC Trade Barriers Regulation Committee.

European Commission (1999), "TBR Proceedings Concerning Brazilian Practices affecting Sorbitol and Carboxymethylcellulose (CMC) Exports", Report to the EC Trade Barriers Regulation Committee.

Finger, M., and L. Shuknecht (1999), "Market Access Advances and Retreats: The Uruguay Round and Beyond", World Bank, Washington, DC.

Greenway, D and C. Milner (1993), *Trade and Industrial Policy in Developing Countries*, The Macmillan Press Ltd.

Krueger, A. (1974), "The Political Economy of the Rent-Seeking Society", *The American Economic Review*.

Krueger, A. (1978), "Foreign Trade Regimes and Economic Development", A Special Conference Series on Foreign Trade Regimes and Economic Development, New York.

Laird, S. (2000), "Multilateral Market Access Negotiations in Goods and Services." Centre for Research in Economic Development and International Trade, University of Nottingham.

Michalopoulos, C. (1999), "Trade Policy and Market Access Issues for Developing Countries: Implications for the Millennium Round", World Bank.

Nortel Networks (1999), "Import Licensing for Information Technology Products", submission to the WTO Committee on Import Licensing by Dave McGuire, Senior Manager, International Trade Global Logistics.

PricewaterhouseCoopers (2001), "Identification and Analysis of Trade Barriers in Indonesia, Thailand, Malaysia and the Philippines".

Pruzin, D. (2001), "Licensing Rules Can Hamper IT Trade, Canada Tells WTO", *International Trade Reporter*.

Roberts, D., T.E. Josling and D. Orden (1999), "A Framework for Analysing Technical Trade Barriers in Agricultural Markets", USDA, Washington, DC.

Spencer, B. (1996), "Bureaucratic Import Licensing, Rent-Seeking Quality Effects and the High Cost of Imported Capital-Goods", University of British Columbia, IBTF working paper 01-01.

Stewart, T. (1996), "Multilateral Trade Framework for the 21st Century and US Implementing Legislation", American Bar Association, Washington, DC.

Vinod, T and J. Nash (1991), "Best Practices in Trade Policy Reform", World Bank, Washington, DC.

Wade, Robert (1990), *Governing the Market : Economic Theory and the Role of Government in East Asian Industrialization*, Princeton University Press, Princeton, New Jersey.

WTO (n.d.), Agreement on Import Licensing, http://www.wto.org/english/docs_e/legal_e/23-lic.pdf.

WTO (1998), "Goods: Rules on NTMs", Module 3.

Chapter 4

Customs Fees and Charges on Imports

by

Michael Engman

This chapter examines the nature and the extent of the use of customs fees and charges that affect imports at borders. It draws on data collected from WTO Trade Policy Reviews, non-tariff barrier notifications to the Negotiating Group on Market Access (NAMA), and the UNCTAD TRAINS database and country notes. It reveals that most types of customs fees and charges on imports are applied *ad valorem* rather than on the basis of the underlying costs of the services rendered. The use of customs fees and charges has evolved over time. The use of both customs surcharges and consular invoice fees has declined markedly over the last two decades. More countries nowadays charge importers fees for the use of various customs-related services.

Introduction

This chapter examines the nature and the extent of use of customs fees and charges that affect imports at borders. It provides background material and analysis of a category of potentially trade-distorting measures that are among those relatively frequently mentioned by WTO members in notifications submitted to the Negotiating Group on Market Access (NAMA) and for which further clarification has been sought by the Council on Trade in Goods (CTG).

Customs fees and charges may constitute a nuisance to traders or act as an outright barrier to trade, depending on their nature and extent. This chapter seeks to provide as clear a picture as possible of the use made of different types of customs fees and charges collected on imports and the problems they may cause for traders. Some countries collect customs fees and charges to increase government revenue. Others may use them as a means to protect their domestic markets. Such motives may be in violation of GATT Article VIII, which states that fees and charges in connection with importation shall be "limited in amount to the approximate cost of services rendered and shall not represent an indirect protection to domestic products or a taxation of imports or exports for fiscal purposes".

The chapter draws heavily on data that have been systematically collected from Trade Policy Reviews (TPRs) published since the establishment of the TPR mechanism in 1995. Other data have been collected from existing studies and databases, including from the non-tariff barrier notifications to NAMA, the UNCTAD TRAINS (Trade Analysis and Information System) database and country notes, the Market Access Sectoral and Trade Barriers Database[1] and previous studies.[2]

In this chapter, an overview of relevant WTO disciplines follows a presentation of the definitions, scope and methodology. Then, the data found in TPRs, NAMA notifications and other reports are reviewed. The following section contains the main analysis, with discussions of the characteristics and patterns of use of customs fees and charges; trends in high- and low-income countries; motivations and effects of imposing customs fees and charges; and related provisions in regional trade agreements (RTAs). Finally, some conclusions are drawn.

Definitions and methodology

Customs fees and charges belong to a broader group of non-tariff barriers commonly referred to as para-tariff measures. The *Dictionary of Trade Policy Terms* (Goode, 2003) states that the term "para-tariff" is "sometimes used for charges levied on imports instead of, or in addition to, tariffs. These can consist of service fees, additional import surcharges or other fees levied on imported products inside the market." Different classifications are available and different names are frequently used to refer to some types of fees and charges.

In UNCTAD's TRAINS database para-tariffs are described as "other measures that increase the cost of imports in a manner similar to tariff measures, *i.e.* by a fixed percentage or by a fixed amount, calculated respectively on the basis on the value and the quantity". In the UNCTAD coding system of trade control measures (TCM),[3] para-tariff measures are divided into four main groups, with a fifth for miscellaneous items (see Table 4.1 for the classifications and Annex 4.A1 for definitions). The UNCTAD TCM coding system of para-tariff measures was introduced in 1994. The subsequent evolution of the various customs fees and charges applied on importers may have rendered certain categories obsolete or may merit the creation of new categories.

Table 4.1. UNCTAD coding system of trade control measures

TCM Code			Description*
2000			**Para-tariff measures**
	2100		**Customs surcharges**
	2200		**Additional taxes and charges**
		2210	*Tax on foreign exchange transactions*
		2220	*Stamp tax*
		2230	*Import licence fee*
		2240	*Consular invoice fee*
		2250	*Statistical tax*
		2260	*Tax on transport facilities*
		2270	*Taxes and charges for sensitive product categories***
		2290	*Additional charges n.e.s.*
	2300		**Internal taxes and charges levied on imports**
		2310	*General sales taxes*
		2320	*Excise taxes*
		2370	*Taxes and charges for sensitive product categories***
		2390	*Internal taxes and charges levied on imports n.e.s.*
	2400		**Decreed customs valuation**
	2900		**Para-tariff measures n.e.s.**

* The shaded area indicates the measures studied in this chapter.

** Including: 2X71: Charges to protect human health; 2X72: Charges to protect animal health and life; 2X73: Charges to protect plant health; 2X74: Charges to protect environment; 2X75: Charges to protect wildlife; 2X76: Charges to control drug abuse; 2X77 Charge to ensure human safety; 2X78: Charges to ensure national security; 2X79: Charges for purposes n.e.s. (X = 2, 3).

Source: Based on UNCTAD.

The TRAINS database is structured around the TCM coding system and provides very limited information on para-tariff measures. Countries that submit their bound and applied tariff schemes annually to UNCTAD are encouraged to submit information on their para-tariff schemes, but this voluntary practice has so far failed to create a comprehensive and continuously updated record of the rich and sometimes complex para-tariff schemes that exist in many countries.

The TCM coding system was based on the categories of fees and charges identified in GATT Article VIII, as shown in Annex 4.A2, but the WTO Negotiating Group on Market Access employs a broad and vaguely defined classification for its "inventory of non-tariff measures", which was created to provide a framework for future non-tariff barrier notifications (WTO, 2003a). Sub-category VI of this inventory is "Charges on Imports" and includes:

1. Prior import deposits.
2. Surcharges, port taxes, statistical taxes, etc.
3. Discriminatory film taxes, use taxes, etc.
4. Discriminatory credit restrictions.

5. Border tax adjustments.

This classification of import charges includes some sub-groups that are not necessarily related to the sub-categories in the TCM coding system, but items b) and c) seem to be directly related to category 2100 (customs surcharges) and 2200 (additional taxes and charges). Category e) may occasionally have an effect equivalent to a discriminating import fee or charge. The TCM coding system is arguably the most widely accepted detailed classification scheme for customs fees and charges.

To maintain manageability, this chapter focuses on the customs fees and charges regulated by GATT Article VIII "Fees and Formalities connected with Importation and Exportation".[4] It also focuses on customs fees and charges *on imports* and assessed or payable *at borders* since the classification schemes concern imports. The customs fees and charges examined in this chapter are shaded in grey in Table 4.1.

Overview of WTO disciplines

GATT Article VIII, "Fees and Formalities connected with Importation and Exportation" provides a legal framework for fees and charges on imports. Its legally binding provision [paragraph 1(a)] states that "All fees and charges of whatever character (other than import and export duties and other than taxes within the purview of Article III) imposed by contracting parties on or in connection with importation or exportation shall be limited in amount to the approximate cost of services rendered and shall not represent an indirect protection to domestic products or a taxation of imports or exports for fiscal purposes."[5]

Article VIII states that "contracting parties recognise the need for reducing the number and diversity of fees and charges" [paragraph 1(b)] and that "contracting parties also recognise the need for minimising the incidence and complexity of import and export formalities and for decreasing and simplifying import and export documentation requirements" [paragraph 1(c)]. However aside from paragraph 1(a) GATT Article VIII contains no binding restrictions on the use of fees and charges, which helps explain why complex schemes of fees and charges still exist. There is also no provision requiring member states to notify regularly their customs fees and charges to a central registry.

Article VIII additionally requires WTO members to "review the operation of its laws and regulations in the light of the provisions of this article" at the request of other members (paragraph 2) and prohibits the imposition of "substantial penalties for minor breaches of customs regulations or procedural requirements" (paragraph 3). Moreover, paragraph 4 sets forth an illustrative list of the types of fees and charges that fall within the scope of Article VIII; category 2200 of the TCM coding system is basically structured around this list (see Annex 4.A2).

There is an interpretative note to Article VIII (WTO, 2002) which states that "the use of taxes or fees as a device for implementing multiple currency practices is inconsistent with Article VIII, but creates an exception, in accordance with Article XV:9(a) of the GATT, for circumstances in which a Member uses multiple currency exchange fees for balance of payments reasons with the approval of the IMF". Any member imposing customs surcharges for balance-of-payment (BOP) purposes is required to hold periodic consultations with the WTO and the international Monetary Fund (IMF) to determine whether the use of restrictive measures is necessary or desirable to address its difficulties. The country must specify the period for which the import surcharges will be applied and then reduce and eliminate them as the situation improves. Several transition economies

– Poland, Hungary, Slovak Republic, Czech Republic, Bulgaria, Romania, Sri Lanka and South Africa – applied import surcharges for BOP reasons in the 1990s. Most of these measures were abolished in the second half of the 1990s; Romania and the Slovak Republic lifted their restrictions in 2001 (OECD, 2004).

GATT Article II:1(b) refers to the term "other duties and charges" (ODCs), which includes "all taxes levied on imports in addition to the customs duties which are not in conformity with Article VIII".[6] The Uruguay Round produced an understanding on the interpretation of Article II:1(b), stating that members agreed to record the nature and level of any ODCs levied on bound tariff items (as referred to in Article II) in the schedules of concessions annexed to the GATT 1994 against the tariff item to which they applied. These ODCs were bound on 15 April 1994 and any failure to notify ODCs before the deadline meant that they had to be eliminated.

The aim was to ensure greater transparency in terms of the legal rights and obligations with respect to the nature and level of any ODCs levied on bound tariffs items. The legal character of recorded ODCs did not change. Thus, the WTO Consolidated Tariff Schedules (CTS) database does not prejudice whether bound ODCs included are consistent or not with rights and obligations under the GATT 1994. The ODC register is an illustrative source of information, although it should be noted that the data are ten years old and the ODCs are not now necessarily applied at the indicated rates.[7] A quick review of Annex 4.A3 indicates that in 1994 ODCs were common in developing countries and virtually absent in OECD member countries. Fifty countries notified ODCs to the WTO: 27 were African, 12 were South American, Central American or Caribbean, eight were Asian, and three were European (Cyprus, Malta and Romania). Half of the countries applied ODCs with simple averages of 10% or higher, and four had simple averages around 100% or higher.

Para-tariff disputes have typically concerned issues relating to the application of internal sales taxes and excise taxes and very few dispute settlement cases are related to the customs fees and charges on imports included in the scope presented above. The GATT Panel on "United States – Customs User Fee"[8] examined complaints concerning the "merchandise processing fee", an *ad valorem* charge applied for the processing of commercial merchandise entering the United States. The Panel findings noted that "Article VIII:1(a) states a rule applicable to all charges levied at the border, except tariffs and charges which serve to equalize internal taxes. It applies to all such charges, whether or not there is a tariff binding to the product in question. The rule of Article VIII:1(a) prohibits all such charges unless they satisfy the three criteria listed in that provision: (a) the charge must be limited in amount to the approximate cost of services rendered; (b) it must not 'represent an indirect protection to domestic products'; (c) it must not 'represent … a taxation of imports … for fiscal purposes'." (GATT, 1994) The Panel concluded "that the *ad valorem* fee was not compatible with the plain meaning of the text or with the objectives of the GATT".

A 1998 panel, "Argentina – Textiles and Apparel", reasoned that "An *ad valorem* duty with no maximum fee, by its very nature, is not "limited in amount to the approximate cost of services rendered … high-price items necessarily will bear a much greater tax burden than low-price goods, yet the service accorded to both is essentially the same. An unlimited *ad valorem* charge on imported goods violates the provisions of Article VIII because such a charge cannot be related to the cost of the service rendered."[9]

It should be noted that the *ad valorem* fees and charges discussed in this chapter do not exclusively refer to Article VIII and thus are not necessarily incompatible with

GATT. In addition to the provisions in GATT Articles II and VIII, the fees and charges presented may be covered by Article III. These fees and charges have a clear fiscal purpose and are WTO-consistent if they are applied in a non-discriminatory fashion. The data in the TPRs are such that, in the interpretation and classification carried out during data collection, fees and charges that correspond to similar fees and charges applied domestically may occasionally be included.

Review of data on use of customs fees and charges

This section draws mainly on information and data collected from the latest WTO TPRs. Ninety countries were reviewed for the period from the start of the Trade Policy Review Mechanism in 1995 until mid-September 2004. Section III of each of the TPRs: "Trade policies and practices by measure", was examined, and Table 4.2 offers a snapshot of the customs fees and charges countries were imposing on imports when the reviews were undertaken (see also Annex 4.A4). [10]

Customs fees and charges in the WTO Trade Policy Reviews (1995-2004)

With some slight modifications, the UNCTAD TCM coding system of sub-category 2100 and 2200 is used here to classify the data collected from the WTO TPRs (see Table 4.1).

An additional category was created for so-called "community levies" (Com. levy), *i.e.* fees applied by RTA administrations. Category 2290 "Additional charges n.e.s." has been further subdivided into two groups: fees related to customs procedures (2290 Service); and a subgroup comprising all the other fees and charges belonging to 2290 as described under 2200 in Annex 4.A1. In addition, taxes for "special funds" have been registered as surcharges (2100) rather than "additional charges n.e.s." (2290) as suggested by UNCTAD. [11]

Table 4.2 provides information on the existence of fees and charges in different countries and shows whether the fees are specific or *ad valorem* in nature[12] (see Annex 4.A4 for more detailed information about the customs fees and charges accounted for in the TPRs).

Customs surcharges (2100)

Customs surcharges added to customs duties are also commonly referred to as surtaxes, special import taxes or additional duties. Data retrieved from the TPRs show that customs surcharges are predominantly *ad valorem* in nature (25 of 29 cases). Two out of five low-income and upper-middle-income economies imposed surcharges at the time of the reviews (Table 4.3). Many "temporary" surcharges were in fact fairly persistent: some countries applied temporary surcharges without setting a fixed end date (*e.g.* Bangladesh and Senegal), continuously extended the end date (*e.g.* Gabon and Trinidad and Tobago), or phased out the surcharge over an extended period of time (Trinidad and Tobago). For example, Papua New Guinea introduced a temporary import duty surcharge of 1.5% on all imports as a drought relief measure in the 1998 budget and then extended the surcharge for six months in 1999 before terminating it.

Table 4.2. Customs fees and charges on imports at the time of the latest trade policy reviews

Table 4.2a. High-income economies (16)

	TPR	2100	2210	2220	2230	2240	2250	2260	2270	2290	2900 Service	Com. levy
Australia	2002	..	..	..	..	..	..	..	..	..	S	..
Bahrain	2000	..	..	..	..	..	..	..	..	..	..	..
Brunei Darussalam	2001	..	..	..	..	..	..	..	..	..	..	..
Canada	2003	..	..	..	..	..	..	..	..	..	..	..
European Communities	2002	..	..	..	..	..	..	..	..	..	..	..
Hong Kong, China	2002	..	..	..	..	..	..	..	..	..	S	..
Iceland	2000	..	..	..	..	..	..	..	..	..	..	..
Israel	1999	AV	..	..	..	..	..	..	AV	..	..	..
Japan	2002	..	..	..	..	..	..	..	..	..	..	..
Korea	2004	S	..	..	..	..	..	..	..	AVS	..	..
Macao, China	2001	..	..	..	S	..	..	..	AV	..	..	..
New Zealand	2003	..	..	..	..	..	..	..	..	..	..	..
Norway	2000	..	..	..	..	..	..	..	AV	..	AV	..
Singapore	2004	..	..	..	..	..	..	..	..	..	..	..
Switzerland & Liechtenstein	2000	..	..	..	S	..	..	..	..	S	..	..
United States	2004	..	..	..	..	..	..	..	AV	..	..	..	SUM
Specific (S)		1	..	..	2	..	..	..	1	..	2	..	6
Ad valorem (AV)		1	..	..	..	..	..	2	2	..	1	..	6
Ad valorem & specific (AVS)		..	..	..	..	..	..	..	..	1	..	..	1
Unspecified (X)		..	..	..	..	..	..	..	..	..	..	..	0

Table 4.2b. Upper-middle-income economies (19)

	TPR	2100	2210	2220	2230	2240	2250	2260	2270	2290	2900 Service	Com. levy
Antigua & Barbuda	2001	..	AV	..	..	..	..	..	S	..	AV	..
Argentina	1999	AV	..	..	..	..	AV	..	..	..	AV	..
Barbados	2002	..	..	..	..	..	..	..	S	..	..	..
Belize	2004	..	..	..	..	..	..	..	AV	AV	..	..
Botswana	2003	..	..	..	..	..	..	..	..	..	..	..
Chile	2003	AV	..	..	..	..	..	AV	..	AV	..	..
Costa Rica	2001	AV	..	..	..	..	..	..	..	AV	X	..
Dominica	2001	AVS	..	..	..	..	..	..	AVS	..	AV	..
Gabon	2001	AV	..	..	..	..	..	..	..	..	..	..
Grenada	2001	..	..	..	S	..	..	..	AVS	..	AV	..
Malaysia	2001	..	..	..	..	..	..	..	..	..	S	..
Mauritius	2001	..	..	..	S	..	..	..	S	AVS	S	..
Mexico	2002	..	..	..	..	..	..	..	..	..	AV	..
St Kitts & Nevis	2001	..	..	..	..	..	..	..	S	..	AV	..
St Lucia	2001	..	..	..	..	..	..	..	X	..	AV	..
St Vincent & the Grenadines	2001	..	..	..	..	..	..	..	S	..	AV	..
Trinidad & Tobago	1998	AV	..	..	..	..	..	..	..	..	..	..
Uruguay	1998	AV	..	..	..	..	..	..	..	..	AV	..
Venezuela	2002	AV	..	..	..	..	..	..	..	..	AV	..	SUM
Specific (S)		..	..	..	2	..	..	..	5	..	2	..	9
Ad valorem (AV)		7	1	..	..	..	1	1	1	3	10	..	24
Ad valorem & specific (AVS)		1	..	..	..	..	..	..	2	1	..	..	4
Unspecified (X)		..	..	..	..	..	..	..	1	..	1	..	2

Table 4.2. Customs fees and charges on imports at the time of the latest trade policy reviews (cont.)

Table 4.2c. Lower-middle-income economies (26)

	TPR	2100	2210	2220	2230	2240	2250	2260	2270	2290	2900 Service	Com. levy
Bolivia	1999	..	..	..	..	..	..	..	..	..	AV	..
Brazil	2000	S	..	..	..	..	..	..	..	..	AVS	..
Bulgaria	2003	..	..	..	S	..	..	..	..	..	..	..
Colombia	1996	..	..	..	..	..	..	..	..	..	..	..
Dominican Republic	2002	..	..	..	..	S	..	..	..	AV	..	..
Egypt	1999	AV	..	..	..	..	..	..	..	..	AV	..
El Salvador	2003	..	..	..	..	..	..	..	..	AV	..	..
Fiji	1997	..	..	..	..	..	..	..	..	..	..	..
Guatemala	2002	..	..	..	..	..	..	..	..	..	..	..
Guyana	2003	..	..	..	..	..	..	..	S	..	..	..
Honduras	2003	..	..	..	..	..	..	..	..	..	..	..
Indonesia	2003	..	..	..	..	..	..	..	..	..	..	..
Jamaica	1998	..	..	AVS	S	..	..	..	..	..	..	..
Maldives	2003	..	..	..	..	..	..	..	..	..	..	..
Morocco	2003	..	..	AV	..	..	..	..	S	AVS	AVS	..
Namibia	2003	..	..	..	..	..	..	..	..	..	..	..
Paraguay	1997	..	..	..	..	AVS	..	AV	..	..	..	..
Peru	2000	AV	..	..	..	..	..	..	..	..	AV	..
Philippines	1999	..	..	..	..	..	..	..	..	..	X	..
Romania	1999	AV	..	..	..	..	..	..	..	..	AV	..
South Africa	2003	..	..	..	S	..	..	..	S	..	..	..
Sri Lanka	2004	AV	..	..	AV	..	..	AV	..	..	AV	..
Suriname	2004	..	..	..	..	..	AV	..	..	AV	..	..
Swaziland	2003	..	..	..	AV	..	..	..	..	..	..	..
Thailand	2003	X	..	..	..	..	..	..	..	..	S	..
Turkey	2003	AV	..	..	..	..	..	..	..	..	S	.. SUM
Specific (S)		1	..	..	3	1	..	..	3	..	2	.. 10
Ad valorem (AV)		5	..	1	2	..	1	2	..	3	5	.. 19
Ad valorem & specific (AVS)		..	..	1	..	1	..	..	..	1	2	.. 5
Unspecified (X)		1	..	..	..	..	..	..	..	..	1	.. 2

Table 4.2d. Low-income economies (29)

	TPR	2100	2210	2220	2230	2240	2250	2260	2270	2290	2900 Service	Com. levy
Bangladesh	2000	AV	..	..	AVS	..	..	..	..	..	AV	..
Benin	2004	S	..	..	..	..	AV	S	..	..	S	AV
Burkina Faso	2004	..	..	..	..	..	AV	..	..	S	AVS	AV
Burundi	2003	AV	..	..	..	..	..	..	..	..	AV	..
Cameroon	2001	..	..	..	..	..	..	..	AVS	S	..	..
Côte d'Ivoire	1995	..	..	..	..	..	AV	..	..	..	AVS	..
The Gambia	2004	..	..	..	S	..	..	..	S	..	AV	AV
Ghana	2001	AV	..	..	..	..	..	..	..	..	AV	AV
Guinea	1999	AV	..	..	..	..	..	..	..	AV	AV	AV
Haiti	2003	AV	..	..	..	..	..	..	..	..	AV	AVS ..
India	2002	..	..	..	..	..	..	..	..	..	AV	..
Kenya	2000	AV	..	..	..	..	..	..	..	..	AV	..
Lesotho	2003	..	..	..	..	..	..	..	..	..	..	..
Madagascar	2000	..	..	AV	..	..	AV	..	..	AVS	..	..
Malawi	2002	..	..	..	..	..	..	..	..	..	AV	..
Mali	2004	..	..	..	..	..	AV	..	..	..	..	AV

Table 4.2. **Customs fees and charges on imports at the time of the latest trade policy reviews (cont.)**

Table 4.2d. Low-income economies (29) (cont.)

	TPR	2100	2210	2220	2230	2240	2250	2260	2270	2290	2900 Service	Com. levy
Mauritania	2002	..	..	..	..	..	AV	..	..	..	..	..
Mozambique	2001	AV	..	..	..	..	..	..	..	..	S	..
Nicaragua	1999	..	..	..	..	AV	..	..	..	..	S	..
Niger	2003	..	..	S	..	..	AV	..	..	..	AV	AV
Nigeria	1998	AV	..	..	..	..	..	..	..	..	AV	..
Pakistan	2002	..	..	..	..	..	..	..	..	X	..	..
Papua New Guinea	1999	..	..	..	..	..	..	..	..	..	..	..
Senegal	2003	AV	..	..	..	..	AV	..	..	..	..	AV
Solomon Islands	1998	AV	..	..	..	..	..	..	..	..	S	..
Tanzania	2000	..	..	..	..	..	..	..	..	..	..	..
Togo	1999	AV	..	AVS	..	..	AV	S	..	..	..	AV
Uganda	2001	..	..	..	AV	..	..	..	..	..	..	..
Zambia	2002	..	..	..	..	..	..	..	..	..	..	..
												SUM
Specific (S)		1	..	1	1	..	..	2	..	2	4	..	11
Ad valorem (AV)		11	..	1	1	1	9	..	1	3	9	9	45
Ad valorem & specific (AVS)		..	..	1	1	..	..	..	1	1	3	..	7
Unspecified (X)		..	..	..	..	..	..	..	..	1	..	..	1

1. For an explanation of TCM codes see Table 4.1.

Several countries applied surcharges to finance infrastructure projects, development funds or other special causes and institutions. Peru levied surcharges to pay for its Agricultural Development Fund: the 5% tariff surcharge was introduced on 331 agricultural products in 1997. The number of tariff lines was subsequently increased to 350 in late 1997, and then to 352 in 1999 when the surcharge was increased to 10% for meat products. Uruguay applied a 0.25% fee on imports transported by sea to finance the severance packages of its National Ports Administration personnel. Brazil charged a Merchant Marine Renewal tax to modernise and improve its merchant fleet and a Dock Worker Severance pay surcharge to indemnify workers whose registration had been cancelled. Benin charged a specific fee on imports for its National Dockers' Council and Haiti collected a tax of 2% (calculated on the basis of import duties and taxes paid) for its fund for the "Management and Development of Local Communities". Nigeria applied a Port Development Tax (5%), a "Raw Materials and Development Council" surcharge (1%), and a Shippers' Council surcharge (1%). Senegal applied a 0.2% levy for the Senegalese Loaders' Council and a Livestock Fund levy. Bangladesh introduced a temporary infrastructure development surcharge of 2.5% in 1997 that was still in place three years later. Turkey applied a Mass Housing Fund levy of 3% to imports of fish and fishery products to finance its low-cost housing schemes for poor and middle-income families. Costa Rica applied a 1% tax on most imports, with the proceeds earmarked for welfare, medical and child-care centres.[13]

Some countries applied surcharges on the importation of used goods. Chile and Dominica had special surcharges on used vehicles. Burundi applied a 20% surcharge on imports of certain textile products to protect the Bujumbura Textile Complex from international competition. Nicaragua also introduced a temporary protection surcharge in 1994 to "counter effects from asymmetries resulting from the preferential trade treatment granted by CACM members to Nicaragua" as well as to support the "strengthening of the economy". In 1999, the surcharges still ranged between 5% and 20%. The Solomon Islands introduced a temporary surcharge of 10% in 1998 for revenue reasons. To ensure price stability, Korea levied surcharges on petroleum and Mozambique on sugar, cement and steel. Mozambique's sugar surcharge (averaging 25%) varied depending on the world market price. The Mozambique government negotiated the price policy with investors to ensure profitable local investment.[14]

In 1992, Israel started to apply "safeguard levies" on certain agricultural imports, although it lacked safeguard legislation within the meaning of Article XIX of the GATT 1994 and the Agreement on Safeguards. In 1999, 0.8% of the total number of tariff lines was still affected by these measures.

Several countries apply various types of advance income payments and withholding taxes at their borders. These taxes are not included in the scope of this study, but they may act as proxies for import surcharges in cases where importers are not in a tax-paying position, *e.g.* in instances where companies make losses or enjoy tax holidays. For example, Bangladesh levied an advance income tax on all importers at the rate of 3% (c.i.f. value) and Burundi applied a 4% levy on the customs value of imports by taxpayers in arrears as an advance payment on income tax. Burundi's transaction tax was applied on domestic and imported goods alike but in the case of agricultural, fisheries and stockbreeding products, local products were taxed at a lower rate than imports. Both Uganda and Pakistan applied withholding taxes of 6% and 4%, respectively, on imports.

Temporary surcharges were sometimes used to compensate for the negative revenue impact of tariff reductions, for example in the form of imposition of common external tariffs (CET) in RTAs. Senegal, for example, imposed several surtaxes to compensate for the revenue reduction following the introduction of the WAEMU CET. In St Kitts and Nevis, the reduction of the CET among members of the Organisation of Eastern Caribbean States (OECS) led to the imposition in 2001 of a 5% increase in the consumption tax on imports and a 2% increase in the customs service charge.

Tax on foreign exchange transactions (2210)

There is scant evidence of countries imposing taxes on foreign exchange transactions related to importation. The only case in the data examined concerns Antigua and Barbuda, which in 2001 applied a foreign exchange transaction tax of 1% on all transactions.[15]

Stamp tax (2220)

Four African countries and Jamaica applied stamp taxes or duties. Madagascar charged a customs stamp duty of 1%, Morocco collected a 5% verification and stamp tax on carpets and Niger applied a specific stamp tax which discriminated between WAEMU and non-WAEMU countries. However, the fees charged in Niger were small. Togo and Jamaica charged both specific and *ad valorem* stamp duties. Jamaica charges an additional stamp duty on customs warrants inward to protect local production of certain product categories such as primary aluminium products (20-25%), vegetables and beans (35%), alcoholic beverages (34%) and tobacco products (56%). Importation of refined sugar was subject to an additional stamp duty whenever the c.i.f. price plus the customs duty fell below an established benchmark. Several countries either abolished or transformed/merged their customs stamp taxes into existing tariff schemes or other forms of fees and charges during the 1990s. For example, Belize removed its 14% stamp duty in

1996 and Barbados abolished a 20% stamp duty levied on imports from non-CARICOM member states in 1997.[16]

Import licence fee (2230)

Import licence/import permit fees were applied in countries independent of income level: the frequency ratio was 10-20% across the board. Most fees were specific, but *ad valorem* import licence fees were applied in Bangladesh (2.5% on imports valued above BDT 100 000), Sri Lanka (0.1% on 474 items), Swaziland (0.05%) and Uganda (2% on all imports). Most other countries charged small fees to cover the administrative costs of issuing import licences. In the high-income economy group, Macao, China; Switzerland and Liechtenstein did so.[17]

Consular invoice fee (2240)

Consular invoice fees were rare and only applied in Caribbean, South and Central American countries. The Dominican Republic levied a specific consular invoice fee to approve transactions and Nicaragua charged an *ad valorem* fee of 0.05%. Paraguay introduced a consular tax in 1972 that was still applied 25 years later. It was applied at a rate of 7.5% on total merchandise value. Special consular fees, ranging from USD 10 to more than USD 100, also affected compulsory document registration, additional copies and airmail charges for sending documentation to Paraguay.[18]

Statistical tax (2250)

All 11 countries that applied statistical taxes applied *ad valorem* fees. Statistical taxes were applied mainly in low-income economies: Benin, Burkina Faso, Mali, Niger and Senegal levied fees of 1% on imports from non-ECOWAS and non-WAEMU countries. Madagascar, Côte d'Ivoire, Mauritania and Togo applied statistical taxes of between 2% and 3%. Suriname charged 0.5% on the c.i.f. value of all imports except those of bauxite companies for which the statistical tax was quadrupled. In 1998, Argentina reduced its statistical tax on non-Mercosur countries from 3% to 0.5% following a decision by a WTO panel.

Both Côte d'Ivoire and Mauritania applied statistical taxes on most, but not all, products. Suriname also discriminated between product categories.

Tax of transport facilities (2260)

The application of taxes on transport facilities is seemingly independent of countries' income levels. Airport taxes (Chile, Sri Lanka) and port taxes (Benin, Israel, Paraguay, Sri Lanka and the United States) are mostly *ad valorem* and the predominant measure used. The United States has levied an *ad valorem* tax on port use since 1986 when the Harbor Maintenance Tax of 0.125% was introduced. The user fee applies to imports, admissions into foreign trade zones, domestic cargo shipped through a port, as well as passengers. Exports have been exempted since 1998. In Israel, importers were charged a 1.1% wharfage fee/port use fee while exporters paid 0.2%.

Taxes and charges for sensitive product categories (2270)

Taxes and charges for sensitive product categories include several types of fees and charges, and the variety makes the category rather difficult to define. Almost half of the upper-middle-income economies are identified as using taxes and charges for sensitive product categories, while the prevalence is low in high-income countries – where consumption rather than imports tends to be taxed – and even lower among low-income and lower-middle-income economies. The great majority of fees were specific although eight of the countries applied *ad valorem* fees. Three cases were found in the high-income economy group.

Various forms of environmental taxes were most common. Imported beverages in containers are a popular focus of taxation, especially in the Caribbean (Antigua and Barbuda, Dominica, Grenada, Guyana, and St Kitts and Nevis). It should be added that the tax paid at the border was frequently repaid in return for the empty containers. Some countries applied environmental taxes on gasoline/petroleum/heating oils (Dominica, Switzerland and Liechtenstein) or on new or used vehicles (Grenada, St Kitts and Nevis, and St Vincent and the Grenadines). Korea applied environmental waste charges on certain plastics; domestic producers were charged a specific fee while foreign imports were subject to an *ad valorem* fee (0.7%).

Additional taxes cover inspection fees for animals or plants (Cameroon; Gambia; Macao, China; Mauritius; Morocco; South Africa; Switzerland; and Liechtenstein). In Norway, plant inspection was subject to a fee of 0.8% of the value of inspected imports. Barbados charged a specific environmental levy for waste disposal. Belize charged an environmental tax of 1% on most imported products, and Grenada applied a similar 1% environmental levy on a range of goods.[19] Both Barbados and Belize's environmental levies were applied on imports but not on the same type of products produced domestically.

Additional charges n.e.s. (2290)

Additional charges not elsewhere specified include a range of fees of various forms. They were prevalent in 15-24% of the studied low-income, lower-middle-income and upper-middle-income economies. The fees included an administrative charge (Belize, 1.5%); a social fee in commercial free zones (Belize); specific taxes on particular product categories (Burkina Faso on rice, sugar, vehicles and hydraulic cement, Cameroon on certain meats, Mauritius on tea [20%], El Salvador on empty sacks and bags of synthetic fibre [80%], and Morocco on cement and wood); and a dispatch tax on merchandise exempt from import duties (Chile, 5%). There were various import taxes on new and used vehicles (Costa Rica, Dominican Republic, Haiti and Pakistan), a para-fiscal tax (Morocco, 0.25%), a consent fee (Suriname, 1.5%), and regulatory duties (Pakistan[20]).[21]

Fees related to customs procedures (2290 [Service])

Various fees are applied for customs-related procedures. They do not necessarily provide utility to the importer, and in three out of four cases they were *ad valorem*. Many countries do not charge special customs service fees but cover the costs through other customs measures. Private inspection companies paid by the governments of countries to which the goods are to be exported frequently conduct pre-shipment inspection in low-income and lower-middle-income countries.

Some countries applied an *ad valorem* customs "service fee" (1% in Bangladesh and Venezuela; 0.35-1.1% in Uruguay; 2% in Dominica; 4% in St Lucia and St Vincent and the Grenadines; and 5% in Antigua and Barbuda, Grenada and St Kitts and Nevis),[22] while others applied specific fees (Brazil, Mozambique and Nicaragua).[23] Other countries specified and charged for the type of service rendered. *Ad valorem* fees were common for import inspection or pre-shipment inspection of imports (Argentina, Bolivia, 1.92%;

Burkina Faso, 1%; Ghana, 1%; Guinea, 1.05%; Haiti, 4%; Malawi, 0.85%; Mauritius: specific fee; Niger, 1%, Nigeria, 1%; and Peru: up to 1%). There were also cases of "processing fees" (Gambia, 1.05%; Mexico, 0.8%; and the Philippines).[24] In Peru, the pre-shipment inspection fee varied and had to be negotiated with the inspection company. In Norway, imports of agricultural products were subject to inspection or foodstuff taxes of 0.58-0.82%.

Egypt applied a service and inspection fee of 1% plus an additional service charge of 2% on goods subject to import duties of 5-29%, and 3% on goods with duties of 30% or higher. Burundi levied a 6% service tax on all imports in addition to a pre-shipment inspection fee (for imports worth more than USD 5 000) which amounted to 1.5% of customs value. Côte d'Ivoire applied a 0.6% service fee on imports carried by sea, and inspection firms charged an additional 0.75%. Romania applied a 0.5% customs commission in 1998.

Morocco charged an administrative specific fee based on the tonnage of shipments. Peru applied *ad valorem* charges for customs clearance. Australia, Costa Rica, Thailand and Turkey also applied various service charges to cover costs. Warehouse or storage fees were applied in countries such as Bolivia, Brazil, Haiti, Morocco and Nicaragua.

Computer service fees were applied in some African countries: Benin, Burkina Faso, Côte d'Ivoire, Mauritania and Morocco all charged specific fees for submitting import declarations. Hong Kong, China, also used a mandatory electronic system (electronic data interchange – EDI) for trade declarations for which there was a HKD 11 charge in 1999. Kenya applied an import declaration fee of 2.75% on the customs value of all imports.

Community levies

Two West African RTA Secretariats imposed discriminatory customs fees and charges to fund their activities. The ECOWAS Secretariat refers to the principle of financial autonomy, and the resources generated by the community levy partly finance their community activities.[25] One-third of the WAEMU budget was funded by the community solidarity levy in 1998 (Grimm, 1999).

- ECOWAS[26] members Benin, Burkina Faso, Gambia, Ghana, Guinea, Mali, Niger, Senegal and Togo applied an ECOWAS customs community levy of 0.5% on imports from non-ECOWAS members.

- WAEMU[27] members Benin, Burkina Faso, Mali, Niger and Senegal applied the WAEMU community solidarity levy of 1% on imports from non-WAEMU countries. The TPR of Togo stated that the country charged a WAEMU community solidarity levy of 0.5% in the beginning of 1998.

In addition, Niger applied a special import tax (TCI: *taxe conjoncturelle à l'importation*) of 10% on rice during the period 2000-02. The TCI applied if the customs value was lower than the trigger price set by the WAEMU Commission. The TCI is a domestic protection mechanism established by the WAEMU and it is applied on agricultural, agro-industrial, livestock and fisheries products (with the exception of fish and fish products). Its purpose is to mitigate the effects of sharp fluctuations in international prices on community production and to counteract "unfair" practices. It is applied on products imported from third countries in two ways: as 10% of the trigger price or by equalisation.[28]

Notifications of customs fees and charges in the Negotiating Group on Market Access

In the autumn of 2002, WTO members were invited to notify non-tariff barriers (NTBs) that their exporters face in various markets. The NAMA received such notifications from 30 countries (and customs territories) between March 2003 and March 2004; a summary of the notifications related to customs fees and charges on imports is presented in Annex 4.A5.[29] Two-thirds of the notifying countries raised the issue of customs fees and charges (without revealing the identity of the imposing country or countries). Almost the entire range of fees and charges discussed above were notified. Norway notified nearly every category in the TCM coding system.

The NTB notifications seem to confirm some of the general trends identified in the analysis of TPR data. Customs surcharges and various fees related to customs procedures were the two most frequently notified categories. Six countries notified port fees, others pointed to fees related to documentation, and some countries noted that certain service fees did not necessarily reflect the cost of rendering the service. Generic or all imports were the most notified group and several product-specific categories, such as metals, plastics, chemicals, medicines, automobiles, fluorescents lamps, textiles and clothing, watches, fish, drinks and forestry products, were notified as well. Food products or agricultural produce was notified only once. A few countries reported variable import fees and charges (notifications by Malaysia and Mexico), some of which "fluctuated excessively" according to Singapore. Argentina reported that special duties on iron and steel products raised the applied tariff by up to 100% in certain cases, and the United States notified that express delivery services were affected by discriminatory customs treatment in the form of unequal fees and taxes.

Analysis of the data on customs fees and charges

A few of the categories in the TCM coding system appear to have negligible impact in the context of the information on which this chapter draws. Only one country was found to charge taxes on foreign exchange transactions (2210). Consular invoice fees (2240) were also infrequent and seem to be non-existent in the great majority of countries. Elctronic data interchange (EDI) may be increasingly adopted by customs authorities, but the TPRs did not note many fees related to the use of EDI systems to submit import declarations.[30] The category "Additional charges n.e.s." (2290) contains by far the most fees and charges, yet the title reveals nothing about their nature. This category may usefully be further subdivided into two or more groups since it includes types of fees and charges that appear more common than those falling under 2210 and 2240, for example. This review has found that the most frequently recorded types of customs fees and charges relate to customs inspection, processing and servicing. Most West African countries also charge community levies of yet other types.

Trends in high- and low-income countries

Table 4.3 shows the number of countries that apply different customs fees and charges as identified in the TPRs (see Table 4.1 for definitions of the categories of fees and charges). The first line reveals that fees related to customs procedures (2290 [Service]) are most prevalent and identified in nearly half the countries. The number would most likely have been higher if the TPRs accounted more strictly for the many small specific fees applied for services related to documentation, inspection, testing, etc.[31] Customs surcharges (2100) were applied in one-third of the countries and taxes on sensitive product categories (2270) were found in one-fifth. Taxes on foreign exchange transactions (2210) and consular invoice fees (2240) were applied in only a few cases; stamp taxes, import licence fees, statistical taxes, taxes on transport facilities, additional charges n.e.s. and community levies were less frequently identified.

Table 4.3. **Number of countries imposing various customs fees and charges**

Country group (no. of countries)	2100	2210	2220	2230	2240	2250	2260	2270	2290	2900 (Service)	Com. levy
All countries (90)	29	1	5	12	3	11	7	18	15	42	9
High-income economies (16)	2	0	0	2	0	0	2	4	0	3	0
Upper-middle-income economies (19)	8	1	0	2	0	1	1	9	4	13	0
Lower-middle-income economies (26)	7	0	2	5	2	1	2	3	4	10	0
Low-income economies (29)	12	0	3	3	1	9	2	2	7	16	9

Source: WTO Trade Policy Reviews, 1995 to -mid-September 2004.

A similar study of 63 developing countries conducted two decades earlier found customs surcharges in 63% of the countries, other fiscal charges in 17%, foreign exchange levies in 14%, stamp taxes in 13%, consular fees in 43%, licence fees in 8%, statistical taxes in 13%, transport taxes in 21%, and other service taxes in 19% of the countries (Kostecki and Tymowski, 1985). While both data sets have methodological shortcomings, the findings still point to some general trends:

- The number of countries that apply customs surcharges is significantly smaller today than 20 years ago, or down from two-thirds to one-third of the countries.

- There has been a considerable drop in the number of countries that apply consular invoice fees, and the imposition of taxes on foreign exchange transactions is also less frequent.

- The number of countries that apply various service fees related to customs procedures seems roughly to have doubled.

- The trend is less clear for stamp taxes, import licence fees, statistical taxes and taxes on transport facilities. The numbers seem to have been fairly stable over the time period.

This seems to indicate that countries have moved slowly in the direction laid out in GATT Article VIII:1(b) which states that "contracting parties recognise the need for reducing the number and diversity of fees and charges". The data do not allow for a comparison of the absolute levels of customs fees and charges but high *ad valorem* charges were most widespread in the group of customs surcharges, and the data indicate a significant downturn in the imposition of surcharges. However, while the number of customs fees and charges has declined over the last decades, a great variety of fees and charges are still applied, and most are proportional to the value of the imported goods.

The TPRs also indicate that several countries have reformed their customs schemes of fees and charges applied at borders. For example, in Cameroon until 2000, a temporary import surcharge of up to 30% could be levied for a period of three years on products that were previously subject to quantitative restrictions (cement, flour and polypropylene bags, for example), and a number of fees and charges were eliminated by the Budget Law of 2000/01. These included an import inspection fee of 0.95% on imports in excess of XAF 1 million (with a minimum charge of XAF 110 000); a computer user fee of 1.5% used to finance the national computer office; and a levy of 0.3% collected on river and maritime freight originating in and imported from non-members of the Customs and Economic Union of Central Africa (UDEAC).

In Bangladesh, regulatory duties and surcharges on imports were replaced by a supplementary excise duty, which is largely a trade-neutral consumption tax. In 1995, Uruguay combined all customs duties, surcharges, service and other charges in a unified customs charge (TGA), which is levied on the c.i.f. value of imports with the exception of goods subject to the Minimum Export Price Regime. The TGA is the sum of three components: the minimum surcharge (0-6%), the additional surcharge (0-8%) and the single customs tax on imports (0-10%). Brazil has also reformed its customs measures and since 1996 eliminated import licence fees, a document surcharge for non-preferential customers and a tax for the organisation and regulation of the rubber market.

Table 4.3 reveals the following breakdown: [32]

- *Low-income economies:* 55% applied various fees related to customs procedures, 41% applied customs surcharges, and 31% applied statistical taxes and community levies.

- *Lower-middle income economies:* 38% applied various fees related to customs procedures at borders, 27% applied customs surcharges and 19% statistical taxes. This income group also had the highest share of import licence fees and consular invoice fees, but both were relatively infrequent and found in less than a fifth of the countries.

- *Upper-middle-income economies:* Seven out of ten charged various fees related to customs procedures and just under half applied customs surcharges and taxes on sensitive product categories. Six categories of fees and charges were recorded only once or not at all.

- *High-income economies:* In general, few fees and charges were recorded although taxes and charges for sensitive product categories and various fees related to customs procedures were identified for a few countries. Six categories of fees and charges were not found in any country.

The shift from customs surcharges to the application of fees related to customs procedures would be welcome if the latter reflected the costs of the services rendered. However, Table 4.4 shows that a great majority of the fees related to customs procedures are, like the group of customs surcharges, *ad valorem* fees.

Ad valorem *vs. specific customs fees and charges*

Customs fees and charges applied on imports are assessed on either an *ad valorem* or a specific basis. *Ad valorem* fees are proportional to the customs value of imports and the value is normally calculated as cost, insurance and freight (c.i.f., or occasionally of the f.o.b. value).[33] Specific fees are either fixed or based on weight or volume. Some countries apply *ad valorem* fees with a fixed minimum or maximum. Table 4.4 shows the frequency of the two types. Customs surcharges (2100), statistical fees (2250) and community levies are predominantly, or only, of the *ad valorem* type. A great majority in the groups of taxes on transport facilities (2260), "Additional charges n.e.s." (2290), and fees related to customs procedures (2290 [Service]) are also *ad valorem*. Import licence fees (2230) and taxes and charges for sensitive product categories (2270) tend to be specific.

The information contained in the TPRs shows some patterns that are worth highlighting: *e.g.* poorer countries seem more likely to apply *ad valorem* fees. While 54% of the fees and charges applied by high-income economies were *ad valorem*, the corresponding figures were between 71% and 76% in the upper-middle income and lower-middle income economies, and 83% in low-income economies.[34] OECD member countries had few *ad valorem* fees and these are generally less than 1% and targeted at specific products (*e.g.* agricultural products in Norway or plastics in Korea).

Table 4.4. **Fee structure of customs fees and charges on imports**

	2100	2210	2220	2230	2240	2250	2260	2270	2290	2900 (Service)	Com. levy
Specific (S)	3	0	1	8	1	0	2	9	2	10	0
Ad valorem (AV)	24	1	2	3	1	11	5	4	9	25	9
Ad valorem and specific (AVS)	1	0	2	1	1	0	0	4	3	5	0
Unspecified type (X)	1	0	0	0	0	0	0	1	1	2	0

Source: WTO Trade Policy Reviews, 1995 - mid-September 2004.

Many *ad valorem* customs fees and charges do not differ from customs duties other than by the name and the procedural and legal grounds on which they are used (Kostecki and Tymowski, 1985). Several low- and middle-income countries use high *ad valorem* fees and charges that may obstruct trade with high-income countries and other low- and middle-income countries alike. Although panel reports contain some discussion of the reference to "approximate cost of services rendered", the overview of various fees and charges that countries apply suggests that the relation between "services rendered" and the cost imposed on the imported products warrants further clarification. The administrative burden for customs is not necessarily related to the value of the imported goods. The customs services offered to an importer of a container of mobile phones or telephone directories is an example: an *ad valorem* service fee would be considerably higher for the mobile phone importer even if the services rendered at customs take the same amount of time and involve similar procedures. Clearer guidelines for calculating customs fees and charges would remove some of the uncertainties regarding the legality of their application.

Box 4.1 describes the policies of 14 Arab countries, many of which are not members of the WTO or included in the TPRs. As of the late 1990s, these countries applied a plethora of fees and charges. Measures such as Sudan's defence tax and Libya's artificial river tax did not break WTO rules since neither country was a member of the WTO. Tunisia applied a duty on goods that competed with similar local products to assist its "Development and Competitiveness Fund". Egypt's para-tariffs were relatively low compared to its applied *ad valorem* tariffs, but they still increased the effective rate of duty collected on average by about 10%.[35] Zarrouk (2000) observed that transparency was a real problem: detailed data on specific surcharges were not available in most of the countries surveyed.

Box 4.1. Customs fees and charges on imports in selected Arab countries

The findings of a study of para-tariff measures in 14 Arab countries relating to customs fees and charges on imports are summarised below. The author collected the information from the Arab Trade Information Network, the Program for Arab Trade Financing, the TRAINS database, and from reports by UNCTAD, the World Bank and the WTO. Moreover, customs authorities were surveyed in some cases to verify the information, and a number of Egyptian importers replied to a questionnaire about taxes and charges in the Arab world.

Egypt: Service charges affecting importers included: *i)* a statistical tax of 1% (on f.o.b. value); *ii)* a customs surcharge collected at the rate of 2% or 3% of the import value of goods subject to *ad valorem* rates between 5-29% and 30% or more, respectively; *iii)* X-ray, health and food control charges levied on foodstuffs at USD 1 per ton; and *iv)* progressive certification and stamp duties collected on the imported value. In addition, a specific surcharge (EGP 25 per ton) was levied on imported goods to control standards and quality of exports.

Iraq: Import charges were collected to assist exports at the rate of 0.5% (on c.i.f. value) of capital goods and 0.75% (on c.i.f. value) of consumer goods.

Jordan: Service charges affecting importers included: *i)* fees for customs overtime wages that were levied on all imported goods at 0.2% (on c.i.f. value); *ii)* legalisation charges of JOD 2 for certifying import invoices and certificates of origin and their attachments were levied (on f.o.b. value) on imports ranging between JOD 1 000 and JOD 10 000, and the certification fee was JOD 20 for import values exceeding JOD 10 000; and *iii)* additional specific duties were expressed as a fixed monetary amount per physical unit of the product imported.

Lebanon: Service charges affecting importers included: *i)* additional customs duties levied on imported cars at 20% for the first LBP 25 million (c.i.f. value) and 35% for the balance of the c.i.f. value of the imported car; *ii)* specific duties on alcoholic beverages and beer; and *iii)* stamp fees on all imports at the rate of LBP 3 per each LBP 1 000 of the c.i.f. import value.

Libya: Service charges affecting importers and internal taxes and charges violating the national treatment of imports were not found. However, a 15% additional import tax called the "artificial river tax" was levied on the c.i.f. value of imports. The tax was paid upon opening a letter of credit by the importer with his local bank.

Morocco: A 0.25% para-fiscal tax (on c.i.f. value) was collected on all imported goods except those exempted from or subject to minimum customs tariffs. The tax was collected to assist standards and quality inspections of export-oriented goods, the Moroccan crafts industry, the Moroccan Centre for Export Promotion, and the Industrial Development Council. Specific import duties on timber were levied at the rate of 6% (on c.i.f. value).

Sudan: Special import taxes complementing tariffs included a defence tax collected at the rate of 4% (on c.i.f. value) of all goods except staples; and a business profit tax of 5% (c.i.f. value plus the customs tariff and other customs duties) levied on imported goods competing with locally produced goods.

Syria: Import licence fees were collected at the rate of 2% (on c.i.f. value) on all imported goods in the private sector. Consular invoice fees were collected at a minimum of 4% on the first SYP 1 000, 3% on the next SYP 1 000 and 0.4% on the additional value of imports. The collected consular invoice fees differed by country and shipment. Additional import taxes were levied on all imported goods. The rates were progressive and *ad valorem* at rates between 6% and 35%.

Tunisia: Service charges affecting importers included: *i)* a 3% customs service charge of the total amount of collected tariffs and other import taxes and charges (or a fee of TND 5 per section of the customs declaration for tariff exempted goods); and *ii)* a computer data word-processing fee of TND 2 per page of customs declaration. A duty to assist the "Development and Competitiveness Fund" was levied at 1% (on c.i.f. value) on imported goods that competed with similar local products.

United Arab Emirates: Specific surcharges were levied on imported tobacco and its derivatives.

For *Bahrain, Kuwait, Qatar* and *Saudi Arabia*, no para-tariffs were identified.

Source: Zarrouk (2000).

The lack of a comprehensive and trusted central registry of customs fees and charges raises transparency issues for importers, as they must spend time and money to search for the relevant information but still receive surprises at borders, particularly in poorer countries where the fees and charges may change without notice, thereby increasing financial risks and hampering trade. As TPRs point out, one reason why customs fees and charges are so frequent in low- and middle-income countries is that taxation of imports constitutes an important source of revenue for many governments. "Temporary surcharges" are also applied for long periods of time but result in few legal challenges.

Motivations and effects of imposing customs fees and charges

Governments pursue trade policies for a variety of reasons, such as to raise revenue, to protect specific industries, to shift the terms of trade, to attain certain foreign policy or security goals, or to restrict the consumption of specific goods (Hoekman and Kostecki, 2001). Although many of the fees and charges presented so far are clearly applied to cover costs for services rendered, some governments would have great difficulty in arguing that their high permanent *ad valorem* fees – those without ceilings, domestic equivalents, and not related to BOP concerns – are related to services rendered and not used for reasons such as raising revenue or protecting industries. Surcharges are sometimes used to stabilise low commodity prices. Several countries also charge importers to help finance various funds that have little, or indeed nothing, to do with the services rendered.

Article VIII does not define the meaning of "service" in the provision that "all fees and charges ... imposed by contracting parties on or in connection with importation ... shall be limited in amount to the approximate cost of services rendered". Some of the fees and charges that are identified in this chapter do not provide any direct value to traders. They would include, for example, community fees and taxes on foreign exchange transactions. Some services, such as statistical taxes and taxes on sensitive product categories, may provide a service that could be regarded as a public good. However, para-tariff measures such as some customs surcharges or community fees are arguably neither a useful service for traders nor a public good. A more precise definition of what constitutes a "service" in Article VIII:1(a) would remove some of the uncertainties in the interpretation of the article and potentially lead to a reduction in the costs of trading.

Customs fees and charges not only apply direct costs on importers, they also entail a range of indirect additional costs. The imposition of customs fees and charges may lead to delays, and transparency is an issue because of the lack of comprehensive and up-to-date registers. Fees and charges, and the regulations governing their application, tend to change over time, and some developing countries have been shifting and changing their fees and charges for various reasons.

Lack of transparency, frequent changes and lax controls on the administration of fees at customs create opportunities for bribery and corruption. Some countries require importers to make advance payments on fees, which increases the financial risk of cross-border trade. In addition, domestic taxes are often calculated on the import price inclusive of additional fees and charges. Calculating a tax on the basis of the sum of c.i.f. value, import duty, surcharge, cess and excise duty amplifies the increase in consumer prices.

Provisions in RTAs and discrimination

Annex 4.A6 provides a review of selected RTAs and their provisions concerning customs fees and charges. The great majority of these RTAs state that no new customs fees and charges shall be introduced and existing ones shall be abolished either immediately or progressively over a number of years. Exceptions are frequent and refer to particular product categories that are not included or for which the elimination of fees is to take place over time. Some RTAs include a provision allowing members to renegotiate their commitments (*e.g.* in former Soviet Republics). Other RTAs state that existing fees and charges shall not be raised and no new ones introduced. Several agreements also include a provision that allows for the application of fees to cover costs for services rendered. A general observation is that many recent RTAs define "customs duties" as including (non-tariff) customs fees, and charges and provisions concerning customs duties thus affect all other fees and charges similarly.

Measures to increase transparency and provisions to prohibit bilateral discrimination in the application of additional fees and charges are occasionally included. The United States-Chile RTA and the United States-Bahrain RTA include a simple but very useful transparency provision stating that: "Each Party shall make available through the Internet or a comparable computer-based telecommunications network a current list of the fees and charges it imposes in connection with importation or exportation."

The data in the TPRs provide very little evidence of arbitrary discrimination in the application of fees and charges among trading partners, except in the case of RTAs. Discrimination is observed mainly where the customs fees and charges are being abolished on a preferential basis among members of RTAs, and this preferential elimination will affect an increasing share of world trade in the wake of the current proliferation of RTAs. Examples include the US merchandise processing fee, which is abolished in recent bilateral trade agreements; Grenada's application of licence fees to non-CARICOM countries; and Chile's abolition of customs fees on imports originating from countries with which it has free trade agreements. In the case of two West African RTAs – ECOWAS and WAEMU – specific community fees are levied only on trade transactions involving non-member countries.

In November 1997, the Mercosur common external tariff was increased by 3% following Argentina's proposal to replace a 3% statistical tax that had been condemned by a WTO panel. In January 1998, Argentina, Brazil, Paraguay and Uruguay implemented the new tariff. The higher rate was originally set to be discontinued in December 2000 but was subsequently lowered to 2.5% in 2000 and to 1.5% in 2001. In November 2002, Mercosur decided to extend the application of this additional duty until December 2003.[36]

A few other cases of selective application of fees and charges were noted. In 1999, Israel applied fees that discriminated between exporter countries. Korea's surcharge on petroleum imports was levied to provide funds to ensure adequate supply and price stability. The Korean government also promoted diversification of oil imports to reduce dependency on Middle Eastern oil and increase imports from other regions including the Americas, Africa and Europe. Surcharges on oil imports other than from the Middle East were to be lowered to offset higher transport costs at the time of the review. A few examples not related to country of origin include Suriname, which applied a statistical fee that was four times higher for bauxite companies than for others, and Egypt, which applied an additional *ad valorem* service charge that increased with the level of tariff protection.

The data presented in Annex 4.A4 indicate that agricultural products, petroleum and vehicles are singled out for various customs fees and charges. One explanation may be that petroleum and vehicles represent a large share of imports in many poor countries. The agriculture sector is also heavily protected in general and represents a larger share of the economy in poor than in rich countries.

Concluding remarks

Customs fees and charges on imports in WTO member states are required by GATT Article VIII to be limited in amount to the approximate cost of services rendered and not to represent indirect protection to domestic products or a taxation of imports for fiscal purposes. This chapter has shown that various types of customs fees and charges continue to affect world trade, particularly in low- and middle-income countries. Fees and charges related to customs inspection, processing and similar services are applied by half of the 90 reviewed WTO members and various customs surcharges in a third.

If one compares this more recent information with data collected in the early 1980s, it is clear that the use of both customs surcharges and consular invoice fees has declined markedly. On the other hand, more countries now charge importers fees for the use of various customs-related services. The present study has discerned no clear trend concerning the use of stamp taxes, import licence fees, statistical taxes and taxes on transport facilities. Taxes on foreign exchange transactions observed to be in place in the early 1980s now seem to be abolished.

Ad valorem fees are more frequently applied than specific fees: customs surcharges, statistical taxes and community fees are predominantly of the *ad valorem* type. Taxes on transport facilities and fees related to customs procedures are also mostly *ad valorem*. Import licence fees and taxes on sensitive product categories are the only categories of primarily the specific type. Poorer countries seem more likely to use *ad valorem* fees than richer countries.

Many low- and middle-income countries apply high *ad valorem* fees and charges. Several countries appear to employ customs fees and charges for reasons other than to provide services. RTAs tend to include provisions which either abolish customs fees and charges between members or freeze and prohibit the introduction of new such measures. There is no indication that the proliferation of RTAs is providing impetus for a widespread reduction or removal of fees and charges that would also benefit the countries that are not members of RTAs.

An additional issue is transparency. The few market access databases available do not offer comprehensive and continuously updated data on customs fees and charges. This lack of information increases the financial risk for traders and may affect trade, especially for SMEs without the means and infrastructure to keep themselves informed. In addition, the price effect of customs fees is amplified in some countries because domestic taxes are frequently calculated on top of the import value and all additional fees and charges.

Annex 4.A1

Descriptions of Fees and Charges in the UNCTAD TCM Classification

I. **2100 Customs surcharges:** are levies added to the normal customs duties; and they are commonly referred to as surtaxes or additional duties. Customs surcharges are sometimes used to improve a current account deficit, to raise fiscal revenue or to protect domestic industry.

II. **2200 Additional taxes and charges:** are levied on imported goods in addition to customs duties and surcharges that have no internal equivalent. Various other taxes, such as taxes for special funds, municipal taxes, registration fees on imported motor vehicles, customs formality taxes, etc., are classified as additional charges, n.e.s. (not else specified).

III. **2300 Internal taxes and charges levied on imports:** general sales taxes levied on imports are the equivalent of those internal taxes that are applied to all or most products. There are three types of internal taxes: the sales tax is *ad valorem* and based on the gross receipts of sales of goods; the turnover tax, or multiple sales tax, is imposed at more than one level of production and distribution and is based on gross receipts; and the value-added tax (VAT) is a modified turnover tax based on the net value added. The excise tax levied on imports is the equivalent of the excise tax levied on domestic products. This tax is an internal tax imposed on selected types of commodities, usually of a luxurious or non-essential nature, and it is levied separately from, and in addition to, the general sales tax.

IV. **2400 Decreed customs valuation:** customs duties and other charges on selected imports can be levied on the basis of a decreed value of goods. This practise practice is presented as a means to avoid fraud or to protect domestic industry.

Annex 4.A2

UNCTAD's TCM Coding System in Relation to the GATT

General Agreement on Tariffs and Trade (GATT)	UNCTAD TCM code
Art. VIII:1(a) – All fees and charges of whatever character (other than import and export duties and other than taxes within the purview of Article III) imposed by contracting parties on or in connection with importation or exportation shall be limited in amount to the approximate cost of services rendered and shall not represent an indirect protection to domestic products or a taxation of imports or exports for fiscal purposes. **Art. VIII:4** – The provisions of this Article shall extend to fees, charges, formalities and requirements imposed by governmental authorities in connection with importation and exportation, including those relating to:	See 2100 See 2200
a) consular transactions, such as consular invoices and certificates	See 2240
b) quantitative restrictions	
c) licensing	See 2230
d) exchange control	See 2210
e) statistical services	See 2250
f) documents, documentation and certification	See 2220
g) analysis and inspection	See 2290
h) quarantine, sanitation and fumigation	See 2270
Art. II:2 – Nothing in this Article shall prevent any contracting party from imposing at any time on the importation of any product: (a) a charge equivalent to an internal tax imposed consistently with the provisions of paragraph 2 of Article III in respect of the like domestic product or in respect of an article from which the imported product has been manufactured or produced in whole or in part; (c) fees or other charges commensurate with the cost of services rendered. **Art. III:1** – The contracting parties recognize that internal taxes and other internal charges, and laws, regulations and requirements affecting the internal sale, offering for sale, purchase, transportation, distribution or use of products, and internal quantitative regulations requiring the mixture, processing or use of products in specified amounts or proportions, should not be applied to imported or domestic products so as to afford protection to domestic production. **Art. III:2** – The products of the territory of any contracting party imported into the territory of any other contracting party shall not be subject, directly or indirectly, to internal taxes or other internal charges of any kind in excess of those applied, directly or indirectly, to like domestic products. Moreover, no contracting party shall otherwise apply internal taxes or other internal charges to imported or domestic products in a manner contrary to the principles set forth in paragraph 1.	See 2300
Art. VII:2 – (a) The value for customs purposes of imported merchandise should be based on the actual value of the imported merchandise on which duty is assessed, or of like merchandise, and should not be based on the value of merchandise of national origin or on arbitrary or fictitious values. (b) "Actual value" should be the price at which, at a time and place determined by the legislation of the country of importation, such or like merchandise is sold or offered for sale in the ordinary course of trade under fully competitive conditions. To the extent to which the price of such or like merchandise is governed by the quantity in a particular transaction, the price to be considered should uniformly be related to either (i) comparable quantities, or (ii) quantities not less favourable to importers than those in which the greater volume of the merchandise is sold in the trade between the countries of exportation and importation. (c) When the actual value is not ascertainable in accordance with sub-paragraph (b) of this paragraph, the value for customs purposes should be based on the nearest ascertainable equivalent of such value.	See 2400

Annex 4.A3

Bound Other Duties and Charges for All Products

Import markets	Other duties and charges Simple average	Maximum	Import markets	Other duties and charges Simple average	Maximum
Angola	0.1	0.1	Madagascar	190.2	
Argentina	3.0	3.0	Malawi	11.8	
Bahrain	0.0	2.0	Maldives	0.0	
Bangladesh	2.2	2.5	Mali	19.0	
Barbados	98.3	246.0	Malta	0.4	
Belize	14.2	106.0	Mauritania	5.4	
Benin	6.8	19.0	Mauritius	13.7	
Burkina Faso	17.8	50.0	Morocco	15.0	
Burundi	18.8	30.0	Mozambique	100.0	
Central African Republic	15.3	16.0	Niger	37.1	
Costa Rica	1.0	1.0	Nigeria	80.0	
Côte d'Ivoire	4.7	70.0	Qatar	3.0	
Cyprus	0.2	6.0	Romania	0.5	
Djibouti	99.6	100.0	Senegal	7.2	
Dominican Republic	0.7	60.0	Sierra Leone	43.1	
Gabon	18.2	48.0	Sri Lanka	0.9	
Gambia	10.0	10.0	St. Kitts and Nevis	17.8	
Ghana	0.2	15.0	Suriname	27.0	
Guinea	8.8	93.0	Tanzania	0.3	
Guinea-Bissau	46.8	80.0	Thailand	0.0	
Guyana	31.4	85.0	Trinidad and Tobago	14.2	
Haiti	12.6	21.0	Tunisia	0.7	
Indonesia	0.1	25.0	Uganda	3.5	
Jamaica	14.1	200.0	Uruguay	3.0	
Kuwait	15.0	15.0	Zimbabwe	9.4	

Countries with simple average and maximum equal to 0.0: The OECD member states, Albania, Antigua and Barbuda, Bolivia, Brazil, Darussalam, Bulgaria, Cameroon, Chad, Chile, China, Colombia, Dem. Rep of Congo, Croatia, Cuba, Dominica, Ecuador, Egypt, El Salvador, Estonia, Fiji, Grenada, Guatemala, Honduras, Hong Kong (China), India, Israel, Jordan, Kenya, Kyrgyz Rep., Latvia, Lesotho, Lithuania, Macao (China), Malaysia, Moldova, Mongolia, Myanmar, Namibia, Nicaragua, Oman, Pakistan, Panama, Papua New Guinea, Paraguay, Peru, Philippines, Singapore, Slovenia, Solomon Islands, South Africa, St. Vincent and the Grenadines, Swaziland, Chinese Taipei, Togo, United Arab Emirates, Venezuela and Zambia.

Source: WTO, World Trade Report 2003.

Annex 4.A4

Customs Fees and Charges in the WTO Trade Policy Reviews

2100: Customs surcharges

Argentina [99]:[37] In 1997, minimum surcharge levels, ranging from 8% to 16% depending on the cylinder capacity of the engine, were set for private importers of Category A vehicles.

Bangladesh [00]: In 1997, an infrastructure development surcharge of 2.5% was introduced as a temporary measure. It applies to 98.4% of total tariff lines and it has effectively counteracted the fall in the overall applied MFN tariff level.

Benin [04]: A levy for the Benin National Dockers' Council (XOF 400/t on imports) is calculated on volume.

Brazil [00]: A Merchant Marine Renewal Tax is charged on imports transported by sea at 25% of ocean freight charges. The tax is used to modernise and improve the Brazilian merchant fleet. In addition, there is a Dock Worker Severance Pay Surcharge that varies according to the type of cargo. The surcharge aims to "indemnify workers whose registration has been cancelled".

Burundi [03]: Imports of certain textile products are subject to a 20% surcharge on the customs value of the goods to provide additional protection for the Bujumbura Textile Complex.

Chile [03]: Used goods bear a surcharge of 50% above the relevant import duty.

Costa Rica [01]: There is a 1% tax on customs value of imports.

Dominica [01]: An import surcharge of 15% is applied on apples, fresh grapes, pears and motorcycles, and there is a surcharge of XCD 2 500 on the importation of reconditioned vehicles older than five years.

Egypt [99]: A 2% or 3% surcharge is levied for imports subject to customs duties of between 5% and 29% or 30% and above, respectively.

Gabon [01]: Since 1994, Gabon has availed itself of a provision allowing CACEU member countries the possibility of imposing a temporary surcharge on certain products. The surcharge concerned two categories of goods: *i)* those subject to quantitative restrictions in the member states in 1994, to be abolished in 1996 at the latest; and *ii)* those included on a list to be abolished in June 2000 at the latest. In 2001, Gabon had not yet finally abolished the temporary surcharge because of opposition by local producers of identical or directly competing products. The temporary surcharge is set at 20%, and affects 25 Gabonese tariff lines, notably vegetable fats and oils.

Ghana [01]: The temporary introduction of a special import tax of 20% in 2000 mainly on consumer goods and covering 7% of tariff lines has effectively added a fifth tariff rate of 40% and raised the average applied MFN tariff to almost 15% currently.

Guinea [99]: A 0.25% (c.i.f. value) tax is levied for payment to the Chamber of Commerce. A consumption surcharge has been levied on "luxury products" since 1986: on imports, the surcharge is *ad valorem* and comprises eight rates ranging from 5% to 70%. The surcharge is also levied on locally manufactured products, but the method of taxing local products differs from that for imports of identical products: *e.g.* beer produced locally is subject to a specific tax of GNF 20 per bottle with a content of 50 cl or less, while imported beers are taxed at a rate of 70%. Imports are more heavily taxed than locally produced goods.

Haiti [03]: A tax of 2% calculated on the basis of the import duties and taxes paid is levied as a contribution to the Fund for the Management and Development of Local Communities.

Israel [99]: So-called safeguard levies are collected on a number of imported goods although Israel has no safeguard legislation within the meaning of Article XIX of the GATT 1994 and the Agreement on Safeguards. The safeguard levy is partly used as an instrument to enhance flexibility of the tariff system. In 1994, based on agricultural policy considerations, Israel imposed safeguard levies on a wide range of agricultural products. In 1999, 81 items at the HS 8-digit level, equivalent to 0.8% of the total tariff lines, were subject to such surcharge, down from 268 items, equivalent to some 2.7% of tariffs lines, in 1992. The rate differs depending on the origin; imports of US origin are generally subject to a lower safeguard levy than other imports.

Kenya [00]: A fee of 1% is collected on the c.i.f. value of agricultural imports to support the Kenya Plant Health Inspectorate Service. In addition to customs tariffs, "suspended" (stand-by) duties ranging up to 70% on maize, rice, wheat, sugar, and milk are imposed on some 17% of all tariff lines in agriculture and manufacturing.

Korea [04]: A surcharge is levied on petroleum imports to provide funds to ensure adequate supply and price stability. Petroleum refiners and oil importers pay the surcharge, currently set at KRW 14 per litre.

Mozambique [01]: Since 1997, Mozambique levies a variable surcharge on sugar (25% on average), and a fixed one on cement and on steel (12.5%). The import surcharge on sugar varies depending on the world price with government and investors negotiating price policies to assure profitability.

Nigeria [98]: A surcharge of 7% is levied on the customs duty payable. The surcharge comprises a Port Development Tax (5%), a Raw Materials and Development Council Surcharge (1%) and a Shippers' Council Surcharge (1%). A National Automotive Council tax of 2% is also levied on the c.i.f. value of imported vehicles and parts. In addition, Nigeria's position as an important transhipment point for neighbouring countries suffers from high port charges and customs fraud which drive business away. As of 1998, multiple fees and charges levied illegally at various stages of discharging cargo resulted in overall shipping charges and port duties that were approximately 45% of the total cost of clearance.

Peru [00]: A 5% tariff surcharge on 331 agricultural products was introduced in 1997. Changes introduced later that year increased the number of tariff lines subject to the surcharge to 350. In 1999, two more lines were added and the surcharge was increased to 10% for meat products. The tariff surcharge is applied on the c.i.f. value of imports before tax and the revenue is channelled to the Agricultural Development Fund. Tariff surcharges apply also to imports under preferential agreements; in this case the margin of preference is applied to the sum of the base and surcharge rates.

Romania [99]: In 1998, Romania introduced a surcharge of 6% on imports by OU22/1998 until the end of the year 2000. The surcharge was reduced to 4% for 1999.

Senegal [03]: A temporary surcharge of 10% to 20% is levied on imports of several agricultural goods. No timetable had been fixed for the abolition of these temporary surcharges. In addition, there is a 0.2% levy for the Senegalese Loaders' Council and a special import tax for some agricultural goods from non-WAEMU countries. There is also a livestock fund levy, which is imposed on imported goods and has no counterpart at the domestic level. A 1% tax is payable on imported fabrics, without any counterpart at the domestic level.

Solomon Islands [98]: In 1998, a temporary 10% surcharge was introduced on all duty rates for revenue reasons.

Sri Lanka [04]: Most imports, with the exception of basic goods, were subject to a 20% surcharge (on the c.i.f. value and import duty) effective in 2003. This surcharge was reduced from 40% in 2002. The authorities were planning to phase it out by the end of 2003, but this period has been extended. In addition, imported tobacco and tobacco products are subject to import cess. A cess of 1% is levied on imports of plastic. Imports subject to a tariff higher than 45% are subject to a 10% import cess used to finance the Export Development Board.

Thailand [03]: Certain product-specific surcharges are imposed; for example, a surcharge is levied on out-of-quota imports of corn and certain fish-meals.

Togo [99]: The MFN import duty includes a tax for the protection and maintenance of the infrastructure.

Trinidad and Tobago [98]: Temporary import surcharges, which replaced quantitative restrictions in 1990, apply to a handful of products: *e.g.* poultry, sugar and assorted fruits and vegetables. It was planned to eliminate them for some products in 1999, for others they were to continue to apply. For example, a 100% surcharge on various poultry parts was to be reduced to 86% by 2004, but an import surcharge of 60% on sugar (75% for icing sugar) will not be reduced.

Turkey [03]: A Mass Housing Fund levy is applied since 1984 to imports of fish and fishery products (3% of the tariff lines or 555 items at the HS 12-digit level, up from 514 tariff lines in 1998) to finance the government's low-cost housing schemes for poor and middle-income families.

Uruguay [98]: The unified customs charge, which is levied on the c.i.f. value, is the sum of three components: the minimum surcharge (up to 6%), additional surcharge (up to 8%) and the single customs tax on imports (up to 10%). A tax of 0.25% based on the c.i.f. value is levied on imports transported in ships, to finance the severance packages of the National Ports Administration's personnel.

Venezuela [02]: In 2001, a 1% tariff surcharge was imposed on the f.o.b. value of imports for a five-year period. As of 2002, the surcharge had still not been applied since no regulation had been issued for its implementation.

2210: Tax of foreign exchange transactions

Antigua and Barbuda [01]: A foreign exchange transaction tax of 1% is levied on all foreign exchange transactions.

2220: Stamp tax

Jamaica [98]: Stamp duties are levied on the c.i.f. value of imports at the rate of JMD 5 for imports with a c.i.f. value of less than JMD 5 500, and JMD 100 for imports of over JMD 5 500. Additional Stamp Duties on Customs Warrants Inward are levied on the duty-paid value of imports. The aim is to protect local production of selected product categories. On primary aluminium products, applied rates of additional stamp duty (excluding the customs duty) are in the 20-25% range. Some agricultural products are charged additional stamp duty rates of 35% (vegetables, beans). The range for agricultural products is between 65% and 90%. A non-specific additional stamp duty must be paid on imported refined sugar, whenever the c.i.f. price plus the customs duty fall below an established benchmark (currently USD 0.22 per pound), to cover this difference. The additional stamp duty on alcoholic beverages is 34%, while tobacco products are subject to a 56% duty

Madagascar [00]: Customs stamp duty of 1%.

Morocco [03]: A 5% verification and stamp tax on carpets.

Niger [03]: WAEMU imports are charged stamp taxes amounting to XOF 9 000. Non-WAEMU imports are charged stamp taxes equalling XOF 12 000.

Togo [99]: A customs stamp is collected at the rate of 4% on the taxes where the product enters with exemption from the fiscal import duty. The costs of the various formalities are: a XOF 500 stamp levy for nationals and citizens of the ECOWAS countries, and XOF 20 000 for others.

2230: Import licence fee

Bangladesh [00]: A 2.5% letter of credit authorisation/import permit fee is levied on the value of all imports above BDT 100 000, unless exempted by the Import Policy Order. All industrial consumers and commercial importers must register with the Chief Controller of Imports and Exports. Registration and annual renewal fees are based on the value of annual imports: BDT 500 for imports up to BDT 0.5 million; BDT 1 500 up to BDT 1.5 million; BDT 3 000 up to BDT 5 million; and BDT 5 000 for above BDT 5 million.

Bulgaria [03]: Licensing fees are charged to cover administrative expenses on the processing of documents and are independent of the value of imports or exports.

The Gambia [04]: GMD 50 is charged for the issuance of an import permit for agricultural products.

Grenada [01]: A number of products originating in non-CARICOM countries are subject to automatic and non-automatic licensing. A fee of XCD 5 is charged for an import licence.

Jamaica [98]: Import licences for motor vehicles, in the case of an individual importer, are granted every three years, subject to a maximum fee of JMD 776.32.

Macao, China [01]: Importers of pharmaceutical products and medicines must be licensed by the Health Service. A fee of MOP 3 000 is charged to the importer/firm for the licence; the annual renewal costs are MOP 400.

Mauritius [01]: Import permits cost MUR 50 per permit.

South Africa: A cost-related fee of ZAR 60 (per import permit) is charged for issuing import permits by the Directorate of Veterinary Public Health.

Sri Lanka [04]: In 2003, 474 items at the HS 8-digit level were subject to import licensing. Licences are issued at a fee of 0.1% of c.i.f. value; they are valid for six months from the date of issue. Import licences are a policy instrument used by the government from time to time to control domestic supply and prices; import licences, especially on agricultural goods, are removed and imposed frequently.

Swaziland [03]: An administrative charge is levied on import permit goods at the rate of SZL 1.00 per SZL 2 000 of value (0.05%).

Switzerland and Liechtenstein [00]: Applications for licences must be submitted three to five days in advance of importation. Fees are to be paid for the administration of data on tariff quotas (CHF 8 per consignment) and for the allocation of tariff quota shares (CHF 30 per allocation). Special allocations (upon special request) are subject to a fee of CHF 80 per allocation. According to the authorities, the fees cover the cost of administrative services involved.

Uganda [01]: An import licence commission of 2% is collected on all imports.

2240: Consular invoice fee

Dominican Republic [02]: The cost of the consular invoice approving a transaction is USD 34 for transaction values below USD 1 000 and USD 82 for transaction values above USD 1 000.

Nicaragua [99]: Since 1980, consular fees, set at specific amounts (USD 20-USD 50) depending on the range of the import value and corresponding to at least 0.05% *ad valorem*, have affected shipments of a c.i.f. value exceeding USD 50. A maximum in-range fee of USD 50 per shipment (from c.i.f. value of USD 10 000 to USD 100 000) is added to every additional tranche of USD 100 000.

Paraguay [97]: Since 1972, a consular tax, currently at a rate of 7.5% on total merchandise value, has been levied on all imports (with a few exceptions). Special consular fees affect compulsory document registration, additional copies and air mail charges for sending the documentation to Paraguay; the fees are levied at fixed rates ranging from USD 10 (copies) to more than USD 100 (registration). In 1994 and 1995 the authorities raised USD 8 million a year from these charges.

2250: Statistical tax

Argentina [99]: In 1998, the statistical tax was reduced from 3% to 0.5%, while most import duties were increased by 3 percentage points. The tax, which is levied on the c.i.f. merchandise value of all imports originating in countries other than those of Mercosur and its associate members has been changed frequently according to the fiscal situation. In July 1998, Argentina proposed to modify the statistical tax as of January 1999; a maximum ceiling of USD 500 was to apply to each import transaction.

Benin [04], Burkina Faso [04], Mali [04], Niger [03] and Senegal [03]: A statistical fee is levied solely on imports from non-WAEMU and non-ECOWAS countries at 1% *ad valorem*.

Côte d'Ivoire [95]: The statistical tax is levied at the rate of 2.5% on most products.

Madagascar [00]: There is an import statistics tax of 2%.

Mauritania [02]: There is a uniform statistical fee of 3% on the majority of tariff lines.

Suriname [04]: A statistical fee of 0.5% (c.i.f. value) is levied on all imports except those of bauxite companies, which are subject to a statistical fee of 2%.

Togo [99]: There is a 3% statistical tax on all imports (c.i.f. value).

2260: Tax on transport facilities

Benin [04]: Port charges such as docking and handling (XOF 1 000/t), port commission (XOF 1 300/t) and the fee for placing seals (XOF 25 per seal) are calculated on volume.

Chile [03]: An additional airport tax of 2% of the applied duty applies to all imports transported by air (*i.e.* the tax is currently 0.12%). However, goods originating in Canada, Costa Rica, El Salvador and Mexico are exempt from this tax, as provided by their free-trade agreements with Chile.

Israel [99]: Another border charge is the wharfage fee. Until 1995, Israel's port authorities charged importers 1.5% of the c.i.f. cost of imports into Israel for the use of ports, whereas exporters using the same services faced no charges. This implied that importers were subsidising the use of such services by exporters. Since then, the "playing field" has levelled between exporters and importers, as the importer fee has been reduced to 1.1% and exporters are charged a fee of 0.2% on the c.i.f. value of containers.

Paraguay [97]: Port fees and other charges for shipping services differentiate between imports and exports for handling charges. Exports stored in ANNP-owned warehouses benefit from rates, set on an *ad valorem* basis, which are 50% lower than imports; in 1992 the full rates applicable to imports ranged between 0.75% and 3%.

Sri Lanka [04]: Imports are subject to the Ports and Airports Development Levy (PAL) at a rate of 1%.

Togo [99]: The infrastructure protection and maintenance tax on all imports was XOF 2 000/tonne.

United States [04]: The United States maintains an *ad valorem* tax on port use. The Harbor Maintenance Tax (HMT), introduced in 1986, is an *ad valorem* levy of 0.125% collected by the Customs and Border Protection (CBP) (formerly the US Customs Service) on port use. The authorities indicated that the HMT applies to imports, admissions into foreign trade zones, domestic cargo shipped through a port, as well as passengers. The tax has not been collected on exports since 1998, when the US Supreme Court ruled that the portion of the HMT levied on exported cargo violated the Export Clause of the Constitution, which bans taxes on exports, but not user fees.

2270: Taxes and charges for sensitive product categories

Antigua and Barbuda [01]: Imported beverages in glass and plastic containers are subject to an environmental (returnable) tax of XCD 0.25 per container.

Barbados [02]: Sales of certain imported (but not domestic) goods from all countries are subject to an environmental levy for the purpose of defraying the cost of disposing of specific goods. The levy is charged on the c.i.f. value of the goods and rates vary from BBD 1.00 to BBD 150 per item.

Belize [04]: The environmental tax is applied on virtually all imports at the rate of 1%. Domestic products are not subject to the environmental tax.

Cameroon [01]: Live animals, fresh products and salted, dried, smoked, preserved and semi-preserved products are subject to an *ad valorem* or specific veterinary inspection tax.

Dominica [01]: Dominica imposes an environmental surcharge on certain imported goods. A charge of XCD 0.25 per container is levied on non-alcoholic and alcoholic beverages. A charge of XCD 0.12 per gallon is applied on gasoline, and a 5% charge is levied on some domestic appliances, electric heaters and television receivers.

The Gambia [04]: The Department of State for Agriculture carries out sample tests to verify that the imports are free from infestation, before issuing a phytosanitary certificate for exports or a certificate of clearance for imports. Inspection fees depend on the type and quantity imported and the type of analysis to be performed; fees range from GMD 10 to GMD 500 per consignment. Fumigation of infested consignments is charged at GMD 100 per tonne. In addition, an environmental tax of GMD 1 000 is applied on second-hand vehicles.

Grenada [01]: An environmental levy per container is charged on imported water and all types of beverages in plastic and glass bottles, and in other containers. The levy is partly refundable and amounts to XCD 0.50 per plastic or glass container and XCD 0.25 for other containers. An environmental levy of 1% of the c.i.f. value is charged on a range of other goods. An environmental levy is also charged on imported vehicles; new vehicles are charged a levy equivalent to 2% of the c.i.f. value. A levy of 30% of the c.i.f. value is charged on imported vehicles over five years old. In the case of imported used trucks over five years old, the levy is 5% of the c.i.f. value for trucks between 1 and 10 tonnes, 10% for trucks between 11 and 20 tonnes, and 20% for trucks of 21 tonnes and over.

Guyana [03]: Guyana imposes a levy of GYD 10 on every unit of imported non-returnable metal, plastic, glass or cardboard container of any alcoholic or non-alcoholic beverage.

Korea [04]: Korea imposes environmental waste charges on imports of certain products, materials and containers that contain harmful substances and are difficult to recycle. It applies equally to domestic goods. The environmental waste charge on plastics is set at either KRW 3.8 or KRW 7.6 per kg of the plastic or synthetic resin used for domestic goods, and at 0.7% of the imported price for imports.

Macao, China [01]: Imports of species listed in Annexes I, II and III of the Convention on International Trade in Endangered Species of Wild Fauna and Flora (CITES), regardless of country of origin, are subject to a charge of 0.5% on the c.i.f. value in patacas. Live animals and food products of animal origin, edible ice, animal fodder, fruit, mushroom spawn, plants and vegetables are subject to sanitary or phytosanitary inspection upon arrival in Macao, China. Sanitary and phytosanitary inspections are subject to a fee, which varies according to product and municipality.

Mauritius [01]: A permit from the ministry responsible for agriculture is required prior to the importation or exportation of plants and their by-products, animals and animal products. Inspection fees are specific.

Morocco [03]: Veterinary sanitary inspection tax (MAD 0.02 to MAD 20 per unit) or inspection of plants (MAD 0.01 to MAD 0.3/kg).

Norway [00]: Consignments of plants, including fruit and vegetables, are required to be accompanied by a phytosanitary certificate issued by the plant inspection authorities of the exporting country, in accordance with FAO standards, which must specify if disinfection of any kind has taken place in the exporting county. Plant inspection is subject to a fee corresponding to 0.8% of the value of inspected imports.

South Africa [03]: Food products are routinely analysed in specialised laboratories in South Africa to determine their composition, microbiological contamination and pesticide residue levels. Inspection fees range from ZAR 35 per 30 minutes to ZAR 104 per hour or portion thereof; fees payable for testing range from ZAR 12 to ZAR 122 per test or sample.

St Kitts and Nevis [01]: Imposes a deposit levy of XCD 0.30 per container of imported beer, stout, malt, ale and aerated drinks in non-returnable bottles. There is an environmental levy on importation of second hand cars: XCD 2 500 for cars imported less than two years after the date of manufacture; XCD 3 500 for cars imported between two and four years after the date of manufacture; and XCD 5 000 for cars imported four years or more after the date of manufacture.

St Lucia [01]: The 1999/2000 budget introduced an environmental levy on a group of imported goods, expected to yield XCD 7 million in revenue.

St Vincent and the Grenadines [01]: An environmental tax of between XCD 2 000 and XCD 3 000 per car, depending on the size of the engine, is levied on the importation of used vehicles older than five years.

Switzerland and Liechtenstein [00]: For items subject to import licensing, applications for authorisation must be submitted to the Federal Phytosanitary Service. A fee of CHF 5 per application is charged. Imports, transit and exports of animals and animal products are subject to a permit based on veterinary and species protection regulations. A fee of CHF 15 per application is charged. Under the 1983 Federal Law relating to the Protection of the Environment (as amended up to 1997), certain taxes are collected on volatile organic compounds and "extra light" heating oils for environmental protection purposes.

2290: Various other fees and charges

Belize [04]: Imports to commercial free zones are exempt from duties, a social fee of 1.5% must be paid on the value of all imported goods except fuel, for which the fee is 10%.

Burkina Faso [04]: Other taxes are levied on imports of any origin. The toll per tonne imported is composed of the following: XOF 500 in general; XOF 75 for sugar, rice and hydraulic cement; XOF 3 000 for vehicles; and XOF 150 for articles of metal.

Cameroon [01]: Imports of bovine, ovine, caprine, and pork meat are subject to a fixed tax of XAF 100 per 100 kg.

Chile [03]: A dispatch tax of 5% on the customs value applies to merchandise that has been partially exempt from duties. The dispatch tax is not levied on goods originating in countries with which Chile has trade agreements.

Costa Rica [01]: There is a used vehicle transfer tax of 2.5% of the import value.

Dominican Republic [02]: The specific tax on vehicles ranges from 0% to 80%, depending on and applied to the vehicle's c.i.f. value.

El Salvador [03]: Empty sacks and bags of synthetic fibre, produced in or imported into El Salvador, are subject to an 80% tax on the reference price for sacks made of coarse fibre.

Guinea [99]: A 3% flat-rate levy is due on all imports by natural or legal persons not registered for VAT. A registration tax on imports under the Investment Code is levied at the rate of 0.5%. A 1% storage tax is levied on goods placed in a warehouse.

Haiti [03]: The first registration tax applies to imported new or used automobiles, buses, lorries and vans. The rates are 5%, 10%, 15% and 20 % and apply to the customs value; the minimum rate of 5% applies to vehicles valued at less than HTG 35 000 while the maximum rate of 20% applies to vehicles whose value exceeds HTG 75 000. A single rate of 5% is applicable to lorries not exceeding 2 tonnes and minibuses with a capacity not exceeding 24. Lorries weighing over 2 tonnes and minibuses carrying more than 24 people are exempt. A tax called the tourist tax is also levied on the import of used vehicles at a single rate of 10% calculated on the customs value.

India [02]: A special additional duty (SAD) of 4% was introduced on most imports in the 1998/99 budget to tax imports "similarly" to state sales taxes. As the SAD is an across-the-board 4% tariff on most goods, it may not be equivalent to local sales taxes imposed on similar domestically produced goods, some of which may face higher or lower rates of sales tax.

Madagascar [00]: There is an import tax, ranging from zero to 30%. Goods exempt from duties are charged USD 50 for each importation.

Mauritius [01]: A cess is levied on imports of tea at MUR 0.20 per kg, and a 20% fee is collected on the c.i.f. value.

Morocco [03]: A 0.25% para-fiscal import tax applies to imported goods with certain exceptions. The following also apply: a special tax on cement (MAD 50/tonne); a tax on imported wood (12%); proportional duties on tobacco imported by individuals authorised by the Tobacco Authority (65% plus additional taxes depending on the product); and a tax on the marketing of dried beet pulp (MAD 10/quintal net weight).

Pakistan [02]: Regulatory duties "appear" to have been reinstated (for imports of edible oil and oil seeds for crushing). In addition, a capital-value tax is levied on imported motor vehicles.

Suriname [04]: All imports are subject to a consent fee of 1.5%. The fee is assessed on the c.i.f. value of imports.

2290 (Service fees): Fees related to customs procedures

Antigua and Barbuda [01]: A customs service tax of 5% is charged on all imported goods.

Argentina [99]: Pre-shipment inspection (PSI) requirements affect merchandise of an f.o.b. value of USD 3 000 and over. Inspection costs consisting of a commission of 0.8% of the f.o.b. value of inspected goods (minimum USD 250) plus a bonus of 5% on the amount of increased tax collection from import duties and the statistical tax (up to 0.2% of the f.o.b. value of inspected items) are covered by the authorities; an auditing company charges an additional 0.64% of the value of goods included in its sample monitoring.

Australia [02]: Fees for cargo handling, customs clearance and post-clearance compliance activities are set on a cost-recovery basis since 1997.

Bangladesh [00]: A 1% service charge is levied on the value of imported goods.

Benin [04]: Since 2000, a computer fee of XOF 2 000 has been levied for each customs declaration. This applies to all goods imported into Benin and to all goods exported or re-exported.

Bolivia [99]: Private inspection companies charge 1.92% of the f.o.b. value of merchandise. A 0.5% customs warehouse fee is charged on the c.i.f. value of merchandise remaining in warehouses for up to 30 days; thereafter a monthly 2% demurrage fee is charged.

Brazil [00]: There is a fixed administrative commission of USD 50 per transaction. An import declaration, for which there is a USD 5 fee, must be submitted to the customs authorities. Warehousing charges are assessed on the full value of customs duties or on the commercial value of duty-free goods; generally, charges range between 0% and 15% of value.

Burkina Faso [04]: Importers have to pay a contribution to the import inspection programme corresponding to 1% of the f.o.b. value of all imports above a certain threshold. A detailed declaration must either be written or sent by computer (98% of customs transactions); in the latter case, a computer fee of XOF 5 000 is payable.

Burundi [03]: A 6% service tax is levied on imports regardless of origin. Pre-shipment inspection fees for imports worth more than USD 5 000 amount to 1.5% of the customs value of the goods. The inspection firm Société Générale de Surveillance (SGS) charges a minimum fee (flat rate) per inspection of CHF 275; Baltic Control charges USD 105.

Costa Rica [01]: Imports are subject to charges connected with customs formalities, *e.g.* cost of forms, storage and handling.

Côte d'Ivoire [95]: The charge for services rendered by the Ivorian Shippers' Office (0.6%) is levied on imports carried by sea (some 90% of the value of the imports); and the inspection firm SGS charges a 0.75% *ad valorem* fee (f.o.b. value). The SYDAM fee is a payment for a computer service rendered of XOF 1 000 per declaration, invoiced by the shipper to the exporter at XOF 9 750.

Dominica [01]: The government levies a 2% customs service tax on imports. The customs service tax was increased from 1% effective 2000.

Egypt [99]: A service and inspection charge of 1% is charged on the c.i.f. value of all imports. According to the authorities, an additional service charge of 2% or 3% is levied on goods subject to import duties of 5% to 29%, or 30% and above, respectively; the fees are used to improve customs services.

The Gambia [04]: A 1.05% processing fee is applied to all imports.

Ghana [01]: An inspection fee of 1% of the c.i.f. value of imports is levied on behalf of inspection agencies to cover the costs of providing inspection services.

Grenada [01]: Imports are generally subject to a customs service charge at the rate of 5% on the c.i.f. value of imports.

Guinea [99]: Importers are charged for pre-shipment inspection at a minimum sum set at CHF 430 and 1.05% for importation for goods worth more than USD 29 252.

Haiti [03]: Imports are subject to inspection fees which amount to 4% of the c.i.f. value of goods. A storage duty is levied on goods in warehouses before the payment of duties and taxes or before their reshipment. This duty amounts to 2% of the customs value per month of storage.

Hong Kong, China [02]: All trade declarations must be submitted via electronic data interchange (EDI) and the import declaration charge as of 1999 was HKD 11 for electronic declaration.

Kenya [00]: An import declaration fee of 2.75% is collected on the customs value of all imports to Kenya. The Kenya Bureau of Standards (KBS) tests and inspects products to ensure conformity to national standards and issues certificates. The inspection fee is 1% of the c.i.f. value of imports or the sale price of locally produced goods.

Malawi [02]: Malawi requires pre-shipment inspection of all imports with a f.o.b. price of USD 2 000 and above. A pre-shipment inspection fee of 0.85% is levied on the c.i.f. value of inspected imports.

Malaysia [01]: Handling charges at the rate of MYR 0.20 per 100 kg are levied for weighing all dutiable goods for assessment purpose, if such weighing is not conducted by the importers.

Mauritania [02]: A computer fee of MRO 2 000 is imposed on each declaration irrespective of the customs regime.

Mauritius [01]: Inspection and certification fees range from MUR 10-100 per consignment.

Mexico [02]: The customs processing fee (DTA) varies according to the origin and nature of imports. The general DTA is 0.8% of the declared customs value; imports under temporary regimes carry a reduced rate of 0.176%, or under certain conditions a specific amount of MXN 159 per transaction. In principle, definitive importation from preferential partners is exempt from DTA.

Morocco [03]: Administrative fees for verifying the manifest (MAD 0.50 or MAD 0.75/tonne deadweight tonnage, with a maximum of MAD 1 500 or MAD 3 000 respectively; MAD 0.20 to MAD 0.5/tonne if the tonnage of the goods loaded is less than one quarter of the deadweight tonnage). Storage tax (2% to 10% depending on the length of storage on customs premises). There is a fee for use of the computer system (MAD 500 for each summary declaration; MAD 100 for each import declaration; and MAD 6 for each page of status reports or management statements).

Mozambique [01]: Customs charges an administrative charge of USD 50 per bill of entry on products exempted from customs duty.

Nicaragua [99]: As of 1997 Nicaragua has levied a customs services tax of USD 0.50 per tonne and a warehousing fee of USD 2 per tonne per day for merchandise stored for more than 12 days after arrival at the warehouse.

Niger [03]: An import inspection tax amounting to 1% of the customs value is levied on imports subject to the import verification programme.

Nigeria [98]: In 1996, importers were made to pay for pre-shipment inspection (PSI), previously paid by the government, at a rate of 1% of the f.o.b. value to be charged on the Import Duty Report. This fee is payable only on shipments from certain countries where the PSI service has not been phased out.

Norway [00]: Imports of agricultural products are subject to inspection or foodstuff taxes levied at various rates (0.58% to 0.82%). Some products are affected by both the inspection and the foodstuff taxes.

Peru [00]: The pre-shipment inspection fees are negotiated between the company and importer; a maximum fee of 1% of the f.o.b. value of inspected merchandise is set by law. Charges for customs clearance amount to 0.6668% of the UIT (fiscal unit) for imports under the general regime, or half this amount for imports under the simplified regime. Handling fees on international air cargo remain twice as high as those on national air shipments.

The Philippines [99]: Other charges specifically imposed on imports are fees for various forms, processing fees on ordinary claim for refund, registration fees for participation in public auction sales and brokerage fees for licensed customs brokers. Other charges specifically imposed on imports include laboratory fees for services rendered by the Customs Laboratory Unit.

Romania [99]: Imported products are assessed a customs commission of 0.5%.

Solomon Islands [98]: Fees are levied by customs on importers to partially recover the costs of customs services. Hourly attendance and clearance fees, ranging from SBD 22-28 and SBD 60-100, respectively, apply for services provided outside normal working hours. Examination fees of SBD 14-22 per examination also apply. In addition, rent and charges are applied as demurrage on a per cubic metre basis.

Sri Lanka [04]: Imports used solely for processing and re-export are subject to a levy at 0.5%.

St Kitts and Nevis [01]: A 5.0% customs service charge is levied on all imports (c.i.f. value).

St Lucia [01]: A customs service charge of 4% is applied on the c.i.f. value of all imports.

St Vincent and the Grenadines [01]: A customs service charge of 4% is applied on the c.i.f. value of imports.

Thailand [03]: The Customs Department collects fees for customs services; these include fees for documentation, and charges for attendance at Customs House on holidays or after office hours.

Turkey [03]: The format of the Turkish customs declaration has been aligned on the single administrative document (SAD) used in the EU for customs procedures. Form EUR1 is required for imports from non-EU countries with which Turkey has free-trade agreements. The fee is TRL 150 000 for the SAD, and TRL 120 000 for the EUR1.

Uruguay [98]: The *Banco de la República Oriental del Uruguay* (BROU) charges a commission for the services rendered related to the import procedures. A commission of 1.1% is levied on imports of less than USD 10 million, 0.65% on imports between USD 10 million and USD 20 million, and 0.35% on imports that exceed USD 20 million. The Executive may authorise the BROU to increase the commission to 3%. Temporary admission of merchandise to be used in trade shows and for other specific purposes has to be authorised by the Ministry of Economy and Finance. The entry of merchandise to be transformed or elaborated is authorised by the Technological Laboratory of Uruguay (LATU), which also regulates and monitors the entry of merchandise under the regime. The fees charged by LATU for these services are set according to the cost of the services rendered; however, since 1996 this fee has been fixed at 0.6% of the c.i.f. value of the goods admitted under the regime.

Venezuela [02]: Venezuela levies a customs service charge of 1% on the value of all imported merchandise.

Community levies

WAEMU and ECOWAS members: Benin [04], Burkina Faso [04], Mali [04], Niger [03] and Senegal [03]: Goods not originating in the WAEMU are subject to a number of supplementary duties, for example: the community solidarity levy (PCS) of the WAEMU, at a rate of 1%, and the ECOWAS community levy (CL) at a rate of 0.5%. The basis for all these supplementary duties and levies is customs value.

Togo [99] charged a community solidarity levy of 0.5% (imports from outside WAEMU) and a community levy of 0.5% (imports from outside ECOWAS) on c.i.f. value in March 1998. **Niger [03]** had also introduced a special import tax (TCI) on rice of 10% during the period 2000-02. The TCI applies if the customs value is lower than the trigger price (threshold price) set by the WAEMU Commission. It is imposed at a rate of 10% of the value calculated as from the trigger price. For this purpose, the duties and taxes payable apply to the same trigger price (the trigger price is calculated according to the following formula: PD = (0.3*CM + 0.7*CPI) with PD being the trigger price; CM = the global price of the product; and CPI = cost of domestic production of the product).

ECOWAS members: The Gambia [04], Ghana [01] and **Guinea [99]**: An ECOWAS customs levy of 0.5% is applied to imports from non-ECOWAS members.

Annex 4.A5

Non-tariff Barrier Notifications to NAMA on Customs Fees and Charges[38]

Argentina has notified:
- Iron and steel products (generic): Three special duties (special, additional, special additional) apply as well as a basic duty. These considerably raise the applied tariff and even double the amount in certain cases.

Australia has notified:
- Metals, in particular lead and zinc and products thereof: ODCs, surcharges, advance income tax payments, special additional duties, security charges and import licensing requirements.
- Plastics/chemicals: Excessive port handling charges.

Bangladesh has notified:
- Juices/drinks, jam/jelly, pickles, spices and snacks: Attestation fees BDT 13 000 to BDT 14 000.

Bulgaria has notified:
- Generic: Existence of multiple, high-value taxes related to border checkpoint passing.
- Medicines: Additional fees and charges for customs clearance documents. Prolonged check-control procedures and demurrage at the border, even in the case of availability of all necessary certificates: 5-6 days. High storage taxes in the areas under customs control.

China has notified:
- All commodities: Overhead, 0.15% of declared value is levied by customs.

Egypt has notified:
- Several products: Exaggeration in imposing the custom levies and charges for services obtained at ports and airports which are considered a burden on the exported products. High cost of accreditation of commercial invoices. Not accrediting the commercial invoices of Egyptian exports.

India has notified:
- All exports: Imposition of high levels of port fees and taxes significantly add to the cost of exports. Fees for authentication of export documents by the consulates of the importing countries similarly add to cost. The necessity for imposition of the fees and taxes as well as the need to have consular authentication procedures must be linked to the administrative necessity for the same.

Kenya has notified:
- Various imports: Exports accompanied by prior cash deposits.

Korea has notified:
- Automobiles, electric and electronic products: Unduly long time and excessive fees are required in acquiring certification marks.
- Majority of products: Excessive customs use fee and harbour maintenance fee.

Malaysia has notified:
- Food and beverage products: Despite progress in recent years, the participant's import clearance procedures remain slow and cumbersome. User fees remain high and customs processing hours of operation are short.
- All products: Trade documents for exports to a group of Participants/WTO applicants are subject to

endorsement by their respective embassies. The endorsement fees charged are high and vary with different embassies.

- Fluorescents lamps: Massive documentation and high cost of endorsement fee. Certificate of origin needs to be certified by their consulate in Kuala Lumpur and cost MYR 400 to MYR 600.
- Service charge for export receipts: Businessmen have to bear a 20% across-the-board government service charge for all export receipts, which are collected by the banks.
- Brochures and printed materials: Printed materials brought into the territory of this participant for free distribution are subject to import duty of 20% by weight.

Mexico has notified:

- Textiles and clothing: One member imposes a significant number of variable taxes only on imports, thereby affecting access to textile and clothing products.
- Horizontal: One member imposes import duties, which include, *inter alia*, storage, cargo and maritime transport taxes. One member, in addition to the normal tariff (generally 30%), levies an additional special tax of 4% on the import value (which already includes an import tax).

New Zealand has notified:

- Forestry, logs and downstream products: High internal taxes or charges, charges on imports by some ports and state trading bodies, import surcharges, some arbitrary charges.
- Carpets, leather, fish, forestry, manufactured products, metal, raw materials and unspecified other: High internal taxes or charges.

Norway has notified:

- Fish and fish products (salmon): Special additional duty.
- Generic: Customs fees and surcharges, extra taxes, statistical taxes, high fees related to financial transactions, port taxes, inspection taxes, customs fee for shipments, extra customs duty, solidarity fees, storage taxes, transit taxes, price controls, additional taxes and fees. Currency restrictions, exchange restrictions/control, currency licence required for shipment of goods, foreign currency controlled by domestic central bank.

The Philippines has notified:

- Cuttle fish, dried, salted, in brine, smoked: Advance payment requirements n.e.s. The licence issued should be affixed with a stamp indicating "The charge for issuance of permit should be paid before the applicant acquires the import permit".

Singapore has notified:

- Mechanical machinery, equipment and parts, plastics and plastic articles, sound recorders and reproducers: Port, customs or other levies and fees that fluctuate excessively.

Switzerland has notified:

- Textiles: Fiscal stamp.
- Watches: Luxury tax, *ad valorem* fees, anticipated profit tax, various surcharges, statistical taxes.
- Machines: High fees and import customs clearance costs and lengthy customs clearance procedure.

Turkey has notified:

- All products: Passage fees applied to Turkish transporters are higher than the legal amount paid by other transporters. High passage fees, unnecessary controls at various points.

United States has notified:

- Motion pictures: US industry has reported the prevalence of discriminatory box office taxes, sometimes set at a higher rate for foreign films than for domestic films. Discriminatory levies and taxes at other stages in the distribution of filmed entertainment were also reported.
- Express delivery services: US industry reports a variety of NTBs, which include discriminatory customs treatment in the form of unequal fees, taxes, paperwork and inspection requirements.

Annex 4.A6

Provisions in Selected RTAs Concerning Customs Fees and Charges

RTA	Customs duties, taxes, levies or charges which have equivalent effect	Service fees
AFTA	No new ones shall be introduced.*	
ANCERTA	Shall be abolished.**	X
Armenia - Georgia	Are not imposed.*	
Armenia - Kyrgyzstan	Shall not be applied.	
Australia - Papua New Guinea	Prohibited for certain types of articles.	
Australia - Singapore	Shall be abolished.	X
Australia - Thailand	No new ones shall be introduced, existing ones shall be abolished.	X
Bulgaria - Israel	No new ones shall be introduced, existing ones shall be abolished.	
Bulgaria - Macedonia, FYR	No new ones shall be introduced, existing ones shall be abolished.	
CACM	Shall be prohibited.*	X
Canada - Chile	No new ones shall be introduced, existing ones shall be abolished.**	X
Canada - Costa Rica	No new ones shall be introduced, existing ones shall be abolished.**	X
Canada - Israel	No new ones shall be introduced, existing ones shall be abolished.**	X
CARICOM	Shall not be applied.*	X
Chile - Korea	Shall be limited in amount to the approximate cost (specific) of services rendered.	X
CIS	Shall not be applied.*	X
Costa Rica - Panama	Shall be prohibited.*	
EC - Algeria	No new ones shall be introduced, existing ones shall be abolished.**	
EC - Andorra	No new ones shall be introduced, existing ones shall be abolished over time.*	
EC - Bulgaria	No new ones shall be introduced, existing ones shall be abolished.**	
EC - Croatia	No new ones shall be introduced, existing ones shall be abolished.*	
EC - Egypt	Shall be abolished.**	
EC - Faroe Islands	No new ones shall be introduced; existing ones shall be abolished.	
EC - Iceland	No new ones shall be introduced; exiting ones shall be abolished.**	
EC - Israel	Shall be prohibited.	
EC - Jordan	No new ones shall be introduced, existing ones shall be abolished.**	
EC - Lebanon	Shall be abolished.*	
EC - Macedonia, FYR	No new ones shall be introduced, existing ones shall be abolished.**	
EC - Mexico	Existing ones shall be abolished over time.**	X
EC - Morocco	No new ones shall be introduced, existing ones shall be abolished.**	
EC - Norway	No new ones shall be introduced, existing ones shall be progressively abolished.	
EC - PLO	No new ones shall be introduced, existing ones shall be abolished.**	
EC - Romania	No new ones shall be introduced, existing ones shall be abolished.**	
EC - South Africa	Shall be abolished.	
EC - Switzerland	No new ones shall be introduced, existing ones shall be abolished.**	
EC - Syria	Existing ones shall be abolished over time.** Syria has the right to introduce new fees.	
EC - Tunisia	No new ones shall be introduced, existing ones shall be abolished.**	
EC - Turkey	No new ones shall be introduced, existing ones shall be abolished.	
EFTA	Shall not introduce new ones for fiscal reasons.	
EFTA - Bulgaria	No new ones shall be introduced, existing ones shall be abolished.**	
EFTA - Croatia	No new ones shall be introduced, existing ones shall be abolished.*	
EFTA - Israel	No new ones shall be introduced, existing ones shall be abolished.	
EFTA - Jordan	No new ones shall be introduced, existing ones shall be abolished.*	
EFTA - Macedonia, FYR	No new ones will be introduced, existing ones shall be abolished.*	
EFTA - Morocco	No new ones shall be introduced, existing ones shall be abolished.*	
EFTA – PLO	No new ones shall be introduced, existing ones shall be abolished.	

RTA	Customs duties, taxes, levies or charges which have equivalent effect	Service fees
EFTA - Romania	No new one shall be introduced, existing ones shall be abolished.**	
EFTA - Singapore	No new ones shall be introduced, existing ones shall be abolished.*	X
EFTA - Turkey	No new ones shall be introduced, existing ones shall be abolished.**	
Egypt - Jordan	No new ones shall be introduced, and existing ones reduced.	
El Salvador - Panama	Shall not be applied.	
Georgia - Azerbaijan	Are not imposed.*	
Georgia - Turkmenistan	Are not imposed.*	
Iceland - Faroe Islands	No new ones shall be introduced, existing ones shall be abolished.	
Japan - Mexico	Shall be abolished or reduced.*	X
Japan - Singapore	No new ones shall be introduced, existing ones shall be eliminated.	X
Kazakstan - Georgia	Are not imposed with the exception for fees concerning customs processing.	
Kazakstan - Kyrgyzstan	Shall not be applied*	
Mercosur	Shall be eliminated.	X
Mexico - Chile	Shall be prohibited.	
Mexico-Colombia-Venezuela	No new ones shall be introduced, existing ones shall be abolished.**	
Mexico - EFTA	No new ones shall be introduced, existing ones shall be abolished.*	X
Mexico - Israel	Shall eliminate any *ad valorem* customs users fees.	
Moldova - Kyrgyzstan	Shall not be applied.	
NAFTA	No new ones shall be introduced, existing ones shall be progressively abolished.	
New Zealand - Singapore		X
Norway - Faroe Islands	No new ones shall be introduced. existing ones shall be abolished.	
Russia - Georgia	Are not imposed.	
Russia - Kyrgyzstan	Shall not be applied.	
Switzerland - Faroe Islands	Shall be prohibited.	
Turkey - Bosnia & Herzegovina	No new ones shall be introduced, existing ones shall be abolished.**	
Turkey - Bulgaria	No new ones shall be introduced, existing ones shall be abolished.	
Turkey - Israel	No new ones shall be introduced nor shall existing ones be increased.	
Turkey - Macedonia, FYR	No new ones shall be introduced; existing ones shall be abolished.*	
Turkey - Romania	No new ones shall be introduced, existing ones shall be progressively abolished.	
Ukraine - Georgia	Are not imposed.*	
Ukraine - Kyrgyzstan	Shall not be applied.*	
United States - Bahrain	Consular fees and merchandise processing fees shall be abolished.	X
United States - Chile	Consular fees and merchandise processing fees shall be abolished.	X
United States - Israel	May be maintained based on agricultural policy considerations.	
United States - Jordan		
United States - Morocco	Consular fees shall be prohibited. Morocco may apply a parafiscal tax of 0.25%.	
United States - Singapore	No new ones shall be introduced, existing ones shall be progressively abolished.	X
Uzbekistan - Kyrgyzstan	Shall not be applied*	

* With exceptions or potential exceptions.

** With exceptions and some abolished over time.

Notes

1. http://mkaccdb.eu.int/cgi-bin/stb/mkstb.pl.

2. The following discussion does not claim to provide a complete list of the customs fees and charges that are imposed on imports today. The fees and charges were imposed at the time of the publication of the reviews and reports and it has not been possible to verify whether they are still imposed or whether new ones have been added. The years of publication are presented in both tables and annexes.

3. www.unctad.org/Templates/WebFlyer.asp?intItemID=2177&lang=1.

4. Annex 4.A2 attempts to view the UNCTAD TCM coding system of para-tariff measures in a GATT perspective. While the list of GATT Articles in Annex 4.A2 is not exhaustive, it aims to show that the diversity of the classification scheme implies the involvement of several GATT articles, such as II, III, VII and VIII. Sub-category 2300 is covered by GATT Article III, and internal taxes such as general sales taxes and excise taxes are omitted from the analysis, as is 2400 "Decreed customs valuation". Moreover, general sales and excise taxes are not necessarily collected at borders, the primary focus of the analysis. This leaves 2100 "Customs surcharges" and 2200 "Additional taxes and charges". Sub-category 2900 "Para-tariff measures n.e.s." is dealt with on an *ad hoc* basis depending on the nature of the measures found. It is not clear whether sub-category 2260 "Tax on transport facilities" is regulated by GATT Article VIII and it is not discussed in any depth.

5. Article III concerns national treatment on internal taxation and regulation.

6. www.wto.org/english/thewto_e/whatis_e/eol/e/wto02/wto2_46.htm.

7. Some members, notably African countries, never submitted any information concerning their ODCs to the WTO Secretariat.

8. Panel Report, *US – Customs User* Fee, BISD 35S/245, adopted in 1988. See WTO (2002).

9. Panel Report, *Argentina – Measures Affecting Imports of Footwear, Textiles, Apparel and Other Items ("Argentina / Textiles and Apparel")*, WT/DS56/R, adopted in 1998. See WTO (2002).

10. Section III of the TPRs was examined using a broad set of key words, including fee, charge, surcharge, duty, tax, stamp, statistical, import licence, consular, environmental, computer and foreign exchange.

11. The main reason for this adjustment is that many of the charges directed to special funds are directly referred to as surcharges, and the difference between a surcharge and a special charge for a specific fund is that the destination of the revenue for the "fund charge" is specified.

12. Table 4.2 presents the countries according to their respective income group. Four groups are identified according to 2003 gross national income (GNI) per capita as calculated by the World Bank: low-income economies (USD 765 or less); lower-middle-income (USD 766-3 035); upper-middle-income (USD 3 036-9 385); and high-income (USD 9 386 or more).

13. Ghana's Export Development and Investment Fund Act imposed a 0.5% import levy on all non-petroleum products imported in "commercial quantities" (UNCTAD Country Notes).

14. The Market Access Sectoral and Trade Barriers Database also states that Vietnam (2002) had established a Price Stabilisation Fund that acted as a variable surcharge to raise import prices for a set of products (*e.g.* fertilisers, iron, petroleum and steel). Nicaragua was also reported to apply a variable surcharge levied on 780 imported tariff items (UNCTAD Country Notes). In addition, it imposed a 35% levy on goods and services coming from and originating in Colombia and Guatemala.

15. The UNCTAD TRAINS database classified an excise duty in Singapore as a tax on foreign exchange transactions.

16. The UNCTAD TRAINS Web site noted that Nicaragua, Guatemala, Lebanon and Mali imposed various types of stamp taxes.

17. The UNCTAD country notes observed that Myanmar, the Philippines and Singapore had also notified different forms of import licence fees. Singapore imposed a 0.5% surcharge on licence applications for imports from Albania, Laos, Mongolia and Vietnam.

18. UNCTAD's country notes further note that El Salvador imposed specific consular fees and the Market Access Sectoral and Trade Barriers Database indicated that Russia levied consular fees related to imports or exports on a discriminatory basis. The fees were ten times lower in the Commonwealth of Independent States (CIS) and Baltic countries than in others.

19. TRAINS notes that Singapore imposed specific fees linked to the inspection of plants, crops and plant products and the endorsement of phytosanitary certificates.

20. The *ad valorem* rate in Pakistan was 5% in 2002 according to the Market Access Sectoral and Trade Barriers Database.

21. Nicaragua was reported to apply a municipal tax of 1% (UNCTAD Country Notes). In addition, anecdotal evidence indicates that some countries require importers to pay customs fees and charges in hard currency with potential returns paid in local currency. This practice gives rise to "hidden costs" in countries with high inflation or that lack currency convertibility.

22. Senegal imposed service fees of 6-12% on all imports from non-WAEMU countries (UNCTAD Country Notes).

23. The UNCTAD Country Notes stated that Cambodia levied a specific import declaration fee, a pre-shipment inspection fee at 0.8% and specific registration fees for several products. Laos also charged pre-shipment inspection fees with minimum fees and 1% of goods valued above USD 30 000; Myanmar applied a 0.5% landing charge.

24. The US Bureau of Customs and Border Protection collects a merchandise processing fee of 0.21% on the value of imported goods per transaction. The minimum fee is USD 25 and the maximum fee is USD 485. Shipments falling under selected trade agreements like NAFTA are exempted (Ernst & Young, 2003; Market Access Sectoral and Trade Barriers Database).

25. www.sec.ecowas.int/sitecedeao/english/regional-6.htm.

26. ECOWAS includes Benin, Burkina Faso, Cap Verde, Côte d'Ivoire, The Gambia, Ghana, Guinea, Guinea Bissau, Liberia, Mali, Niger, Nigeria, Senegal, Sierra Leone and Togo.

27. WAEMU includes Benin, Burkina Faso, Côte d'Ivoire, Guinea Bissau, Mali, Niger, Senegal and Togo.

28. Several other WAEMU countries imposed TCIs on agricultural goods, including Senegal (UNCTAD country notes).

29. The notifications are available at the WTO Secretariat (TN/MA/W/25, TN/MA/W/25/Add.1, TN/MA/W/25/Add.2, TN/MA/W/46, and TN/MA/W/25/Add.1). The notification format has some inherent weaknesses since the classification scheme is imprecise (as noted above). Many countries have submitted notifications without categorising the notifications in accordance with the WTO's instructions. Others notified the NTBs using the wrong classification. The notifications presented in Annex 4.A5 include those that conformed to the definitions of fees and charges used in this chapter.

30. EDI does not include the computer fees which are imposed in some developing countries.

31. The TPRs are fairly consistent in accounting for para-tariff measures but they do not necessarily manage to account for every specific fee or charge imposed (and which might vary between customs points) on a strict cost-recovery basis (*e.g.* fees related to documentation and registration).

32. Calculations made with data from the COMTRADE database using 2003 as base year indicate that low-income economies accounted for 2.0% of world goods imports; lower-middle-income economies for 13.7%; upper-middle-income economies for 7.9%; and high-income economies for 76.3%.

33. Goods are valued at the importer's border (*i.e.* the c.i.f. value = transaction value plus the cost of transport and insurance to the frontier of the importing country or territory) or at the exporter's border (*i.e.* the f.o.b. value = transaction value including the cost of transport and insurance to bring the merchandise to the frontier of the exporting country or territory). See WTO (2003c).

34. Calculated as $(\Sigma AV + \Sigma AVS)/(\Sigma AV + \Sigma AVS + \Sigma S)$.

35. Algeria was another Arab non-WTO member that imposed a rich variety of high *ad valorem* fees and charges (UNCTAD country notes).

36. Based on the TPRs and the Market Access Sectoral and Trade Barriers Database.

37. The figures in square brackets represent the years for which the latest TPRs were carried out.

38. WTO documents TN/MA/W/25, TN/MA/W/25/Add.1, TN/MA/W/25/Add.2, TN/MA/W/46, and TN/MA/W/46/Add.1 submitted between 28 March 2003 and 4 March 2004.

References

Ernst & Young (2003), "TradeWatch", Customs and International Trade Practice, September.

GATT (1988), "United States Customs User Fee", L/6264 – 35S/245.

GATT (1994), *Guide to GATT Law and Practice: Analytical Index*.

Goode, Walter (2003), *Dictionary of Trade Policy Terms*, Cambridge University Press, 4th edition, Cambridge.

Grimm, Sven (1999), "Institutional Change in the West African Economic and Monetary Union (WAEMU) since 1994", *Afrika Spectrum*, 34 (1), pp. 5-32.

Hoekman, B.M. and M.M. Kostecki (2001), *The Political Economy of the World Trading System: The WTO and Beyond*, 2nd edition, Oxford University Press.

Kostecki, M.M. and M.J. Tymowski (1985), "Customs Duties versus Other Import Charges in the Developing Countries", *Journal of World Trade Law*, Vol. 19, No. 2, pp. 262-286.

OECD (2004), "Analysis of Non-Tariff Measures: The Case of Prohibitions and Quotas", OECD Trade Policy Working Paper No. 6, TD/TC/WP(2004)28/FINAL.

UNCTAD: United Nations Conference on Trade and Development (1994), *Directory of Import Regimes*, UNCTAD: Geneva.

UNCTAD (n.d.), UNCTAD Coding System for Trade Control Measures, http://r0.unctad.org/trains/ (available online 20 May 2004).

World Bank (2004), Country Groups, www.worldbank.org/data/countryclass/classgroups.htm.

WTO: World Trade Organization (1947), "General Agreement on Tariffs and Trade", GATT 1947.

WTO (2002), "Article VIII of the GATT 1994 – Scope and Application", Council for Trade in Goods, G/C/W/391, WTO, Geneva.

WTO (2003a), "Table of Contents of the Inventory of Non-Tariff Measures", TN/MA/S/5/Rev.1, WTO, Geneva.

WTO (2003b), *World Trade Report 2003*, WTO, Geneva.

WTO (2003c), *International Trade Statistics 2003*, WTO, Geneva.

Zarrouk, Jamel (2000), "Para-Tariff Measures in Arab Countries" in *Trade Policy Development in the Middle East and North Africa*, B.M. Hoekman and Kheir-El-Din, eds., World Bank, Washington.

Chapter 5

Export Duties

by

Jun Kazeki

This chapter takes stock of the present situation for export duties (tariffs) under the GATT/WTO. It clarifies the definition of export duties and examines existing disciplines at both multilateral and regional levels. It analyses factual information on products subject to such duties drawn from WTO Trade Policy Reviews (TPRs) and describes key findings. Export duties are mainly imposed for fiscal reasons or as a means to restrict exports of particular products in order to reserve the domestic supply for local industries and are applied mainly by developing countries and least developed countries (LDCs). Aspects of possible rule-making on export duties are also addressed.

Introduction

Since the creation of the Negotiating Group on Market Access for Non-Agricultural Products in the context of the Doha Development Agenda (DDA), countries have communicated their thoughts about the scope and modalities of the future negotiations, *inter alia* in the non-tariff field. Export duties have been mentioned several times, and they are currently one of the topics being discussed in the context of the implementation of China's WTO accession, as well as in the Working Party on the WTO accession of Russia. Export duties are also raised as an export competition issue in negotiations at the special session of the Committee of Agriculture.

Export duties are mainly imposed for fiscal reasons or as a means to restrict exports of particular products in order to reserve the domestic supply for local industries. They resemble import tariffs in that their primary effect is on the price of traded goods. However, this price effect generally also affects trade volumes and thus contributes to the tendency to discuss export duties under the heading of export restrictions. Export duties appear to be used rarely, although there have been cases in a relatively large number of countries, particularly developing countries and least developed countries (LDCs). Items subject to export duties include forestry products, fishery products, mineral and metal products, leather and hide and skin products, and various agricultural products.

WTO disciplines on export duties are not clearly defined. However, a significant number of regional trade agreements (RTAs) contain provisions prohibiting such measures.

Against this background, this chapter takes stock of the present situation. It first clarifies the definition of export duties and then examines existing disciplines on export duties in the WTO. It also looks at current trends in respect of disciplines at the regional level and in the WTO accession process. Finally, it analyses factual information on products subject to such duties obtained from Trade Policy Reviews (TPRs) and offers some conclusions, including comments on the trade and economic implications. This chapter thus aims to be a factual guide and to provide information to support the process of market access negotiations on non-agricultural products as well as negotiations on agriculture. It may also contribute to other aspects of the WTO process.

Definition

In keeping with generally observed usage, this chapter makes no distinction between the terms "export duties" and "export taxes". Both are used here in the sense of (customs) duties on exports. They do not include tax credit on exports, which might be discussed as export subsidies in the context of the Agreement on Subsidies and Countervailing Measures. A variety of similar or complementary terms also exists, such as export tariffs, export fees, export charges and export levies. However, "export duties" or "export taxes" are preferred to the other terms. To justify this choice, Table 5.1 indicates usage in various sources.

Table 5.1. Examples of usage of terminology for export duties

Export duties	Article VIII of GATT (exclusion of application), TPR reports, *GATT Analytical Index*
Customs duties on exportation	Article I of GATT, EU-Mexico FTA
Duties on exportation	Article XI of GATT (exclusion of application), Article VII of GATT (customs valuation)
Export taxes	Indicative List annexed to Decision on Notification Procedures, NAFTA, TPR reports,[1] *GATT Analytical Index, A Case Book of Intenational Economic Relations*
Taxes on exportation	Article XI of GATT (exclusion of application)
Export charges	Article VIII (all charges) of GATT, TPR reports
Customs charges on exportation	Article I of GATT
Charges on exportation	Artrcle XI of GATT (exclusion of application)
Export fees	Article VIII of GATT (all fees)
Export tariffs	*The Dictionary of Trade Policy Terms*
Export levies	APEC Osaka Action Agenda/Individual Action Plans

1. TPR reports use various terms: export taxes, export duties, export charges, etc. The use of export taxes seems to prevail.

The question also arises whether export duties should be considered a tariff or a non-tariff measure. In the Doha Declaration of 2001, paragraph 16 on market access for non-agricultural products states that negotiations aim to reduce, or as appropriate eliminate, tariffs as well as non-tariff barriers. In discussions on the organisation of these negotiations, the definition of the scope of non-tariff barriers to be included has been a primary concern, while for tariffs (particularly reduction of import tariffs), the coverage and issues for discussion have been well defined. Export duties are sometimes equated with tariffs (and even called export tariffs), perhaps reflecting the fact that they are normally levied by customs in a manner similar to import tariffs.[1] For example, the EU-Mexico free trade agreement (FTA) includes "customs duties on exports" in the chapter on customs duties, rather than in the chapter on "non-tariff measures".

However, the GATT and a number of regional trade agreements (RTAs) tend to consider export duties as non-tariff measures. The "Indicative List of Notifiable Measures" annexed to the Decision on Notification Procedures adopted at the conclusion of the Uruguay Round puts "export taxes" in the category of non-tariff measures. The NAFTA also puts "export taxes" in the section "Non-tariff Measures." A well-known case book uses the term "export taxes" in the chapter entitled "Export Controls under the GATT and National Law" (Jackson *et al.*, 1995).

A further question is the relationship between export duties and fees and formalities. Export duties are explicitly excluded from the application of Article VIII(a) of the GATT 1994, which deals with fees and formalities and prohibits fees and other charges rendered in connection with exportation (or importation) that exceed the costs of the service rendered. The article stipulates that fees and other charges shall not represent an indirect protection to domestic products or a taxation of imports or exports for fiscal purposes. It applies to all fees and formalities of whatever character, but it explicitly states that "export duty" is excluded from the scope of application. Therefore, a distinction should be drawn between export duties and fees or charges, even though in specific cases the substance of the measures may be similar.[2]

Current disciplines in the WTO

Schedules

In launching the Uruguay Round in 1986, the Declaration of Punta del Este stated that "negotiations shall aim to reduce or eliminate non-tariff measures, including quantitative restrictions, without prejudice to any action to be taken in fulfilment of the rollback commitments". By the end of the negotiations, 13 agreements in Annex 1A of the Multilateral Agreements on Trade in Goods (including GATT 1994) dealt with certain aspects of non-tariff measures.

Furthermore, the Marrakech Protocol to the General Agreement on Tariffs and Trade 1994, paragraph 6, defined a mechanism for scheduling non-tariff measures: "In case of modification or withdrawal of concessions relating to non-tariff measures as contained in Part III of the schedules, the provisions of Article XXVIII of GATT 1994 ... shall apply." Article II:1(a) of the GATT 1994 assumes that each member will concede measures on a most favoured nation (MFN) basis in an appropriate part of the schedules (in the case of non-tariff measures, Part III). However, since no definition of non-tariff measures (NTMs) was included, this scheduling mechanism has not been used except for rare instances of import licensing and no country has assumed the obligation of scheduling export duties in Part III of its schedule.

With regard to imports, Article II:1(b) of the GATT 1994 prohibits all import duties other than ordinary customs duties on products bound in schedules of concessions. In contrast, while the MFN principle explicitly applies to export duties (Article I of the GATT 1994), and Article VIII of the GATT 1994 is also relevant to export duties, no provisions specifically require a binding obligation for export duties as it does for import duties. (Nevertheless, as noted above, Article II:1(a) does not exclude this possibility.)

Notifications

Even without a definition or an obligation to schedule export duties, the decisions at Marrakech include a notification procedure with an indicative list of notifiable measures, which includes "export taxes".[3] However, a note to this indicative list states that the list does not alter existing notification requirements in the Multilateral Trade Agreements in Annex 1A to the WTO Agreement or, where applicable, the Plurilateral Trade Agreements in Annex 4 of the WTO Agreement. Moreover, it does not specify the procedures for notification of possible measures beyond the existing requirements. Therefore, even though export taxes are notifiable measures, the actual disciplines of notification for export duties depend on the substantive provisions of agreements in Annex 1A or related WTO decisions.

After the Uruguay Round, a 1995 decision by the Council for Trade in Goods (CTG) created procedures for biennial notification of quantitative restrictions.[4] The format of the notification does not include export duties or taxes, and thus seems to reflect current disciplines of Article XI and relevant provisions which exclude export duties from the application. The other 1995 decision by the CTG established so-called reverse notification procedures to allow members to indicate specific non-tariff measures of other members for transparency purposes, but this process has rarely been used.[5] Therefore, no decision specifically entails an obligation to notify export duties.

Other relevant WTO provisions

Article XI of the GATT 1994 deals with the general elimination of quantitative restrictions, but it states that "No prohibitions or restrictions other than duties, taxes or other charges ... shall be instituted or maintained ..." Therefore, export duties are in principle not subject to Article XI, although export duties by their nature may include export restrictions as discussed below. Indeed, questions remain as to whether prohibitively high export duties or combined schemes of export duties, together with other restrictions, would be subject to Article XI. In such cases, at issue would be whether justifications such as Article XI:2(a) (Critical Storage of Foodstuffs[6]), Article XX (General Exceptions[7]) and Article XXI (Security Exceptions) are invoked.[8]

Article X of the GATT 1994 requires a party in essence: *i)* to publish its trade-related laws, regulations, rulings and agreements in a prompt and accessible manner; *ii)* to abstain from enforcing measures of general application prior to their publication; and *iii)* to administer the above-mentioned laws, regulations, rulings and agreements in a uniform, impartial and reasonable manner. The paramount objective of this article is transparency. In the context of disciplines on export duties, it is clear that the general rule of transparency applies (*e.g.* publication of regulations on export duties), but no more than that; there is no obligation of notification.

In sum, it is clear that there are almost no disciplines on export duties except the MFN principle under Article I of the GATT 1994 and the general transparency requirement (*e.g.* publication of regulations) under Article X. In contrast to the strict scheduling of import duties, countries do not schedule and notify export duties.[9] The accession and TPR processes are probably the only practical WTO sources for revealing information about the nature and application of export duties.

Other international organisations/regional and bilateral disciplines

Before analysing the TPRs, it is useful to consider how other forums deal with NTMs, and notably with export duties. UNCTAD has been quite active in tackling non-tariff measures and it has a Coding System of Trade Control Measures. However, the NTM coding system does not specify export duties or export taxes. For the International Monetary Fund (IMF), export duties are relevant as far as the balance of payment provisions of the WTO are concerned, to which the IMF is a party, but export duties themselves have only rarely been discussed in this context. The IMF's support programme with conditionality is a more relevant mechanism for disciplining export duties. Indeed, trade liberalisation to improve economic performance is one of the elements of the IMF support programmes and structural conditions are an effective way to reduce or eliminate NTMs (IMF, 2001). Following the Asian financial crisis, for example, Indonesia's government scheduled the elimination or reduction of export duties based upon its letter of intent to the IMF, in keeping with the requirements of conditionality.

APEC has been keen to deal with NTMs with a view to achieving its Bogor goal of free and open trade and investment in the Asia-Pacific region by 2010 for industrialised economies and 2020 for developing economies. The Osaka Action Agenda for achieving this goal includes a section indicating that APEC economies will achieve free and open trade, among other things, by "progressively reducing non-tariff measures". The individual action plans for each member economy explain the current situation in a format that includes "export levies".[10] In spite of the transparency afforded by the E-IAP (electronic individual action plan) initiative, the quality of information available varies. For example, while Mexico in its 2002 IAP states in the column for export levies that "export taxes on sugar and corn flour have been eliminated", the column is empty for China, Malaysia and Russia. Chinese Taipei declares its fees under GATT Article VIII in this column. The Philippines and Thailand state that they do not impose export levies, although the TPR reports note their export taxes, as mentioned below. It seems that the issue of export levies has received little attention in the APEC process (Table 5.2).

Table 5.2. Export levies in APEC individual action plans in 2002

No export levies	13 economies out of 21
Descriptions of measures	5 economies (Canada,[11], Indonesia, Papua New Guinea, Chinese Taipei, Viet Nam)
The column is empty	3 economies (China, Malaysia, Russia)

Note: There is no definition of export levies in the IAPs. Notification is based upon each economy's interpretation.

In some regional trade agreements, in contrast to the WTO and other forums, disciplines on export duties are quite clear. Many RTAs prohibit export duties. For instance, NAFTA,[12] EU-Mexico, ANZCER (Australia and New Zealand Closer Economic Relations Trade Agreement) and JSEPA (Japan-Singapore Economic Partnership Agreement) all prohibit export duties (Table 5.3). The growing tendency in Europe and the Western Hemisphere to restrict export duties is evident in bilateral contexts as well as in regional trade agreements.[13] According to the evolving draft for the prospective Free Trade Area of the Americas (FTAA), export duties would be prohibited.[14] Meanwhile, the EU and Mexico, on the occasion of their bilateral FTA, declared, in addition to the prohibition on export duties, that "Within the context of the multilateral negotiations, both Parties shall seek to establish disciplines for the elimination of export taxes or restrictions that operate to increase the exports of, or the protection afforded to, domestic industries, such as leather."[15]

Table 5.3. Examples of disciplines on export duties in selected RTA

NAFTA	Prohibited (a Mexican exception exists for basic foods in short supply)
Canada-Chile	Prohibited
Canada-Costa Rica	Prohibited (Costa Rica's exception for bananas)
Mercosur	Prohibited
Caricom	Prohibited
EU	Prohibited
EFTA	Prohibited
EU-Mexico	Prohibited
ANZCER (Australia-NZ)	Prohibited
JSEPA (Japan-Singapore)	Prohibited

WTO accession

Since the creation of WTO, the accession process has provided some disciplines on export duties (Table 5.4). In the case of China, 84 specific items were scheduled, with the commitment to eliminate all export duties except on these items. The schedule indicates the rate of bound export duties.[16] Export duties are also one of the topics in the recent discussion on Russia's accession.[17]

Table 5.4. **Examples of disciplines undertaken at the time of WTO accessions**

Bulgaria (1996)	The representative of Bulgaria stated that his government applied export taxes for the relief of critical shortages of foodstuffs or in cases of critically short supply for domestic industry, and that after accession, any such taxes would be applied in accordance with the provisions of the WTO Agreement. He noted that, at the time, Bulgaria applied the export taxes only to the goods and services listed in Annex 2 to the Report. Bulgaria would, after accession, minimise its use of such taxes and confirmed that any changes in the application of such measures, their level, scope, or justification, would be published in the *State Gazette*. The Working Party took note of these commitments (paragraph 39).
Latvia (1999)	The representative of Latvia confirmed that present export tariff rates related only to the goods listed in Annex 3 "Export Duty Tariffs". All customs tariff changes were published in the official journal of the Republic of Latvia, *Latvijas Vēstnesis*. Latvia would abolish all export duties listed in Annex 3 by 1 January 2000 with the exception of the duty on antiques. The timetable for elimination of export duties would be similar for RTA partners and partners to which MFN treatment was applied as indicated in Annex 3. The Working Party took note of these commitments (paragraph 69).
Estonia (1999)	The representative of Estonia confirmed that after accession to the WTO, Estonia would minimise the use of export taxes and any such taxes applied would be in accordance with the provisions of the WTO Agreement and published in the Official Journal, *Riigi Teataja* (State Gazette). Changes in the application of such measures, their level, scope or justification, would also be published there. The Working Party took note of these commitments (paragraph 80).
Georgia (2000)	The representative of Georgia confirmed that after accession to the WTO, Georgia intended to minimise the use of export taxes and any such taxes applied would be in accordance with the provisions of the WTO Agreement and published in the Official Journal. Changes in the application of such measures, their level, scope or justification, would also be published in the Official Journal. The Working Party took note of these commitments (paragraph 82)
Croatia (2000)	The representative of Croatia confirmed that after accession to the WTO, Croatia would apply export duties only in accordance with the provisions of the WTO Agreement and these would be published in the Official Gazette *Narodne Novine*. Changes in the application of such measures, their level and scope would also be published there. The Working Party took note of this commitment (paragraph 101).
China (2001)	The representative of China confirmed that upon accession, China would ensure that its laws and regulations relating to all fees, charges or taxes levied on imports and exports would be in full conformity with its WTO obligations, including Articles I, III:2 and 4, and XI:1 of the GATT 1994. The Working Party took note of this commitment. (paragraph 170): "China shall eliminate all taxes and charges applied to exports unless specifically provided for in Annex 6 of this Protocol or applied in conformity with the provisions of Article VIII of the GATT 1994" (section 11.3. of the protocol). (Annex 6 indicates 84 products and rate of export duties.[1] (ANNEX 5. A2)

1. See WTO accession technical note Annex 3/Protocol on the Accession of the People's Republic of China (WT/L/432) and Report of the Working Party on the Accession of China (WT/ACC/CHN/49) (www.wto.org).

Findings from TPR reports

The WTO's TPRs contain the most systematic information available on export duties. These reports include a section on measures affecting exports and address export taxes, duties, charges and similar measures to a greater or lesser extent. The coverage of "export taxes" varies, in keeping with the differences in the situation of the country being reviewed. Some reports provide a table specifying rates of export duties, while others only touch very briefly on the topic. However, despite these limitations, certain tendencies can be observed.

Pattern of use

Export duties are applied mainly by developing and least developed countries (LDCs), and regional patterns reflect regional efforts to abolish them. A relatively small number of countries in Europe and the Western Hemisphere impose export duties (Table 5.5).

Table 5.5. Number of countries applying export duties/taxes, by regions and other groupings

	Number of countries reviewed by TPRs	Number of countries imposing export duties
Europe/Middle East	29	2
America	26	9
Asia/Pacific	19	11
Africa	26	17
Total	**100**	**39**
LDCs	15	10
OECD	30	3
Others	55	26

Note: TPR reports from 1995 to 2002 (October). Some countries were reviewed two or three times but are here counted once. The EU is counted as 15.

Among the items most often affected are forestry products, fishery products, mineral and metal products, leather and hide and skin products, and various agricultural products (Table 5.6).

Table 5.6. Main product groups on which export duties/taxes are applied

Selected products	Number of countries applying export duties/taxes (out of 39)
Forestry products	13
Fishery products	12
Mineral products, metals, precious stones	17
Leather, hides and skins	9
Agricultural products (sugar, coffee, etc.)	22

Note: TPR reports do not specify HS number of products subject to export duties. Therefore, this table is based upon the description of the products in the TPRs. Hides and skins are grouped with leather rather than agricultural products. The Table is not exhaustive: Further details can be found in Annex 5.A1.

Key findings

Annex 5.A1 provides a detailed description of export duties contained in each TPR. The main findings can be summarised as follows:

- The two main reasons for imposing export duties are: i) fiscal receipts or revenue; and ii) promotion of downstream processing industries, by providing domestic manufacturing and processing industries with cheap raw materials and other inputs.

- Export duties may be seen as a reliable source of revenue, in particular in the LDCs. These countries at times face difficulty in collecting domestic taxes, while the relative efficiency and ease of implementing tax regulations through customs procedures make this an attractive option for governments.

- When the objective is the promotion of downstream processing industries, export duties are seen as a means of gaining competitive advantage. They are then closely linked to other export-restrictive measures such as minimum export pricing. In certain cases, governments introduce export duties on raw materials to encourage FDI in downstream industries. In others, governments promote FDI in export industries by exempting export duties.

- Some developing countries argue that measures to promote processing industries are justified by the existence of tariff escalation in developed countries.

- Importing countries argue that export taxes in the dominant producing countries discriminate against foreign buyers by raising the level of export prices (*i.e.* world prices) and make it difficult for such buyers to obtain essential raw materials and compete internationally.

- Another reason alleged is environmental protection or preservation of natural resources or products, in particular forestry and fishery products, but the effectiveness of export duties for meeting this objective can be questioned.[18]

- Export duties are also used in rare cases as a measure in bilateral negotiations or undertakings to offset countervailing duties or to avoid imposition of duties to address the exporting country's subsidy on the product.

- Various bilateral and regional agreements show a growing tendency to abolish export duties.[19] Indonesia's economic and structural reform is a notable example.

Economic implications and selected examples

The economic effects of export duties need to be assessed with regard to their objectives as well as their overall effects on the economies of the trading partners concerned. When the purpose of export duties is essentially revenue, it may be asked whether alternative internal taxation measures would not be equally effective and less trade-distorting. In making such an assessment, it should be recognised that developing countries and LDCs may need technical assistance to help modernise and improve the efficiency of their tax systems.

When the objective is primarily the promotion of downstream industries, the economic implications vary according to the extent to which the exporting country can affect the world market price of the taxed product. However, whether it can or not, an export duty will cause the price available to domestic processors to diverge from the price charged to foreign processors. This price difference provides a competitive advantage to domestic downstream processors *vis-à-vis* foreign processors. This may be justified by the "infant industry" argument, *i.e.* to provide an initial incentive for the development of a processing industry. It may also help improve the country's overall terms of trade and benefit its balance of payments. However, the net result may be a welfare loss, in that export duties penalise exporters of the taxed product while benefiting downstream processing industries, which in turn will have a reduced incentive to become truly competitive internationally. In this sense, an export duty acts as an implicit subsidy for domestic processing industries, providing them with an artificial competitive advantage both in the domestic market and in export markets.

The TPRs illustrate the practice of export duties in the absence of WTO disciplines.[20] In the TPRs of Papua New Guinea (1999) and the Solomon Islands (1998), the issue of export duties was addressed in some detail in the case of logs. The reports argue that export taxes on unprocessed logs are seen as a means of promoting greater domestic value added and encouraging downstream processing. This attempts to encourage direct investment in forestry for downstream processing, creating employment and domestic economic growth. The reports point out that export taxes divert export sales to the home market and reduce the domestic price, thus providing an implicit subsidy to processors, while penalising raw material suppliers. The domestic price will be decreased by the equivalent of the export taxes; if the export taxes are prohibitive, the price is reduced much more. However, the reports indicate that these implicit subsidies tend to protect inefficient processing industries and ultimately cause an economically undesirable situation. This is particularly true in Papua New Guinea, where the processing industry is protected by high import tariffs. Moreover, countries with relatively small production of raw materials have no influence over the world price of these products; when export duties are applied, they cannot raise their export prices and pass the tax on to foreign purchasers; domestic suppliers must fully absorb the taxes themselves. Export taxes also reduce the returns from exports of raw materials, which can adversely affect national economic growth.

The 2001 TPR of Ghana pointed out that, as Ghana appears to be a dominant player on the world market for cocoa, its producers are able to pass the burden of export taxes on to foreign purchasers. In this case, export duties are intended to exploit a country's market power by fully cultivating its dominant position. However, these duties may encourage potential competitors to expand their business so as to profit from the higher world price, with the risk of weakening the position of the price-making country over time.

The lack of multilateral disciplines on the use of export duties has effects at another level as well. Traders may be subject to the sudden and arbitrary introduction of such duties or to changes in their levels or modalities of application. The lack of transparency and predictability in this area is particularly noticeable in comparison to other aspects of the overall trade regime that have come under multilateral disciplines, especially as a result of the Uruguay Round.

Some possible orientations for future disciplines

In light of the current patterns of use of export duties and the various trade-distorting effects that may arise, it would be useful to reflect on possible orientations for strengthened multilateral disciplines.

Although the main policy objectives identified in the case of export duties – government revenue and promotion of processing industries – are generally legitimate and defensible, the measures applied to achieve them may in certain cases lead to abuse or may be unnecessarily trade-restrictive. In particular, the lack of transparency and of predictability in the use of export duties could be seen as an element of unfinished business in the WTO.[21]

In contrast, more and more bilateral and regional trade agreements have introduced disciplines to prohibit export duties. In the WTO, recent accessions have provided a multilateral framework for making progress with respect to individual countries, as in the case of China.

One approach might be to introduce general disciplines on export duties as on import tariffs. Another approach would be sectoral.[22] Regardless of the choice made, possible elements for consideration would be scheduling, notifications, product coverage, country coverage, possible special and differentiated treatment (SDT), rates of duties and period of implementation. New rules and disciplines in the GATT are one option, although a separate sectoral agreement or decision might work without substantially amending the current regime, as in the case of the Information Technology Agreement of 1996, where the commitment of each member was ultimately reflected in national schedules under Article II of the GATT 1994. In this case, members would have to describe their commitments in Part III of the schedule (Concessions on non-tariff measures). In any event, in the DDA context, various possibilities might be envisaged under the single undertaking structure.

It should also be noted that the specific effects of export duties may be difficult to separate from the effects of overall export regimes, which may include other measures applied in conjunction with export duties to achieve the same policy objectives. As mentioned in the TPRs, other types of export controls that are sometimes used along with export duties include minimum export pricing, export prohibitions, export licensing, export quotas, export cartels and export processing zones. It therefore appears that effective orientations for strengthened multilateral disciplines would require an overall assessment of export regimes. Chapter 6 offers a more detailed discussion of the different kinds of export restrictions.

Annex 5.A1

Descriptions of Export Duties/Taxes in TPR Reports

Europe/Middle East	
Bahrain (2000)	Bahrain abolished all its export duties on 1 September 1986. However, export fees are charged on ready-made clothes. According to the State Budget for FY 1999, export fees on ready-made clothes amounted to BHD 100 000 (about USD 300 000) (Ministry of Finance and National Economy, 1999).
Cyprus (1997)	Not clear.
Czech Republic (OECD) (2001)	No export taxes.
European Union (15) (2002)	No export duties.
Hungary (OECD) (1998)	No export duties.
Iceland (OECD) (2000)	No export taxes.
Israel (1999)	No export taxes.
Liechtenstein (2000)	No export taxes.
Norway (OECD) . (2000)	Exports of fish and fish products are subject to a levy, which varies according to the species and stage of processing of the product. This levy is used to finance part of the activities of the Norwegian Seafood Export Council which assists in the marketing of fish and fish products, both in Norway and abroad
Poland (OECD) (2000)	No export taxes.
Romania (1999)	No export taxes.
Slovak Republic (OECD) (2001)	No export taxes.
Slovenia (2002)	No export taxes. It had notified to the WTO the list of items on which it levied export taxes, as pre-existing "grey-area" measures covered by Article 11 of the Agreement on Safeguards, along with the timetable for the phase-out of such measures. Taxes of 10% or 15% were levied on exports of wood and wood products, and of 25% on ferrous, aluminium and copper wastes and scrap. According to the authorities, the measures were aimed at addressing shortages in the domestic market. On 1 January 1997, Slovenia abolished the export taxes for all notified products, except for wood in the rough. For this product, the export tax was reduced from 10-15%, and eliminated one year later on 1 January 1998.
Switzerland (OECD) (1996) (2000)	Export taxes on metal and steel scrap were removed in July 1993. The last remaining taxes, affecting some animal products were abolished with effect from 1 January 1995. No export taxes.
Turkey (OECD) (1998)	The number of commodities covered by export taxes has decreased since the previous Trade Policy Review from seven to two (in 1993, hazelnuts, figs, liquorice root, pumice stone, raw leather, rye and untreated olive oil). Currently, export taxes apply to hazelnuts in the form of deductions payable to the Support and Price Stabilisation Fund (SPSF) at the rate of USD 0.04 per kg for unshelled hazelnuts and USD 0.08 per kg for shelled hazelnuts. Exports of semi-processed leather are subject to a tax of USD 0.5 per kg for environmental reasons, but the measure should also be beneficial to the leather goods industries.
Asia/Pacific	
Australia (OECD) (2000)	No export taxes.
Bangladesh (LDC) (2000)	According to the authorities, exports are at present not subject to any taxes. However, the Export Policy Order 1997-2002 stipulates that "Tax at source will be deducted at the rate of 0.25%."
Brunei Darussalam . (2001)	No export taxes. Note however that export prohibitions and restraints apply to several products, often to ensure adequate domestic supplies as in the case of rice and sugar.
Fiji (1997)	For revenue purposes, Fiji imposes modest export taxes on sugar and gold. Sugar and gold exported from Fiji are both subject to a 3% export duty. Custom revenue from export duties in 1995 was FJD 11.4 million, equal to 3.5% of total customs revenue.
Hong Kong, China . (1998)	No export taxes, but it is noted that, like imports, all exports other than certain items are subject to a trade declaration charge. For exports of Hong Kong manufactured clothing and footwear items specified in the Schedule to the Industrial Training Ordinance, there is a clothing training levy of HKD 0.3 in respect of each HKD 1 000 value or part thereof in addition to the declaration charge. The levies are used to finance the Clothing Industry Training Authority, a statutory non-profit-making organisation with a mandate to provide training facilities for persons employed in the clothing industry

India (2002)	Since the previous review, India removed export taxes on all products except hides, skins and leathers, tanned and untanned (not including manufactures of leather). The export duty on these products was raised from 15% to 60% in 2000 as a consequence of India having to adhere to a WTO ruling requiring abolition of quantitative licensing controls on these products. According to the authorities, the export duties are maintained to ensure export of high value-added leather goods. However, insofar as such taxes (or other export restrictions) depress the domestic prices of such leather items, they constitute implicit assistance to domestic downstream processing of such items.
Indonesia (1998)	Prior to the currency crisis, export taxes affected about 80 products, covering a wide range of forest products (notably logs, sawn timber and rattan), agricultural products (crude palm oil and coconut oil), and mining and metal products (ores and concentrates of copper, lead, tin and platinum, aluminium waste, etc.). While most rates were set at 30% *ad valorem*, specific taxes, with prohibitively high *ad valorem* equivalents, were imposed on log, sawn timber, rattan and other wood products. Export taxes are in principle levied on the declared f.o.b. price of the products, and check prices, set bi-annually by the Ministry of Industry and Trade, were used, particularly for wood. Use of check prices, intended to prevent under-invoicing by exporters, added a discretionary element to the system of export taxes, reducing transparency. In its second Letter of Intent, the Government committed itself to phase out "punitive" export taxes; as of 1 February 1998, export taxes on leather, cork, ores and waste aluminium were abolished. For natural resources, the Government has decided to reduce gradually their level and replace them by "resource rent taxes" as appropriate. The aim is to reduce the anti-export bias of the policy while at the same time preventing over-exploitation of the resource and deterioration of the environment. In a first step, in April 1998, the *ad valorem* rates of export taxes on logs, sawn timber, rattan and minerals were reduced to a maximum of 30%, and resource rent tax was imposed. Further reductions of export taxes on these products are scheduled (a reduction to 20% by the end of 1998, to 15% by the end of 1999 and to 10% by the end of 2000). The temporary export ban on palm oil, imposed in the context of domestic shortages, was replaced in March 1998 by an *ad valorem* export tax of 40%.
Japan (OECD) . (2000)	No export taxes
Korea (OECD) (2000)	No export taxes.
Macao, China (2001)	No export taxes.
Malaysia (2001)	Out of 10 368 tariff lines, 710 lines are subject to export duties. They include certain fish, birds' eggs, certain fruit and nuts, palm seeds, gum and resin, rattan, crude and semi-processed palm oil, palm kernel, animal feeds, slags, magnesite, petroleum oil, rough wood, articles of stones, certain precious metals, ferrous wastes and scraps, certain base metals and their waste. Of which nine are specific and 701 are *ad valorem* ranging from 2.5% to 30%. There are certain duty rebates or exemptions for export under certain schemes. Rubber and tin are subject to a research and development cess. The bulk of export duties was derived for from crude petroleum, which accounted for 97% of total export duties collected in 2000. The authorities maintain that promoting the use of locally produced commodities in domestic downstream industries is one of the main objectives of export duties; in the case of forestry products, export duties are also regarded as an effective means of forestry management. Export restrictions may not the best way to tax resource rents and thereby ensure the sustainability of Malaysia's forests; more efficient alternative include, for example, the auctioning of logging quota or the imposition of stumpage fees. According to the authorities, however, export duties are used by the federal government because such alternatives cannot be imposed on the state governments, within whose jurisdiction taxation of natural resources, like forestry, apparently lies, although some states do use tendering for logging quotas, in combination with fixed premium charges, and incorporate stumpage value into royalty calculations.
New Zealand (OECD) (1996)	No export taxes.
Pakistan (1995) (2001)	There has been a considerable reduction in the use of these instruments. At the time of the earlier review, 25 product groups, mainly agricultural items, were subject to *ad valorem* rates ranging from 10% to 45%, specific or compound duties, for revenue reasons or to discourage exports of raw materials. Despite WTO information suggesting the elimination of export duties, including tax on cotton and minimum prices as from July 1999, regulatory duties on exports of crushed bones (10%), uncrushed bones (5%) and raw/wet blue hides and skins (20%) are still in force. Minimum price requirements now affect cotton yarn only and are set by the All Pakistan Textile Association. Such restraints on exports tend to reduce the prices of the goods covered and are therefore an implicit subsidy to domestic users of these goods.
Papua New Guinea (1999)	Export taxes principally for revenue purposes, on the f.o.b. value of a range of products, payable before shipment. Taxes of 5% apply to exports of sea cucumbers, mineral ores and concentrates, and crocodile skins, 15% on rattan (cane), when exported unprocessed; and higher progressive rates on round logs. Exports of sandalwood attract a flat rate tax of 15%. Export taxes were lifted on marine products, except for beche de mer. Progressive export taxes on logs were introduced in 1996. Export taxes, 95% of which come from logs, represented around 10% of government tax revenue. This was expected to fall to 3% for 1998.

Philippines (1999)	Export taxes only for logs. The export of logs is generally banned; however, when exports of logs are permitted they are subject to an export tariff of 20% of their f.o.b. value, which is levied for the purpose of conserving the country's natural resources. In addition to export duties, a premium duty has occasionally been levied on exports of certain wood, mineral, plant and vegetable products, depending on the prevailing prices of export products in the world market. Since the previous Trade Policy Review, there have been minimum export price regulations.
Singapore (2000)	No export taxes.
Solomon Islands (LDC) (1998)	Export taxes principally for revenue purpose. Export tax remissions and exemptions, especially on fish products and until recently on logs, have benefited certain activities and producers and reduced export tax levels to well below scheduled rates (*e.g.* 50% remission of export duties for temporary relief from the slump in log export prices and to help clear stockpiled logs). It was announced in the 1998 budget that export taxes would be raised by 2 percentage points on certain items, including palm oil and copra. Export taxes represent a significant share of government revenue, mainly from taxes levied on fish and log exports. These export taxes are used to capture the resource rents associated with natural resource-based products, and to promote downstream value added. However, like import tariffs, export taxes are distortive and an inefficient means of taxing resource rents; they may also constitute a disincentive to conserve natural resources since they do not discourage over-production. Export taxes compound the anti-export bias inherent in the Solomon Islands' system of import duties. They also encourage inefficient domestic downstream processors by providing access to raw materials, such as fish and round logs, at below world prices and special measures may be required to control tax evasion.
Sri Lanka (1995)	Silica quartz, steel, tea, rubber, coconut, cashew nuts in shell, raw hide and skins, and leather of bovine and equine animals. The duties on exports of silica quartz and certain hides and skins appear not only intended to raise revenue, but also to lower input prices for and thus promote, downstream processing activities. The cess of other items are destined for sector-specific activities.
Thailand (1999)	Export taxes consist of statutory rates stipulated in Part III of the Customs Tariff, and applied rates. The level of applied export taxes continued to be very low over the period under review, and their contribution to government revenue almost negligible. Developments since the last review include for the purpose of preventing countervailing duties in the EU. The persistence of relatively high statutory export taxes, nevertheless, leaves an element of uncertainty in Thailand's trade regime, as statutory export taxes on important products such as rice or rubber could in principle be reintroduced without the need for legislative approval. Products listed in Part III of the Customs Tariff are: rice and glutinous rice (10%); metal scraps of any kind (50%); hides of bovine animals; rubber of genus Hevea in various forms such as sheets or slabs (40%); wood, sawn wood and articles made of wood; raw silk (not thrown), silk yarn and yarn spun from waste silk and noil silk (THB 100 per kg.); fish (pulverised or baked) unfit for human consumption (75%); and goods not elsewhere specified or included in the export tariff listing. The last category has no statutory export duty.
Africa	
Benin (LDC) (1997)	Export duties were suspended in1993 for most products. However, they have not been repealed. The fiscal duty on exports is currently levied only on diamonds, precious stones and metals, cocoa beans and crude oil at a rate of 1.04% of the f.o.b. export value.
Botswana (1998)	Not clear.
Burkina Faso (LDC) (1998)	Export taxes only for livestock products are imposed both on exports and domestic sales. Note that export of raw sheep and goat hides and skins is prohibited in order to encourage their processing locally.
Cameroon (2001)	Export taxes on eight agri-industrial products: cocoa, cotton, medical plants, sugar, and rubber (15%); coffee (25%); palm oil (30%); and bananas were eliminated because they created serious distortions in the structure of incentives and were considered a major constraint on export. Since July 1999 only exports of forestry products have been subject to export taxes. In 2000, export taxes on dressed and semi-dressed timber were also eliminated, but not on logs. An export taxes of 17.5% is levied on the f.o.b. value of log exports and 3% or 4% for transformed forestry products. Taxes on logs remain in place to encourage local processing of wood and hence value added.
Côte d'Ivoire (1995)	Rough timber, plywood, coffee, raw cocoa, cola nuts, and uranium ores and concentrates thereof. The report indicates that duties on coffee and cocoa are for fiscal purposes.
Egypt (1999)	No export taxes.
Gabon (2001)	The Gabonese authorities have provided the WTO Secretariat, for the purposes of its trade policy review, with a list of exit duties applicable to exported products in force in 1999, which have remained in place in 2000 and 2001.These are mainly manganese (3%) and unsquared tropical woods (15%), such as Okoume and ozigo. Squared tropical woods are exempt from exit duty so as to encourage squaring of the wood locally.
Ghana (2001)	Traditional exports are taxed while non-traditional products are exempt. The tax is mainly applied to cocoa, but exports of gold, bauxite, manganese and certain processed timber are also taxed at 6% of the f.o.b. value. An export tax is also levied on aviation jet fuel.

Guinea (LDC) (1999)	A fiscal export duty of 2% of the f.o.b. value is levied on the export of all products, apart from mineral products and derivatives (*e.g.* gold, diamonds and scrap) and coffee. Scrap exports are subject to a specific fiscal export duty of GNF 25 000 per tonne. Exports of handicraft gold and diamonds are subject to a fiscal export duty of 3% of f.o.b. price; duty of 2% on exports by the Central Bank of Non-industrial Gold. The coffee export tax is set at USD 13 per tonne and is designed to finance coffee-promotion activities and the payment of Guinea's contributions to the Inter-African Coffee Organisation. A tax of 2% of the f.o.b. value is likewise levied on the re-export of all products (on leaving Guinea). Taxes are also collected by the Central Bank on exports of bauxite and alumina and paid into a special account as an advance payment on the various taxes payable by the Guinea Bauxite and Alumina Company (CBG) and FRIGUIA (which produces alumina). These advance payments are from USD 8 to 9 per tonne of bauxite (they vary according to the world price for this product) and amount to USD 1.75 per tonne of alumina. The tax (advance payment) on alumina is actually collected at the rate of USD 0.5 per tonne of the bauxite consumed in producing it.
Kenya . (2000)	Kenya levies an export tax on timber and on fish. The tax rate on fish is 0.5%. The WTO Secretariat has not been informed of the rate on timber. Other export duties and taxes collected on certain goods, including agricultural and mineral products, were abolished in June 1994. According to the authorities, Kenya has no other export duties
Lesotho (LDC) (1998)	Export taxes on rough, unpolished diamonds.
Madagascar (LDC) (2001)	Effective 1 May 1997, Madagascar eliminated export duties and taxes on all except wood products. For raw logs (raw timber and hardwoods), there is a 4% fee on the f.o.b. value; the fee for processed wood products is 1.5% of the f.o.b. value. During the period immediately prior to 1 May 1997, only vanilla was subject to export duties and taxes. Vanilla was subject to the following export duties and taxes: 1994/95 – 35% *ad valorem* tax; 1995 – specific tax of MGA 85 000/kg. net; 1996 – specific tax of MGA 85 000/kg., modified by a 25% *ad valorem* tax.
Mali (LDC) (1998)	Export taxes only of 3% on gold and a specific duty on fish. These taxes are also levied on domestic sales of these products. Export duties and taxes were abolished on most products in 1991. After devaluation, the export tax on livestock products was abolished in order not to compromise opportunities for development and market access of these products in the sub-region.
Malawi (LDC) (2002)	Dutiable products are tobacco, tea and sugar. However, since April 1998 the rate of export tax has been zero. Temporary export duties were previously applied for revenue reasons to tobacco and sugar from April 1995, initially at a rate of 10%, but reduced to 8% from April 1996 and to 4% from April 1997, when coffee was also included.
Mauritania (LDC) (2002)	Export taxes only for pelagic fisheries products. Export taxes on products other than fisheries products existed on paper but were not applied in practice and were officially abolished in 2000. They applied to various products such as live animals, meat and edible meat offal, certain dairy products, gum arabic, salt, mineral ores, slag and ash, hides and skins.
Mauritius . (2001)	No export taxes
Morocco (1996)	At present, hydrocarbons are subject to 5% export duty and crude phosphate is subject to a specific prospecting tax of MAD 34 per tonne exported.
Mozambique (LDC) (2001)	No export taxes except on cashews for which the rate was 18% as of 31 July 2000. The raw cashews surcharge resulted from intense domestic pressure from the cashew processing industry.
Namibia (1998)	No export taxes.
Nigeria (1998)	The authorities indicated that an administrative levy of USD 5 per tonne is applied to exports of cocoa, and USD 3 per tonne of other raw material exports.
South Africa (1998)	Export taxes on unpolished diamonds.
Swaziland (1998)	Not clear.
Tanzania (LDC) (2000)	In 1996, Tanzania reinstated an export tax on non-traditional products and minerals at a rate of 2%, for revenue purposes and enhancement. However, as a result of further liberalisation of the trade sector, the Tanzanian government no longer imposes any export duties or taxes. Voluntary crop boards such as the Cotton Board and the Cashew Nuts Development Fund levy a fee of 1-2% on their members' exports to finance research, extension services and training.
Togo (LDC) (1999)	No export taxes. The export tax on phosphates, of XOF 1 000 per tonne, has been abolished and replaced by the mining royalty fixed and collected by the Directorate of Mines. Taxes on coffee, cocoa and cotton formerly existed but were never applied.
Uganda (LDC) (2001)	Export taxes only for coffee, 1% cess collected by the Uganda Development Authority on coffee exports.
Zambia (LDC) (2002)	No export taxes.

Americas

Argentina (1999)	In the past, export taxes affected a wide range of products, mostly unprocessed agricultural products, mainly to ensure the supply of raw materials to domestic processing industries; the authorities also indicated that such taxes were a response to tariff escalation in export markets. These were also an important source of fiscal revenue. At present, export taxes apply only to raw materials of cattle, including raw hides and skins, at rates of 5% to Mercosur and 10% to third country markets for 1998, as well as unprocessed oilseeds at a rate of 3.5%.
Antigua and Barbuda (2001)	Export taxes on lobsters and fish. Total revenue collected is small and has been declining.

Barbados (2002)	No export taxes.
Bolivia (1999)	No export taxes. Note that the exportation of national cultural treasures, narcotics, dangerous substances, and goods and products pertaining to national security is prohibited. In addition, export prohibitions on unprocessed forestry products are being introduced.
Brazil (2000)	All exports are subject to a tax of 30% which can be decreased or increased up to 150% if the executive deems it necessary. Exports may be exempt from this tax according to their destination. The authorities noted that these taxes are usually not applied.
Canada (OECD) (1998)(2000)	No export taxes. The Export and Import Permit Act governs the use of export controls, including the imposition of export taxes. However, all of Canada's free trade agreements, including NAFTA, prohibit participating countries from maintaining or introducing any tax, duty or charge on exports to another participating country's territory, unless the same levy is also collected on the product in the domestic market.
Chile (1997)	No export taxes.
Colombia (1996)	Export taxes levied on coffee, crude oil, gas, coal and ferro-nickel.
Costa Rica (2001)	The revenue from exports is relatively large and equivalent to 1% of total revenue. From 1995 to 1999, Costa Rica levied taxes on exports of coffee, meat and bananas. On 31 December 1999, the taxes on meat and coffee were abolished. At the end of 2000, only bananas were subject to export taxes. In 1999, the *ad valorem* equivalent of the taxes on banana exports represented 2.8% of their f.o.b. value. Part of the revenue from these taxes was returned to the banana producers through the Banana Producers' Price Compensation Fund.
Dominica (2001)	No export taxes.
Dominican Republic (2002)	For environmental reasons Decree No. 11-01 of 11 November 2001 established export taxes for live fish, molluscs and crustaceans. The tax is DOP 0.03 per kg for fish and 5% *ad valorem* for molluscs and crustaceans. Furthermore, under Art. 119 of the Mining Law, mineral substances in their natural state or in the form of metalliferous concentrates which are destined for export, are subject to a specific tax of 5% f.o.b. According to the authorities no other export taxes are applied.
El Salvador (1996)	No export taxes. Export taxes on sugar and shrimp were abolished in 1989, and on coffee in 1992.
Guatemala . (2002)	Export taxes only for coffee. 1% for f.o.b. value of exports, part of which is paid to municipalities. The banana export taxes expired in 2000
Grenada (2001)	No export taxes.
Jamaica (1998)	No export taxes.
Mexico (OECD) (2002)	In general, Mexico does not apply export taxes, except for some cases like sub-products of endangered species (particularly turtles) and certain plants and human organs (see Official Gazette, 18 January 2002).
Nicaragua (1999)	Not clear: Export prohibitions have affected timber of two species (cedar and mahogany) as from 1997, lobsters in reproductive phase, and estuary shrimps in larval stage, as from 1991; these measures are to protect the environment and natural resources.
Paraguay (1997)	No export taxes.
Peru (2000)	No export taxes. For statistical purposes only, a notional 0% tax is applied.
St. Kitts and Nevis (2001)	Export taxes are applied on live animals, lobster and cotton.
St. Lucia (2001)	No export taxes. Exports of bananas are subject, in principle, to a 5% customs duty, in accordance with the Fourth Schedule to the Customs Duties Act No. 23 of 1990. The authorities noted, however, that this export tax is not applied. St. Lucia applies no other taxes or levies on exports.
St. Vincent and the Grenadines (2001)	No export taxes.
Trinidad and Tobago (1998)	No export taxes.
United States (OECD) (2001)	No export taxes.
Uruguay (1998)	Exports of dry, salted and pickled hides are subject to a 5% tax. The purpose of this tax is to ensure the supply of leather for the domestic leather industry, while promoting higher value-added activities. Other agricultural goods are also subject to taxes and/or fees used to finance bodies such as the Uruguayan Wool Secretariat and the National Meat Institute. Exports of bales of wool are subject to a 1.6% tax on their f.o.b. value; processed wool is subject to USD 0.03 per exported kilogramme and exports of wool clothing and apparel are also subject to USD 0.03 per kg of wool contained in the item. Exports of meat are subject to a 0.6% tax on the f.o.b. value. The domestic tax on transactions involving agricultural goods (IMEBA) is levied on some export items, *i.e.* exports are not excluded from the payment of the tax. The rate varies according the product but in each case a maximum rate is stipulated. The IMEBA is levied on the f.o.b. price of the export. Export taxes for live animals (bovine, ovine and equine), boned beef and grease were eliminated in 1993-94
Venezuela (1996)	Not clear.

Note: Descriptions are drawn from TPR reports, but in some cases have been abbreviated or changed as appropriate to meet the analytical objective of this paper. For further details, see the TPR reports.

Annex 5.A2

China's Accession Schedule: Products Subject to Export Duty

No.	HS No.	Description of products	Export duty rate (%)
1	03019210	Live eels fry	20.0
2	05061000	Ossein and bones treated with acid	40.0
3	05069010	Powder and waste of bones	40.0
4	05069090	Bones and horn cores, unworked, defatted, simply prepared (but not cut to shape), treated with acid or degelatinised, excl. Ossein and bones treated with acid	40.0
5	26070000	Lead ores & concentrates	30.0
6	26080000	Zinc ores & concentrates	30.0
7	26090000	Tin ores & concentrates	50.0
8	26110000	Tungsten ores & concentrates	20.0
9	26159000	Niobium, tantalum & vanadium ores & concentrates	30.0
10	26171010	Crude antimony	20.0
11	28047010	Yellow phosphorus (white phosphorus)	20.0
12	28047090	Phosphorus, nes	20.0
13	28269000	Fluorosilicates and fluoroaluminates and complex fluorine salts, nes	30.0
14	29022000	Benzene	40.0
15	41031010	Slabs of goats, fresh, or salted, dried, limed, pickled or otherwise preserved, but not tanned, parchment-dressed or further prepared, whether or not dehaired or split	20.0
16	72011000	Non-alloy pig iron containing by weight <0.5% of phosphorus in pigs, blocks or other primary forms	20.0
17	72012000	Non-alloy pig iron containing by weight >0.5% of phosphorus in pigs, blocks or other primary forms	20.0
18	72015000	Alloy pig iron and spiegeleisen, in pigs, blocks or other primary forms	20.0
19	72021100	Ferro-manganese, containing by weight more than 2% of carbon	20.0
20	72021900	Ferro-manganese, nes	20.0
21	72022100	Ferro-silicon, containing by weight more than 55% of silicon	25.0
22	72022900	Ferro-silicon, nes	25.0
23	72023000	Ferro-silico-manganese	20.0
24	72024100	Ferro-chromium containing by weight more than 4% of carbon	40.0
25	72024900	Ferro-chromium, nes	40.0
26	72041000	Waste & scrap, of cast iron	40.0
27	72042100	Waste & scrap, of stainless steel	40.0
28	72042900	Waste & scrap of alloy steel, other than stainless steel	40.0
29	72043000	Waste & scrap, of tinned iron or steel	40.0
30	72044100	Ferrous waste & scrap, nes, from turnings, shavings, chips, milling waste, sawdust, filings, trimmings and stampings, whether or not in bundles	40.0
31	72044900	Ferrous waste & scrap of iron or steel, nes	40.0
32	72045000	Remelting scrap ingots of iron or steel	40.0
33	74020000	Copper unrefined; copper anodes for electrolytic refining	30.0
34	74031100	Cathodes & sections of cathodes, of refined copper, unwrought	30.0
35	74031200	Wire bars, of refined copper, unwrought	30.0
36	74031300	Billets, of refined copper, unwrought	30.0
37	74031900	Refined copper, unwrought, nes	30.0
38	74032100	Copper-zinc base alloys (brass), unwrought	30.0
39	74032200	Copper-tin base alloys (bronze), unwrought	30.0
40	74032300	Copper - nickel base alloys (cupronickel) or copper-nickel-zinc base alloys (silver), unwrought	30.0
41	74032900	Copper alloys, unwrought (other than master alloys of heading, 74.05)	30.0
42	74040000	Waste &scrap, of copper or copper alloys	30.0
43	74071000	Bars, rods & profiles of refined copper	30.0
44	74072100	Bars, rods & profiles, of copper-zinc base alloys	30.0
45	74072200	Bars, rods & profiles, of copper - nickel base alloys or copper-nickel-zinc base alloys	30.0

No.	HS No.	Description of products	Export duty rate (%)
46	74072900	Bars, rods & profiles, of copper alloy nes	30.0
47	74081100	Wire of refined copper, of which the maximum cross-sectional dimension >6 mm	30.0
48	74081900	Wire of refined copper, of which the maximum cross-sectional dimension ≤6 mm	30.0
49	74082100	Wire of copper-zinc base alloys	30.0
50	74082200	Wire of copper-nickel base alloys or copper-nickel-zinc base alloy	30.0
51	74082900	Wire of copper alloy nes	30.0
52	74091100	Plate, sheet & strip, thickness >0.15 mm, of refined copper, in coil	30.0
53	74091900	Plate, sheet & strip, thickness >0.15 mm, of refined copper, not in coil	30.0
54	74092100	Plate, sheet & strip, thickness >0.15 mm, of copper-zinc base alloys, in coil	30.0
55	74092900	Plate, sheet & strip, thickness >0.15 mm, of copper-zinc base alloys, not in coil	30.0
56	74093100	Plate, sheet & strip, thickness >0.15 mm, of copper-tin base alloys, in coil	30.0
57	74093900	Plate, sheet & strip, thickness >0.15 mm, of copper-tin base alloys, not in coil	30.0
58	74094000	Plate, sheet & strip, thickness >0.15 mm, of copper – nickel base alloys or copper-nickel-zinc base alloy	30.0
59	74099000	Plate, sheet & strip, thickness >0.15 mm, of copper alloy nes	30.0
60	75021000	Unwrought nickel, not alloyed	40.0
61	75022000	Unwrought nickel alloys	40.0
62	75089010	Electroplating anodes of nickel	40.0
63	76011000	Unwrought aluminium, not alloyed	30.0
64	76012000	Unwrought aluminium alloys	30.0
65	76020000	Aluminium waste & scrap	30.0
66	76041000	Bars, rods & profiles of aluminium, not alloyed	20.0
67	76042100	Hollow profiles of aluminium alloys	20.0
68	76042900	Bars, rods & profiles (excl. hollow profiles), of aluminium alloys	20.0
69	76051100	Wire of aluminium ,not alloyed, with the maximum cross-sectional dimension >7 mm	20.0
70	76051900	Wire of aluminium, not alloyed, with the maximum cross-sectional dimension ≤7 mm	20.0
71	76052100	Wire of aluminium alloys, with the maximum cross sectional dimension >7 mm	20.0
72	76052900	Wire of aluminium alloys, with the maximum cross sectional dimension ≤7 mm	20.0
73	76061120	Plates & sheets & strip, rectangular (incl. square), of aluminium, not alloyed, 0.30 mm ≤ thickness ≤0.36 mm	20.0
74	76061190	Plates & sheets & strip, rectangular (incl. square), of aluminium, not alloyed, 0.30 mm > thickness >0.2 mm	20.0
75	76061220	Plates & sheets & strip, rectangular (incl. square), of aluminium alloys, 0.2 mm < thickness <0.28 mm	20.0
76	76061230	Plates & sheets & strip, rectangular (incl. square), of aluminium alloys, 0.28 mm ≤ thickness ≤ 0.35 mm	20.0
77	76061240	Plates & sheets & strip, rectangular (incl. square), of aluminium alloys, 0.35 mm < thickness	20.0
78	76069100	Plates & sheets & strip, of aluminium, not alloyed, thickness >0.2 mm, n.e.s.	20.0
79	76069200	Plates & sheets & strip, of aluminium alloys, thickness >0.2 mm, nes	20.0
80	79011100	Unwrought zinc, not alloyed, containing by weight ≥ 99.99% of zinc	20.0
81	79011200	Unwrought zinc, not alloyed, containing by weight < 99.99% of zinc	20.0
82	79012000	Unwrought zinc alloys	20.0
83	81100020	Antimony unwrought	20.0
84	81100030	Antimony waste and scrap; Antimony powders	20.0

Note: China confirmed that the tariff levels included in this Annex are maximum levels which will not be exceeded. China confirmed furthermore that it would not increase the presently applied rates, except under exceptional circumstances. If such circumstances occurred, China would consult with affected members prior to increasing applied tariffs with a view to finding a mutually acceptable solution.

Notes

1. *The Dictionary of Trade Policy Terms* defines "export tariffs" as "a levy on goods or commodities at the time they leave the national customs territory" (Goode, 1998).

2. It may also be noted that the term "export levies" is used, for example, in APEC's Individual Action Plans (IAPs), but no definition is given and notifications of export levies under IAPs are considered too diverse to determine their nature (see below). While the distinction between export tax or duty and export fee, charge or levy seems to be easier, the difference between tax and duty is not recognised under the current regime. *The Black Law Dictionary* states that "customs duties" are "taxes on the importation and exportation of commodities, merchandise and other goods" and include "export taxes as well". The *GATT Analytical Index* also seems to use both terms with the same meaning. In the context of analysis of the national treatment of internal taxation, the word "tax" seems to be preferred, and in the context of customs-related matters, "duty" is used, but in any event, export duties and export taxes have the same substance and meaning in the current trade regimes. On this basis, and for analytical purposes, this chapter gives the term export duties the same meaning as export taxes.

3. Notifiable measures: Tariffs (including range and scope of bindings, GSP (general system of preferences) provisions, rates applied to members of free-trade areas/customs unions, other preferences); Tariff quotas and surcharges; Quantitative restrictions, including voluntary export restraints and orderly marketing arrangements affecting imports; Other non-tariff measures such as licensing and mixing requirements; variable levies; Custom valuation; Rules of origin; Government procurement; Technical barriers; Safeguard actions; Anti-dumping actions; Countervailing actions; Export taxes; Export subsidies, tax exemptions and concessionary export financing; Free trade zones, including in-bond manufacturing; Export restrictions, including voluntary export restraints and orderly marketing arrangements; Other government assistance, including subsidies, tax exemptions; Role of state-trading enterprise; Foreign exchange controls related to imports and exports; Government-mandated countertrade; Any other measure covered by the Multilateral Trade Agreements in Annex 1A to the WTO Agreement. (Ministerial Decision on Notification Procedures adopted by the Trade Negotiating Committee on 15 December 1993)

4. G/L/59: "Members shall make complete notification of the quantitative restrictions which they maintain by 31 January 1996 and at two-yearly intervals thereafter…".

5. G/L/60, "Decision on Reverse Notification of Non-Tariff Measures". This decision terminated the old inventory of Non-tariff Measures created in 1968 (which also included export taxes as one of the measures) and launched the new inventory for use by members, who have rarely used it. WTO, "Table of Contents of the Inventory of Non-tariff Measures", TN/MA/S/5.

6. Article 12 of the Agreement on Agriculture (Disciplines on Export Prohibitions and Restrictions) stipulates when this exception is to be applied. So-called food security issues are relevant to this argument.

7. For example, (g) relating to the conservation of exhaustible natural resources if such measures are made effective in conjunction with restrictions on domestic production or consumption; (i) involving restrictions on exports of domestic materials necessary to ensure essential quantities of such materials to a domestic processing industry during periods when the domestic price of such materials is held below the world price as part of a governmental stabilisation plan; *Provided* that such restrictions shall not operate to increase the exports of or the protection

afforded to such domestic industry, and shall not depart from the provisions of this Agreement relating to non-discrimination; (j) essential to the acquisition or distribution of products in general or local short supply; *Provided* that any such measures shall be consistent with the principle that all contracting parties are entitled to an equitable share of the international supply of such products, and that any such measures that are inconsistent with the other provisions of the Agreement shall be discontinued as soon as the conditions giving rise to them have ceased to exist …".

8. With regard to the applicability of the Agreement on Subsidies and Countervailing Measures, the issue is, among other things, whether the measure is a "subsidy" as defined by the ASCM Article 1. It is argued that export duties on raw materials are *de facto* subsidies benefiting the domestic processing industry because they enable the industry to obtain low-cost raw materials. A subsidy under Article 1 of the ASCM agreements only exists if: *i)* a financial contribution is provided *and ii)* the contribution is made by a government or public body *and iii)* that contribution confers a benefit. It seems that export duties *per se* have not so far been challenged under the ASCM/WTO, but in any event, interpretation is beyond the scope of this chapter. Furthermore, in the case of the introduction of drastic export duties, the concept of non-violation, nullification and impairment of Article XXIII of the GATT 1994 may arguably provide a basis for challenging measures that fundamentally undermine other concessions that have been made.

9. One exception is the notification by Slovenia on export taxes as the pre-existing measures subject to elimination under Article 11.1 of the Agreement on Safeguards (G/L/338), the so called "grey measures" subject to elimination. Slovenia eliminated special export taxes on certain items such as wood, non-ferrous metals in 1997 and 1998.

10. The individual action plans for each APEC economy can be found at www.apec-iap.org/.

11. Canada has declared: "As part of a comprehensive strategy to improve the health of Canadians by reducing tobacco consumption, Canada introduced a tobacco tax structure in April 2001 to reduce the incentive to smuggle Canadian-produced tobacco products back into Canada from export markets, the main source of contraband in the past. The main element of this tax structure is an export tax on Canadian tobacco products. This measure is fully compliant with Canada's WTO commitments."

12. Article 314 of NAFTA imposes a prohibition on export taxes, subject to a Mexican exception for basic foods set out in Annex 314. Under the GATT, export restrictions may be imposed in situations of short supply, for the conservation of natural resources where domestic production or consumption is constrained, or in conjunction with domestic price stabilisation programmes.

13. One historical example is leather in Argentina. A dispute regarding Argentina's export restrictions on leather began with the US contention that the measures were trade-distorting and resulted in the introduction of export duties as an alternative measure in 1979. However, because the export duties had an effect similar to the export restriction, the United States and the EU raised the issue again in the 1990s. They argued that export-restrictive measures, including export duties, made it difficult for foreign processors to obtain sources of raw bovine hides and gave an advantage to Argentina's domestic processors.

14. For example, the United States has signalled interest in export duties by describing its position on FTAA negotiation, which is to "eliminate discriminatory export taxes" (www.ustr.gov/). The Organization of American States (OAS) also provides relevant information (www.sice.oas.org/).

15. http://europa.eu.int/, Joint Declaration VI No. 4104. In another sectoral example, in the context of the steel agreement under the Agreement on Partnership and Co-operation between the EC and the Russian Federation (PCA), export duties on ferrous waste and scrap are

prohibited. In response to Russia's introduction of export taxes on ferrous scrap in breach of the agreement, the EC was to take countermeasures (http://europa.eu.int/).

16. The EC has made inquiry with China concerning its implementation of this commitment in the China's Transitional Review Mechanism (G/MA/W/33).

17. In the accession process of Russia, export duties on minerals, petrochemicals, natural gas, raw hides and skins, ferrous and non-ferrous metals and scraps, etc. are being discussed. WTO Members argue that in the case of dominant supplier in Russia, third country buyers would suffer from increased cost because of the high price of the product and the insufficient supply of the goods. They point out that the loss of relative competitiveness in the global market for downstream products vis-à-vis Russian products should be taken into account.

18. In Indonesia's 1998 TPR, this argument is made with respect to logs. In response, the report points out that lowering domestic log prices by applying export taxes encourages processors to expand production but reduces the financial incentives for them to adopt efficient, less wasteful technology and processing practices and diminishes the incentives for owners of natural resources to engage in conservation practices. Therefore, export taxes risk reducing incentives both for owners and processors to conserve and use natural resources efficiently.

19. A comparison of TPRs in 1989-94 and in 1995-98 suggests that export taxation increased slightly in countries for which information is available in both periods (Michalopoulos, 1999). However, recent TPRs indicate that quite a number of the countries examined have eliminated export duties, reflecting regional efforts in this regard.

20. In addition to the cases discussed below, the 2002 TPR of India raised the issue of India's export duties of 60% on hides, skins and leathers, which might artificially inflate world prices of these products and distort international competition. India stated that "India has lifted all export restrictions on exports of hides, skins and leathers. There is no tax on export of finished leather. However raw hides and skins and semi-finished leather are taxed at varying rates for export purposes. These taxes are WTO compatible." However the report points out that "insofar as such taxes (or other restrictions) depress the domestic prices of such leather items, they constitute implicit assistance to domestic downstream processing of such items."

21. In the Negotiating Group on Market Access, the EC, the United States, New Zealand, Japan, Korea, Norway, Singapore, Canada and India had tabled communications by the end of October 2002. With respect to NTBs, in September 2002 the Negotiating Group agreed with the Chairman's proposal that he write to participants requesting them to start notifying, within a specified time frame, NTBs which their economic operators were encountering when exporting to various markets (TN/MA/4). On export restrictions, and in particular export duties, the EC has stated that "a bold initiative on tariffs will only maximise market openness if non-tariffs barriers are tackled up-front through approaches that allow also for discussion of specific non-tariff measures on a case-by-case basis and – as necessary – of horizontal rules minimising their negative effects and fostering transparency, as we shall indicate in our forthcoming submission on this particular issue. A level playing field does, furthermore, require the removal of export restrictions, and in particular export duties, which are the flip-side to tariff escalation." The EC also proposed that "all export restrictions on raw materials [be] removed"(TN/MA/W/11). India, on the other hand, has stated that it "attaches great significance to the removal of specific non-tariff barriers on tariff lines of particular interest of developing countries. By their nature, NTBs do not lend themselves to securing commitments that can be easily defined or monitored. To the extent there can be some creative ideas in this regard it would be useful. Compilation of comprehensive data with regard to NTBs is an essential requirement for furthering discussion in this area. India, however, has cautioned against the inclusion of legitimate instruments that developing countries may use under the various WTO agreements for development of their industries. For instance, export tariffs or levies are generally used to generate resources to develop an industry by diversification in the product profile and development of value added products for exports. Therefore, the

suggestion that 'export duties' be negotiated is perceived to be outside the Doha mandate" (TN/MA/W/10). This chapter was drafted in late 2002, but the state of play surrounding the negotiations had not changed by the time of this publication in 2005. In the framework agreement concluded in July 2004 (WT/L/579), countries were urged "to make notifications on NTBs by 31 October 2004 and to proceed with identification, examination, categorization, and ultimately negotiations on NTBs" (Annex B – Framework for Establishing Modalities in Market Access for Non-Agricultural Products, paragraph 14). On agriculture, the framework agreement mentioned "differential export taxes" under "Other Issues" for negotiations in Annex A – Framework for Establishing Modalities in Agriculture, paragraph 49).

22. In the joint declaration at the occasion of the EU-Mexico Free Trade Agreement, both parties agreed to seek to establish disciplines for the elimination of export taxes or restrictions that operate to increase the exports of, or the protection afforded to, domestic industries, such as leather, within the context of multilateral negotiations (http://europa.eu.int/, Joint Declaration VI No. 4104). Meanwhile, the US proposal on market access on agricultural products in July 2002 included the following proposal on export taxes: "1. Other than provided in paragraph 2, no Member shall establish or maintain an export tax on any agricultural products. 2. A developing country Member may apply an export tax only in conformity with the following provisions: a. The export tax shall apply to all agricultural products. b. The export tax shall be applied to at a uniform rate across all agricultural products. c. The export tax shall be applied without modification for a period of at least one year. Any subsequent modification shall apply for a period of at least one year from the date of such modification. d. Any developing country Member applying, proposing, or modifying an export tax shall supply such information to the Committee on Agriculture prior to the application or modification." (www.ustr.gov/)

References

Asia-Pacific Economic Cooperation (2002), *APEC Individual Action Plan 2002*, www.apec-iap.org/

Black's Law Dictionary (1991), West Publishing Co.

GATT (1994), *Analytical Index Guide to GATT Law and Practice.*

Goode, Walter (1998), *The Dictionary of Trade Policy Terms*, Centre for International Economic Studies, University of Adelaide.

IMF: International Monetary Fund (2001), *Trade Policy Conditionality in Fund-Supported Programs*, www.imf.org/.

Jackson, John H., William J. Davey and Alan O. Skyes, Jr. (1995), *Legal Problems of International Economic Relations, Cases, Materials, and Text*, Third Edition.

Michalopoulos, C. (1999), *Trade Policy and Market Access Issues for Developing Countries: Implications for the Millennium Round*" World Bank.

OECD (1999), *Foreign Direct Investment and Recovery in Southeast Asia*, OECD, Paris.

WTO: World Trade Organisation, Trade Policy Review country reports (1995-2002), www.wto.org/.

WTO (2001), Accession Technical Note, www.wto.org/.

WTO (2001), Protocol on the Accession of the People's Republic of China, WT/L/432, www.wto.org/.

WTO (2001), Report of the Working Party on the Accession of China, WT/ACC/CHN/49, www.wto.org/.

WTO (2002), Report of the Trade Policy Review Body for 2002, WT/TPR/W/29, www.wto.org/.

Chapter 6

Export Restrictions

by

Jun Kazeki

This chapter provides an overview of current disciplines on export restrictions under the GATT/WTO, including the scope of exceptions. Disciplines at the regional level are also reviewed, and information provided by WTO Trade Policy Reviews (TPRs) on the use of different types of export restrictions and the products affected is analysed. The chapter describes some of the rationales for export restrictions and the nature of justifications invoked for exceptions, in particular for economic reasons. It also considers whether current transparency disciplines are sufficient in terms of predictability and whether there is room for strengthening disciplines in this area, on either a horizontal or a sectoral basis.

Introduction

Since the launch of the Doha Development Agenda (DDA) in 2001, export restrictions have been mentioned several times in communications from WTO members to the Negotiating Group on Market Access for Non-Agricultural Products and the Committee on Agriculture in Special Session. In the non-agricultural field, some WTO members have indicated their interest in specific non-tariff measures (NTMs). Members are also working to agree on negotiating modalities and expect further analytical elaboration of specific type of measures. Export restrictions, together with export duties, are among the issues to be pursued.

This chapter focuses on export restrictions other than export duties and provides an overview of existing disciplines on these restrictions in the WTO and other relevant regimes. It then presents information on products subject to various types of export restrictions and comments on their pattern of use and their trade and economic effects. The primary objective is to support the process of market access negotiations for non-agricultural products and the negotiation of further liberalisation of trade in agriculture. The study may also contribute to other trade policy discussions related, for example, to future WTO accessions.

Export restrictions under the GATT/WTO

In the GATT, export restrictions, sometimes considered a synonym for export controls[1] or export restraints,[2] are a fundamental issue for trade in goods. While reducing import tariffs and restrictions has been a primary goal of market access negotiations, export-related measures have also been addressed in contexts such as export prohibitions, quantitative export restrictions, export quotas, voluntary export restraints[3] and export duties.

The recent WTO Trade Policy Reviews (TPRs) include a section on "measures directly affecting exports". Under this heading, besides export-incentive measures (*i.e.* export subsidies; duty and tax drawback; export processing zones; export finance, insurance and guarantees; and other export promotion measures), the TPRs cover export-restrictive measures (typically, export prohibitions, export quotas, export licensing, export duties and levies, and minimum export prices). There are various other relevant sub-headings.[4] The current WTO disciplines are surveyed below with a view to identifying which types of measures are subject to disciplines and which are not and the main issues to be addressed in negotiations and other relevant processes.

Summary of WTO disciplines

Article XI of the GATT 1994 is a key provision which stipulates a general prohibition of quantitative restrictions. It states that "no prohibitions or restrictions other than duties, taxes or other charges, whether made effective through quotas, import or export licences or other measures, shall be instituted or maintained by any contracting party on the importation of any product destined for the territory of any other contracting party". There are, however, certain exceptions to this general prohibition such as Article XI:2, (a)(critical shortage of foodstuffs), (b)(restrictions necessary to the application of standards, etc.); Article XX (General Exceptions), in particular, (g), (i), and (j)[5] and Article XXI (Security Exceptions). Article XIII of the GATT 1994 stipulates that when export restrictions are used, they must be applied on a non-discriminatory basis.

Article XII of the GATT 1994 (Article XVIII in the case of developing countries) allows members to apply restrictions to safeguard the balance of payments.[6]

On the procedural side, Article X of the GATT 1994 establishes a general transparency requirement (*e.g.* publication of regulations). Article VIII addresses fees and formalities, prohibition of fees and other charges rendered in connection with exportation (or importation) that exceed the costs of the services rendered, and the need to minimise the incidence and complexity of formalities and decrease documentation requirements.

As a result of the Uruguay Round, so-called "grey measures", including voluntary export restraints, are prohibited under the Agreement on Safeguards. The Agreement on Trade-related Investment Measures (TRIMs) prohibits the use of such measures if they are inconsistent with Article III (national treatment) and Article XI (general elimination of quantitative restrictions), *i.e.* typically local content requirements for exports and export balancing requirements. With respect to state trading, while Article XVII of the GATT 1994 stipulates general obligations,[7] the "Understanding on the Interpretation of Article XVII of the GATT 1994" at the end of the Uruguay Round provided working definitions of state trading enterprises which have to be notified,[8] and established a Working Group to study the issue. Its work is ongoing.

Article 12 of the Agreement on Agriculture (disciplines on export prohibition and restrictions) stipulates when the exception in Article XI:2(a) of the GATT 1994 is to be applied. It requires members introducing new export restrictions on foodstuffs to give due consideration to the effects of such restrictions on the importing member's food security. Members, except non-net exporting developing countries, must notify the Committee on Agriculture before introducing new export restrictions on foodstuffs, and must consult with affected members.[9]

Regarding the possibility of scheduling commitments concerning export restrictions, Chapter 5 points out that paragraph 6 of the Marrakech Protocol to the GATT 1994 created a mechanism for scheduling non-tariff measures: "In case of modification or withdrawal of concessions relating to non-tariff measures as contained in Part III of the schedules, the provisions of Article XXVIII of GATT 1994...shall apply." However, the scheduling mechanism has been used only in a few instances and no country has scheduled export restrictions in Part III of its schedule.

In sum, while Article XI stipulates strict prohibitive disciplines on export restrictions, there are rather broad exceptions or justifications under provisions relating to non-economic reasons (*e.g.* security, public health and safety). The Uruguay Round provided strengthened disciplines in many respects, but issues in the area of export restrictions may remain for either economic or non-economic reasons, although as long as a relevant case is not justified by Article XX (General Exceptions) or Article XXI (Security Exceptions), it is governed by the general principle of elimination of export restrictions established by Article XI. In contrast with import regulations, where tariffication of quantitative import restrictions has been strongly encouraged over several rounds of multilateral negotiations, export restrictions have not been substantially discussed, except for the prohibition of voluntary export restraints. Perhaps this reflects the difficulty of dealing with issues such as national sovereignty over natural resources (*e.g.* petroleum) and national financial policy for tackling inflation by controlling adequate domestic supplies of key products, although importing countries clearly have a strong interest in ensuring access to supplies of raw materials or products.

Notifications after the Uruguay Round

As Chapter 5 noted, the Uruguay Round created a Notification Procedure. The indicative list of notifiable measures includes: quantitative restrictions; other non-tariff measures such as licensing; export taxes; and export restrictions, including voluntary export restraints and orderly marketing arrangements. Pursuant to a decision taken in December 1995 by the Council for Trade in Goods (CTG), procedures for detailed biennial notification of quantitative restrictions by members were put in place. Another December 1995 CTG decision involved reverse notification procedures, so far rarely used, which allow members to notify specific non-tariff measures of other members for transparency purposes.

The implementation of WTO notification obligations regarding quantitative restrictions seems to have been far from satisfactory in terms of the transparency objective. Currently, only half of the members have submitted quantitative restriction notifications (Table 6.1). In addition, among members having submitted notifications, and some have notified that they had none.[10] It seems that some members have interpreted the notification obligation as relating only to WTO-inconsistent quantitative restrictions, while others have notified details of many existing quantitative restrictions for transparency purposes even though these measures can be justified under Articles XX or XXI.

Table 6.1. Number of members having submitted notifications on quantitative restrictions

	Number of relevant WTO members at the time of the CTG review	Number of WTO members having submitted notifications on quantitative restrictions
LDCs	30	8
OECD	30	25
Others	80	39
Total	140	72

Note: Notifications in accordance with the WTO decision (G/L/59). Based upon the record of Council for Trade in Goods from 1995 to 2001 (G/L/223/Rev.8, 5 June 2002). EU is counted as 15.

The number of notifications by developing and least developed countries (LDCs) is relatively low and may be due to capacity problems. Moreover, although notified information is stocked in a database in the WTO and available to members, it can be consulted only on request to the WTO Secretariat. Given the variety of the measures described in the TPRs, it is not clear whether a publicly available database would be feasible and adequate under the current structure.

Overall, while the Uruguay Round has resulted in strengthened disciplines on export restrictions (*e.g.* for voluntary export restraints), a number of issues remain. Procedural aspects could be pursued in the context of the agenda on trade facilitation under the DDA. State trading, in particular of agricultural products, might be dealt with in the broader context of the implications of imports and exports and competition policy, as in the case of export cartels. In market access negotiations on non-agricultural and agricultural products, however, export restrictions and export taxes for economic reasons appear to have been most often discussed so far. This chapter thus addresses these export restrictions.

Because of the broad exceptions to the general prohibition on export restrictions, the main questions to be dealt with are: the nature of the justifications invoked for exceptions, in particular in the case of economic reasons; whether current transparency disciplines are sufficient in terms of predictability; and whether there is room for strengthening disciplines in this area, on either a horizontal or a sectoral basis. In order to pursue these points, the following sections analyse practices in various areas.

Sources of information on possible disciplines

WTO accession

Disciplines agreed to in WTO accession processes provide information on possible disciplines in the field of export restrictions, such as scheduling of certain products and notification requirements. Some observations may be made concerning so-called commitment clauses in accession agreements (see Annex 6.A1 for details):

- Most of the commitments include compliance with provisions on export restrictions of Articles XI, XII, XIII, XVII, XVIII, XIX, XX, and XXI of the GATT 1994, the Agreement on Agriculture, and the Agreement on Safeguards.

- The transparency requirements of Article X are emphasised.

- Some cases reflect specific interests of certain members in products of acceding countries, e.g. Mongolia (raw cashmere, ferrous and non-ferrous metal); Albania (raw hides and skins and leather); and Moldova (unbottled wine) (see Annexes 6.A1 and 6.A2).

- An additional commitment beyond GATT in terms of transparency (besides export duties[11]) is provided for in the case of China, where remaining non-automatic restrictions on exports are to be notified to the WTO annually.

Regional and bilateral disciplines

In regional trade agreements (RTAs),[12] disciplines on export restrictions are mostly in line with the structure of the GATT, allowing Article XX and XXI types of exceptions to the general prohibition on quantitative restrictions. However, efforts have been undertaken to enhance transparency by specifying justifiable export regulations in the agreements and in annexes or subsequent regulations.

In the EU, Article 29 of the Treaty establishing the European Community stipulates that quantitative restrictions on exports, and all measures having equivalent effect, shall be prohibited between member states. Article 30 addresses exceptions from prohibitions or restrictions on grounds of public morality, public policy or public security. Subsequent directives, regulations, decisions and cases have enhanced predictability of the rules. With regard to exports to third countries, the general principle of EU policy is freedom from quantitative restrictions.[13]

In Europe, disciplines on exports are in line with the GATT. For example, Article 7 of the European Free Trade Association (EFTA)[14] states that quantitative restrictions on imports and exports and all measures having equivalent effect, shall be prohibited between the member states, with general exceptions (Article 13) and security exceptions (Article 39).

In the case of the Europe Agreements[15] as well, quantitative restrictions on exports and all measures with equivalent effect are to be abolished by the date of the entry of the Agreement into force, except for measures explicitly mentioned in the annex, which however are to be abolished by the end of the fifth year after entry of the Agreement into force (Article 14).[16] No new quantitative restrictions on exports or measures having equivalent effect are to be introduced, nor are existing ones to be made more restrictive (Article 26).[17] Europe has long tackled quantitative restrictions on the free movement of goods in the integrated market and emphasised their elimination in the region's disciplines.

In the chapter on non-tariff measures of the EU-Mexico Agreement, Article 12 prohibits quantitative restrictions on trade between the Community and Mexico. Annex IV sets out the exceptions. Article 16 (the shortage clause) allows the possibility of export restrictions in the case of a critical shortage of foodstuffs, but it also requires that the measure shall not operate to increase the exports of or protection afforded to the domestic processing industry concerned. In addition, the EU and Mexico, in addition to prohibiting export duties, declared that "Within the context of the multilateral negotiations, both Parties shall seek to establish disciplines for the elimination of export taxes or restrictions that operate to increase the exports of, or the protection afforded to, domestic industries, such as leather."[18]

The North American Free Trade Agreement (NAFTA) stipulates export disciplines in the section on non-tariff measures. It provides general rules in line with Article XI of the GATT 1994 while its annex indicates the exceptional export restrictions maintained by each party.[19] Article 315 further specifies the conditions of exceptions in Articles XI:2(a) or XX(g), (i), or (j) of the GATT 1994 by articulating detailed requirements such as comparison of trade volumes.[20] With regard to security exceptions, Part Eight of the NAFTA covers general exceptions and national security. Overall, these provisions at least help to enhance transparency and narrow the scope of unpredictability by articulating regulations in annexes and detailed requirements in the provisions.

Western Hemisphere RTAs (*e.g.* Canada-Chile, Canada-Costa Rica, available draft of FTAA, etc.) adopt a structure similar to the NAFTA by stipulating basic provisions in line with the GATT 1994, and include in annexes additional disciplines such as specific requirements relating to general exceptions and prohibitions on export taxes and minimum price requirements. This increases transparency.

The Australia and New Zealand Closer Economic Relations Trade Agreement (ANZCER) prohibits all quantitative export restrictions. This provisions is contained in Article 9 of the 1983 CER Agreement in conjunction with 1988 CER Protocol on the Acceleration of Free Trade in Goods, under which all transitional arrangements and temporary exceptions to the basic free trade rule were eliminated as of 1 July 1990.[21] Article 18 allows standard exceptions from its provisions, which are similar to the general exceptions and security exceptions under the GATT 1994.

As Chapter 5 mentions, APEC has set itself the goal of achieving free and open trade and investment in the Asia-Pacific region by 2010 for industrialised economies and 2020 for developing economies. With the Osaka Action Agenda, APEC economies have pledged to reach this goal, among other things by "progressively reducing non-tariff measures". The individual action plans (IAPs) for each member economy explain the planned steps of voluntary liberalisation. Four categories in the section on NTMs relate to export restrictions: export levies, quantitative export restrictions/prohibitions, discretionary export licensing, and voluntary export restraints.[22]

Notifications in the IAPs vary, but the following findings on export restrictions can be drawn from the records of 21 member economies:[23]

- Most economies notify that they do not impose voluntary export restraints; others just leave the relevant column blank or refer to relevant international agreements.

- The distinction between export restrictions/prohibitions and discretionary export licensing is not necessarily clear, with each country choosing a column on the basis of its interpretation.

- A few economies choose to notify that they do not maintain quantitative export restrictions or prohibitions that are inconsistent with WTO rules, rather than to describe details of justifiable export regulations; many other economies notify, though some are detailed and others are brief, existing export controls schemes in accordance with international obligations such as the Convention on International Trade in Endangered Species CITES) and the Basel Convention, and other reasons including security, public health and safety.

- Most economies simply describe existing regulations and seldom undertake additional commitments. Indonesia is a rare exception and gives several reasons for export restrictions in addition to making a unilateral commitment to gradually reduce export taxes on logs, sawn timber, rattan and minerals.[24]

- Most economies provide multiple enquiry points for export restrictions in the electronically available E-IAPs, including e-mail address, and telephone and fax numbers of relevant authorities, to the extent possible.

In sum, structures similar to those of the GATT on export restrictions have been envisaged on some points. However, in the APEC context, disciplines have generally not been as extensive on export restrictions as on export duties, which increasingly tend to be abolished in Europe and the Western Hemisphere. Export restrictions are too varied for a simple streamlined discipline, and issues such as national sovereignty over natural resources may be difficult to address, although a more transparent approach in annexes to the agreements would be helpful. While the annexes rarely include commitments to eliminate certain export restrictions, they describe detailed regulations of a binding nature and definitely enhance transparency and predictability compared to justifications based simply on exceptions under Articles XX and XXI. As noted, the EU-Mexico Agreement hints at a sector-specific approach with respect to leather.

Findings based on the TPRs

The most systematic information available on export restrictions appears in the section on "measures directly affecting exports" in the WTO's TPRs. In assessing the economic impact of export restrictions, the TPRs include much useful information. Basic information such as HS lines of applicable products is limited, but certain tendencies can be observed from the reports. Since export duties were surveyed in Chapter 5, this section reviews other types of restrictions, namely minimum export prices, export quotas and export prohibitions/export licensing.

Minimum export prices

Minimum export prices, or in certain cases index prices, tend to be used as complementary measures aimed at achieving target export prices which are set to control world market prices for certain dominant products, or at obtaining a competitive advantage for domestic downstream industries by allowing them to obtain locally available inexpensive raw materials. Few reference are made to minimum export prices in the TPRs. Rather, they are discussed with export duties. They are also mentioned in the context of voluntary export restraints, orderly marketing, export cartels and state trading. However, since the Agreement on Safeguards was introduced, the so-called grey measures have been abolished, so that the relevant situations are likely to involve export cartels and state trading. Table 6.2 compares the groups of countries applying minimum exports prices with those applying export duties and taxes. The key findings on minimum export price measures from the relevant section of the TPRs are:

- Around one-third of members applying export duties maintain minimum export price requirements as a supplementary measure to implement or calculate export duties and to achieve objectives such as maintenance of world prices or price differentiation for domestic downstream industries *vis-à-vis* world competitors.

- Developing countries are the main users, with LDCs making relatively less use of these measures; this reflects the difficulty in valuation of prices.

- Examples of products affected are forestry products, mineral and metal products, and various agricultural products.

- It is not clear in some cases whether minimum export prices are binding in nature or reference prices.

Table 6.2. **Number of countries applying export duties/taxes and minimum export prices, by regions and other groupings**

	Number of WTO members reviewed by TPRs	Members imposing export duties	Members imposing minimum export prices
Europe/Middle East	29	2	0
America	26	9	6
Asia/Pacific	19	11	6
Africa	26	17	2
Total	100	39	14
LDCs	15	10	1
OECD	30	3	0
Others	55	26	13

Note: TPR reports from 1995 to 2002 (October). Some members were reviewed two or three times, but are here counted as one. The EU is counted as 15.

Export quotas

Export quotas are, in the *Dictionary of Trade Policy Terms*, "restrictions or ceilings imposed by an exporting country on the total volume of certain products. They are designed to protect domestic producers and consumers from temporary shortages of these products or to improve the prices of specific products on world markets by shortening their supply. The latter is only possible where a country, or a group of countries, is the dominant exporter of a product." The scope of the descriptions of export quotas in the TPRs varies. Sometimes, quotas are discussed in the same context as export restrictions, quantitative restrictions and licences. Here, the key findings are drawn from the relevant sections of the TPRs:

- Around 20 members describe legitimate export quotas in response to restrictions by importing members under the WTO Agreement on Textiles and Clothing.[25]
- International commodity agreements or arrangements are stated justifications for measures taken for agricultural products, such as sugar and coffee, and on crude oil.
- For certain agricultural items (in the absence of international arrangements), the objective of the measure may be to respond to an importing country's legitimate import-restrictive measures or to stabilise domestic prices and meet domestic needs.
- In the case of forestry products, hides and skins and leather, and non-ferrous metals, there may be an economic reason for fostering domestic downstream industries.
- Linkage to export cartels and voluntary orderly marketing is pointed out in certain cases, though the latter measure is currently prohibited by the Agreement on Safeguards.

Export prohibitions/export licensing

The TPRs describe export prohibitions and export licensing in various ways. Because the relevant sections in the reports vary in length and level of detail, it would be hard to analyse this area quantitatively, although certain tendencies can be observed. The difference between automatic and non-automatic export licensing is not treated substantially in these reports; export prohibitions and licensing are reviewed together. It should also be noted that export duties, minimum export prices and export quotas are specific aspects of export restrictions in a broader sense, so that overall assessments of measures are sometimes necessary. Box 6.1 presents a tentative classification drawn in particular from sections on export prohibitions and export licensing. The key findings are:

- Where there are multilateral agreements or arrangements, the legitimacy of export restrictions is well recognised, in particular in such areas as security, life, public health, safety, social and religious reasons.
- In the case of certain commodities such as sugar, coffee and petroleum, international mechanisms affect the use of export restrictions.
- Following the introduction of the Agreement on Safeguards, so-called grey measures tend to be removed.[26]
- It seems clear that restrictions on foodstuffs are inevitable in cases of drought in LDCs. When the alleged reason for restrictions is to secure an adequate domestic supply of foodstuffs in developed as well as developing countries, it should be a matter of overall assessment and balance.[27]
- Export restrictions for quality control are essentially export promotion activities to meet minimum standards in importing countries and to maintain the reputation of goods.
- Questions remain when export restrictions are applied for economic reasons or mixed reasons in the absence of certain international arrangements. They can be summarised as follows:
  - Hides and skins and leather: the primary reason is to encourage downstream industries.

- Mineral products, metals and precious stones: the reason alleged is generally conservation of natural resources, but in some cases it is the promotion of downstream processing industries.

- Fishery products: the main reason alleged is conservation of natural resources (including seasonal restraint).

- Forestry products: the environmental reason is often strongly invoked, but in some cases, promotion of downstream processing industries is a major reason.

• Importing countries argue that export restrictions by dominant producing countries discriminate against foreign buyers by raising the level of export prices (*i.e.* world prices) and making it difficult for buyers to obtain essential raw materials and compete internationally.

• Some developing countries argue instead that measures to promote processing industries are justified by the infant industry argument and by the existence of tariff escalation in developed countries.

• In relation to export regulations for economic reasons, governments sometimes exempt export restrictions (*e.g.* exemptions of licensing requirements in an export process zone) to promote foreign direct investment in export industries, particularly in developing countries.

• Lack of transparency of regulations and licensing systems is frequently indicated in the case of developing members.

Export restrictions for economic reasons

In general

When export restrictions are imposed for economic reasons (see Box 6.1), the type of instrument used is basically a regulatory choice, *e.g.* whether to apply export duties supplemented by export price requirements, export quotas and export prohibitions or export licensing on a product-by-product basis.

Where the objective is primarily the promotion of downstream industries, export restrictions create a gap between the production costs of domestic processors and those of foreign processors using the same inputs. This gives domestic downstream processors a competitive advantage with respect to foreign processors. When export prohibitions or export quotas are used, the effect may be greater than in the case of export duties, since they also limit the amount of competition.

As with import restrictions, export restrictions to promote downstream industries may be justified by the "infant industry" argument, *i.e.* to provide an initial incentive for the development of a processing industry. This may bring further benefits, such as increased employment. However, assessment of the net result needs to take into account that these measures may penalise exporters of the regulated product while benefiting downstream processing industries, which then have less incentive to become truly competitive internationally. If a relevant case is not justified by Article XX (General Exceptions) and Article XXI (Security Exceptions), the general principle of elimination of export restrictions established by Article XI governs the case. In negotiating its accession, Albania invoked the infant industry justification, but ultimately committed to abolish its export restrictions on hide and skins and leather (see Annex 6.A2).

Box 6.1. Illustrative list of rationales for export restrictions in TPRs

1. Export restrictions for non-economic reasons: security:

- The United Nations Security Council Resolutions (e.g. sanctions against particular countries).
- The Convention on Chemical Weapons.
- The Treaty on Nuclear Non-Proliferation.
- Multilateral export control arrangements: the Australia Group (to prevent the spread of chemical and biological weapons); the Missile Technology Control Regime; the Nuclear Suppliers Group; the Zangger Committee (control of nuclear materials and related high technology); the Wassenaar Arrangement (control of exports of conventional weapons and dual use products).

2. Export restrictions for non-economic reasons: other international treaties or arrangements, and life, public health, safety, social and religious reasons:

- The Basel Convention on the Transboundary Movement of Hazardous Wastes and their Disposal.
- The Convention on International Trade in Endangered Species of Fauna and Flora (CITES).
- The Montreal Protocol on Substances that Deplete the Ozone Layer.

3. Export restrictions for economic reasons but in accordance with international or bilateral agreements or arrangements:

- The Agreement on Textile and Clothing. (All restrictions under this agreement were eliminated at the end of 2004.)
- International commodities agreements on sugar, coffee and petroleum.
- General System of Preferences and other arrangements related to preferential treatment.
- In the process of counteracting countervailing duties of an importing country.

4. Export restrictions for food security reasons (prevention of critical shortage):

- Staple products such as maize to cope with drought in particular in LDCs (including seasonal regulations).

5. Export restrictions: for environmental reasons; for conservation of exhaustible natural resources; to maintain an adequate supply of essential products; or to promote downstream industries (either non-economic or economic reasons):

- Forestry products (such as log, timber).
- Fishery products (including seasonal restraint for a biological rest period of fish).
- Mineral products, metals, precious stones.
- Hides and skins and leather.
- Other agricultural products (seasonal measures are introduced in some cases).

6. Export restrictions for quality controls and regulatory aspects:

- Patent- or copyright-infringing products.
- Sanitary quality controls or standards assurance to meet importer's demands or to maintain international reputation (*e.g.* SPS quality of foods, quality of diamonds, etc.).

7. Export restrictions: others:

- Gold (financial security).
- Exchange control related.
- Heritage goods (to protect national treasures).
- Statistical and monitoring purposes.

In the case of export restrictions whose objectives are combined with environmental considerations, as in the case of forestry products, the relation to a domestic conservation programme is a key factor in justifying the measures. If conservation of natural resources rather than promotion of domestic downstream industries is the main reason for applying export restrictions, the existence of a domestic conservation plan that affects domestic players and foreign buyers equally may be a justifiable factor. Article XX(g) stipulates a general exception relating to the conservation of exhaustible natural resources if such measures are made effective in conjunction with restrictions on domestic production or consumption.[28]

Development dimension (including a South-South factor)

It should be pointed out that, in the long run, export-distorting measures do not benefit the developing world. Nevertheless, it was found that export duties and minimum export pricing are mainly undertaken by developing countries and LDCs, a pattern that also applies to other types of export restrictions.[29] A World Bank study (Hertel and Martin, 1999) emphasised that almost 40% of developing-country exports of manufactures were destined for other developing economies and that this share had been increasing steadily over time, so that these intra-developing-country exports would account for over half within a decade.[30] Moreover, 70% of duties collected on developing countries' exports are levied by developing countries themselves. Developing countries thus have a particular interest in reducing barriers that currently hamper South-South trade. Although a similar figure is not available to indicate the importance of the South-South dimension in assessing the effects of export restrictions, it is likely to be significant, since export restrictions applied in one developing country will impede economic development in others, particularly in poor or geographically isolated countries with limited alternative supplies.

Though certain export-restrictive policies have decreased in developing countries, export restrictions still remain, in particular in the area of promotion of downstream industries. This may penalise exporters of raw materials and protect inefficient downstream industries by providing an implicit subsidy. Shifting from export restrictions to export duties and scheduling their phase-out has been a way to address this inefficiency and to secure greater predictability for business. The solution after the EC-Pakistan dispute on Pakistan's export prohibition on hides and skins resulted in the replacement of the prohibition by a 20% export duty.[31] India has also removed export restrictions on hides and skins and leather and introduced export duties on these products as a consequence of a WTO ruling requiring abolition of quantitative licensing controls on these products (TPR India, 2002).

In other cases, a rollback from export duties to export restrictions has occurred, although questions have been raised: the TPR on Ghana (2001) states: "Government policy has been to replace export taxes on logs progressively with export prohibitions, to encourage downstream processing of timber products and to help preserve forests. The efficacy of using export prohibitions to achieve such economic objectives as well as to meet environmental concerns is, however, questionable."

With regard to implications for investment policy, export restrictions may sometimes be an incentive to encourage FDI in processing industries, as in the forestry sector of a few developing countries.[32] On the other hand, exemptions from export restrictions may be an incentive for investment in other areas, as in the case of waivers granted for export licences in export processing zones. However, such exemptions cause problems of non-transparency, arbitrary treatment and discrimination.

Possible orientations for future disciplines

In light of the current patterns of use of export restrictions, it would be useful to reflect on possible orientations for strengthened multilateral disciplines. In the case of export duties, the possibility hass been suggested of general disciplines taking the form of prohibition and scheduling, on either a horizontal or a sectoral basis. In the case of China, the WTO accession process adopted a practical scheduling solution. Prohibition of export duties is a clear trend in regional disciplines. In the broader case of export restrictions, while regional efforts have been moderate compared with those relating to export duties, the same approach can be taken when these measures are introduced for economic reasons.

Sectors in which multilateral or regional agreements or arrangements are lacking could be priority areas for attempts to strengthen disciplines. Such sectors might include hides and skins and leather, forestry products, certain mineral products and certain agricultural products. The availability of alternatives to export restrictions is also a factor in assessing the use of these restrictions. For the promotion of downstream industries, other domestic measures might be effective. However, a rollback from export duties to other types of export restrictions may increase economic distortion.

From the legal point of view, export restrictions could be included in the schedule of Part III (Concessions on non-tariff measures). In accordance with current disciplines, one scenario might be the scheduling of shared understandings on disciplines (*e.g.* scheduling export restrictions for economic reasons). Shared understandings, such as strengthened disciplines relating to general exceptions, as seen in RTAs and co-ordination mechanisms, *e.g.* Article 12 of the Agreement on Agriculture, could be as binding, through scheduling, as a decision or a rule under the WTO. Another scenario could be sector-specific disciplines,[33] which could also ultimately be reflected in the schedules or be a decision or a rule under the WTO if members wish. A request- and offer-based sectoral concession together with other market access concessions might be another possibility, as in the accession process. Special and differential treatment could also considered.

In the "Export Restrictions" section of the WTO overview paper in the negotiations on agriculture,[34] outstanding issues are described as including: "(a) Whether export restrictions shall be prohibited, and, if so, (i) for all Members, or (ii) for all Members except developing countries?; (b) Alternatively, whether export restrictions should be converted into export taxes and subsequently bound in Members' schedule and subjected to reduction commitments?; (c) Whether export taxes shall be prohibited and, if so, (i) for all Members except developing countries, or (ii) for all Members except developing countries unless they are net exporters of the foodstuffs concerned (an alternative special and differential treatment proposal that has been submitted would allow developing countries to apply an export tax subject to strict conditions)?"[35]

Regardless of the approach, the question of transparency in dealing with any kind of non-tariff measure remains. Today, the lack of transparency and predictability in this area is particularly noticeable in comparison to other aspects of the overall trade regime that have come under multilateral disciplines, especially as a result of the Uruguay Round. The current situation of notification of quantitative restrictions in the WTO could be improved. The share of notifying members is small despite the obligation to notify; furthermore, some members notify that they do not maintain quantitative restrictions while others indicate justifiable measures. The annex-style negative list or committed restrictions list widely used in regional arrangements represents an improvement, although it is not a schedule and does not commit members to reductions or elimination. The lack of transparency and of predictability of export restrictions should be considered unfinished business of the WTO.

Annex 6.A1

Examples of disciplines undertaken at the time of WTO accession

Ecuador (1996)
The representative of Ecuador indicated that his Government would eliminate by the date of accession all non-tariff import and export restrictions (including all quantitative restrictions currently in place in the agricultural sector) that cannot be justified specifically under WTO provisions (*e.g.* bans, quotas, permits and licences), in particular the Agreements on Agriculture,... and Article XI of the GATT 1994 .... The Working Party took note of this commitment (paragraph 34).

Bulgaria (1996)
In conclusion the representative of Bulgaria confirmed that, in the context of its accession to the Agreement Establishing the WTO, the Bulgarian Government would use its authority to suspend or prohibit imports and exports or otherwise restrict their quantities in conformity with the provisions of the GATT 1994 in particular Articles XI, XII, XIII, XIX, XX and XXI. The Working Party took note of this commitment (paragraph 49).

Mongolia (1997)
The representative of Mongolia said that Mongolia commits that, from the date of accession, the authority of its Government to suspend imports and exports or to apply licensing requirements that can be used to suspend trade in the products under licence would be applied in conformity with the requirements of the WTO, in particular GATT 1994 Articles VI, XI, XVIII, XIX, XX and XXI, and the Multilateral Trade Agreements on Agriculture, ...and that his government would not maintain from the date of accession non-tariff import measures, including bans, quotas, permits and licences, that cannot be justified specifically under WTO provisions.... The Working Party took note of these commitments (paragraph 20).

The representative of Mongolia also stated that his government would maintain the prohibition on the export of raw cashmere only until 1 October 1996, when an export duty at the rate of not more than 30% *ad valorem* would be introduced. That export duty would be phased out and eliminated within ten years of the date of Mongolia's accession to the WTO. The representative of Mongolia also stated that export licensing requirements for ferrous and non-ferrous metals would be removed by 1 January 1997. The Working Party took note of these commitments (paragraph 24).

Panama (1997)
The representative of Panama confirmed that, from the date of accession, the authority of his Government to suspend imports and exports or to apply licensing requirements that could be used to suspend, ban or otherwise restrict the quantity of trade would be applied in conformity with the requirements of the WTO, in particular Articles XI, XIII, XVIII, XIX, XX, and XXI of the GATT 1994, and the Multilateral Trade Agreements on Agriculture, ... Safeguards,.... The Working Party took note of these commitments (paragraph 42).

The representative of Panama stated that following accession to the WTO, his Government would only apply export controls in conformity with relevant WTO provisions including Article XI paragraph 2(a) of the GATT 1994. The Working Party took note of this commitment (paragraph 71).

Kyrgyz Republic (1998)	The representative of the Kyrgyz Republic confirmed that the legal authority of the Government of the Kyrgyz Republic to suspend imports and exports or to apply licensing requirements that could be used to suspend, ban or otherwise restrict the quantity of trade would be applied from the date of accession in conformity with the requirements of the WTO, in particular Articles XI, XII, XIII, XIX, XX and XXI of the GATT 1994, and the Multilateral Trade Agreements on Agriculture, ... Safeguards, ... The Working Party took note of these commitments (paragraph 60). He also stated that the Kyrgyz Republic would ensure that its system of export licensing was in conformity with the requirements of Article XI of the GATT 1994 as from the date of accession. The Working Party took note of this commitment (paragraph 79).
Latvia (1999)	The representative of Latvia confirmed that the legal authority of the Government of Latvia to suspend imports and exports or to apply licensing requirements that could be used to suspend, ban, or otherwise restrict the quantity of trade will be applied from the date of accession in conformity with the requirements of the WTO, in particular Articles XI, XII, XIII, XVIII, XIX, XX and XXI of the GATT 1994, and the Multilateral Trade Agreements on Agriculture, ... Safeguards,.... The Working Party took note of these commitments (paragraph 59).
Estonia (1999)	The representative of Estonia confirmed that any remaining export control requirements were fully consistent with WTO provisions, including those contained in Articles XI, XVII, XX and XXI of the GATT 1994. The Working Party took note of this commitment (paragraph 83).
Jordan (2000)	The representative of Jordan confirmed that the legal authority of the Government of Jordan to suspend imports and exports or to apply licensing requirements that could be used to suspend, ban, or otherwise restrict the quantity of trade will be applied from the date of accession in conformity with the requirements of the WTO, in particular Articles XI, XII, XIII, XVIII, XIX, XX and XXI of the GATT 1994, and the Multilateral Trade Agreements on Agriculture, ... Safeguards,.... The Working Party took note of these commitments (paragraph 88). He further confirmed that any export control requirements remaining in place on the date of accession would be fully consistent with WTO provisions, including those contained in Articles XI, XVII, XX and XXI of the GATT 1994. The Working Party took note of this commitment (paragraph 116).
Georgia (2000)	The representative of Georgia confirmed that any remaining export control requirements would be applied in a manner fully consistent with WTO provisions, including those contained in Articles XI, XVII, XX and XXI of the GATT 1994. The Working Party took note of this commitment (paragraph 86).
Albania (2000)	The representative of Albania confirmed that at the time of accession any remaining export control requirements in place would be fully consistent with WTO provisions, including those contained in Articles XI, XVII, XX and XXI of the GATT 1994. In this regard, Albania had lifted the export bans on items listed in the document WT/ACC/ALB/34/Rev.1, with the Decision of the Council of Ministers "For the Export-Import of Goods from and into the Republic of Albania", No. 450 dated 16 September 1999 (see Annex 6.A2). He stated that from the date of accession export restrictions would only be imposed in conformity with the WTO Agreement. The Working party took note of these commitments (paragraph 90).

Oman (2000)	The representative of Oman confirmed that any export control requirements remaining in place on the date of accession would be fully consistent with WTO provisions, including those contained in Articles XI, XVII, XX and XXI of the GATT 1994. The Working Party took note of this commitment (paragraph 77).
Croatia (2000)	The representative of Croatia confirmed that the legal authority of the Government of Croatia to suspend imports and exports or to apply licensing requirements that could be used to suspend, ban, or otherwise restrict the quantity of trade will be applied from the date of accession in conformity with the requirements of the WTO, in particular Articles XI, XII, XIII, XVIII, XIX, XX and XXI of the GATT 1994, and the Multilateral Trade Agreements on Agriculture, … Safeguards, …. The Working Party took note of these commitments (paragraph 73).
	He further confirmed that Croatia had eliminated all export quotas, bans and other forms of export restrictions as of 1 January 1999, and said that from the date of accession, export restrictions would only be imposed in conformity with relevant provisions of WTO Agreements, including Article XI of the GATT. The Working party took note of this commitment (paragraph 105).
Lithuania (2001)	The representative of Lithuania confirmed that the legal authority of the Government of Lithuania to suspend imports or exports or to apply licensing requirements that could be used to suspend, ban or otherwise restrict the quantity of trade would be applied from the date of accession in conformity with the requirements of the WTO, in particular Articles III, XI, XII, XIII, XIX, XX and XXI of the GATT 1994, and the Multilateral Trade Agreements on Agriculture, …, Safeguards, … and the Understanding on Balance-of-Payments Provisions of the GATT 1994. The Working Party took note of these commitments (paragraph 71).
	He further confirmed that from the date of accession export restrictions would only be imposed in conformity with the provisions of Article XI of the GATT 1994. The Working Party took note of this commitment (paragraph 97).
Moldova (2001)	In response to questions, the representative of Moldova said that Moldova no longer maintained the temporary export restriction on unbottled wine intended to promote the quality image of Moldovan wine. Because the restriction had proved ineffective to achieve this objective it had been removed. The representative of Moldova said that if any of these policy instruments were introduced in the future, they would be fully consistent with the relevant WTO provisions. The Working Party took note of this commitment (paragraph 101).
China (2001)	Some members of the Working Party noted that there were a large number of non-tariff measures in existence in China, both at the national and sub-national levels, which appeared to have a trade-restrictive or trade-distorting effect. Those members requested that China undertake a commitment to eliminate and not to introduce, re-introduce or apply non-tariff measures other than those specifically identified and subject to phased elimination in Annex 3 to the Draft Protocol. The representative of China confirmed that China would not introduce, re-introduce or apply non-tariff measures other than listed in Annex 3 (on import restrictions) of the Draft Protocol unless justified under the WTO Agreement. The Working Party took note of this commitment (paragraph 122).
	The representative of China confirmed that the list of all entities responsible for the authorisation or approval of exports would be updated and republished in the official journal, the MOFTEC Gazette, within one month of any change thereto. The Working

Party took note of this commitment (paragraph 157).

The representative of China confirmed that China would abide by WTO rules in respect of non-automatic export licensing and export restrictions. The Foreign Trade Law would also be brought into conformity with GATT requirements. Moreover, export restrictions and licensing would only be applied, after the date of accession, in those cases where this was justified by GATT provisions. The Working Party took note of these commitments (paragraph 162).

The representative of China confirmed that upon accession, remaining non-automatic restrictions on exports would be notified to the WTO annually and would be eliminated unless they could be justified under the WTO Agreement or the Draft Protocol. The Working Party took note of this commitment (paragraph 165)

See WTO accessions technical note Annex 3 (www.wto.org).

Annex 6.A2

Examples of disciplines on export restrictions from a document regarding the Accession of Albania

Prohibitions on exportable products, by type: justification, and phase-out period		
Article and description by harmonised code and corresponding legislation or regulation	Justification/rationale for the prohibition	Phase-out period
I . 41.00 Raw hides and Skins (other than fur skins) and leather		
41.01 Hides of cattle as fresh, dried, limed, salted, stretched or otherwise treated but not tanned or pergaminated, prepared and cleaned (these are for hides of cattle other than those of horses) **41.02** Raw skins of sheep and lambs as fresh or salted, pointed or otherwise treated, but not tanned or prepared (including skins with wool, stretched or un-stretched) **41.03** Other hides and skins as fresh or salted, dried, limed in salted water or otherwise treated, but not tanned and pergaminated or processed further (including wool or hair and stretched or unstretched)	During the transition period, Albania's leather processing industry suffered serious disruptions and losses in investment. Leather processing has traditionally been a sector in which Albania has had productive economic activity and is expected to be competitive in the future. **The ban on hides is an attempt to protect this industry which finds itself in its infancy.** The current ban allows the more than ten existing domestic enterprises (those with or without foreign joint ventures) to have access to the raw materials needed to produce the intermediate and/or the final products.	The Ministry of Economic Co-operation and Trade in conjunction with the Ministry of Finance has prepared a draft of the Decision of the Council of Ministers **to repeal the prohibitions on exports of scraps of rawhide, skins and leather.** Approval from the Council is in progress and should be enforced by the end of September 1999.

Note: This table draws on a document [WT/ACC/ALB/34/Rev.1, 14 June 1999] regarding the accession of Albania with a view to providing examples of disciplines of export restrictions. Emphasis added in bold.

Notes

1. *The Dictionary of Trade Policy Terms* defines "export controls" as "measures instituted by exporting countries to supervise export flows. Reasons for them can be many, including, but not exhaustively, compliance with United Nations economic sanctions, adherence to voluntary restraint arrangements, observance of export quotas under international commodity arrangements, management of strategic exports and administration of rules concerning dual purpose exports as well as a policy preserving some raw materials and other articles for domestic production or consumption" (Goode, 1998).

2. A panel under the WTO Dispute Settlement Understanding, in the context of the application of the Subsidies and Countervailing Measures Agreements, delineated the scope of "export restraint" as "a border measure that takes the form of a government law or regulation which expressly limits the quantity of exports or places explicit conditions on the circumstances under which exports are permitted, or that takes the form of a government-imposed fee or tax on exports of the products calculated to limit the quantity of exports" (WT/DS194/R).

3. A voluntary export restraint is undertaken when a country agrees to limit its exports to another country on certain sensitive products only to the extent that the exporting country wishes to avert a threat to its trade with the partner. The character of the restriction is different from other export-restrictive measures in that it includes the other country's interest to limit the import. In any event, voluntary export restraints are prohibited under the Agreement on Safeguards.

4. While the TPRs attempt to use uniform sub-headings, there are many variations owing to differing practices and realities. Examples of sub-headings include: procedures, registration and documentations, export taxes, charges, levies, index prices, minimum reference prices, export prohibitions, export licensing, export restrictions and controls, export permit requirements, access-related export quotas, export cartels, voluntary restraints, surveillance, retention schemes and export performance requirements.

5. For example, "(g) relating to the conservation of exhaustible natural resources if such measure are made effective in conjunction with restrictions on domestic production or consumption; (i) involving restrictions on exports of domestic materials necessary to ensure essential quantities of such materials to a domestic processing industry during periods when the domestic price of such materials is held below the world price as part of a governmental stabilisation plan; *Provided* that such restrictions shall not operate to increase the exports of or the protection afforded to such domestic industry, and shall not depart from the provisions of this Agreement relating to non-discrimination; (j) essential to the acquisition or distribution of products in general or local short supply; *Provided* that any such measures shall be consistent with the principle that all contracting parties are entitled to an equitable share of the international supply of such products, and that any such measures, which are inconsistent with the other provisions of the Agreement shall be discontinued as soon as the conditions giving rise to them have ceased to exist…".

6. With regard to the applicability of the Agreement on Subsidies and Countervailing Measures, at issue is, *inter alia*, whether the measure is a "subsidy" under the ASCM Article 1. There is a question whether export restrictions on raw materials could be a *de facto* subsidy for the domestic processing industry because they enable the industry to

obtain raw materials at low cost. A subsidy under Article 1 of the ASCM agreements only exists if: *i)* a financial contribution is provided *and ii)* the contribution is made by a government or public body *and iii)* that contribution confers a benefit. Furthermore, for example in the case of the introduction of new drastic export restrictions, the concept of non-violation nullification and impairment based on Article XXIII of GATT 1994 may arguably provide a basis for challenging measures that fundamentally undermine other concessions that have been bargained for. The aim of this chapter is not interpretation, and these issues are simply mentioned in connection with export restrictions.

7. The basic obligation with respect to state-trading enterprises as contained in Article XVII of the GATT 1994 is that enterprises which are state-owned, or receive exclusive or special privileges from the state, shall act in a manner consistent with the general principles of non-discriminatory treatment, that is, should make any purchases or sales strictly on the basis of commercial considerations. Members are required to notify the relevant products.

8. The working definition is "governmental and non-governmental enterprises, including marketing boards, which have been granted exclusive rights or privileges, including statutory or constitutional powers, in the exercise of which they influence through their purchases or sales the level or direction of imports or exports".

9. The rules and disciplines on export restrictions of the GATT 1994 apply both to non-agricultural and to agricultural products, and the section on export measures in the TPRs deals with both categories of measures; this chapter thus includes all products. However, in the context of the negotiations under the DDA, additional disciplines on agricultural products under Article 12 of the Agreement on Agriculture should be taken into account. The scope of agricultural products is defined in Annex 1 (product coverage) of the Agreement on Agriculture. These products are the subject of negotiations in the Committee on Agriculture in Special Session; other products are dealt with in the Negotiating Group on Market Access for Non-agricultural Products.

10. A note by the WTO Secretariat reports that 24 members indicated that they do not maintain any quantitative restrictions. (G/MA/NTM/QR/W/1)

11. See Chapter 5, Table 5.4 and Annex 5.A2.

12. See relevant government sites and the Organization of American States (OAS) (www.sice.oas.org/) for information on specific provisions.

13. Council Regulation 2603/69, as amended. Exceptions include measures to prevent a critical situation arising from a shortage of essential products; these may be limited to exports from certain regions of the Community or only to certain destinations. See TPR of the European Union (2002).

14. Iceland, Liechtenstein, Norway and Switzerland.

15. Before its expansion from 15 to 25 members, the European Union concluded these with Bulgaria, Czech Republic, Estonia, Hungary, Latvia, Lithuania, Poland, Romania, Slovak Republic, and Slovenia.

16. For industrial products.

17. Article 32 and Article 34 enable the use of exceptional measures under given conditions, such as serious shortage of essential products.

18. http://europa.eu.int/, Joint Declaration VI, No. 4104.

19. See Part Two, Section C, Non-Tariff Measures, Article 309-315 and the Annex. For example, each party reserves the right to apply export controls on logs of all species.

20. Article 315 (Mexico is exempted by Annex 315): "a Party may adopt or maintain a restriction otherwise justified under Article XI:2(a) or XX(g), (i) or (j) of the GATT with

respect to the export of a good of the Party to the territory of another Party, only if: (a) the restriction does not reduce the proportion of the total export shipments of the specific good made available to that other Party relative to the total supply of that good of the Party maintaining the restrictions as compared to the proportion prevailing in the most recent 36-month period for which data are available prior to the imposition of the measure, or in such other representative period on which the Parties may agree; (b) the Party does not impose a higher price for exports of a good to that other party than the price changed for such good when consumed domestically, by means of any measure, such as licences, fees, taxation and minimum price requirements. The foregoing provision does not apply to a higher price that may result from a measure taken pursuant to subparagraph (a) that only restricts the volume of exports; and (c) the restriction does not require the disruption of normal channels of supply to that other Party or normal proportions among specific goods or categories of goods supplied to that other Party."

21. WT/REG111/R/B/2, G/L/540, 13 May 2002.

22. The full text of the footnote on NTMs in the Osaka Action Agenda is as follows: "[N]on-tariff measures include but are not restricted to quantitative import/export restrictions/prohibitions, import/export levies, minimum import prices, discretionary import/export licensing, voluntary export restraints and export subsidies." Note that voluntary export restraints are still relevant despite prohibition under the Agreement on Safeguards since Russia and Viet Nam are APEC members but not yet WTO members.

23. For detailed information on export levies, see Chapter 5, Table 5.2.

24. According to Indonesia's IAP (2002), "Indonesia has undertaken unilateral action to remove or reduce non-tariff barriers which are not included in the Uruguay Round commitments; ..., gradual reduction of export taxes on logs, sawn timber, rattan and minerals." As the IAP explains, "Export bans and prohibition covers several products such as fisheries, wildlife, hide and skins of certain animals such as reptiles, rubber materials (notably rubber block) and variety of waste and scrap products. The aim is to protect endangered species of wild flora and fauna as well as to prevent export of hazardous materials. Apart from imposing textiles quotas with importing countries, ... these export restrictions are based on (i) protection of natural resources and endangered species; (ii) promotion of higher-value-added downstream industries; (iii) upgrading the quality of export products; (iv) ensuring adequate supply of 'essential products', and (v) imposing controls on textiles and clothing under MFA. Export restrictions will be further eliminated." It should also be noted that the IMF's support programme for Indonesia following the Asian financial crisis called for removal of export-restrictive measures as a way to improve the country's economic performance.

25. All restrictions under this agreement were eliminated at the end of 2004.

26. Several reports mentioned the existence of surveillance and monitoring mechanisms, but interpretation of the agreement is not the subject of this chapter.

27. Article 12 of the Agreement on Agriculture stipulates a certain co-ordinating scheme between these conflicting interests.

28. In the Transitional Review Mechanism of China, the United States, joined by Japan, raised an issue of export restrictions of raw materials and stated that "fluorspar" is an example of a raw material that is still subject to this type of export restriction. China imposes quota and licence fees on fluorspar exports, apparently to support China's domestic users of fluorspar, which face no comparable restrictions. China responded that "China maintains export administration of a small number of products for the purposes of protecting public interest, avoiding shortage in domestic supply, conserving the exhaustible natural resources, or undertaking obligations under international treaties or intergovernmental agreements, which are in conformity to Article XX of GATT 1994." From 1 January 2002,

China gave up export administration of Chinese chestnut, reed mat, red bean, honey, colophony, tung wood and boards (to Japan), vitamin C, etc. As of 2002, there were still 54 products subject to export administration, including live bovine and beef (to Hong Kong, China and Macao, China), live swine and swine meat (to Hong Kong, China and Macao, China), fowl and meat (to Hong Kong, China and Macao, China), garlic, tea, wheat, corn, rice, liquorice roots and their products, rushes and their products, sugar, bauxite, light (dead)-burned magnesia, talc, fluospar, rare earth, tungsten ores and products, antimony ores and products, tin, zinc, coal, coke, crude oil, processed oil, paraffin wax, artificial corundum, heavy water, ozonosphere-depleting materials, chemicals under supervision and control, chemicals used to produce narcotics, sawn wood, silk, greige, cotton, woven fabrics, silver, platinum, certain steel products (to the United States), etc. These export administrative measures have been notified to the WTO. (G/C/W/435, G/C/W/430, G/C/W/438, 2002)

29. A study focusing on the development dimension conducted a comparison between TPRs in 1989-94 and in 1995-98. It found, for example, that export taxation increased slightly in countries for which information is available in both periods (Michalopoulos, 1999). However, recent TPRs indicate that quite a number of reviewed countries have eliminated export duties, partly reflecting regional efforts in this regard (see Chapter 5).

30. WTO Director General Dr. Supachai Panitchpakdi in a speech at the occasion of the Partnership Summit 2003 in India, stated the following: "I hope that India will also be looking at market access opportunities in other developing countries. South-South trade has risen significantly over the last ten years from 30% in 1990 to 40% today, but trade barriers tend to remain high. For example, the average tariff on textile and clothing in developing and transition economies is 29%, this is over three times the average tariff on textiles and clothing in the Quad (the United States, Canada, the European Union and Japan." (8 January 2003, www.wto.org/)

31. WT/DS107, TPR Pakistan (2001).

32. In the TPR of Papua New Guinea in 1999 and Solomon Islands in 1998, the issue of export duties on logs was addressed in detail. The reports argued that export taxes on unprocessed logs are seen as a means of promoting greater domestic value added and encouraging downstream processing. This attempts to encourage direct investment in forestry for downstream processing, creating employment and domestic economic growth. The reports point out that export taxes divert export sales on to the home market and reduce the domestic price, thus providing an implicit subsidy to processors, while penalizing raw material suppliers. The domestic price would be decreased by the equivalent of the export taxes; if the export taxes are prohibitive, the effect of reducing price is much larger. However, the reports indicate that these implicit subsidies tend rather to protect inefficient processing industries and ultimately to cause an economically undesirable situation. This is particularly the case in PNG where the processing industry is protected by high protective import tariffs. Moreover, countries with relatively small production levels of raw materials have no influence over the world price of these products; when export duties are applied, they thus cannot raise their export prices and pass the tax on to foreign purchasers; the domestic suppliers must fully absorb the taxes themselves. Export taxes also reduce the returns from exports of raw materials, which could adversely affect national economic growth.

33. In the joint declaration issued at the conclusion of the EU-Mexico Free Trade Agreement, both parties agreed to seek to establish disciplines for the elimination of export taxes or restrictions that operate to increase the exports of, or the protection afforded to, domestic industries such as leather within the context of multilateral negotiations (http://europa.eu.int/, Joint Declaration VI No. 4104).

34. TN/AG/6, 18 December 2002.

35. The framework agreement agreed in July 2004 (WT/L/579) mentioned that "…disciplines on export prohibitions and restrictions in Article 12.1 of the Agreement on Agriculture will be strengthened" (Annex A: Framework for Establishing Modalities in Agriculture, paragraph 50). In the meantime, concerning non-agricultural products, the framework agreement encouraged members "to make notifications on NTBs by 31 October 2004 and to proceed with identification, examination, categorisation and ultimately negotiation on NTBs (Annex B: Framework for Establishing Modalities in Market Access for Non-Agricultural Products, paragraph 14). By early 2005, the negotiations were still under way.

References

Asia-Pacific Economic Cooperation (APEC) (2002), APEC Individual Action Plan 2002, www.apec-iap.org/

Black's Law Dictionary (1991), West Publishing Co.

GATT (1994), Analytical Index Guide To GATT Law and Practice.

Goode, Walter (1998), The Dictionary of Trade Policy Terms, Centre for International Economic Studies, University of Adelaide.

Hertel, Thomas W. and Will Martin (1999), Developing Country Interests in Liberalizing Manufactures Trade, Purdue University and World Bank.

International Monetary Fund (IMF) (2001), Trade Policy Conditionality in Fund-Supported Programs, www.imf.org/.

Jackson, John H., William J. Davey and Alan O. Skyes, Jr. (1995), Legal Problems of International Economic Relations, Cases, Materials, and Text, Third Edition.

Martin, Will (2001), Trade Policies, Developing Countries, and Globalization", World Bank, Washington, DC.

Michalopoulos, C. (1999), Trade Policy and Market Access Issues for Developing Countries: Implications for the Millennium Round, World Bank.

OECD (1999), Foreign Direct Investment and Recovery in Southeast Asia, OECD, Paris.

WTO: World Trade Organisation, Trade Policy Reviews (1995-2002), www.wto.org/.

WTO (2001), "Protocol on the Accession of the People's Republic of China", WT/L/432, www.wto.org/.

WTO (2001), "Report of the Working Party on the Accession of China", WT/ACC/CHN/49, www.wto.org/.

WTO (2002), "Report of the Trade Policy Review Body for 2002", WT/TPR/W/29, www.wto.org/.

Chapter 7

Non-tariff Barriers of Concern to Developing Countries

by

Barbara Fliess and Iza Lejarraga

> This chapter identifies non-tariff barriers (NTBs) faced by developing countries in their trade with developed countries and in South-South trade. The goal is to raise awareness of barriers that interfere with the ability of developing countries to build up trade. Data collected and analysed consist of the academic literature, notifications by developing countries to the Negotiating Group on Market Access for Non-Agricultural Products (NAMA) of the Doha Development Agenda (DDA), business surveys, and records relating to trade disputes brought before the World Trade Organization (WTO) and regional dispute settlement mechanisms. The chapter identifies the categories and types of measures that are most reported and the products affected by the reported measures. Attention is also drawn to developing countries' forward-looking export strategies and related potential barriers. Overall, the chapter highlights similarities and differences in NTBs reported in the data reviewed and compares NTBs reported for trade with developed countries and for trade among developing countries.

Introduction

For developing countries, integration into global markets offers the potential for more rapid growth and poverty reduction.[1] Yet tariff and non-tariff barriers may hamper key developing-country exports, making it difficult for them to take full advantage of this opportunity.

The issue of improved market access for goods has been taken up by successive GATT rounds. Significant progress in reducing tariff barriers overall has been counterbalanced by persisting non-tariff barriers (NTBs) that may even be on the increase in new and possibly more discrete forms.[2] It is often hard to evaluate the importance of NTBs owing to the lack of transparency concerning their scope and effects. In addition, measures that traders encounter may or may not be legitimate under WTO agreements.

With the Doha Development Agenda (DDA), the use of NTBs is once again the subject of multilateral negotiations.[3] Opportunities to address developing country concerns relating to NTBs are also provided by regional and other forums that pursue trade liberalisation.

Against this background, this chapter analyses data that identify NTBs of concern to developing countries in trade both among themselves and with developed countries. A clearer idea of these barriers should allow WTO members to better understand developing countries' concerns and their implications and thus respond with an appropriately proactive and positive agenda. More specifically, consideration could be given to attaching priority to NTBs found to affect products in which developing countries have a comparative advantage when market access commitments are negotiated in the WTO Negotiating Group on Market Access for Non-Agricultural Products (NAMA) and other WTO bodies.

Similarly, identification of NTBs of particular concern to developing countries could help determine priority targets for strengthening special and differential treatment (SDT). To help boost their exports, developing countries have requested SDT, including in the field of NTBs. A review of SDT-related assistance is also called for by the Doha Ministerial Declaration.

Finally, the chapter aims to help raise general awareness of NTBs maintained by developing countries which interfere with their ability to trade with each other and to build trade among themselves. Overall, the results presented can serve as benchmarks against which policy makers in developing countries may wish to examine the particular situation of their economies and their negotiating objectives.

Recent trends in developing countries' export performance

As background for examining NTBs of concern to developing countries, it is useful to review their recent export trends. Export data show that these countries are increasingly important players in world trade. In the last decade, their share in world merchandise exports increased from 17% to 27%.

Most developing country exports go to high-income countries, but trade with other developing countries is increasingly important and dynamic, although it is becoming more concentrated on regional markets. This is particularly noticeable in Sub-Saharan Africa, where intra-regional exports increased from approximately 20% in 1993 to almost half of the region's total exports to other developing countries.

In terms of export structure, the share of manufactured products has grown steadily over the past two decades, whereas the share of primary commodities has declined. Developing countries are clearly striving to diversify their export activity, as shown by the shift in the export pattern from low value-added manufactured goods towards higher value-added goods such as electrical and electronic products, industrial equipment and machinery. The exception is the group of least developed countries (LDCs), whose export structure has not evolved to the same extent.[4]

Annex 7.A1 provides a detailed statistical overview of developing countries' export performance over the last decade.

Analysis of NTBs: data availability and methodology

Data on NTBs are extremely limited, particularly in developing countries. One source of fairly comparable and comprehensive data is the UNCTAD Database on Trade Control Measures, which has, however, a number of well-known definitional and methodological limitations. A few regional groupings of developing countries (*e.g.* ALADI, SIECA, ASEAN, SAARC) and individual developing countries maintain their own databases on trade measures or barriers of various types. Particularly lacking are data on NTBs that affect low-income countries, including LDCs.

Besides these databases, there are no widely accepted tools or approaches for capturing non-tariff measures that limit market access. Researchers and analysts have resorted to various methodologies in an effort to identify and assess the most prevalent and restrictive barriers, including frequency measures derived from the databases, as well as empirical analyses based on surveys of exporters or data drawn from WTO trade policy reviews (TPRs). The advantages and shortcomings of each of these approaches have been well documented (Andriamananjara *et al.*, 2004; Dean *et al.*, 2003; Bora *et al.*, 2002; McGuire *et al.*, 2002; Michalopoulos, 1999; Deardorff and Stern, 1998; OECD, 1997).

Acknowledging such data and methodological shortcomings, this chapter draws on several sources of information in an attempt to provide useful insights for traders and trade negotiators. The result is an analytical framework based on four elements of research:

- A brief review of literature on existing NTBs.

- Analysis of recent NTB notifications by developing country governments to the WTO.

- A review of private-sector perceptions of NTBs through available surveys.

- Analysis of trade disputes involving NTBs brought before multilateral and regional dispute settlement mechanisms.

These approaches are combined to provide a unified basis for analysis. The term NTBs is used to refer broadly to all measures (public and private) other than tariffs that have the potential for distorting international trade flows in goods.

The next section reviews some of the main findings from available literature on NTBs affecting developing countries, covering both South-North and South-South trade. Subsequently, the NTB notifications made to date made by non-OECD countries to the WTO Negotiating Group on Market Access for Non-Agricultural Products (NAMA) are analysed. The following section reviews disputes brought to the WTO and to tribunals of regional trade arrangements (RTAs) among developing countries. Finally, available surveys reporting private-sector perceptions of NTBs are examined. Various supporting materials and data are compiled in the annexes to this chapter.

Literature review

A great deal of research has shown that developing countries still have an important market access agenda in the aftermath of widespread tariff liberalisation undertaken by developed and developing economies. This section summarises the available literature on non-tariff market issues that affect developing countries in both a South-North and a South-South trade perspective. It first looks at the global level, and then turns to a region-based overview of NTBs affecting intra-regional trade among developing countries. Relevant literature and case studies undertaken by scholars, trade analysts, governments and international organisations were examined. Studies based on private-sector perceptions are excluded, as these are reviewed separately.

Global trends in NTBs affecting developing countries

The existing literature describes a few key findings and trends pertaining to developing countries. Most analysts observe that the utilisation of certain types of NTBs affecting developing countries, such as quantitative restrictions, has decreased markedly in the post-Uruguay Round (UR) setting (McGuire *et al.*, 2002; Stephenson, 1999; PECC, 1995; Estevadeordal and Robert, 2001; Alexander and Yeats, 1995[5]). The remaining post-Uruguay NTBs, according to frequency ratio analyses conducted by Michalopoulos (1999) and others, appear to be more prevalent in developing-country than in developed-country markets, although they have decreased over time. Michalopoulos (1999) notes that frequency ratios of quantity and price control measures tend to be higher in countries with lower levels of per capita income and lower degrees of openness. A seemingly greater prevalence of these NTBs in trade among developing countries is however difficult to demonstrate given that the literature focuses predominantly on barriers to developing-country trade in their major export markets, which are generally OECD markets (Bhattacharryya, 2002; COMESA, 2003; ECLAC, 2001; Haveman and Shatz, 2004).

Although the literature takes a range of approaches to identifying measures of concern to developing countries, it frequently focuses on quantity control measures: non-automatic import licensing, quotas and tariff rate quotas. These measures may also attract attention because their effects are by nature easier to quantify and analyse than most other types of NTBs. Researchers report that post-UR NTBs are far more frequent for processed goods than for primary commodities.

Laird (1999) finds that the primary NTBs affecting developing-country access to both OECD and non-OECD markets are essentially the same, primarily import licensing systems (including allocation of tariff quotas); variable levies and production and export subsidies (in the agricultural sector); import/export quotas (in textiles and clothing sector) and local content and export balancing requirements (automotive industry); export subsidies to develop non-traditional manufacturers (administered as tax breaks or subsidised finance, as direct subsidies have almost disappeared under fiscal pressures); and state trading operations.

Another perspective comes from research that identifies the prevalence of various types of NTBs differently, according to whether developing countries trade with developed countries or among themselves, as described below.

Observations regarding NTBs in trade with developed countries

The literature suggests that technical regulations, price control measures and certain other measures are very often subject to concerns about access to developed-country markets.

Technical barriers to trade: While recognising that technical measures may serve legitimate purposes, it is also evident that they can be important obstacles to exports to developed countries whose technical regulations, standards and conformity assessment procedures may effectively serve as border-protection instruments (Wilson, 1996; Stephenson, 1997; Michalopoulos, 1999). In spite of their adverse effects, Nixon (2004) argues that these measures can also have a positive effect on developing countries by spurring new competitive advantages and investment in technological capability, if enterprises in developing countries act offensively. This scenario is less likely to materialise in LDCs, given the technological and financial constraints they face.

Sanitary and phytosanitary measures: The literature also reveals that animal health and plant protection measures may, in some cases, appear unnecessarily protectionist. These measures are of special importance to developing countries given the level of their agricultural exports. A quantitative analysis of the impact of a specific SPS standards implemented in the EU found a decrease in African exports to this market of 64% or USD 670 million (Otsuki *et al.*, 2001). The emergence of biotechnology, and international trade in biotechnology, has recently spurred the use of restrictive measures that are costly and burdensome for developing countries (Zarrilli and Musselli, 2004).

Other measures: The literature shows a growing concern about measures in developed-country markets that may have trade-restrictive effects. At issue are rules and regulations associated with environmental, national security, labour and other social standards (Michalopoulos, 1999; Bhattacharyya, 1999; Bhattacharyya and Mukhopadhyaya, 2002; Dasgupta, 2002; Chatuverdi and Nagpal, 2003; Bharucha, 2000). While these are legitimate areas for regulation, bioterrorism rules, child labour clauses, and environmental standards are at times perceived as being more trade-restrictive than necessary to achieve intended goals. Discussion of this area is highly politicised: few objective studies quantify or thoroughly examine the impact of these measures on developing countries' exports.

NTBs in trade among developing countries

As mentioned above, there is a dearth of studies on intra-developing country trade from the perspective of NTBs. There is a growing tide of research interest in issues affecting trade among developing countries; however, existing analyses still focus on tariffs and tariff liberalisation (Lucke, 2004; Priyadarshi, 2003; Australian Government, 2004) or more generally on avenues for co-operation among developing countries (UNCTAD, 2004; South-South Centre, 1996).

Given the void with respect to NTBs, the best sources of information are studies on barriers to trade among developing countries participating in RTAs (*e.g.* Berlinski, 2002; ACS, 2003; Soontiens, 2003; Bhattacharyya and Mukhopdhyaya, 2002). However, the findings drawn from these studies reflect barriers to intra-regional exports (which concentrate on Asia and Latin America) and not barriers to trade with developing countries in other regions (a significant portion of trade for the Middle East and Africa).

A few general observations can be made and are noted below. Specifically, customs procedures, para-tariff measures, and some other forms of NTBs are observed to slow the pace of liberalisation and improved market access in intra-developing country trade.

Customs and administrative procedures: The literature on intra-developing country trade reports significant problems associated with cumbersome and inefficient customs and administrative bureaucracy. Customs procedures are generally not automated; customs valuation tends not to be based on market prices; the customs clearance process is long and complex; and weak customs administration leads to border smuggling. Such inefficient procedures and excessive formalities may result in a high degree of non-official trade that is not reflected in South-South trade statistics (Daly *et al.*, 2001).

Para-tariff measures: Where intra-regional tariffs have been lowered or eliminated as a result of regional co-operation, RTAs among developing countries witness an upsurge of import surcharges and other additional charges. This seems to reflect the fiscal dependence of developing countries and LDCs on imports and their need to set new charges to compensate for the loss of tariff revenue. This type of NTB is particularly prevalent among smaller developing countries and LDCs (Daly *et al.*, 2001).

Other obstacles: The literature identifies other barriers that are not considered conventional NTBs. Geographical and infrastructural features emerge as sizeable barriers to trade among developing countries, particularly landlocked countries (Coulibaly and Fontagne, 2003). Growth in trade among developing countries also depends on improvements in property rights, good governance and sound institutions (Agatiello, 2004).

Regional trends in the use of NTBs

A country's major trading partners and the composition of its exports to those markets determines the NTBs that a country faces. Therefore, the identification of NTBs warrants detailed analysis, as the large number of region-specific studies available indicate. Findings from regional studies point to subtle differences among the NTBs that affect the exports of a given region:

- For the Asia-Pacific region, where trade has been characterised by labour-intensive products, particularly textiles and garments, *tariff quotas* applied under the Multi-Fibre Arrangement (MFA), which has since expired, and *technical regulations (especially labelling)* emerge as being the most significant NTBs in terms of the volume of exports affected (ESCAP, 2000; Bhattacharyya, 1999; Bhattacharyya and Mukhopadhyaya, 2002; Bhattacharyya, 2002).

- In the case of Latin America and the Caribbean, which are competitive agricultural exporters, *SPS standards* and agricultural *export subsidies* emerge as the main issues impeding market access to major OECD markets (ECLAC, 2003, 2001, 1999). A quantitative analysis of the incidence of non-tariff measures (NTMs) in Latin American countries shows a growing incidence of technical measures (Inter-American Development Bank, 2002). Also, issues relating to antidumping, particularly for steel, are reported to affect the larger economies of the region (Brazil, Mexico, Argentina, Chile) (Scandizzo, 2002).

- Studies on Africa and the Middle East indicate that key NTBs faced by exports from these regions – such as *quantitative restrictions* and *special import charges* – do not have a significant restrictive effect but instead reveal that certain NTBs – notably MFA quotas and voluntary export restraints (VERs) – have helped their exporters by shielding them from competition from other developing regions (Gugerty and Stern, 1997; Arnjadi and Yeats, 1995; Yeats, 1994). More than complaining about the effect of a particular NTB, these documents reflect concern about the heavy concentration of an array of NTBs on strategic products of export interest to the region, namely the energy sector.

- Finally, focusing on the EU as the principal export market and the possibility of future accession, studies covering Europe and Central Asia register strong concerns about barriers pertaining to *stringent TBT and SPS rules* (Hanspeter et al., 2001). For this region, there is very little literature.

Annex 7.A2 offers further details on the findings from the literature addressing NTBs by developing region.

Analysis of notifications of NTBs to NAMA

A more systematic account of developing countries' perceptions of non-tariff barriers comes from the notification process established under the auspices of NAMA. WTO members were invited to submit notifications on NTBs that directly affect their exports. From March 2003 through October 2004, a total of 11 OECD countries and 21 non-OECD countries submitted lists describing barriers to their exports in foreign markets.[6] Notifications were made according to the NAMA Inventory of Non-tariff Measures, which provides for a broad and comprehensive coverage of NTBs (see Annex 7.A3).[7]

The following section analyses the notifications made by non-OECD developing countries, with a view to identifying frequently reported barriers and the products affected.

Data set

The 21 non-OECD countries made a total of 1 200 notifications that, in their view, represent NTBs affecting various export sectors.[8] These countries represent a geographically and economically diverse and balanced sample of developing countries. In terms of income level, 19% are high-income economies; 28% upper-middle-income; 28% lower–middle-income; and 24% low-income (of the latter, one country, Bangladesh, is a LDC).[9] In 2002, the total value of merchandise exports from these 21 countries was USD 1 132 567 million and represented approximately 57% of total developing-country exports and 18% of total global exports.[10]

While the data set is fairly representative in terms of developing countries and their aggregate exports, the context in which it was collected must be considered. Moreover, some notifications lack precision and clarity or have missing or incomplete information. The methodology used by countries to identify the NTBs is not documented. The inventory itself has certain shortcomings, namely the lack of clear definition and demarcation of some types of NTBs (for example, in the areas of import licensing and rules of origin). Furthermore, as some potential types of barriers are not explicitly listed in the inventory, countries may not have reported on them. This chapter does not make any judgement about whether the policies or measures notified are legitimate or not.[11]

There is insufficient information to ascertain whether notifications are made with regard to developed- or developing-country markets.[12] To the extent that most developing-country exports are destined for developed markets, it would seem reasonable to view this analysis in that perspective.

Types of barriers reported

As shown in Figure 7.1, TBTs represent the NTB category with the highest incidence of notifications with 530 entries, or almost half of the total, followed by Customs and Administrative Procedures (380 entries) and SPS measures (137 entries). Quantitative restrictions, trade remedies, government participation in trade, charges on imports, as well as other barriers amount to less than 5% of total NTB entries.

Figure 7.1. Frequency of notifications by NTB category

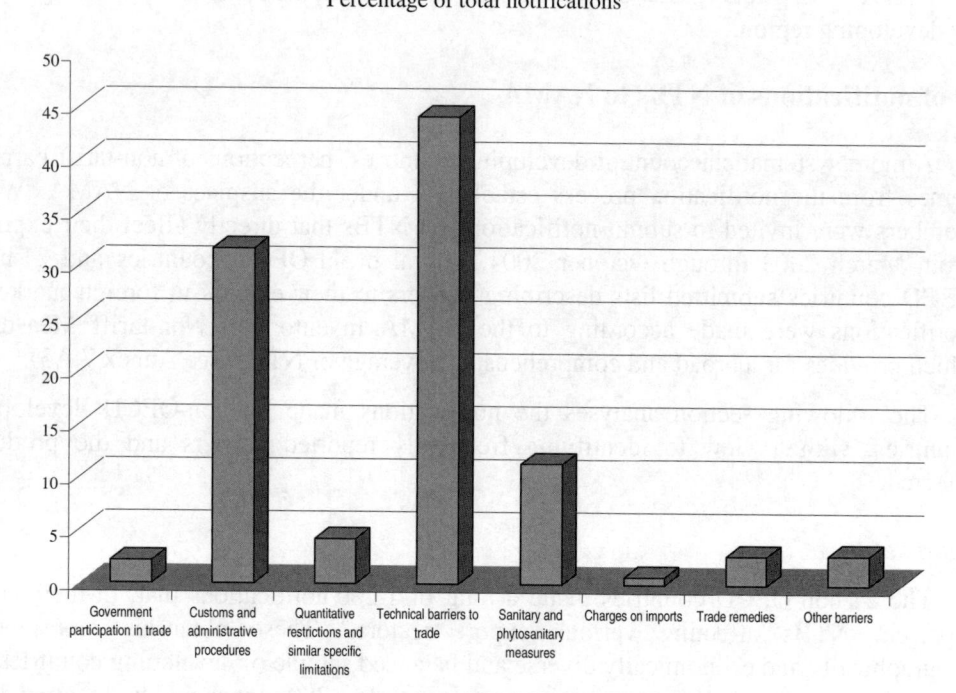

Percentage of total notifications

Source: OECD, based on submissions to NAMA (TN/MA/W*).

Technical barriers to trade

TBTs were the principal reported barrier for 12 of the 21 countries, and the second most reported barrier for five others. Almost half of the complaints in this area concerned technical regulations and standards (46%), followed by testing and certification arrangements (26%) and by marking, labelling and packaging requirements (16%). A commonly reported trade impact of these barriers is an unnecessary (and often significant) increase in costs that effectively impedes exports.

Several notifying countries comment that technical regulations and standards applied by certain WTO members are more stringent than those specified by relevant international bodies and that no legitimate explanation has been provided. Moreover, upward revision of these standards at regular intervals makes it difficult for developing countries to keep up with and adapt to changing requirements. Another complaint relates to differing technical requirements among members because common international standards have not been adopted, thus raising compliance costs and discouraging developing countries from diversifying their export markets. Countries indicate that equivalence agreements on standards across WTO members would benefit developing-country exporters by reducing financial burdens as well as the risk of uncertainty.

Many complaints pertain to the area of testing and certification. Reported concerns are a general absence of information and lack of transparency on the procedural norms and regulations regarding specifications as well as methods of sampling, inspection and testing.

Notifying countries maintain that testing methods specify exceedingly high levels of sensitivity that may not be justified on the grounds of health and safety issues, thereby making testing costs disproportionately high and even prohibitive. Sometimes levels of sensitivity are raised only because better technology or testing equipment becomes available, and not because of evidence that higher sensitivity is required to meet a health objective. Aside from cost concerns, countries report that they lose customers simply as a result of the time required for further testing by importing country laboratories before the required certificates are completed and shipments released from customs.

Other reported problems in conformity assessment procedures include: applying exhaustive pre-inspection measures at national boundaries, which consume large amounts of time and money; providing quality certificates that are valid only for one year and only renewable annually; examining the production process in the country of origin by experts of the importing country, the developing country manufacturer (exporter) having to pay for travelling expenses and accommodation of experts; and registration that is costly, time-consuming, arbitrary and not always granted.

Other TBTs subject to a significant number of notifications are marking, labelling and packaging requirements that are noted as being burdensome, complicated to implement, and often not equally applied to similar products of domestic origin. It is claimed that such requirements may entail the use of highly developed technological systems that developing countries cannot afford. Labelling for genetically modified organisms (GMO), in particular, increases costs for developing country producers, owing to very stringent procedures in the absence of solid scientific evidence on the risks to humans of consuming GMOs. Other countries report that abrupt changes in packaging requirements result in entire shipments being held back at the distributor's warehouse.

Overall, the fact that developing-country suppliers may have more difficulty adapting to new, legitimate requirements argues for technical assistance and capacity building. WTO members can also explore avenues for reducing the effects of these different TBT-related measures through international standards, more common approaches to test methods and conformity assessment, among other mechanisms.

Customs and administrative procedures

The second most-reported NTB is customs and administrative procedures, which accounts for almost a third of the total notifications. For nine countries, these are the primary barrier, and for six others the second most reported barrier. Within this broad category, the two most prominent barriers are rules of origin and import licensing (both automatic and non-automatic), each responsible for more than one-third of notifications. Other areas exhibiting a high to moderate number of notifications under this category are customs valuation, formalities and, to a lesser extent, classification. There are also notifications pertaining to pre-shipment inspection and consular formalities and documentation.

Some notifying countries report that rules of origin are discriminatory, unreasonable or inconsistent. This entails extra formalities and costs or administrative difficulties. Rules of origin can be preferential or non-preferential. While most notifications do not elaborate on the type of rules of origin at issue, there seems to be some concern on the part of countries that fail to obtain originating status under preferential rules of origin, with the result that their products are not covered by the preferences.

Notifications testify that import licensing procedures frequently have the effect of delaying or hampering imports. Some notifying countries complain about the introduction of additional requirements, such as supporting documents, for automatic licences issued by the importers. Other complaints hold that much of the time, the issuing of import licences is not expressly stipulated and lacks transparency.

Customs valuation rules are also perceived to act as trade barriers on some occasions. Most complaints describe overestimation of prices for customs purposes, particularly through the use of discriminatory and arbitrary valuation methods. The use of minimum and reference prices, rather than transaction prices, is widely criticised. Notifying countries also report that the requirement of a minimum amount of imports for customs valuation prohibits developing-country producers from exporting small volumes.

Other complaints relate to inconsistent and varying customs classification, including the right of customs officers to exercise excessive discretion when classifying goods. In some countries, customs clearance is reported to be deliberately delayed to increase transaction costs and thus reduce competition with similar domestic products. Notifications also reveal excessive requirements for customs formalities, another factor that contributes to delaying trade and increasing costs.

Sanitary and phytosanitary measures

SPS measures constitute the third most frequently reported barrier for non-OECD exports. Complainants recognise that risk to consumers is an important concern at international level, but they claim that certain countries tend to establish onerous standards without first conducting comprehensive risk assessments. These measures include chemical residue limits, freedom from disease and specified product treatment, among others (74% of SPS entries). Approximately 17% of complaints in this area pertain specifically to testing, certification and other conformity assessment measures related to SPS.[13]

While SPS measures may serve legitimate purposes, the notifying countries report extra formalities, time and costs that restrict or inhibit exports. Obtaining SPS approvals also reportedly involves tedious and substantial documentation and bureaucratic procedures. For instance, one notifying country reported that its exports for a specific product were reduced by 70% in both value and volume because a detector required to comply with SPS measures was too expensive to purchase.

Quantitative restrictions

Quantitative restrictions and specific limitations account for 51 notifications (4% of total). Half of the barriers reported under this category represent strictly quantitative restrictions (QRs). Other measures in this category that are reported relatively often include embargoes and similar restrictions (20%), exchange controls (12%), tariff rate quotas (10%) and discrimination resulting from bilateral agreements.

Government participation in trade

Instances of government participation in trade account for 26 notifications (2%). The bulk of these notifications falls into the category of restrictive practices tolerated by governments (65%), which often are not further specified but which are reported to protect domestic producers from foreign competition and to distort trade. Other complaints that have similar effects regard government assistance, state trading and monopolistic practices, and government procurement.

Charges on imports

Charges on imports represent the category of NTBs subject to the fewest number of NAMA notifications in the sample of developing countries (0.8%). Import surcharges in this category include: high taxes for border passage; high storage taxes; port taxes; statistical taxes; variable taxes; cargo and maritime transport taxes; attestation fees and legalisation fees; and fees for authentication of export documents. Countries report that the imposition of high fees and fluctuating taxes adds significantly to export costs, results in uncertainty and may create conditions for corruption.

Products affected by the reported NTBs

For the sample of developing countries, the product groups most frequently notified as being hampered by NTBs are *live animals and products* (309 notifications), *machinery and electronics* (215), *chemical and allied industry products* (124), and *textile and textile articles* (93). Figure 7.2 displays the percentage of notifications by product group. Annex 7.A4 provides a more detailed account of reported barriers and products falling under each of the broad commodity groups.

The product group with the most reported NTBs, live animals and products, is primarily affected by SPS measures (114 notifications) and customs and administrative barriers (106), in particular rules of origin (79% of total notified customs problems).[14] Within this product category, reported measures are highly concentrated on fish and fisheries products, including shrimp and prawns, octopus, crab and tuna. These products represent the largest number of NTB notifications in the data set.[15]

Machinery and electronics is the product category recording the highest incidence of technical barriers to trade (142 notifications), most of them relating to technical regulations and standards. Affected products are mostly electrical apparatus (*e.g.* telephones, televisions, calculators, microwaves); the rest are mechanical machinery (*e.g.* computer and parts of computers, palm mould milling machinery) and accessories such as various kinds of cables. These products also show the largest number of complaints about import licensing procedures (a total of 40 notifications or 69% of the notifications relating to customs problems).

For chemical products, the exports of concern to developing countries, as reflected in their notifications, are mostly pharmaceutical products (23%) and perfumery, cosmetics and toilet preparations (20%), followed by fertilisers, inorganic and organic chemicals, explosives and matches, and soap and washing preparations. This category of exports is significantly affected by TBTs (77 notifications), and to a lesser extent, by import licensing procedures and customs formalities.

Figure 7.2. NTB notifications by product group

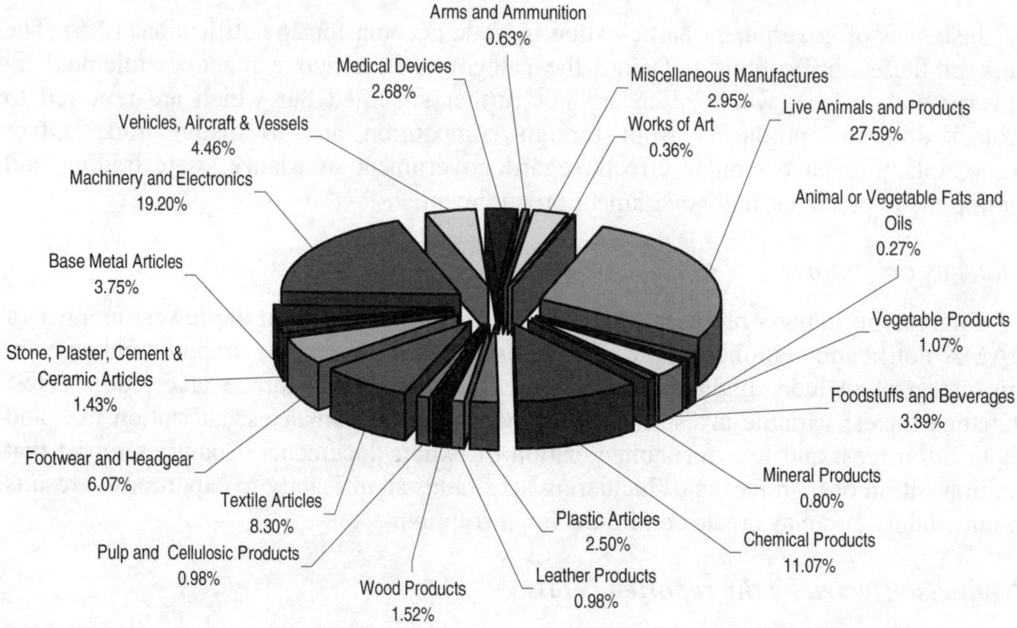

- Arms and Ammunition 0.63%
- Medical Devices 2.68%
- Vehicles, Aircraft & Vessels 4.46%
- Machinery and Electronics 19.20%
- Base Metal Articles 3.75%
- Stone, Plaster, Cement & Ceramic Articles 1.43%
- Footwear and Headgear 6.07%
- Textile Articles 8.30%
- Pulp and Cellulosic Products 0.98%
- Wood Products 1.52%
- Plastic Articles 2.50%
- Leather Products 0.98%
- Miscellaneous Manufactures 2.95%
- Works of Art 0.36%
- Live Animals and Products 27.59%
- Animal or Vegetable Fats and Oils 0.27%
- Vegetable Products 1.07%
- Foodstuffs and Beverages 3.39%
- Mineral Products 0.80%
- Chemical Products 11.07%

Source: OECD, based on notifications to NAMA (TN/MA/W*).

Another important export sector for the sample of developing countries, textiles and textile articles, is also the subject of a significant number of notifications, relating particularly to TBTs (42 notifications) and customs procedures (37). In the latter category there are many complaints about customs valuation (43% of notified customs problems), second only to the still higher number of notifications of valuation problems affecting footwear, handbags and related products (where customs valuation is 89% of customs-related barriers). Textiles receive the highest number of complaints concerning quantitative restrictions (9 notifications), which may be related in part to the complaints on import licensing. The main commodities reported to be subject to these restrictions are apparel and clothing accessories.

The list of products mentioned in the above findings is not exhaustive. Other notified manufactures are vehicles and ships; wood and wood products; optical, medical and surgical supplies; and prepared foodstuffs. Most of these product groups mainly face TBTs, although the nature of the TBTs varies from one product category to the other. For instance, prepared foodstuffs and beverages are notably affected by marking, labelling and packaging requirements, which make up 46% of TBT complaints. This is not the case for vehicles and for wood products, which record few notifications relating to marking and labelling requirements (4% and 5%, respectively) but many notifications concerning testing (34%) and certification arrangements (35%), followed by technical regulations (31%) and standards (30%). Notifications regarding the export of optical, medical and surgical equipment, in contrast, pertain exclusively to the issue of enforcement of technical regulations and standards (86% of TBT notifications).

In several other product categories, however, customs and administrative procedures register more notifications than TBTs: this is the case for the categories of miscellaneous manufactures (where 45% of the reported barriers relate to customs), plastic and plastic products (46% of reported barriers), and metals and metallic products (41% of reported barriers). For plastics and rubber articles, the main complaint pertains to rules of origin (46% of reported customs-related problems), while in the general category of miscellaneous manufactures (comprising furniture, toys, etc.), notifications refer mostly to excessive use of import licensing (43%). With respect to metal exports (mostly iron and steel) there is a relatively high number of references to trade remedies, in addition to customs and administrative barriers.

Table 7.1. NTBs reported for specific product groups

	1	2	3	4	5	6	7	8	9
Live animals and products	2	106	5	79	114	1	0	2	309
Vegetable products	0	1	0	4	6	1	0	0	12
Animal or vegetable fats and oils	0	1	0	0	2	0	0	0	3
Prepared foodstuffs & beverages	2	12	4	17	2	1	0	0	38
Mineral products	1	2	1	4	1	0	0	0	9
Chemical/allied industry products	3	24	6	77	1	1	5	7	124
Plastics and rubber articles	0	13	2	10	0	0	2	1	28
Leather products	1	5	1	3	1	0	0	0	11
Wood and articles of wood	0	3	0	13	0	0	0	1	17
Pulp of wood / fibrous celluloid material	0	2	1	7	0	0	0	1	11
Textile and textile articles	0	37	9	42	4	1	0	0	93
Footwear, headgear & related articles	2	19	0	41	0	1	5	0	68
Articles of stone, plaster, cement, ceramic	1	5	1	8	0	0	1	0	16
Pearls and precious stones and metals	0	0	0	0	0	0	0	0	0
Base metals and articles of base metal	2	17	3	6	0	1	13	0	42
Machinery and electronics	0	59	3	142	2	2	3	4	215
Vehicles, aircraft, vessels	2	17	3	26	0	0	2	0	50
Optical, photographic, medical/surgical	0	7	0	22	0	1	0	0	30
Arms and ammunition	0	3	2	2	0	0	0	0	7
Miscellaneous manufactured articles	0	13	2	12	2	0	2	2	33
Works of art & pieces and antiques	0	3	0	0	0	0	0	1	4
All products & many products	8	25	5	11	0	3	2	10	64
Not classified	1	2	1	5	0	0	0	3	12
Total	25	376	49	531	135	13	35	32	1 196

1. Government participation in trade.
2. Customs and administrative procedures.
3. Quantitative restrictions & similar specific limitations.
4. Technical barriers to trade.
5. Sanitary and phytosanitary measures.
6. Charges on imports.
7. Trade remedies.
8. Other barriers.
9. Total.

Source: OECD, based on notifications to NAMA (TN/MA/W*).

NTBs and products identified in national export strategies

Most developing countries make export promotion and development a priority in order to achieve economic development goals. This typically involves identification of existing and new products that have a potential to emerge as drivers of growth of a nation's exports.

While the success of export strategies is affected by many domestic factors, it is also affected by conditions of world trade, including barriers to market access.[16] Therefore, to provide a forward-looking perspective for the analysis of potential barriers to trade, an effort is made here to identify the products and sectors that feature particularly in developing-country export sectors. The objective is to draw attention to specific NTBs associated with these sectors or products that may impede the achievement of developing countries' export goals.

Data were collected from available national export strategies or programmes of non-OECD countries and other sources, in order to construct an indicative, non-exhaustive list of products and sectors of export interest to an important segment of developing countries. The inventory is presented in Annex 7.A5.

The merchandise products/sectors identified relatively frequently as having potential for helping to spur and sustain future export growth are *textiles and apparel, fish and fisheries products, chemicals and pharmaceuticals, information technology (IT) products, and electrical and other heavy machinery*. In addition, the data suggest that countries are increasingly looking to provision of *services* as an activity with a potential to drive their export performance. Drawing on this information and the data on NTBs contained in the notifications made to NAMA, a number of observations can be made about strategic sectors and potential barriers to their exports.

Textiles and apparel

Reported NTBs affecting exports are essentially of three types: technical barriers to trade, customs and administrative procedures, and quantitative restrictions. Technical regulations and standards as well as testing and certification arrangements are the main problems reported for TBTs, while customs valuation is the predominant problem reported in the area of customs and administrative procedures. For details see Annex 7.A4, Section C.

Fish and fisheries products

Reported NTBs in this sector consist of SPS measures, customs-related procedures and TBTs. While some SPS measures take the form of conformity assessment requirements, other measures cannot be further specified. Most reported problems relating to customs-related procedures refer specifically to rules of origin; the rest relates mainly to import licensing. For details see Annex 7.A4, Section A.

Chemicals and pharmaceuticals

Most reported NTBs affecting exports concern a broad range of TBTs, covering technical regulations and standards, testing and certification arrangements, and marking, labelling and packaging requirements. Various problems with customs and administrative procedures (import licensing, customs formalities, valuation, and consular fees and documentation) are also reported. For details see Annex 7.A4, Section D.

Information technology (IT) products

While notifications to NAMA offer little information on IT products, data on barriers to trade in IT products have been collected by the WTO Secretariat through submissions made by the Committee of Participants on the Expansion of Trade in Information Technology in the context of their Non-tariff Measures Work Programme. The responses from the four developing members that have participated in these submissions[17] indicate that the most serious barriers to market access in IT products are standards and conformity assessment (including testing and certification). Other reported NTBs in this sector relate to rules of origin, lack of transparency and availability of information, process and production methods, and on-site service by IT professionals.[18]

Electrical and other heavy machinery

The main NTB reported for this sector is TBTs, with a prevalence of technical regulations over other forms of TBTs. Customs and administrative barriers are also frequently reported and pertain primarily to import licensing requirements and procedures. For details see Annex 7.A4, Section F.

Analysis of dispute settlement cases concerning non-tariff import measures

Over the past several years, developing countries have filed a growing number of cases under the WTO's Dispute Settlement Understanding (DSU), some of which voice important market access concerns in the area of NTBs. The true number of grievances may be still higher: for many developing-country complainants, preparing and presenting a case at the WTO represents a significant task.[19] Filing of legal challenges is often constrained by a lack of financial resources and technical expertise in working through the process of settling disputes.[20] Therefore, NTBs introduced into a dispute settlement mechanism are likely indicative of serious trade-impeding effects.

The following analysis examines trade dispute activity with a view to identifying the barriers and affected products that have posed serious concerns to developing countries.[21] It first reviews cases brought to the DSU (1995-2004) by non-OECD countries, *i.e.* requests for consultations under Article 4 of the Uruguay Round Understanding on Rules and Procedures Governing the Settlement of Disputes (DSU) presented by developing countries. In order to gain further insight into NTB-related concerns in developing-country forums, the analysis then turns to an examination of complaints raised among Parties to the Andean Community and some other regional dispute mechanisms. The Andean Community was chosen as a case study because of the large number of complaints submitted to this standing tribunal.

WTO cases concerning non-tariff import measures

During the ten years of the WTO's DSU, 24 non-OECD countries have filed a total of 90 cases pertaining to non-tariff barriers.[22] Of these complainants, 50% are lower-middle-income economies, and 17% are low-income economies. Only one least developed country (Bangladesh) submitted a complaint on NTBs, in 2004. Half of the complainants are Asian countries and the other half are Latin American. No cases on NTBs have been filed by developing countries in Africa, Europe, Central Asia or the Middle East.[23]

While two-thirds of all NTB cases have been filed against OECD members (hereafter referred to as South-North disputes), there is a noteworthy upsurge in complaints filed against other non-OECD countries (hereafter referred to as South-South disputes). As

Table 7.2 shows, during the second half of the DSU's existence, South-South disputes over NTBs have increased by 188%, in sharp contrast to the increase in recorded South-North disputes (19%). Annex 7.A6 shows the trend in NTBs complaints filed by non-OECD countries chronologically, against both OECD members and other DC members.

Table 7.2. Number of NTB cases initiated by non-OECD countries

Respondent	DSU first period 1995-99	DSU second period 2000-04	Percent increase
Non-OECD countries	8	23	188
OECD countries	27	32	19
Total	35	55	57

Source: OECD, compiled from WTO Dispute Settlement Understanding.

The NTBs that register the largest number of disputes presented by developing countries are trade remedies (43 cases), quantitative restrictions (18), customs and administrative barriers (13), and charges on imports (12). There are also a not insignificant number of cases in the area of TBTs (9 cases) and government participation in trade (7).

The number of cases concerning customs and administrative procedures increased fourfold in the period 2000-04 with respect to the period 1995-99 (Figure 7.3). Substantial increases are also evident for cases on trade remedies (50%), charges on imports (50%), and SPS measures (100%). In contrast, cases regarding QRs decreased by two-thirds during this period of time.

There are noticeable distinctions between the types of NTBs subject to South-North and South-South disputes. Contrary to the traditional association of trade remedies as measures erected by OECD countries against developing countries, the WTO dispute record shows non-OECD countries as increasingly applying these measures against each other. In fact, the frequency of these occurrences warrants describing this more as a phenomenon characterising trade relations among developing countries. Disputes over surcharges also have a high incidence in trade among developing countries, and may reflect in part developing countries' dependence on alternative revenues in the aftermath of tariff erosion. On the contrary, disputes over quantitative restrictions, customs and administrative-related procedures, and TBTs are primarily (though not exclusively) directed against OECD countries, while government aid and SPS measures feature only in South-North disputes.

A close examination of legal cases reveals that the concerns often involve *procedural aspects* of a measure's application. For example, in the case of *trade remedies*, complaints gravitate around the process of the investigation, including determination of dumping, increased imports, serious injury and threat thereof, and causal link. In the case of safeguards, complaints concern both procedures and the extent of the measure; in some cases these are tantamount to an import prohibition. One developing country complained of a safeguard blocking the country's ability to register any imports in the desired export market.

Similarly, important procedural issues are sometimes raised with respect to the application of *quantitative restrictions*. In particular, notification procedures and import licensing systems create unpredictability and uncertainty for developing-country exporters. Grievances also frequently refer to discriminatory allocation of quotas, as well as problems in the administration of tariff rate quotas. With MFA quotas on trade in textiles and clothing having been eliminated in 2005, the incidence of cases in this area should decrease.

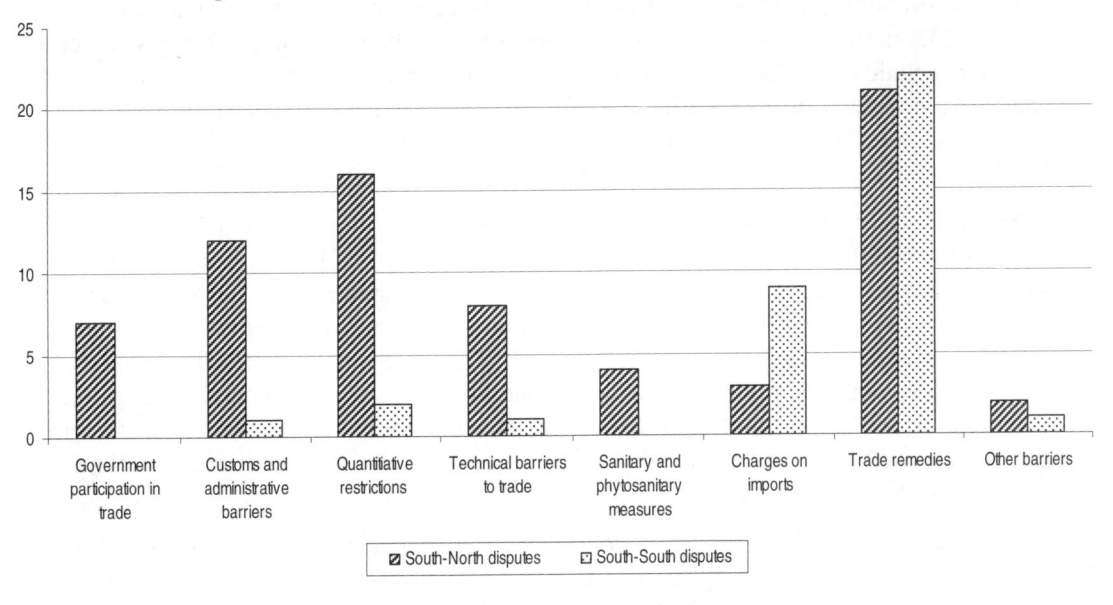

Figure 7.3. Number of DSU cases 1995-2004, categorised by NTBs

NTB category	South-North disputes	South-South disputes
Government participation in trade	7	0
Customs and administrative barriers	12	1
Quantitative restrictions	16	2
Technical barriers to trade	8	1
Sanitary and phytosanitary measures	4	0
Charges on imports	3	9
Trade remedies	21	22
Other barriers	2	1

Note: Disputes refer to instances in which countries have requested consultations under Article 4 of the DSU.
Source: OECD, compiled from records of WTO Dispute Settlement Understanding.

In the area of *customs and administrative barriers*, import licensing presents procedural obstacles such as unnecessary delays and unpredictability in issuance of licences. Also subject to dispute have been customs-related complaints regarding the measures implemented by customs procedures, such as cases in which customs reclassification rules have allegedly forced developing-country exports to be subject to higher tariff rates than the bound rates. Similarly, complainants take issue with OECD countries' application of certain rules of origin that are perceived to protect their markets from import competition.

Various types of *charges on imports* give rise to disputes, particularly when higher than surcharges applied locally. Plaintiffs testify to the existence of an equalising excise tax (EET) in some OECD markets which, applied discriminatorily, protects national products and restricts imports of key developing-country products. Among developing-country trading partners, disputes revolve around discriminatory and unfavourable treatment in the form of selective consumption taxes, general sales taxes, and specific internal taxes. Other practices deemed restrictive include stamps that must be affixed in the importing country, or posting of a bond as a prerequisite to importation of specific products.

With the exception of one case involving intra-developing country trade, complaints regarding *technical barriers to trade* are largely aimed at regulations maintained by OECD countries. Complainants argue that OECD members are adversely affecting competitive conditions for developing countries by applying less favourable technical regulations and standards to imported than to domestic products. Some disputes refer to the introduction of stringent restrictions in the trade descriptions that can be used for marketing imports, relegating developing-country products to a trade description associated with lower quality and market price. Other cases report the existence of unduly burdensome packaging and labelling requirements that are unjustified on environmental or safety grounds.

It is worth noting that the lack of prominence of TBTs in legal cases, versus their role in the NAMA notifications exercise, may result from the difficulty of assessing whether a particular technical regulation or standard is lawful. It may be difficult for a country to challenge the validity of the justification of a TBT, even when it entails significant trade-restrictive effects, and countries tend not to initiate cases when there is little likelihood of liberalisation of the measure through a dispute resolution process (Bown, 2004).

Similarly, in cases involving *sanitary and phytosanitary measures* it is difficult for plaintiffs to challenge a respondent's right to regulate matters of human health and safety. The few cases submitted by non-OECD countries in this area allege that SPS measures prohibit their exports to OECD markets without any prior assessment of risks or scientific principles, and/or are unnecessarily restrictive. The cases also often claim that SPS measures are applied discriminatorily. In addition, there are concerns regarding procedural aspects, such as alleged difficulties in obtaining an administrative document, lack of transparency in the publication of SPS requirements, and authorities' failure to furnish the pertinent information.

Complaints brought in respect of *government participation in trade* question OECD countries' export subsidies applied to primary products, as well as export credits and guarantees, applied generally to higher value-added products.

In many of the preceding cases, complainants hold that a measure has been applied without due consideration of their special situation as a developing country. Further examination of special and differential treatment in relevant NTB areas therefore seems warranted.

Table 7.3 lists the export products of the sample of 24 developing countries involved in the disputes. The sectors most frequently affected are *agriculture and textiles*.

Agricultural products are subject to QRs and import licensing, SPS measures and charges on imports. Sugar, among other agricultural products, is particularly prone to safeguards, export and other types of subsidies applied by OECD countries.

Exportation of textiles and cotton products is also hindered by multiple NTBs, particularly rules of origin, quantitative restrictions, antidumping duties and safeguards. Of note, safety matches feature frequently in the dispute record, facing barriers such as customs clearance procedures, import licensing, TBTs, and environmental measures.

Different product groups are affected by a particular NTB depending on the market maintaining the measure that is challenged, whether this concerns South-South or South-North country trade. This appears to be the case for trade remedies, which are applied mainly to developing-country exports of steel and iron to OECD markets. Non-OECD markets, in contrast, apply trade remedies to agricultural products and foods, textiles and footwear, and pharmaceutical products.

Certain products from developing countries are subject to disputes primarily among non-OECD countries. Other developing countries allegedly apply significant surcharges to tobacco and cigarettes. In the case of pharmaceuticals, barriers are encountered exclusively in trade among non-OECD countries and relate to conformity assessment procedures and antidumping duties.

Table 7.3. Products subject to NTBs cases, DSU 1995-2004

Government participation in trade		
Export subsidies & subsidies	South-North (6 cases)	Sugar, cotton, and other agricultural products; civilian aircraft
Export credits & loan guarantees	South-North (1 case)	Regional aircraft
Customs and administrative procedures		
Customs valuation	South-North (2 cases)	A wide range of products
Customs classification	South-North (2 cases)	Frozen boneless chicken
Customs clearance	South-North (1 case)	Matches (safety matches)
Rules of origin	South-North (1 case)	Textile and apparel products
Import licensing	South-North (6 cases)	Fresh fruits (banana, papaya, plantain) and vegetables; black beans; poultry products; safety matches; fishing vessels
Quantitative restrictions and similar specific limitations		
Tariff rate quotas, prohibitions, and similar import restrictions	South-North (13 cases)	Fresh fruits (bananas) and vegetables; ground nuts; poultry products; shrimp and shrimp products; textile and clothing products; cotton products; automobiles
	South-South (2 cases)	Canned tuna with soybean oil
Technical regulations and standards		
Technical barriers to trade	South-North (7 cases)	Sardine and scallops; wine; safety matches; gasoline
	South-South (1 case)	Pharmaceutical products
Sanitary and phytosanitary measures	South-North (4 cases)	Fresh fruits (banana, pineapple, others) and vegetables; black beans
Charges on imports		
Charges on imports	South-North (9 cases)	Processed orange and grapefruit products; bananas; rice
	South-South (3 cases)	Apples, grapes, and peaches; beverages; tobacco and cigarettes; lubricants and fuels; automobiles
Trade remedies		
Antidumping duties	South-North (10 cases)	Iron and steel products (steel plates, steel and iron pipe fittings, iron tube or cast fittings, oil country tubular goods); silicon metal; electric transformers; paper; cotton typed bed linen; unbleached cotton fabrics
	South-South (8 cases)	Vegetable oils; poultry; pasta (macaroni and spaghetti); jute bags; batteries; pharmaceutical products
Countervailing	South-North (3 cases)	Carbon steel products, steel plates; salmon
	South-South (3 cases)	Desiccated coconut and coconut milk powder; footwear; buses
Safeguard measures	South-North (8 cases)	Steel products; poultry products; cotton yarn; brooms and corn brooms; woven wool shirts and blouses; wool coats
	South-South (11 cases)	Sugar and fructose; agricultural products; mixed edible oils; preserved peaches; medium density fibre; polyester filaments; woven fabric of cotton and cotton mixtures; footwear
Other barriers		
Pricing measures	South-North (1 case)	Many products
Approval and marketing measures	South-North (1 case)	Agricultural biotechnology products
Environmental measures	South-North (1 case)	Safety matches
Intellectual property rights	South-North (1 case)	Not specified

Source: OECD, compiled from records of WTO Dispute Settlement Understanding www.wto.org/english/tratop_e/dispu_e/dispu_status_e.htm), as of 31/10/2004.

Cases on non-tariff import measures in trade among developing countries: Andean Community

In order to elucidate the nature of NTBs that have given rise to disputes among developing-country trading partners, this section analyses legal cases submitted to the Court of Justice of the Andean Community (AC).[24] In particular, it reviews the complaints of non-compliance (*Dictámen de Incumplimiento*), which represent the pre-litigation phase before an action may be brought to Court.[25]

Compared to the process of settling disputes pursuant to the DSU in the WTO, this procedure is much less costly for countries to engage in and does not bear the same burdensome demands with regard to technical expertise, given that the General Secretariat of the Andean Community is charged with the administrative (*i.e.* pre-litigation) investigation. This may explain members' more frequent use of this mechanism. Furthermore, the scope of intra-regional activity regulated by the Andean Community is broader than that of multilateral trade rules; hence a broader set of NTB-related complaints is captured in the disputes.

During the period 1997-2004, a total of 104 legal cases covering NTBs were initiated among members of the Andean Community. Figure 7.4 shows the incidence of various types of barriers that have been subject to complaints. Although tariffs among AC members were eliminated in 1993, the rise of intra-regional exports has been a modest 0.1%.[26] This draws attention to the potentially significant role of NTBs and possibly other factors in inhibiting trade in a tariff-free environment.

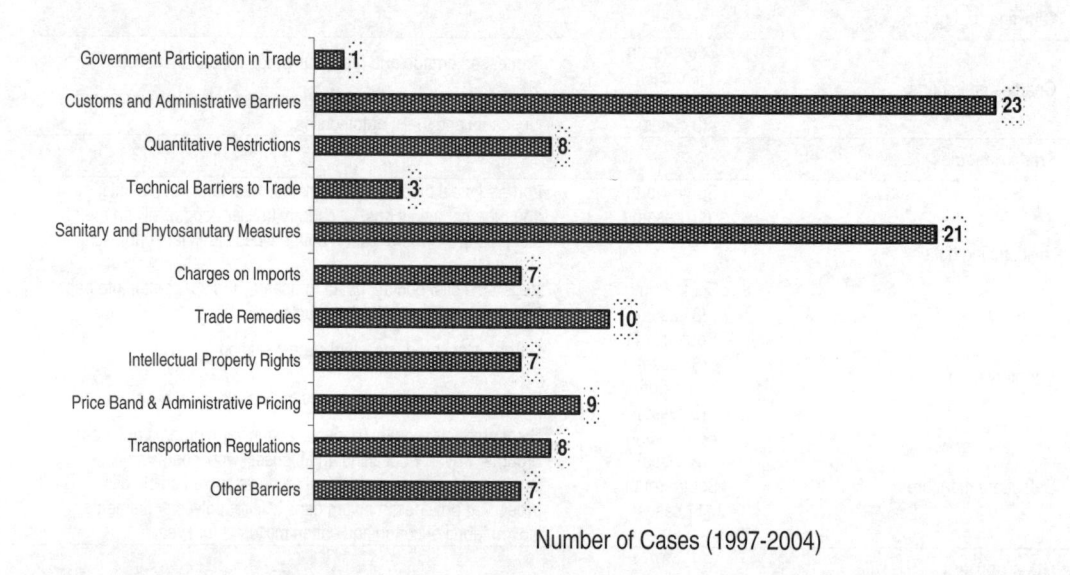

Figure 7.4. NTB cases in the Andean Community

Category	Number of Cases
Government Participation in Trade	1
Customs and Administrative Barriers	23
Quantitative Restrictions	8
Technical Barriers to Trade	3
Sanitary and Phytosanutary Measures	21
Charges on Imports	7
Trade Remedies	10
Intellectual Property Rights	7
Price Band & Administrative Pricing	9
Transportation Regulations	8
Other Barriers	7

Number of Cases (1997-2004)

Source: OECD, compiled from records of the Andean Community (www.sieca.org.gt/SIECA.htm), as of 31 October 2004.

As shown in Figure 7.4, intra-Andean Community trade appears to be consistently hampered by customs and administrative procedures, the most frequent legal complaint among the AC's six member countries. Import licensing alone accounts for 48% of the cases, capturing complaints on consistent overuse of licences and procedural problems in obtaining them, including delays and arbitrary decisions. Next, 27% of the cases reveal problems with proper certification and determination of origin for a wide variety of products. Other areas that generate problems are customs valuation (17% of cases) and classification (4%); these complaints tend to highlight authorities' lack of technical expertise in complying with requisite customs regulations and procedures.

Many complaints concerning sanitary and phytosanitary measures have been lodged, despite the absence of South-South disputes in this area at the multilateral level. The AC's South-South disputes on SPS raise issues of a procedural nature, *e.g.* arbitrary granting of certificates and permissions. Commonly noted procedural issues include:

- Delays of more than five months in granting SPS permissions, while the maximum timeframe for granting permission is ten days.

- Granting SPS permission with a validity limited to 60 days, when the minimum validity period established by AC regulations is 90 days.

- Establishing complementary requirements for granting SPS permission, not provided for in AC legislation.

- Granting permissions only for a small portion of the products, with other products subject to indefinitely pending approval without any stated objections on SPS grounds.

In some instances, the complainant perceives the procedural problem in granting SPS approval as being intentional or a hidden restriction.

Complaints on trade remedies rank third among AC cases, which is consistent with the increase in trade remedy cases observed for developing countries in the DSU. Most of the AC cases (70%) concern safeguards, particularly involving sugar, and state that countries maintain safeguards without showing proof or documenting injury of national producers. With respect to antidumping measures, the intra-regional cases (30%) differ from those brought before the DSU: AC members charge each other with not applying duties on imports of steel and metal from non-member countries, thereby allowing extra-regional partners to engage in dumping practices to the detriment of the competitiveness of regional production.

Similarly, a relatively large number of cases challenge quantitative restrictions, mostly quotas on agricultural products. As in the DSU, there are considerable problems involving government use of surcharges in AC intra-regional trade. These mainly concern large numbers of customs fees. In contrast, very few cases involve TBTs and only one case involves government assistance. This supports the conclusion drawn from the analysis of the DSU that these issues arise mainly in South-North trade.

Several NTBs that appeared infrequently, if at all, in the review of DSU cases appear to pose significant challenges in South-South trade relations. A significant number of AC cases involve intellectual property rights, mostly for pharmaceuticals; they relate to such issues as the lack of protection granted for essential medicines or unclear provisions for patent registration. There are also many cases involving administrative price fixing, particularly for agricultural products, although most are related to the administration of the Andean Price Band. Other cases in this area challenge the practice of fixing minimum import prices at a level that exceeds the price of similar domestic products on grounds of violation of national treatment. Finally, serious problems of intra-regional market access are attributed to the existence of transport barriers, partly because infrastructure is poor and use costly, and partly because government regulations allow only certain cargo carriers to operate in a market.

Other regional dispute settlement bodies

There are very few permanent regional trade dispute settlement bodies. Among the regional trade agreements of developing countries, only the Common Market of the South (Mercosur) and the Common Market for Eastern and Southern Africa (COMESA) have bodies similar to the one in operation in the Andean Community.

In the case of Mercosur, a total of nine commercial disputes among participants have reached the arbitration stage of the dispute resolution mechanism established under the Protocol of Brasilia. While these are the only arbitral panels that have actually issued rulings to date, hundreds of other disputes among members have entered the system, but cases at early stages of proceedings are not published on the Internet and information can only be obtained directly from the Secretariat.

As Table 7.4 shows, all of the nine cases except one (concerning tariffs) challenge alleged NTBs interfering with the free flow of intra-regional trade. As the sample is small and targets a variety of measures ranging from import licensing and quantitative import restrictions to subsidies and trade remedies it is not analysed in greater detail. One interesting observation is the lack of any cases involving technical barriers to trade.

Table 7.4. Controversies submitted to arbitration panel of Mercosur

Date	Complainant	Respondent	Measure	Products
04/04/03	Argentina	Uruguay	Incentives to exports	Wool products
21/05/02	Paraguay	Uruguay	Specific internal tax ('Ímesi')	Cigars
19/04/02	Argentina	Brazil	Obstacles to imports of phytosanitary products (registration system)	Phytosanitary products
09/01/02	Uruguay	Brazil	Import ban (prohibition on the issuance of import licences)	Remolded tyres
29/09/01	Uruguay	Argentina	Restrictions: tariffs (involved controversy over certificate of origin)	Bicycles
21/05/01	Brazil	Argentina	Antidumping duties	Chicken
10/03/00	Brazil	Argentina	Safeguards	Textile products
27/09/99	Argentina	Brazil	Subsidies for production and exports	Pork meat
28/04/99	Argentina	Brazil	Automatic and non-automatic import licensing	Lactate products

Source: OECD, compiled from Mercosur Secretariat (www.mercosur.org.uy/pagina1esp.htm), as of 31 October 2004.

The review of the cases submitted to the Court of Justice of COMESA shows that they often involve issues other than trade measures. For instance, there are cases of alleged defamation (Ref. No. 1/2003) or compulsory acquisition of land (Ref. No. 3/2001), and such cases do not provide insights into the kinds of barriers that might exist within the region. Perhaps the only judgement of the court relevant for an intra-regional analysis of NTBs pertains to the alleged detainment of goods at ports and damages arising from these customs procedures (Ref. No. 1/99).

Analysis of business surveys

Another body of evidence on non-tariff barriers in developing countries consists of survey data on barriers faced by DC exporters of goods in a range of markets. For the purpose of this analysis, a survey is defined as a study that collects enterprise-level data or involves consultation with enterprises.

Annex 7.A7 lists a selection of surveys that are representative of private-sector responses from all developing regions. Concerns about NTBs involve exporters throughout these regions and pertain to OECD markets and global markets (Annex 7.A7, A and B), as well as intra-regional South-South trade in Asia (Annex 7.A7, C), South America (Annex 7.A7, D), Central America and the Caribbean (Annex 7.A7, E), Africa and the Middle East (Annex 7.A7, F), and south-eastern Europe (Annex 7.A7, G). In total, the selection covers responses from over 6 000 exporters of goods from developing countries.

Comparisons of survey data must be made with caution owing to differences in data sets, methodologies and scope of barriers surveyed. Some surveys were open-ended whereas others involved specific questions on a limited set of barriers. The number and profile of respondents also varies. However, despite this heterogeneity, some NTB concerns are evident.

Barriers reported by firms: global markets

A common denominator among survey findings, which is consistent with the analysis of NAMA notifications and the intra-regional AC legal cases, is problems with *customs and administrative procedures* (see the synthesis of surveys in Annex 7.A7). Specifically, the business community in developing countries cites concerns regarding bureaucracy, delays and high costs.

In 2001, the Superintendencia Nacional de Aduanas of Peru conducted a detailed survey of 253 of its users (122 of which were exporters/importers). The survey revealed that 56% of exporters/importers were not well informed about customs rules and procedures.[27] Moreover, 67% of the polled exporters/importers affirmed that custom procedures were not modern or were inefficient, with insufficient personnel, inadequate capacity and non-existent or inefficient controls against corruption and/or arbitrariness. In line with these findings, various other surveys covering trade among developing countries reflect concerns about the lack of business ethics among customs officers and limited computerisation.

Once again, *import licensing* looms as a frequent concern. The surveys also indicate frustration with excessive use of *documentation and formalities*, which further exacerbate the bureaucratic customs and administration obstacles. In terms of specific customs-related barriers by markets, *rules of origin* and *pre-shipment inspection* are more frequently reported to cause obstacles for trade among developing countries than for access to the markets of developed countries. Of note, all surveys on intra-regional trade in Africa signal *customs clearance* as a significant hurdle.

The surveyed business community corroborates that *TBTs* are a major detriment to exportation. Concerns abound regarding divergent and non-harmonised standards, delays and discrimination in TBT application, non-transparency and lack of general information on TBT regulations. In testing and certification arrangements, surveyed companies often complain about the lack of mutually recognised certification bodies and insufficiency of national certificates.

The World Bank Technical Barriers to Trade Survey, administered in 2002 to 698 firms in 17 developing countries, indicates the primacy of technical regulations as a hurdle for major OECD export destinations.[28] The survey findings show that performance standards, product quality standards and testing and certification are perceived to be the most important TBTs, followed closely by consumer safety, labelling, and health and environment measures. Surveyed firms report that TBT compliance involves investment in: additional plant or equipment (38% of firms), one-time product redesign (31%), additional labour for production (30%), product re-design for each export market (26%), additional labour for testing and certification (18%), and workers laid off because of higher costs (11%).

A specialised *survey on packaging and labelling* conducted in 2001 by the Costa Rican Export Promotion Agency (PROCOMER) indicates that 34% of the 215 surveyed businesses state that they are unfamiliar with the packaging requirements for their products in markets to which they currently export, and 63% have no knowledge of these requirements for markets identified as potential export destinations.[29] As for environment-related rules and requirements regulating packaging/labelling, 57% indicate lack of information for their current markets, a percentage that increases to 73% for potential markets. Against this background, 89% of firms express interest in capacity-building and practical assistance with packaging and labelling.[30]

While customs and administrative procedures and TBTs are clearly the most prevalent non-tariff barriers, there is a notable difference in their relative perceived importance depending on whether the surveyed companies are exporting to OECD or non-OECD markets. In surveys covering trade between developing and developed countries, TBTs rank higher as an obstacle to market access. In the surveys on barriers affecting trade among developing countries, on the other hand, customs and administrative-related barriers invariably rank higher. The findings of the Western Balkans Survey (Table 7.5) are representative.

Table 7.5. Ranking of barriers faced by Western Balkan exporters, by market (2004)

Ranking (by importance of barrier)[1]	EU market (extra-DC trade)	South-eastern European market (intra-DC trade)
1	Technical standards and certification	Customs procedures
2	Quality control and consumer protection	Bureaucratic registration
3	Customs barriers	Technical standards and certification
4	----	Quality control and consumer protection
5	Bureaucratic registration	----

1. In descending order by degree of importance. Items in the survey not related to TBTs, customs and administrative procedures are omitted from this table (as indicated by ---).
Source: OECD, based on Western Balkan Survey (2004).

The surveys also illustrate certain problems related to *sanitary and phytosanitary measures* for developing countries, particularly in exporting to OECD markets. A major problem faced by some firms, especially small and medium-sized enterprises, seems to be access to the resources required to comply with SPS standards, given that they are often not available locally. These include information on SPS standards themselves, scientific and technical expertise, appropriate technology, skilled labour and general finance, among others. In a survey of SPS contact/inquiry points in low- and middle-income countries that are members of the WTO and/or Codex Alimentarius, Table 7.6 reports problems related to SPS requirements that were judged to be significant for access to the EU market.

Table 7.6. Problems with meeting SPS requirements in the European Union

Mean score[1]	Factor
1.6	Insufficient access to scientific/technical expertise
2.1	Incompatibility of SPS requirements with domestic production/marketing methods
2.6	Poor access to financial resources
3.0	Insufficient time permitted for compliance
3.1	Limitations in own country's administrative arrangements for SPS requirements
3.1	Poor awareness of SPS requirements amongst government officials
3.5	Poor awareness of SPS requirements within agriculture and food industry
3.9	Poor access to information on SPS requirements

1. Score ranges from 1=very significant to 5=very insignificant. Survey is based on 65 fully completed questionnaires applied to a total of 44 low- and middle -ncome countries, as classified by the World Bank.
Source: University of Reading (2000), Survey on the Impact of Sanitary and Phytosanitary Measures on Developing Countries.

Barriers reported predominantly for trade among developing countries

All of the surveys on intra-regional trade, particularly in Africa and the Caribbean, record concerns regarding an impressive number and variety of *additional charges*, ranging from customs service and harbour and air cargo fees, often deemed to be excessive, to an array of additional taxes and charges such as foreign exchange tax; stamp duty; environmental tax; statistics, consent and inspection fees; and others. Apart from these border and transit charges, companies also report problems with regard to internal taxes and additional charges such as consumption, value added and excise taxes. *Differences in tax regulations* and their lack of transparency are frequently cited as a problem across members of regional groupings.

An interesting finding across the surveys is that companies attach considerable importance to barriers not generally captured in traditional listings of NTBs, particularly in the South-South context (Table 7.7). Among these, respondent firms frequently denounce *transport regulations and costs*, which also feature prominently in disputes in the Andean Community. These concerns relate to poor or unfair regulation of goods transport in the importing country, in addition to various problems pertaining to the quality, frequency and lack of security of road transport and shipping. Moreover, surveyed companies indicate that the costs of international air and maritime transport are high and impede access to foreign markets.

The surveys also indicate that trade is further hampered by *restrictive finance measures*, including the shortage of foreign exchange in developing regions. Private-sector entities underscore the challenges posed by barriers such as banking system weaknesses and restrictive government regulations on exchange requirements, capital controls and finance and payment mechanisms. These seriously affect the export potential of small and medium sized enterprises that lack easy access to external financing sources.

Table 7.7. Non-tariff barriers cited in business surveys

		Asia and the Pacific						Latin America and the Caribbean								Africa and the Middle East				South East Europe		
		India – OECD markets (2004)*	India-non-OECD markets (2004)**	China (2001)*	Thailand (2001)***	Vietnam (1999)**	ASEAN (date unspecified)**	Chile (2000)***	Argentina (1999)*	ALADI (2001)**	Mercosur (2000)**	Andean Community (1997)**	Central America (1999)*	Assoc. Caribbean States (2003)**	CARICOM (2002)**	SADC (2004)**	Morocco (2001)**	MENA (2000)**	COMESA (1999)**	Western Balkans (2004)***	European Commission (2005)	Moldova (2004)
Government participation		√	√		√	√	√		√		√	√			√	√	√				√	
	General				•				•							•	•					
	Subsidies & export subsidies	•														•					•	
	State-trading & monopolistic practices		•			•	•					•			•						•	
	Public procurement													•		•					•	
Customs and administrative procedures		√	√	√	√	√	√	√	√	√	√	√	√	√	√	√	√	√	√	√	√	√
	General		•	•					•	•	•	•				•	•			•	•	
	Customs valuation						•										•				•	
	Customs classification						•														•	
	Customs clearance	•														•	•	•		•	•	•
	Documentation & formalities		•		•	•	•					•	•			•		•			•	
	Import licensing	•		•		•	•	•	•		•		•		•		•			•	•	•
	Rules of origin	•										•							•			
	Pre-shipment Inspection											•					•		•			
Quantitative restrictions		√		√		√			√		√				√	√			√		√	√
	General	•										•										
	Prohibitions and bans	•				•										•			•		•	•
	Quotas	•		•		•					•					•	•				•	
	Tariff rate quotas	•																			•	
	Embargoes	•																				
Technical barriers to trade		√	√	√	√		√	√	√	√	√				√		√	√	√	√	√	
	General			•				•														
	Technical reg. & standards	•					•			•	•	•			•					•	•	
	Testing & certification	•	•								•							•		•	•	

Table 7.7. **Non-tariff barriers cited in business surveys (cont.)**

		Asia and the Pacific						Latin America and the Caribbean								Africa and the Middle East				South East Europe		
		India – OECD markets (2004)*	India-non-OECD markets (2004)**	China (2001)*	Thailand (2001)***	Vietnam (1999)**	ASEAN (date unspecified)**	Chile (2000)***	Argentina (1999)*	ALADI (2001)**	Mercosur (2000)**	Andean Community (1997)**	Central America (1999)**	Assoc. Caribbean States (2003)**	CARICOM (2002)**	SADC (2004)**	Morocco (2001)**	MENA (2000)**	COMESA (1999)**	Western Balkans (2004)***	European Commission (2005)	Moldova (2004)
	Labelling & packaging	•	•		•						•						•					
Sanitary and phytosanitary		√		√				√	√	√				√			√		√		√	
	General	•		•				•	•	•			•				•		•		•	
	Testing and certification																					•	
	Quarantine procedures	•																					
Charges and Fees		√	√			√	√	√			√	√			√	√	√	√	√	√		√	√
	Various charges	•	•			•	•	•			•	•			•	•	•	•	•	•		•	•
Trade remedies		√						√		√					√								
	General							•															
	Antidumping duties	•																					
	Countervailing duties												•			•							
	Safeguards																						
Other barriers		√	√	√	√	√	√	√	√	√	√	√	√	√	√	√	√	√	√	√	√	√
	Import restrictions	•	•			•	•																
	Unilateral sanctions	•																					
	Registration	•	•									•									•	•	
	Intellectual property rights							•				•											
	Environmental measures								•													•	
	Minimum pricing & price control measures				•							•			•								•
	Finance measures			•	•				•	•	•			•		•	•		•	•	•		
	Access to final users																				•		
	Extraterritorial application of the law	•	•																				
	Legal differences	•											•										
	Lack of Information on foreign markets		•	•	•				•					•						•			

Table 7.7. Non-tariff barriers cited in business surveys (cont.)

	Asia and the Pacific						Latin America and the Caribbean								Africa and the Middle East				South East Europe		
	India – OECD markets (2004)*	India-non-OECD markets (2004)**	China (2001)*	Thailand (2001)***	Vietnam (1999)**	ASEAN (date unspecified)**	Chile (2000)***	Argentina (1999)*	ALADI (2001)**	Mercosur (2000)**	Andean Community (1997)**	Central America (1999)**	Assoc. Caribbean States (2003)**	CARICOM (2002)**	SADC (2004)**	Morocco (2001)**	MENA (2000)**	COMESA (1999)**	Western Balkans (2004)***	European Commission (2005)	Moldova (2004)
Competition from other countries				●					●			●									
Transport costs and/or regulations									●	●	●	●	●						●	●	●
Corruption and theft		●										●			●		●				
Political, social, and/or economic instability											●		●		●	●					
Inadequate infrastructure																		●			
Low demand in export markets													●								
Cultural differences			●																		
Linguistic barriers			●	●															●	●	
Unclassified	●	●		●	●		●	●	●			●	●		●		●	●			●

●: Barrier is reported in survey (note: not all surveys include all listed barriers). √: At least one kind of barrier is reported under the NTB category. *: Extra-DC surveys; **: Intra-DC surveys; ***: Global surveys

Source: OECD, compiled from a selection of business surveys.

Most of the surveys also show that enterprises have *limited information on foreign markets* in general and on applicable regulations. In the Western Balkans survey, for instance, 48% of 2 166 polled companies affirm that they are not familiar with the EU market, with only 9% fully informed of its relevant laws and regulations.[31] With respect to intra-regional market access opportunities, over a third (37%) of respondents note a lack of familiarity with south-eastern European markets. This would appear to be a very high number in light of the numerous bilateral free trade agreements between countries of the region and current discussions tending towards a common free trade area.

Finally, in the context of the dynamics of trade among developing countries, the sample of surveys examined reveals *political, social and economic factors* inherent to the environment of the export market that act as obstacles to trade. Exporters participating in these surveys cite various kinds of problems relating to corruption, theft, social unrest and economic volatility.

Conclusions

Review of sources

This study has sought to identify NTBs of concern to developing countries by drawing on four sources of data which provide a variety of perspectives. Each of these sources contributes to a better understanding of the market access concerns of developing countries by documenting various kinds of NTBs. Together, they represent a rich source of information.

The review of the literature, while not generating accurate measures of the extent and effects of NTBs, provides an insightful picture of the trends in the use of NTBs over time, particularly in the aftermath of the Uruguay Round. Most research shows that "core NTBs" (*i.e.* quantity and price control measures) have decreased significantly, while other measures that have come to the forefront of developing countries' concerns. Furthermore, among the sources consulted, the literature provides a differentiated picture of market access barriers by developing regions.

The NAMA notifications represent the most recent and direct reporting exercise undertaken by governments in this field. The set of notifying WTO members is representative of developing countries, given that their aggregate exports account for 57% of total developing-country exports. It is the only source of data for identifying not only the barriers but also the products affected, and therefore gives commodity-specific information on NTBs. These notifications provide a solid foundation for some limited empirical analysis.

The examination of dispute settlement cases has provided a limited data set on developing-country concerns. The analysis shows that NTBs are a source of significant and in fact growing friction, both in South-North trade relations and increasingly in South-South trade. In particular, the compilation of cases from regional dispute settlement mechanisms provides a good account of market access barriers encountered in intra-regional developing-country trade.

Finally, an investigation into private-sector perceptions spanning all developing regions offers testimony concerning difficulties that exporters experience. It reveals that market access challenges faced by developing-country exporters extend beyond traditional NTBs to include other factors obstructing trade (*e.g.* transport costs and regulations) which may warrant more attention. This component also contributes to the identification of barriers affecting developing countries' intra-regional trade.

Findings on barriers of concern to developing countries

While there are variations in the main findings resulting from each data set, certain broadly defined categories of NTBs consistently show up as a source of concern. These are summarised below.

Trade with developed countries

In trade with developed countries, customs and administrative procedures and TBTs emerge as the main NTBs of concern to developing countries. These two categories record the highest frequency of notified barriers in the NAMA analysis. TBTs also received considerable attention. The disputes brought before the WTO include a significant number of cases involving customs issues. In contrast, a much smaller number of cases pertain to TBTs, reflecting perhaps the greater difficulty of legally challenging these measures.

For other barriers, there is less consistency. SPS measures follow in importance in the NAMA notifications, and are also cited frequently in business surveys focusing on access to OECD markets, in particular when developing countries are agricultural exporters. This is identified as one of the main sources of concern in the literature review for Asia and Latin America.

Trade among developing countries

In intra-developing country trade, customs and administrative procedures also rank very high among reported concerns. In fact, these problems appear more pervasive for market access to developing countries than to developed-country markets. Of particular note, the 15 business surveys compiled on barriers to intra-regional trade all report at least one, and normally many, customs and administrative hurdles. These include (often procedural) problems encountered with import licensing. Furthermore, the Andean Community NTB cases reveal that customs and administrative procedures represent the largest number of complaints brought to the dispute settlement mechanism of the Andean Community.

The data sets also provide a rich documentation on charges on imports as the next important barrier in trade among developing countries. They draw attention to the fact that as developing countries have reduced their tariffs as a result of multilateral and regional liberalisation, they have resorted to an array of import charges to compensate for the loss of their tariff revenues. In the analysis of disputes brought before the WTO, the second highest number of disputes among developing countries involves such measures. The Central America Common Market (CACM) offers a telling instance in which developing countries removed tariffs intra-regionally, but maintained or even increased their resort to para-tariff measures. Half of the complaints brought against other CACM members during 2003-04 involved various fees and charges. The phenomenon is not confined to Latin America. The literature and business surveys report widely on charges in other regions, particularly Africa, the Middle East and the Caribbean islands.

There is less consistency for other measures. Technical barriers are less often reported for trade among developing countries. The literature review and business surveys suggest that these measures are more prevalent for intra-regional trade in Asia. This may be partially due to the higher value-added content of exports from Asia relative to exports from Africa or Latin America. More generally, concerns related to TBT issues in trade among developing countries evolve more around issues of weak infrastructure and procedural hurdles. In contrast, TBT complaints focusing on developed countries tend to refer more to the cost of compliance with requirements.

This study also sheds light on impediments to access to foreign markets that generally fall outside discussions of NTBs. For example, business surveys in particular, as well as the disputes brought to the Andean Community, underscore the importance of transport costs and regulations. There are also geographic constraints on trade with neighbouring and other countries, for instance in Africa. Finally, other concerns relate to various restrictive finance measures, including shortages of foreign exchange and capital controls.

Findings on products of interest to developing countries

A further objective of this chapter has been to identify what types of NTBs affect the products of export interest to developing countries. NAMA notifications offer the most comprehensive data set for identifying NTBs by product; these are supported and reinforced by the review of literature, disputes and business surveys.

To the extent that the NAMA notifications are representative of the export profile of developing countries, live animals and related products are the commodity category most deserving attention. For this category, the most often reported NTBs relate to SPS measures, including testing, certification and other requirements of proof of conformity. Customs-related problems, particularly in respect of rules of origin and certification, are also mentioned relatively often.

The highest number of notifications submitted to NAMA identified NTBs affecting fish and crustaceans, molluscs and other fishery products (*e.g.* tuna, trout, octopus, shrimps and prawns). The review of eight developing-country export strategies and promotion programmes reveals that this would be a sector of current and future competitive export interest. From the review of legal cases filed in the multilateral and the regional forums for settling disputes, sugar and fructose and fresh fruits and vegetables are other sectors for which developing-country exports face considerable market access difficulties.

Machinery and electronics, notably electrical machinery and equipment (*e.g.* radios, televisions, cables), are other products often mentioned in developing-country notifications to NAMA. The literature on Asia emphasises that electrical appliances and machinery constitute the product most affected by NTBs. Technical regulations and standards are reported to be the most significant obstacle facing developing-country exports in this sector. In fact, most of the TBT complaints in the NAMA notifications fall into this product category. There is also a high incidence of reported import licensing problems.

NAMA notifications also often concern chemical products and especially pharmaceutical products. Moreover, pharmaceutical products have been subject to disputes among developing countries, as documented by the cases brought to the Andean Community. Among the NAMA notifications for this sector, many complaints focus on technical regulations.

The importance of textiles for developing-country trade, documented by a large pool of studies, is reinforced by the number of multilateral and regional dispute cases involving woven cotton and cotton products or textile and apparel products in general. Some of the literature on NTBs, mostly in the Asia-Pacific context, point to a situation in which developing-country access to foreign markets in this area is obstructed by multiple NTBs. While the literature describes the Multi-Fibre Agreement as the most important barrier, some work (especially for India) draws attention to labelling requirements, and a very large number of NAMA notifications by developing countries suggests the presence of various technical barriers to trade. The NAMA notifications also include many references to customs valuation.

Although not as important an export sector for developing countries, the literature indicates that automobiles and auto parts are the object of many NTBs. Many of the developing-country notifications to NAMA for this sector are specifically about technical regulations. They also express developing-country concerns about rules of origin.

The importance of addressing NTBs in these sectors is underscored by the analysis of developing countries' export strategies, many of which identify the above-mentioned product groups as strategic to their efforts to develop and strengthen their export performance.

Notes

1. Developing countries are those considered as such in the World Trade Organization (WTO).

2. For example, developing countries report having difficulties meeting what they perceive are increasingly complex technical regulations, product standards and SPS measures implemented by developed-country trading partners (OECD, 2002; Henson *et al.,* 2000).

3. WTO Ministers meeting in Doha in 2001 agreed "to reduce or as appropriate eliminate tariffs, including the reduction or elimination of tariff peaks, high tariffs, and tariff escalation, as well as non-tariff barriers, in particular on products of export interest to developing countries. Product coverage shall be comprehensive and without a priori exclusions." In addition to NAMA, issues related to NTBs are supposed to be addressed in negotiations focusing on agriculture and on WTO rules regarding antidumping, subsidies and countervailing measures, and are a matter of examination under the regular work programmes of various WTO bodies that are not directly involved in the DDA process.

4. The LDCs are the countries on the United Nations' list of LDCs. As of 31 October 2004, this list contained 50 countries.

5. These studies vary in their classification of developing countries, and some do not specify the classification used.

6. In the July 2004 Framework Agreement, countries were urged "to make notifications on NTBs by 31 October 2004 and to proceed with identification, examination, categorization, and ultimately negotiations on NTBs" (Annex B, paragraph 14).

7. The Inventory of Non-tariff Measures groups barriers into seven broad categories (see Annex 7.A3). A possible weakness in this inventory is the lack of clear definition and demarcation of some types of NTBs (*e.g.*, discrimination resulting from bilateral agreements, discriminatory sourcing, distribution constraints). Furthermore, as some NTBs, such as environmental and security-related measures, are not directly captured in the inventory, countries do not report on these types of barriers. For the purpose of this analysis, certain adjustments were made, mainly to the structure of the classification employed by the inventory. These are also shown in Annex 7.A3.

8. The sample includes non-OECD countries that submitted notifications as of 1 November 2004. They are from Africa and the Middle East: Egypt, Jordan, Kenya, and Senegal; from Asia and the Pacific: Bangladesh, China, Chinese Taipei, Hong Kong (China), India, Macao (China), Malaysia, Pakistan, the Philippines, Singapore, and Thailand; from Latin America and the Caribbean: Argentina, Trinidad and Tobago, Uruguay, and Venezuela; and from Eastern Europe: Bulgaria and Croatia.

Countries from Asia and the Pacific are the most represented (88% of NTB notifications), with Latin America and the Caribbean and Africa and the Middle East following in the number of barriers reported.

9. Based on the World Bank classification of countries by levels of income.

10. WTO, World Merchandise Exports by Region and Selected Economy 1992-2002, *International Trade Statistics 2003*.

11. Some of the measures in the NTB inventory can clearly serve legitimate purposes (for instance, technical barriers to trade, rules of origin and charges on imports).

12. While countries examined here were invited to specify the "Maintaining Participant" of the barriers notified, none provided this information.

13. A large number of these notifications were made by one country (the Philippines).

14. There are also 79 notifications of TBTs; this may in part reflect the methodological difficulty of determining whether a technical regulation applied to this product category is in fact a TBT or SPS measure.

15. Of the 11 developing countries that have made notifications with respect to fisheries, the Philippines submitted the majority of individual notifications on this item.

16. For many developing countries, poor infrastructure, limited access to finance and marketing and other domestic factors are major obstacles to export success, especially for smaller firms, and formidable challenges for governments that seek to help develop and promote export activities. They are not the focus of this inquiry.

17. The four participants are India; Hong Kong, China; Chinese Taipei; and Mauritius.

18. For a compilation of submissions reporting NTMs in IT products, see the WTO document G/IT/SPEC/Q2/11/Rev.1.

19. Moreover, those NTB areas that are not covered by the legal multilateral framework are not captured in the record of disputed cases.

20. The Advisory Centre on WTO Law (ACWL) corroborates the resource implications of preparing for the process of filing a dispute, even at the initial stage of consultations. Depending on the complexity of the case, a developing country requests on average from 42 to 127 hours of legal assistance for the consultation stage, which are charged at the sponsored rate of CHF 162 to CHF 324 per hour if the country is a member of the ACWL (www.acwl.ch, ACWL/MB/D/2004/3). The rate is higher if the developing country is not a member.

21. The sample of developing countries referred to in the analysis of dispute settlement cases covers the non-OECD countries that have submitted requests for consultation on non-tariff measures. They are: Argentina, Bangladesh, Brazil, Chile, China, Colombia, Costa Rica, Ecuador, Guatemala, Honduras, Hong Kong (China), India, Indonesia, Malaysia, Nicaragua, Pakistan, Panama, Peru, Philippines, Singapore, Chinese Taipei, Thailand, Sri Lanka, Venezuela.

22. The analysis includes all cases initiated by non-OECD countries up to 31 October 2004. Of the 90 cases initiated by these countries, 48 have led to the establishment of a panel; of these, 21 have reached the Appellate Body.

23. The analysis does not capture developing countries' requests to join consultations. They are frequently "interested third countries" in dispute settlement negotiations, an indication of substantial interest in the NTB proceedings of other trading partners.

24. The Andean Community is a customs union formed by Bolivia, Colombia, Ecuador, Peru and Venezuela.

25. The *Dictámen de Incumplimiento* is the Secretariat's judgement on the complaint filed by countries; since the complaints are not readily available, the *Dictamen de Incumplimiento/Cumplimiento* is the first official published report on members' complaints.

26. ECLAC (Economic Commission of Latin America and the Caribbean), *Statistical Yearbook for Latin America and the Caribbean 2002*.

27. *Evaluación de Servios de Aduanas. Estudio Cuantitativo: Principales Resultados, Apoyo Opinión y Mercadeo* on behalf of *Superintendencia Nacional de Aduanas*, November 2001.

28. The countries surveyed are: Bulgaria, Czech Republic, Poland, Argentina, Chile, Honduras, Panama, Iran, Jordan, India, Pakistan, Kenya, Mozambique, Nigeria, Senegal, South Africa and Uganda. The main sectors surveyed are raw foods, processed foods, tobacco,, drugs and liquor, equipment and textiles.

29. *Capacidad Exportadora en Costa Rica: Principales Resultados*, PROCOMER, 2001.

30. The areas suggested by businesses for capacity building relating to labelling and packaging are, in order of perceived importance: technical and environmental requirements; suppliers and types of packaging/labelling; costs of packaging/labelling; methods for quality control; effects of packaging/labelling on sales of product; containers; port management, among others. The products identified as most important are: machines and equipment, tubes and tube products, furniture, fragile products, fruits and confectionery.

31. The survey reveals that the most important areas of EU legislation in terms of relevance to companies' operations are, in this order: product certification and technical standards; rules of origin; consumer protection and producer liability; labels, trademarks, and patents; environmental protection; and food quality and safety.

Annex 7.A1

Statistical Overview of Developing Countries' Export Performance

This annex analyses export data reported by UN ComTrade for the group of low- and middle-income countries, as classified by the World Bank.[1] From 1993 through 2003, total merchandise exports originating from this group of countries increased threefold, from USD 569 billion in 1993 to USD 1.8 trillion in 2003. Overall, the share of developing-country exports in world exports increased by 60% over that decade, from 17% to 27% of world exports. The participation of least developed countries (LDCs) in international trade, however, remains marginal. In 2003, their combined global merchandise exports amounted to about USD 44 billion, or 0.67% of world exports.[2]

In terms of the direction of trade, developing countries as a group export predominantly to high-income countries, which absorb approximately 70% of total developing-country exports. The share of exports to other developing countries has remained constant and amounted to 29% of their total exports in 2003. As the regional breakdown in Figure 7.A1.1 illustrates, developing-country markets are more important export destinations for the Middle East and North Africa (41%) and for Europe and Central Asia (31%) than for Latin America and the Caribbean (24%) and Asia and the Pacific (23%).

The more disaggregated picture of export performance in Table 7.A1.1 shows that some developing regions (especially Sub-Saharan Africa and, to a lesser extent, the countries of the Middle East and North Africa and Latin America and the Caribbean) increased their export dependency on developed-country markets over the period 1993-2003.

While overall trade among developing countries has not undergone significant changes over the last decade, some regions show an important shift in the relative importance of intra-regional trade, which may reflect their efforts to engage in regional and bilateral free trade arrangements. For example, Table 7.A1.1 shows that regional markets in Latin America and the Caribbean and in Europe and Central Asia have absorbed the majority of the respective regions' exports to developing countries, whereas for South Asia and the Middle East and North Africa, the regional market has carried less weight but is becoming more important. Meanwhile, the share of intra-regional exports in Sub-Saharan Africa's exports to developing countries rose dramatically, from 22% in 1993 to 48% in 2003.

---

1. These low-income and middle-income countries are referred to as developing countries for the purpose of this annex. The group of high-income OECD countries included in the World Bank's classification by income are referred to as developed countries.

2. "Market access issues related to products of export interest originating from least-developed countries", WTO WT/COMTD/LDC/W/35 TN/MA/S/12, 13 October 2004.

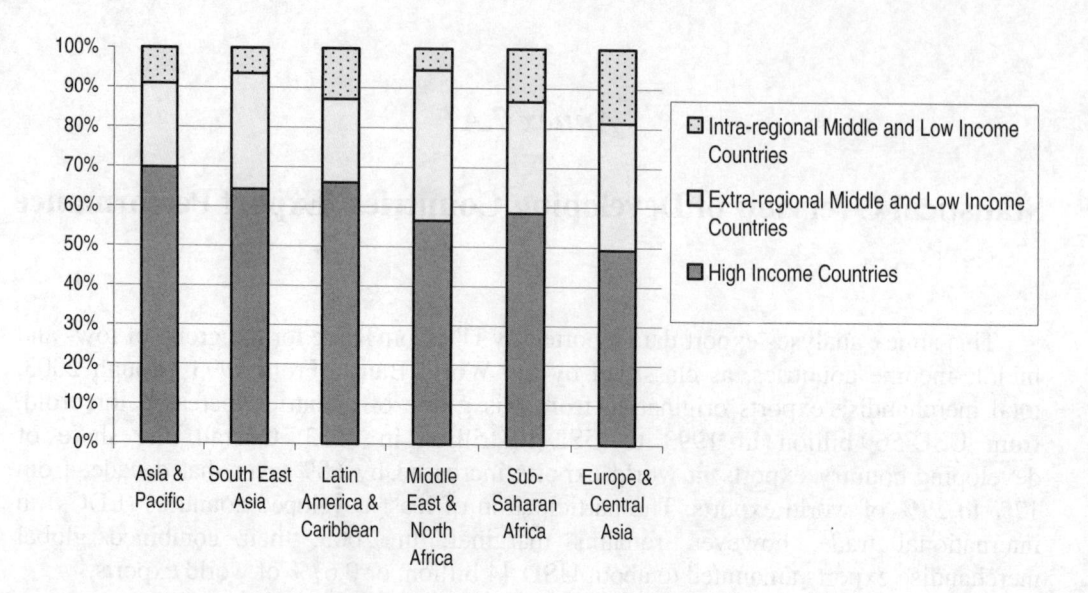

Figure 7.A1.1. Merchandise exports of developing regions, by destination (2003)

Source: UN Commodity Trade Statistics Database (COMTRADE). The data are extracted from World Integrated Trade Solution (WITS), 2004.

The share of manufactured products in developing-country exports has grown steadily over the past two decades, while the share of primary commodities has declined (Hertel and Martin, 1999). As Figure 7.A1.2 shows, manufactured products accounted for more than 60% of developing-country exports in 2003. Moreover, within manufactures, there has been a shift away from low value-added manufactured goods (such as footwear, travel goods, apparel and other products made of rubber, wood, etc.) towards electrical and electronic products, industrial equipment, machinery and other products belonging to the category "machinery and transport equipment". Over the period 1993-2003, the share of products falling into the latter category in total developing-country merchandise exports rose from 20% to 33%, whereas the shares of "manufactured goods" and "miscellaneous manufactures" declined.

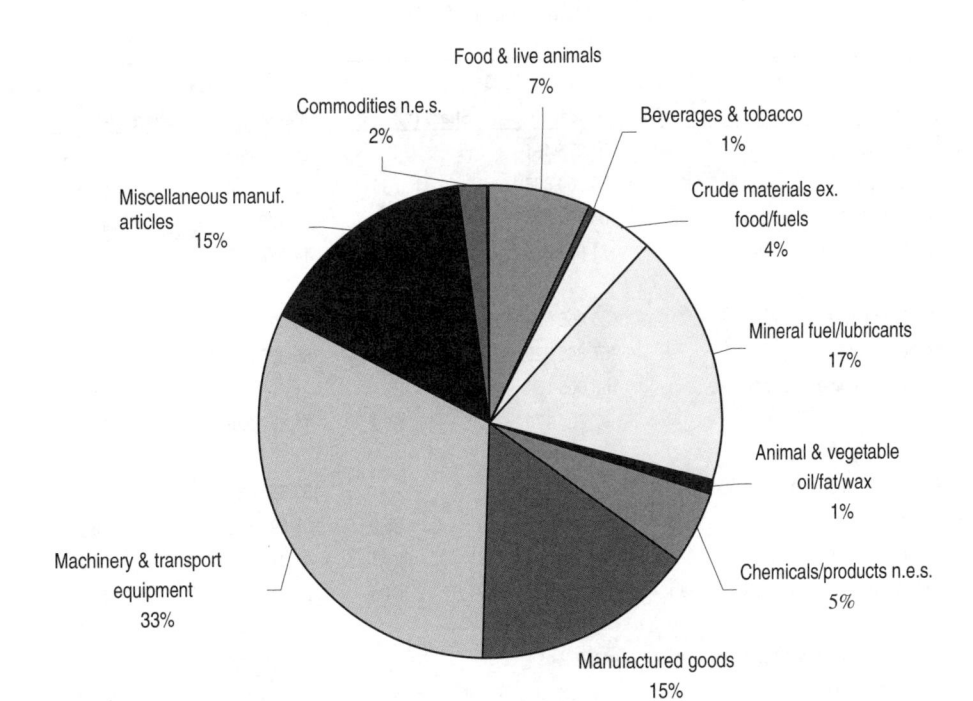

Figure 7.A1.2. Composition of developing-country merchandise exports, 2003

- Food & live animals 7%
- Beverages & tobacco 1%
- Crude materials ex. food/fuels 4%
- Mineral fuel/lubricants 17%
- Animal & vegetable oil/fat/wax 1%
- Chemicals/products n.e.s. 5%
- Manufactured goods 15%
- Machinery & transport equipment 33%
- Miscellaneous manuf. articles 15%
- Commodities n.e.s. 2%

Note: Machinery & transport equipment includes: power generating equipment, industry special machines, metalworking machinery, industrial equipment, telecoms equipment, office/data processing machinery, electrical equipment, road vehicles, railway/tramway equipment. Manufactured goods include: leather articles, rubber products, cork and wood manufactures, paper/paperboard articles, textile/yarn/fabric articles, non-metal mineral manufactures, iron and steel, non-ferrous metals, and metal manufactures. Miscellaneous manufactured articles include: building fixtures, furniture and furnishings, travel goods, apparel clothing accessories, footwear, scientific instruments, photographic equipment, and miscellaneous manufactures n.e.s.

Source: UN Commodity Trade Statistics Database (COMTRADE), using the Standard International Trade Classification (SITC), Rev 3. The data are extracted from World Integrated Trade Solution (WITS), 2004.

There are, however, significant differences across regions. For countries in Africa and the Middle East, manufacturing remains much less important relative to traditional minerals and food exports. In fact, most LDCs have not seen their export structure change much. LDCs rely on a very narrow export base dominated by unprocessed and semi-processed primary commodities and minerals.

Table 7.A1.1. Developing-country export flows

Thousands of USD

	2003 Value	2003 Share (%)	1993 Value	1993 Share (%)	% increase
LMI East Asia and Pacific	724 275 461		224 436 604		222.7
High income countries	555 380 868	76.7	182 957 244	81.5	203.6
Low and middle income countries	168 894 593	23.3	41 479 360	18.5	307.2
intra-LMI East Asia and Pacific	71 601 828	42.4*	14 217 317	34.3	403.6
LMI Europe and Central Asia	425 850 695		59 987 493		609.9
High income countries	257 845 029	60.5	38 660 265	64.4	567.0
Low and middle income countries	168 005 666	39.5	21 327 228	35.6	687.8
intra-LMI Europe	97 707 170	58.2	11 972 285	56.1	716.1
LMI Latin America and Caribbean	364 127 210		150 518 686		141.9
High income countries	276 358 597	75.9	108 593 515	72.1	154.5
Low and middle income countries	87 768 613	24.1	41 925 171	27.9	109.3
intra-LMI Latin America and Caribbean	53 949 847	61.5	28 840 693	68.8	87.1
LMI Middle East and North Africa	107 762 414		67 096 714		60.6
High income countries	64 452 932	59.8	38 248 743	57.0	68.5
Low and middle income countries	43 309 482	40.2	28 847 971	43.0	50.1
intra-LMI Middle East and North Africa	6 384 158	14.7	2 104 490	7.3	203.4
LMI South Asia	85 729 273		34 199 445		150.7
High income countries	58 947 082	68.8	24 453 098	71.5	141.1
Low and middle income countries	26 782 191	31.2	9 746 347	28.5	174.8
intra-LMI South Asia	5 927 062	22.1	1 336 713	13.7	343.4
LMI Sub-Saharan Africa	76 803 799		33 087 102		132.1
High income countries	51 821 829	67.5	18 374 133	55.5	182.0
Low and middle income countries	24 981 970	32.5	14 712 969	44.5	69.8
intra-LMI Sub-Saharan Africa	11 900 094	47.6	3 302 124	22.4	260.4
LMI Total (All regions)	1 784 548 852		569 326 044		213.4
High income countries	1 264 806 337	70.9	411 286 998	72.2	207.5
Low and middle income countries	519 742 515	29.1	158 039 046	27.8	228.9

Note: LMI refers to low- and middle-income countries, as classified by the World Bank.

*Percentage of LMI trade.

Source: UN Commodity Trade Statistics Database (COMTRADE). The data are extracted from World Integrated Trade Solution (WITS), 2004.

Annex 7.A2

Non-tariff-barrier Concerns by Regions

Aggregate trends hide important differences across regions or groups of developing countries. The following synthesis provides a more differentiated picture of barriers affecting developing countries in Asia and the Pacific, Latin America and the Caribbean, Africa and the Middle East, and south and south-east Europe.

Asia and the Pacific

Perhaps the most extensive regional literature identifying non-tariff barriers (NTBs) pertains to Asia and the Pacific region. Studies on APEC offer a comprehensive analysis of frequency and coverage ratios of NTBs for the periods 1984-93 (PECC for APEC, 1995), 1993-96 (Stephenson, 1997), and 2000 (McGuire *et al.*, 2002). Some APEC analyses are also sectoral, identifying, for instance, non-tariff measures (NTMs) in forest products (APEC, 2000). Taken as a whole, these analyses, largely based on TRAINS, show a decline in the frequency and coverage of NTBs. Since APEC includes both industrialised and developing countries, however, the literature would have to be broken down to assess developing-country concerns.

Ongoing work on identifying and eliminating NTBs in ASEAN, which is composed entirely of developing countries, indicates that the most widespread NTBs affecting intra-regional trade are customs surcharges, technical measures, product characteristic requirements, single channel for imports, state trading administration, marketing requirements and technical regulations. The most widely traded products affected by these NTBs are minerals, electrical appliances, and machinery (ASEAN Secretariat). The ASEAN Secretariat has played a central role in efforts to eliminate NTBs, such as removal of surcharges and harmonisation of standards and development of mutual recognition schemes.

Another body of literature draws heavily on case studies, the majority of which focus on NTMs in the most important export destinations for Asia-Pacific countries: the United States, the EU and Japan (Bhattacharyya, 2002, 2000; Bhattacharyya and Mukhopadhyaya, 2002). The region's main exports are labour-intensive products.[3] The NTMs applied most frequently to these products by high-income markets are import quotas under the Multi-Fibre Arrangement (MFA), contingency measures of protection (especially antidumping actions and safeguard measures), technical standards and regulations, including conformity testing requirements, and quarantine and sanitary and phytosanitary (SPS) measures (Bhattacharyya, 2002; Bhattacharyya and Mukhopadhyaya, 2002; Bhattacharyya, 1999).

---

3. Major export products of the Asia-Pacific region include textiles, clothing and footwear, and leather products; a wide range of processed and semi-processed agricultural and fish products; base metals; electrical and non-electrical equipment; and chemicals (ESCAP, 2000).

Anecdotal and other evidence from case studies (Laird, 1999; Michalopoulos, 1999; Stephenson, 1997; McGuire, 2000) appears to challenge the arguments in much of the research-based literature that the use of "core NTBs" has decreased substantially in the post-Uruguay Round trade environment. Case studies for Asia indicate that NTBs remain a significant issue for developing countries. In addition, they reflect the high incidence of non-traditional and less transparent but potentially more detrimental NTBs which are not captured in TRAINS-based analyses (ESCAP, 2000; Bhattacharyya and Mukhopadhyaya, 2002).

A synthesis of the main NTBs faced by exporters in individual Asian countries is displayed in Table 7.A2.1. These findings, resulting from work by the UN Economics and Social Commission for Asia and the Pacific (ESCAP), draw from a variety of data sources, in particular TRAINS, Trade Policy Reviews and other reports of the WTO, and various in-country official databases on foreign barriers to exports.

Table 7.A2.1. NTBs faced by exporters in Asia and the Pacific

Non-tariff barriers	Exports	Export markets
Bangladesh		
MFA quota	Ready-made garments	United States, Canada
Child labour laws	Ready-made garments	United States
Sanitary regulations	Frozen shrimp	European Union
Technical barriers to trade	Many	Many
China		
Antidumping measures	Garlic, honey, bicycles, carbon steel plates, canned mushrooms, others	United States, European Union, Mexico, others
Safeguard quotas	Footwear, porcelain, ceramic tableware, aquatic and textile products, others	European Union, Japan, Others
Technical barriers to trade	Food, porcelain products, leather goods, cigarettes, toys, textiles, garments, machinery, electric and aquatic products	United States, European Union, Japan, Others
SPS regulations	Poultry, aquatic products, goods in wooden packaging	European Union, United States
Packaging and labelling requirements	Toys, electronic goods and machinery	United States
MFA quota	Textiles	United States
India		
MFA quota	Fabrics, apparel, textile	European Union, United States
Labelling requirements	Fabrics, apparel, textile	Not specified
Technical standards	Leather goods; coffee, tea, cigars; pharmaceuticals; electrical machinery	European Union
Anti-dumping measures	Inorganic and organic chemicals, man-made staple fibres, iron and steel bar and rods	European Union
SPS	Meat, fish, dairy products, vegetables, fruit, fish, tea	United States, Japan
Restricted imports	Diamonds, jewellery	Japan
Child labour	Carpets and floor coverings	European Union
Licensing	Fish and fish products; coffee, tea, and spices; hides and skins; fruits and vegetables; wood, lumber and cork; petroleum and products	Australia, Singapore, Malaysia, European Union, China

Non-tariff barriers	Exports	Export markets
Pacific Island countries		
Labelling requirements	Meat; fish and fish products; cereals and preparations; fruit and vegetables; sugar and sugar preparations; coffee, tea, and spices; vegetable oils and fats	Japan, Australia, Malaysia
Testing, inspection, and quarantine requirements	Meat; coffee, tea, and spices; oils, seeds, nuts and kernels	Japan, Philippines, Malaysia
Prior authorisation	Fish and fish products; hides and skins; oils, seeds, nuts and kernels; wood, lumber and cork	European Union, Japan, Malaysia
Product characteristic requirements	Fish and fish products; sugar and sugar preparations; hides and skins; oils, seeds, nuts and kernels; wood, lumber and cork; vegetable oils and fats; word products	Japan
Technical standards	Cereals and preparations; miscellaneous food preparation; electrical machinery	Australia
Quotas	Fish and fish products; coffee, tea, and spices	Japan, European Union, Malaysia, Singapore
Tariff quota	Sugar and preparations; miscellaneous food preparation	United States, China
Prohibitions	Processed tuna	United States
Import ban	Process tuna	United States
Non-automatic licensing	Fruit and vegetables	European Union
Production and export subsidies	Sugar and preparations	United States, European Union
Anti-dumping duty	Sugar and preparations	New Zealand
Administrative pricing	Wood, lumber and cork; petroleum and products	China
Import inspection	Wood, lumber and cork; petroleum and products; sugar and preparations	China
Singapore		
Anti-dumping measures	Ball bearings, refrigerators, compressors, colour TVs	United States, European Union
Orderly market arrangement	Colour TVs	European Union (United Kingdom)
MFA quota	Textiles, clothing	European Union, United States, Canada, Norway, Sweden
Technical barriers to trade	Many (*e.g.* food)	Japan
Sri Lanka		
Variable charges	Coconut	Chile
Agricultural levy	Coconut	Venezuela
Authorisation	Fisheries products, gems and jewellery, rubber manufactures	Japan, European Union, Malaysia, Mexico
Import licence	Natural rubber, coconut, fisheries products, gems and jewellery, textiles and garments, rubber manufactures, non-motallic mineral products, paper products	China, Brazil, El Salvador, Indonesia, Brunei, Hungary, Tunisia, Hungary, Norway, Argentina, Morocco, Mexico, Indonesia, Malaysia
Import suspension	Tea, coconut, fisheries products, non-metallic mineral products, paper products	Algeria
Import authorisation	Natural rubber, textiles and garments, rubber manufactures, non-metallic mineral products	India, Japan
Import monitoring	Textiles and garments	United States
Global quota	Natural rubber, fisheries products, rubber manufactures, rubber manufactures, non-metallic mineral products	China, Brazil, Japan, United States
MFA quota	Textiles and garments	Unites States, Canada
Tariff quota	Textiles and garments	United States
Bilateral quota	Textiles and garments	United States
Prohibitions	Textiles and garments, rubber manufactures	Bangladesh, Oman
MFA consultation agreements	Textiles and garments, non-metallic mineral products	Canada, United States

Non-tariff barriers	Exports	Export markets
MFA export restrictions	Non-metallic mineral products	United States
Non-automatic import licensing	Tea, coconut, gems and jewellery, fisheries products, textiles and garments, rubber manufactures, leather manufactures, non-metallic mineral products, paper products	India, Hungary, India, Peru, El Salvador
Technical regulations	Natural rubber	Brazil
Product characteristic requirements	Natural rubber, coconut, fisheries products, rubber manufactures, non-metallic mineral products	Mexico, Venezuela, Japan, Argentina
Labelling requirements	Fisheries products	Japan
Marking requirements	Textiles and garments	Canada
Sanitary inspection	Fisheries products	Algeria
Anti-dumping measures	Natural rubber, coconut, fisheries products, textiles and garments, rubber manufactures, non-metallic mineral products, paper products	United States, European Union, Canada, Mexico, Australia, Turkey, Argentina
Countervailing measures	Coconut, fisheries products, textiles and garments, rubber manufactures, leather manufactures, non-metallic mineral products, paper products	Brazil, United States, Korea, Canada
Safeguard tariff rate	Leather manufactures	United States
Administrative pricing	Rubber manufactures	China
Minimum import prices	Textiles and garments, rubber manufactures	Tunisia, Morocco
Reference prices	Fisheries products	European Union
Specified points of entry	Fisheries products	Algeria
MFA export restraint	Textiles and garments	Canada
Recommendation system	Textiles and garments	Korea
Special custom formalities	Non-metallic mineral products	Argentina

Source: UN Economics and Social Commission for Asia and the Pacific (ESCAP), 2000.

Latin America and the Caribbean

The literature on barriers to trade for Latin America and Caribbean (LAC) exporters widely acknowledges that tariffs do not constitute a serious impediment to market access for LACs (IDB, 2002; Estevadeordal and Robert, 2001). In 2002, 76.9% of all LAC exports entered duty-free to their principal export market, the United States (ECLAC, 2003). Similarly, tariffs in intra-regional LAC relations have been significantly lowered or eliminated according to a common external tariff (CET) applied in various free trade agreements (FTA) and customs union agreements. The centrepiece of enhanced market access for LAC clearly lies in elimination of NTBs, as Laird (1992) argued in a paper on the importance of NTBs in hemispheric FTA negotiations.

Most authors identifying non-tariff distortions in the region have noted a sweeping eradication of quantitative restrictions and licensing systems over the years (Laird, 1992; Estevadeordal and Robert, 2001). As a result, the incidence of "core NTBs" is quite low overall. In contrast, the literature documents that LACs face more subtle forms of protection which prove difficult to identify. Analytical work on the incidence of NTBs in the region finds a high incidence of technical measures used for protective purposes but reveals that import charges, government participation in trade and customs have a very low incidence in a representative sample of countries (Argentina, Brazil, Paraguay, Uruguay, Bolivia, Colombia, Ecuador, Peru, Venezuela) (Estevadeordal and Shearer, 2002; IDB, 2002).

In trade with developed countries, the UN Economic Commission on Latin America and the Caribbean regularly publishes a report on barriers to LAC exports in the US market, the main destination of LAC exports. The most recent reports (2003, 2001) highlight three areas of particular relevance to LAC:

- Import policies (*e.g.* tariffs and other import surcharges, quantitative restrictions, import licensing, customs barriers).

- Standards, testing, labelling and certification (*e.g.* unnecessarily restrictive application of phytosanitary standards).

- Export subsidies (*e.g.* export financing on preferential terms and agricultural export subsidies that displace other foreign exports in third market countries).[4]

The EU is increasingly looked upon as a principal market for LAC exports, particularly in light of recent and prospective free trade arrangements. Recent work on LAC market access to the EU has been carried out in the framework of the Mercosur-EU dialogue, with some analysts expressing concern that the expected gains from tariff-free market access to the EU may be offset by stringent rules, in particular, SPS measures for food exports from Mercosur countries (Bureau *et al.*, 2003).

Other studies specifically address NTBs in intra-regional trade in various free trade areas and customs unions operating among LAC countries. They appear to indicate that there are important differences in the barriers that prevail in different groupings. The database of the Technical Committee on Non-tariff Restrictions and Measures[5] of Mercosur, for instance, identifies import licensing as the most prevalent NTB in intra-regional trade (Sanguinetti and Sallustro, 2000; Centurion, 2002).[6] The scenario is different for the Caribbean Community (CARICOM), for which an NTB inventory shows customs duties and other charges on imports to be significant constraints on trade liberalisation (Caribbean Export, 2001).

For the Central American Common Market (CACM), SIECA has a notifications mechanism in which countries denounce measures that are maintained by their partners against intra-regional trade which act as obstacles to free intra-regional trade. The SIECA Secretariat mediates between the countries to remove the denounced barriers. As Table 7.A2.2 shows, most of these barriers pertain to customs procedures, various fees and charges, and unjustified allegations of health risks and/or SPS procedural issues (*e.g.* lack of issuance of certification).

---

4. ECLAC's classification of trade barriers is based on the *National Trade Estimate Report on Foreign Trade Barriers* published by the US Trade Representative.

5. Comité Técnico No. 8 sobre Restricciones y Medidas no Arancelarias.

6. There is little analysis on the quantification of the cost of NTBs to intra-regional trade among developing countries. Berlinski (2001) undertakes some analysis along these lines in a study undertaken as part of a project on intra-regional restrictions developed in the framework of Red-Mercosur. Using a model based on Hufbauer and Elliot (1994), Berlinski offers some estimation of the costs of non-tariff protection for member countries of Mercosur.

Table 7.A2.2. Intra-regional NTBs in the Central American Common Market

Complainant	Respondent	Measure denounced
Costa Rica	Honduras	Customs/transit fees
El Salvador	Honduras	Fees to obtain phytosanitary permission that reach USD 9 and USD 10
El Salvador	Honduras	Various fees for issuing permits; harbour; entry/exit of vehicles; business visa
Costa Rica	Guatemala	Customs procedures producing delays and additional costs
El Salvador	Honduras	Restrictions to export chicken products on the grounds of the existence of an influenza
Guatemala	El Salvador	Prohibition of live animals, particularly pork products, alleging risk of pest
Costa Rica	Nicaragua	Prohibition on poultry products
Costa Rica	Nicaragua	Transit fee of USD 10 to transporters
Costa Rica	Nicaragua	Countervailing duties applied to milk
Guatemala	Honduras	Prohibition of potatoes alleging a health risk without scientific evidence
Nicaragua	Honduras	Difficulties in exporting milk products due to non-issuance of certificates even when companies have been re-inspected
Costa Rica	El Salvador	Customs/transit fees
Costa Rica	Honduras	Fines for not having exit permission from trailer
Costa Rica	Honduras	Various customs/transit fees which are unjustified and not provided for under regional regulations
Costa Rica	Honduras	Rejection of poultry products alleging that companies have not been certified or that permissions have expired
El Salvador	Honduras/Nicaragua	Customs fees for custody
El Salvador	Honduras	Erroneous customs classifications of fruit nectars
El Salvador	Nicaragua	Non-acceptance of customs documentation due to inclusion of logos

Source: OECD, compiled from SIECA Secretariat, 2004.

Africa and the Middle East

The literature on NTBs affecting African exports is more limited than that for Asia and Latin America. It is revealing, nevertheless, of the importance and seriousness of invisible barriers to trade, particularly those that are not generally considered as part of the "core NTBs".

A World Bank study focusing on Sub-Saharan Africa (SSA) (Amjadi et al., 1996) identifies the types of measures exports encounter most frequently in OECD markets. Based on COMTRADE records and information from the UNCTAD-World Bank SMART database, findings indicate that quantitative restrictions are the most important type of NTB facing African exports (affecting 8% of Africa exports), followed by price-raising restrictions (covering 4% of African trade). Yeats and Arnjadi (1994) maintain, however, that these measures do not have a significant cost-increasing impact. Of greater concern, the authors argue, is the fact that certain products important to countries in the region, particularly energy, are heavily NTB-ridden and were untouched by the Uruguay Round.[7] Similarly, the fact that fish products were not included in the Agreement on Agriculture affects some SSA countries. Overall, however, the research holds that the UR has had a positive effect on SSA: the NTB ratio covering SSA exports dropped from 11%

---

7. Arnjadi and Yeats show that the NTB coverage ratios applied to OECD energy imports is 7 percentage points higher than for all non-fuel products imported from Africa.

pre-UR to 2% post-UR. Gugerty and Stern (1997) suggest that core restrictions are not a major impediment to African exports.

Sandrey (2003) offers an account of NTBs affecting South African and southern African exports to principal OECD markets, namely the EU, the United States and Japan. The EU, which is the largest importer of African goods, maintains restrictions affecting textiles, agriculture and coal, which of key importance to African countries. Other barriers affecting market access to the EU are rules of origin, cumulation, environmental regulations and SPS issues (COMESA, 1999). The United States also extends tariff preferences to the region through the African Growth and Opportunity Act (AGOA), but these are perceived to be eroded by the use of anti-dumping actions, countervailing and safeguard measures, which have been compounded by recently tightened US borders resulting from national security and foreign policy measures.

Of the products of export interest to South Africa and southern Africa, precious metals and diamonds, as well as copper and aluminium exports, appear to enjoy relatively free market access; forestry products, another important export for the region, are subject to few NTBs outside North Asia. The most heavily NTB-ridden products are automobiles and auto parts, the region's main manufacturing sector. The NTBs that particularly affect trade in this sector are local content rules, import charges, additional charges (such as sales taxes, luxury taxes, statistical fees, purchase and registration fees), investment restrictions and joint venture requirements, and others (Sandrey, 2003).

Studies on NTBs in intra-regional trade in Africa underscore the importance of other kinds of barriers. Burmann (2004) finds four prominent NTBs that emerge as significant. These are, in order of importance: poor infrastructure, including telecommunications; difficulties in customs procedures; political instability; and insufficient product diversification, including dependency on raw materials. As regards infrastructure, analytical work in this area indicates that freight costs are a much more restrictive barrier to African exports than tariffs (Amjadi *et al.*, 1996).

The cataloguing of NTBs by African Development and Economic Consultants (2000) points to the following factors as obstructing intra-DC trade: lengthy and cumbersome bureaucratic clearance procedures, roadblocks erected by security officials, monopoly power granted to government-owned entities for imports or exports, SPS regulations, and quality standards set artificially high to restrict movements of goods. Clearance time through customs is particularly slow, averaging 14 days (Uganda, Kenya) and even up to 18 days (Nigeria) (Wilson and Abiola, n.d.).

An inventory of non-tariff import and export barriers in the Cross Border Initiative (CBI) is of particular importance, given that seven of the 16 CBI members are LDCs. Yet the inventory is limited and records only the categories of import quotas/bans, import licences, state monopolies, and others, with the first two dominating countries' concerns (CBI, 1998).

East and south-east Europe

While research on NTBs in east and south-east Europe is limited, work has recently been undertaken in the context of the enlargement of the EU and the implementation of the region's network of bilateral FTAs. There are widespread calls to eliminate NTBs that may undermine the implementation of 28 bilateral FTAs signed between countries of the region and the pursuit of a single liberalised market in south-eastern Europe.

For post-communist eastern European nations, Bodenstein *et al.* (2003) note an inverse relation between NTBs and capital controls, which they describe as "the two faces of economic transition". The study reports that since 1993, most of the transition countries have lowered trade barriers while increasing capital flow controls. Financial measures are therefore identified as a restrictive practice hampering trade in the region.

The Working Group on Trade Liberalisation and Facilitation under the Stability Pact commissioned a study that identifies NTBs maintained by south-eastern European countries, in both regional and global trade relations, the latter focusing on the EU as the principal export market and aspiration for future accession (Tschani and Wiedmer, 2001). The five countries investigated, including through on-site visits, are Albania, Bosnia and Herzegovina, Croatia and the Federal Republic of Yugoslavia. All are in transition to market economies but are at different stages in the process.

Across the five countries examined, the study reveals that NTBs are a source of concern in the areas of import licensing, customs valuation, functioning of customs, and TBT/SPS measures. Underlying these problems are inadequacies in national laws and provisions, lack of infrastructure and poor training of officials, among others. The study further identifies as less pervasive but important obstacles charges other than duties that have a direct effect on exports/imports by reducing their quantities, making them more expensive and discriminating from domestically produced goods.

The authors also note that the political and constitutional situation presents additional challenges in some of the region's countries. Specifically, they refer to problems in the distribution of power in trade matters (between central/federal authority and other entities) that cause confusion for exporters. There also appears to be a lack of information on trade rules between the public administration and the private sector, which accounts in part for the lack of implementation of trade rules (especially in customs controls and TBT and SPS controls). An inadequate banking system also appears as a major concern that hampers exporters in the region.

While recognising that NTBs deter trade in the region, this study and others agree that NTBs are not systematically used among countries of the region as a tool of trade policy (Tschani and Wiedmer, 2001; World Bank, 2003; European Commission and HTSPE, 2004). Only import licensing and export and import prohibitions are widely used to control trade, particularly in hazardous products (arms, drugs, dangerous wastes) (European Commission and HTSPE, 2004). Other problems derive mainly from the lack of technical capacity and resources to enforce TBT and SPS standards, and from difficulties in customs procedures and administration which result in long delays and corruption (Tschani and Wiedmer, 2001; World Bank, 2003; European Commission and HTSPE, 2004). Table 7.A2.3 summarises the main resource and infrastructure problems affecting trade in the region, which ought to be addressed in the context of eliminating NTBs.

Table 7.A2.3. Problems affecting trade in south-eastern Europe

Customs and administrative procedures
- Inconsistent and non-transparent customs classification.
- Inadequate customs staffing, training, and it equipment (including lack of it links between different national customs administrations and lack of software for data processing).
- Limited legal competences of customs offices, essentially limited to issues of origin.
- Overlapping responsibilities of different agencies at national borders.
- Excessive documentation requirements for the purpose of customs clearance.

Technical barriers to trade
- Severe shortage of accredited laboratories and of competent testing and certification institutes.
- Inability to participate in mutual recognition agreements and international agreements on metrology and conformity assessment.
- Small number of firms that have achieved internationally recognised certification.
- Failure to adapt successfully to international standards, especially EU standards.
- Unnecessary repetition of market inspections; no provision for issue or standard type approvals.

Sanitary and phytosanitary measures
- Insufficient phytosanitary and veterinary inspectors at national borders, and lack of inspection equipment.
- Inadequacy, or in some cases complete lack, of accredited state-level inspection institutions.
- Failure to adapt to EU phytosanitary and veterinary standards due to lack of resources.
- Lack of clarity over standards to be applied and degree to which other countries' standards are acceptable.
- Need to update applicable national laws on food safety and mainstream health and quality control procedures, which are sometimes split between several ministries.

Other problems that affect exports
- Financial and economic problems, such as the inadequacy of national banking systems, lack of adequate facilities and credit insurance schemes, high interest rates, degraded production facilities due to wartime destruction, and inadequacies of tax administration.
- Transport and infrastructure problems, such as inadequate road systems, lack of competition in road transport, lack of professional freight forwarding agents, inability to issue required certification, degraded inland waterway systems, and inefficient rail systems.
- Corruption, increasing transaction costs at national borders, delaying clearance of goods, undermining quality and safety standards, deterring trade by the prospect of delays or pressure to make corrupt payments.

Source: "Helping to Tackle Non-Tariff Barriers in the Western Balkans", The European Union's CARDS Programme for Western Balkans, EU, Brussels (2005).

Annex 7.A3

Categories of Non-tariff Barriers

The following is a listing of the NAMA Inventory of Non-tariff Measures (28 November 2003, TN/MA/S/5/Rev.1) and the adjustments made in the inventory categorisation for the purpose of the analysis of NTB notifications presented in Chapter 7.

NAMA Inventory of Non-tariff Measures	Adjustment made to NAMA categorisation
I. Government participation in trade and restrictive practices tolerated by government	**I. Government participation in trade**
A. Government aids, including subsidies and tax benefits	A. Government assistance, including subsidies and tax benefits
B. Countervailing duties	--
C. Government procurement	B. Government procurement
D. Restrictive practices tolerated by governments	C. Restrictive practices tolerated by governments
E. State trading, government monopoly practices, etc.	D. State trading and monopolistic practices
II. Customs and administrative entry procedures	**II. Customs and administrative procedures**
A. Anti-dumping duties	--
B. Customs valuation	A. Customs valuation
C. Customs classification	B. Customs classification
D. Consular formalities and documentation	C. Consular formalities and documentation
E. Samples	D. Samples
F. Rules of origin	E. Rules of origin
G. Customs formalities	F. Customs formalities
H. Import licensing	G. Import licensing
I. Pre-shipment inspection	H. Pre-shipment inspection
III. Technical barriers to trade	**III. Technical barriers to trade**
A. General	A. General
B. Technical regulations and standards	B. Technical regulations and standards
C. Testing and certification arrangements	C. Testing and certification arrangements
–	D. Requirements concerning marking, labelling and packaging
IV. Sanitary and phytosanitary measures	**IV. Sanitary and phytosanitary measures**
A. General	A. General
B. SPS measures including chemical residue limits, disease freedom, specified product treatment, etc.	B. SPS measures including chemical residue limits, disease freedom, specified product treatment, etc.
C. Testing, certification and other conformity assessment	C. Testing, certification and other conformity assessment

NAMA Inventory of Non-tariff Measures	Adjustment made to NAMA categorisation
IV. Specific limitations	**IV. Quantitative restrictions and similar specific limitations***
A. Quantitative restrictions	A. Quantitative restrictions
B. Embargoes and other restrictions of similar effect	B. Embargoes and other restrictions of similar effect
C. Screen-time quotas and other mixing regulations	C. Screen-time quotas and other mixing regulations
D. Exchange controls	D. Tariff quotas
E. Discrimination resulting from bilateral agreements	E. Voluntary export restraints
F. Discriminatory sourcing	F. Exchange controls
G. Export restraints	G. Export restraints
H. Measures to regulate domestic prices	H. Discrimination resulting from existing bilateral agreements
I. Tariff quotas	**V. Trade remedies**
J. Export taxes	A. Antidumping duties
K. Requirements concerning marking, labelling and packaging	B. Countervailing duties
L. Others	C. Safeguard measures
V. Charges on imports	**VI. Charges on imports**
A. Prior import deposits	A. Prior import deposits
B. Surcharges, port taxes, statistical taxes, etc.	B. Surcharges, port taxes, statistical taxes, etc.
C. Discriminatory film taxes, use taxes, etc.	C. Discriminatory film taxes, use taxes, etc.
D. Discriminatory credit restrictions	--
E. Border tax adjustments	D. Border tax adjustments
	E. Other non-tariff charges
VI. Other	**VII. Other**
A. Intellectual property issues	A. Intellectual property issues
B. Safeguard measures, emergency actions	--
C. Distribution constraints	B. Distribution constraints
D. Business practices or restrictions in the market	C. Business practices or restrictions in the market
E. Other	--
	D. Administrative price fixing
	E. Discriminatory sourcing
	F. Export taxes
	G. Not classified

*Based on typology of non-tariff barriers by Deardorff and Stern (1997).

Annex 7.A4

Analysis of Non-tariff Barriers Notified by Developing Countries, by Product Group[1]

A. Live animals and related products

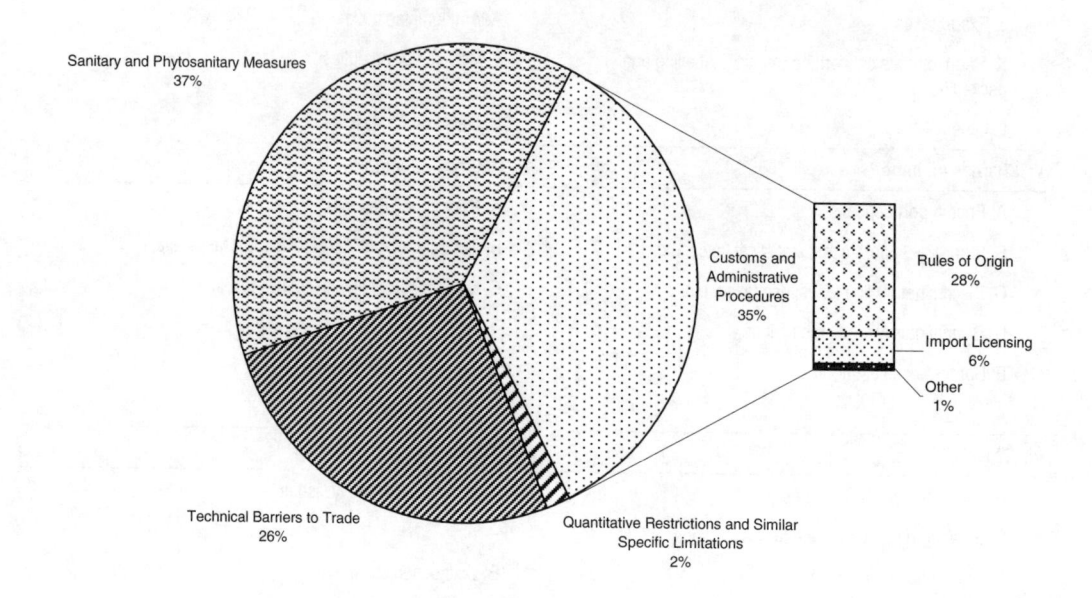

Sanitary and Phytosanitary Measures 37%

Customs and Administrative Procedures 35%
- Rules of Origin 28%
- Import Licensing 6%
- Other 1%

Technical Barriers to Trade 26%

Quantitative Restrictions and Similar Specific Limitations 2%

Data set
Number of notifications under this product group: 309 NTBs.
Developing countries represented by the notifications: Bulgaria, China, Egypt, Hong-Kong (China), Kenya, Malaysia, Pakistan, Philippines, Thailand, Senegal, Venezuela.

Breakdown of product group	
Fish and crustaceans, molluscs, and other aquatic invertebrates	98% of notifications under product group
Dairy products	1% of notifications under product group
Poultry products	1% of notifications under product group

1. In each chart, one of the NTB categories shown is further broken down into sub-categories of measures. The category selected for breakdown does not necessarily correspond to the largest NTB category, but is meant to draw attention to the high incidence of one or several measures that stand out within that NTB category.

B. Prepared foodstuffs and beverages

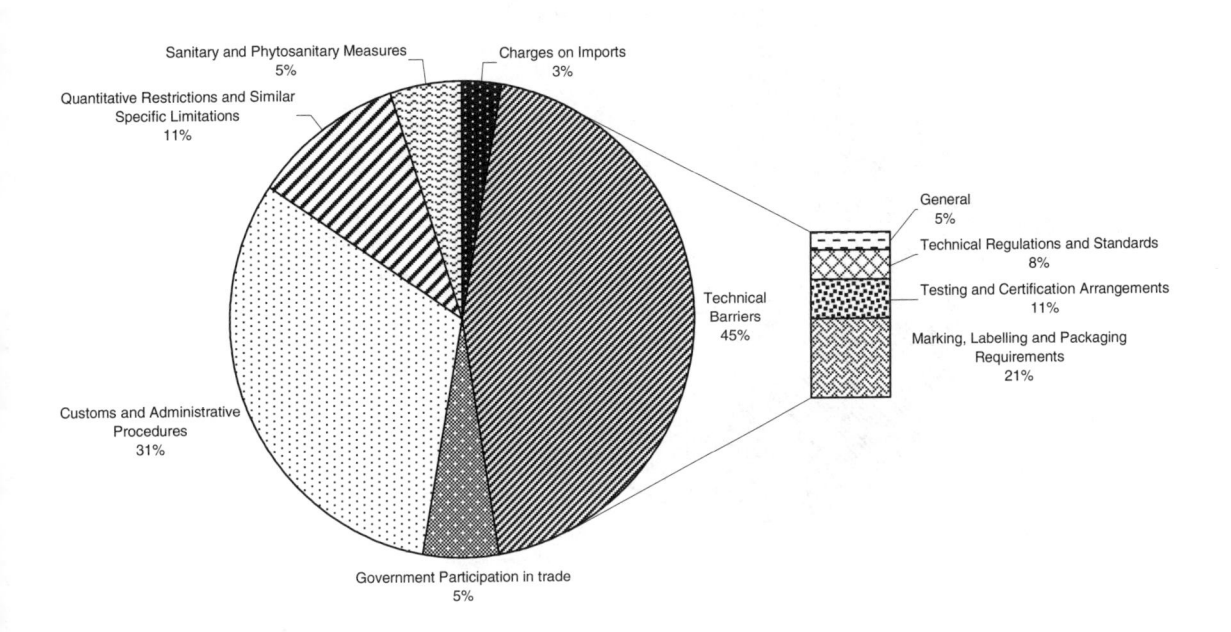

Pie chart segments:
- Sanitary and Phytosanitary Measures: 5%
- Charges on Imports: 3%
- Quantitative Restrictions and Similar Specific Limitations: 11%
- Customs and Administrative Procedures: 31%
- Government Participation in trade: 5%
- Technical Barriers: 45%

Technical Barriers breakdown:
- General: 5%
- Technical Regulations and Standards: 8%
- Testing and Certification Arrangements: 11%
- Marking, Labelling and Packaging Requirements: 21%

Data set
Number of notifications under this product group: 38 NTBs
Developing countries represented by the notifications: Bangladesh, China, Chinese Taipei, Malaysia, Philippines, Thailand Trinidad and Tobago, Uruguay, Venezuela.

Breakdown of product group	
Preparations of meat, of fish, or of crustaceans, molluscs or other aquatic invertebrates	55% of notifications under product group
Preparations of cereals, flour, starch or pastry products	14% of notifications under product group
Beverages and spirits	14% of notifications under product group
Other	17% of notifications under product group

C. Textiles and textile products

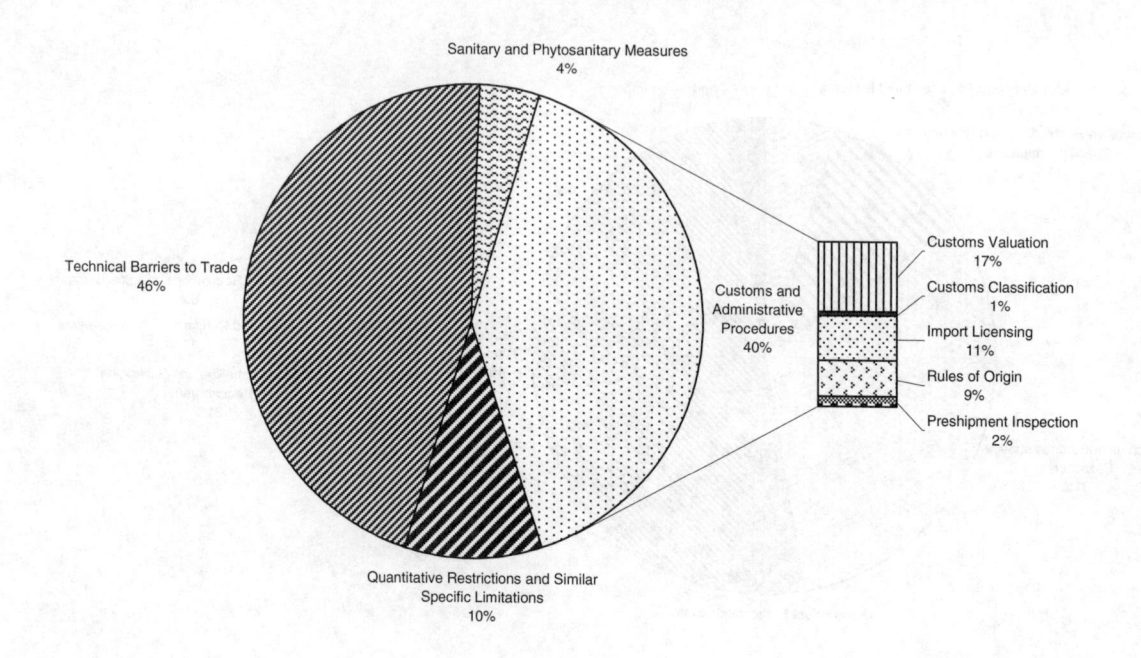

- Sanitary and Phytosanitary Measures: 4%
- Technical Barriers to Trade: 46%
- Customs and Administrative Procedures: 40%
  - Customs Valuation: 17%
  - Customs Classification: 1%
  - Import Licensing: 11%
  - Rules of Origin: 9%
  - Preshipment Inspection: 2%
- Quantitative Restrictions and Similar Specific Limitations: 10%

Data set
Number of notifications under this product group: 93 NTBs
Developing countries represented by the notifications: Argentina, China, Bangladesh, China, Egypt, Hong Kong (China), India, Macao (China), Pakistan, Philippines, Uruguay

Breakdown of product group	
Apparel and clothing accessories	29% of notifications under product group
Generic and miscellaneous	23% of notifications under product group
Other made-up textiles	13% of notifications under product group
Other vegetable and textile fabrics	11% of notifications under product group
Silk, wool and cotton	8% of notifications under product group
Woven fabrics	6% of notifications under product group
Man-made filaments	6% of notifications under product group
Carpets	4% of notifications under product group

D. Chemicals, alloys and related products

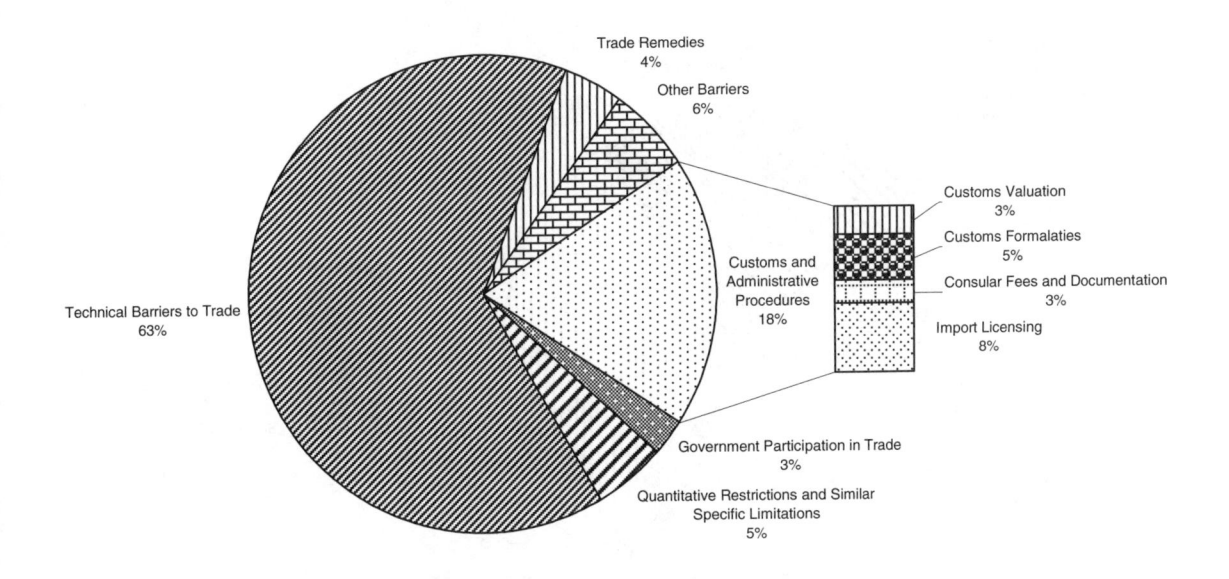

Pie chart values:
- Technical Barriers to Trade: 63%
- Trade Remedies: 4%
- Other Barriers: 6%
- Customs and Administrative Procedures: 18%
  - Customs Valuation: 3%
  - Customs Formalaties: 5%
  - Consular Fees and Documentation: 3%
  - Import Licensing: 8%
- Government Participation in Trade: 3%
- Quantitative Restrictions and Similar Specific Limitations: 5%

Data set
Number of notifications under this product group: 124 NTBs
Developing countries represented by the notifications: Argentina, Bangladesh, Bulgaria, China, Chinese Taipei, Croatia, Jordan, Malaysia, Pakistan, Philippines, Singapore, Uruguay

Breakdown of product group	
Pharmaceutical products	23% of notifications under product group
Miscellaneous chemical products	23% of notifications under product group
Perfumery, cosmetics, and toilet preparations	20% of notifications under product group
Fertilisers	11% of notifications under product group
Soap and washing preparations	7% of notifications under product group
Explosives, matches, and fireworks	6% of notifications under product group
Paints and colouring matter	1% of notifications under product group

E. Metals and metal products

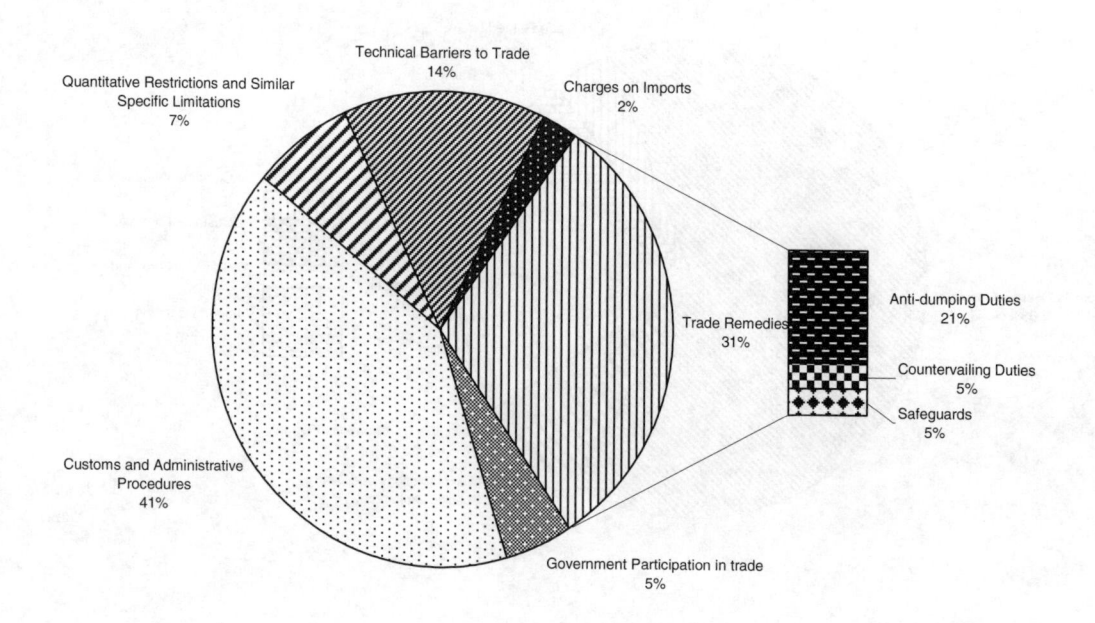

Pie chart:
- Customs and Administrative Procedures: 41%
- Trade Remedies: 31%
  - Anti-dumping Duties: 21%
  - Countervailing Duties: 5%
  - Safeguards: 5%
- Technical Barriers to Trade: 14%
- Quantitative Restrictions and Similar Specific Limitations: 7%
- Government Participation in trade: 5%
- Charges on Imports: 2%

Data set
Number of notifications under this product group: 42 NTBs
Developing countries represented by the notifications: Argentina, China, , Chinese Taipei, Croatia, Jordan, Malaysia, Philippines, Venezuela

Breakdown of product group	
Iron and steel	70% of notifications under product group
Miscellaneous articles of base metals	22% of notifications under product group
Articles of steel and iron	4% of notifications under product group
Aluminium and articles of aluminium	4% of notifications under product group

F. Machinery and electronics

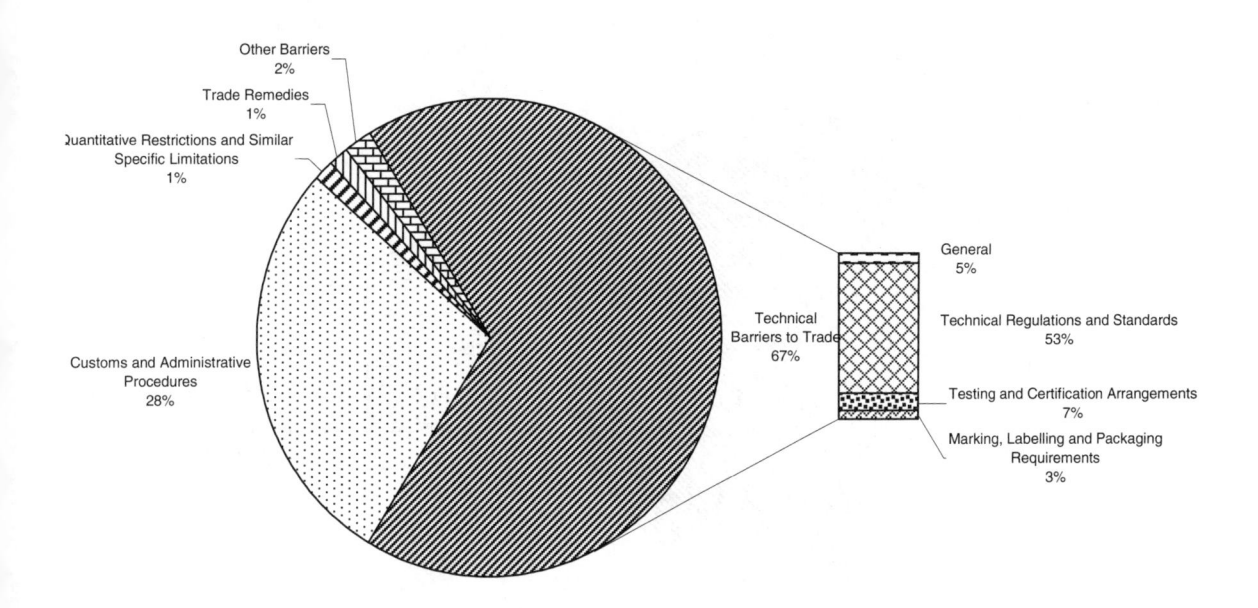

- Other Barriers 2%
- Trade Remedies 1%
- Quantitative Restrictions and Similar Specific Limitations 1%
- Customs and Administrative Procedures 28%
- Technical Barriers to Trade 67%
  - General 5%
  - Technical Regulations and Standards 53%
  - Testing and Certification Arrangements 7%
  - Marking, Labelling and Packaging Requirements 3%

Data set	
Number of notifications under this product group: 215 NTBs	
Developing countries represented by the notifications: China, Croatia, Chinese Taipei, Egypt, Kenya, Malaysia, Pakistan, Philippines, Singapore, Thailand, Trinidad & Tobago	
Breakdown of product group	
Electrical machinery and equipment and parts thereof; television image and sound reproducers, and parts and accessories of such articles	68% of notifications under product group
Nuclear reactors, boilers, machinery and mechanical appliances, and parts thereof	32% of notifications under product group

G. Vehicles, aircraft and vessels

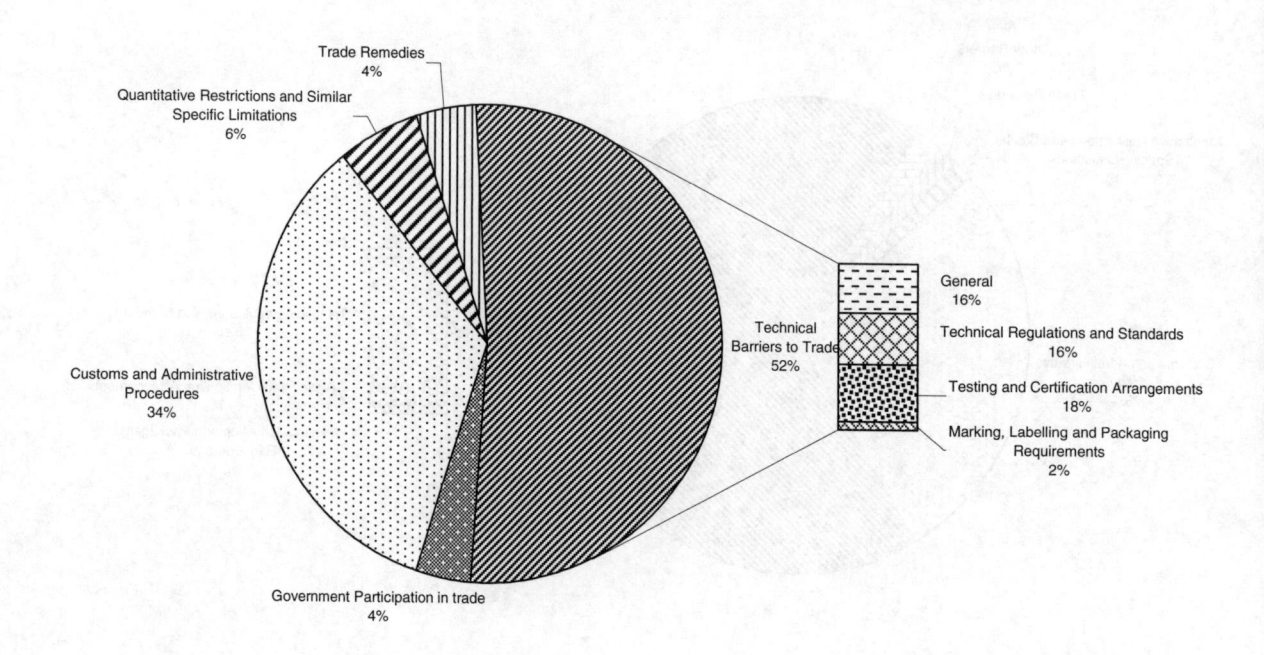

Pie chart:
- Trade Remedies: 4%
- Quantitative Restrictions and Similar Specific Limitations: 6%
- Customs and Administrative Procedures: 34%
- Government Participation in trade: 4%
- Technical Barriers to Trade: 52%
  - General: 16%
  - Technical Regulations and Standards: 16%
  - Testing and Certification Arrangements: 18%
  - Marking, Labelling and Packaging Requirements: 2%

Data set
Number of notifications under this product group: 50 NTBs
Developing countries represented by the notifications: Argentina, China, Chinese Taipei, Philippines, Venezuela

Breakdown of product group	
Vehicles and parts of vehicles	96% of notifications under product group
Ships and boats	4% of notifications under product group

H. Plastics

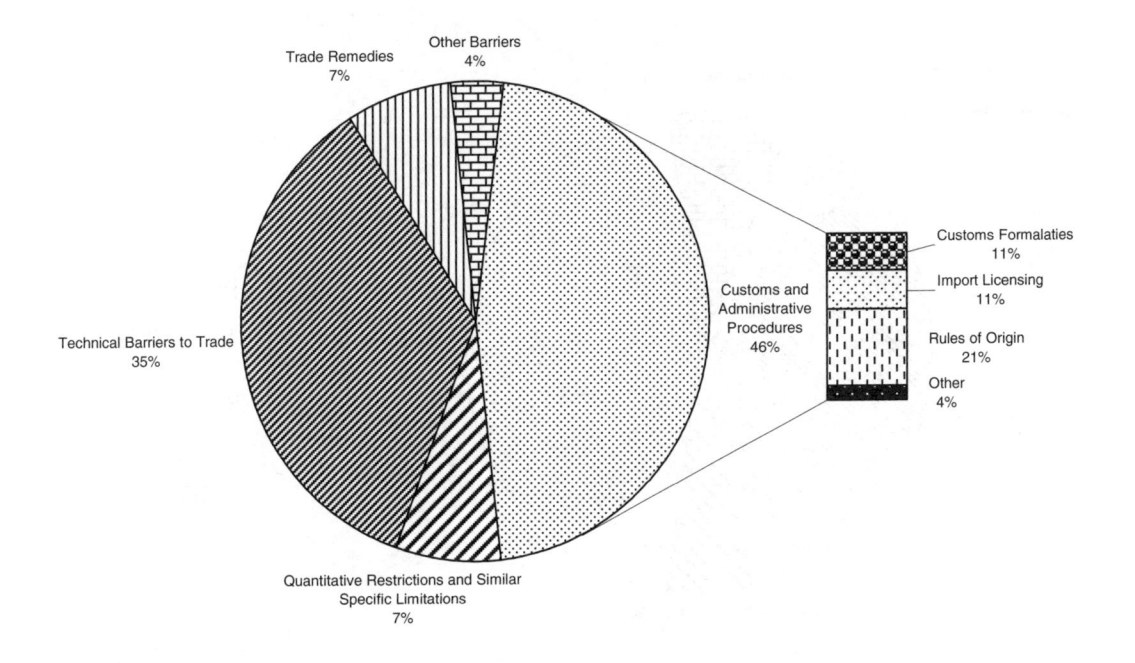

Trade Remedies 7%
Other Barriers 4%
Technical Barriers to Trade 35%
Quantitative Restrictions and Similar Specific Limitations 7%
Customs and Administrative Procedures 46%

- Customs Formalaties 11%
- Import Licensing 11%
- Rules of Origin 21%
- Other 4%

Data set
Number of notifications under this product group: 30 NTBs
Developing countries represented by the notifications: Argentina, China, Malaysia, Philippines, Singapore, Thailand
Breakdown of product group

Plastic and plastic articles	73% of notifications under product group
Rubber and rubber articles	27% of notifications under product group

I. Miscellaneous manufactures

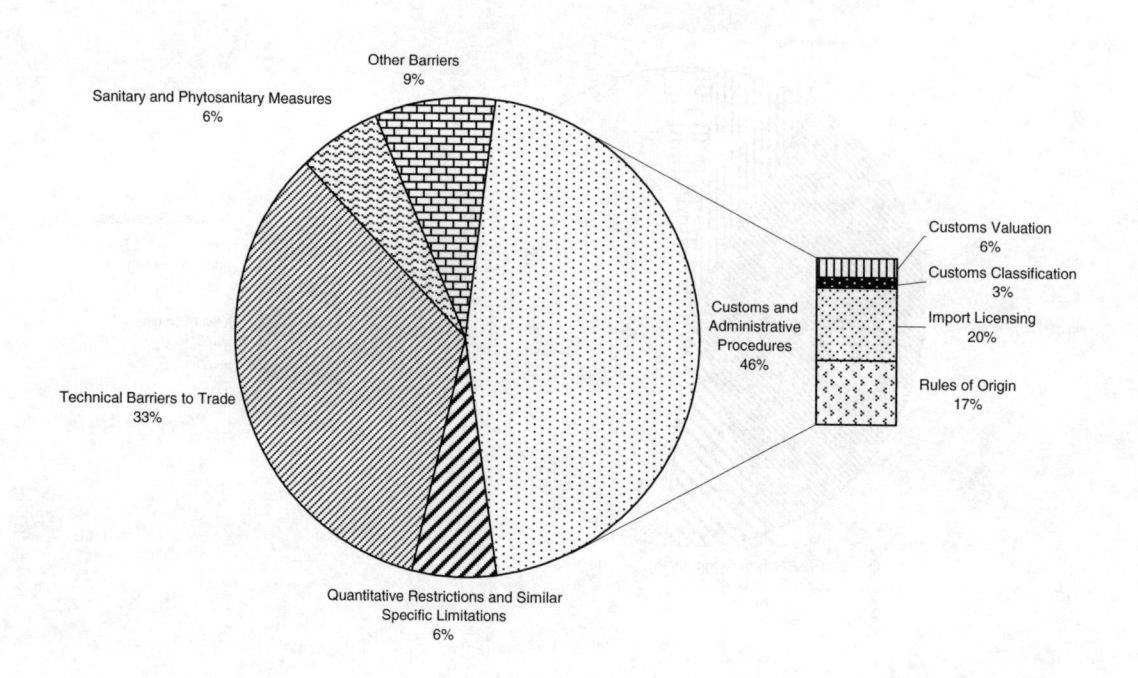

Pie chart segments:
- Other Barriers: 9%
- Sanitary and Phytosanitary Measures: 6%
- Technical Barriers to Trade: 33%
- Quantitative Restrictions and Similar Specific Limitations: 6%
- Customs and Administrative Procedures: 46%

Customs and Administrative Procedures breakdown:
- Customs Valuation: 6%
- Customs Classification: 3%
- Import Licensing: 20%
- Rules of Origin: 17%

Data set	
Number of notifications under this product group: 37 NTBs	
Developing countries represented by the notifications: Argentina, China, Chinese Taipei, Egypt, Malaysia, Philippines,	
Breakdown of product group	
Multi-product submissions	39% of notifications under product group
Furniture and parts of furniture	29% of notifications under product group
Miscellaneous	15% of notifications under product group
Works of art	10% of notifications under product group
Toys	7% of notifications under product group

Annex 7.A5

Strategic Products and Sectors of Interest to Developing Countries

Country(ies)	Export market(s)	Products/sectors
Middle East and North Africa		
Jordan[1]	United States, Algeria, Dubai and selected European, African and other markets	Cosmetics; apparel and garments; pharmaceuticals; food and beverages; information technology; tourism; health services
Saudi Arabia[2]	Developed-country markets and emerging markets in Asia and Latin America	All sectors other than petroleum sector.
Sub-Saharan Africa		
Namibia[3]	Not specified	Fish processing (horse mackerel, tuna, tooth fish etc); mineral processing (dimension stone, white fillers, other industrial minerals); horticulture (fresh fruits and vegetables incl. table grapes, dates, melons, oranges, sub-tropical fruit, asparagus); hides and skins and leather (processed hides and skins, leather garments and products); crafts (wood, textile and metal items, hand woven carpets, gemstone jewellery); cash crops (cotton and oriental tobacco growing)
Community of West African States (ECOWAS)[4]	Intra-regional (ECOWAS)	Aluminium oxide; frozen fish; woven fabrics of cotton; polymers; wood; footwear
14 African countries and 6 Asian countries[5]	Africa-Asia inter-regional trade	Aluminium; coal; nuts; frozen fish; diamonds; iron ores and ferro-alloys
Southern African Development Community (SADC)[6]	Southern African Customs Union (SACU)	Coke or semi-coke of coal; fabrics and apparel; frozen, prepared, preserved fish and crustacean
Southern African Customs Union (SACU)[7]	India	Parts and accessories of automatic data processing machinery; refined sugar, in solid form; transmission apparatus for radiotelephony; medicaments; paper (fine, wood-free, in rolls and sheet)
Southern African Customs Union (SACU)[8]	Mercado común del Sur (Mercosur)	Aircraft parts; motor vehicle parts, components, tires and wheels; fertilizers; filtering machinery; flat rolled products of iron/non-alloyed steel; medicaments; structures and parts for structures; transmission apparatus for radiotelephony; wooden furniture
Latin America and the Caribbean		
Grenada[9]	Not specified	Eco-tourism
	EU	Fish
Jamaica[10]	Not specified	Services, especially entertainment services (music); telecom and information technology; tourism
Peru[11]	Not specified	Agricultural products (such as vegetables; textiles and apparel; fishery and aquaculture; wood products; jewellery; crafts
Antigua and Barbuda[12]	Not specified	Tourism and other services

Country(ies)	Export market(s)	Products/sectors
Asia		
India[13]	Global	Engineering (incl. instruments and items of repair); textiles, gems and jewellery; chemicals and allied; agriculture and allied; leather and footwear items; electronics, electrical and engineering goods
	Latin America (43 countries)	Textiles (incl. ready-made garments, carpets and handicraft); chemical products (incl. drugs/pharmaceuticals)
	United States, EU, Japan	Electronic and electrical products; automobiles and auto components; other engineering items (incl. pumps, electrical machine parts, heating appliances, sports equipment); textiles
	Japan	Marine products (such as frozen and fresh fish, crustaceans, molluscs)
Pakistan[14]	Not specified	with a view to export diversification: fisheries; fruit, vegetables and wheat; marble and granite; engineering goods; healthcare services; poultry; IT software and services; gems and jewellery; chemicals; general services
Philippines[15]	Not specified	13 other sectors, including garments, computer software, construction services, professional services
	Europe	Handicrafts (furniture, ceramics, gifts and house wares)
Cambodia[16]	Not specified	Agriculture (rice etc) ; fisheries; handicrafts; tourism; garments.
ASEAN, selected SAARC countries and China[17]	Intra-regional trade	Digital monolithic integrated circuits; hybrid integrated circuits; fuel oils; rice; parts of electronic integrated circuits; storage units; palm oil; digital processing units
Europe and Central Asia		
Albania[18]	Markets in the region, in Eastern Europe and the EU	In the agricultural and agro-industrial sectors: medicinal plans and herbs; early and late season fruits and vegetables; preserved products such as olives, olive oil, canned tomatoes; tobacco and cigarettes; fresh and processed fish; cheese; meat and meat products; wine; alcoholic beverages, honey and leather.
		Further sectors: garments and footwear; wood products; tourism and sectors such as chromium, gas production, telecommunication, power distribution.
Kyrgyz Republic[19]	WTO countries, CIS countries, ECO countries	Tourism; processing industry; hydropower; information technology; services
5 Central Asian members of the CIS (Kazakhstan, Kyrgyz Republic, Tajikistan, Turkmenistan, Uzbekistan)[20]	CIS intra-regional trade	Textiles and clothing (apparel and clothing accessories of fur skin); heavy machinery (parts of lifting, handling, loading machinery; liquid dialect transformers; parts of harvesting, and other agricultural and mowing machinery; air or gas compressors, hoods; chemicals (Portland cement); natural gas; iron and steel products (flat rolled rod etc.); petroleum oils and oils obtained from bituminous minerals; vehicles (wheeled tractors n.e.s.)

1. "The essential elements of a successful national export strategy. A country paper contributed by the Jordanian Strategy Team". ITC Executive Forum: Competitiveness through Public-Private Partnership: Successes and Lessons Learned, Montreux, September 2004.

2. Arving Gupta, Kingdom of Saudi Arabia: A vision for export promotion. 27 February 2001 (draft)

3. "Namibia – National export strategy: Scope, focus and process". ITC Executive Forum: Small States in Transition – From Vulnerability to Competitiveness, Port of Spain, Trinidad & Tobago, January , 2004.

4. ITC, Economic Community of West African States (ECOWAS): Statistical indicators for sub-regional trade potential. Working document, May 2000.

5. ITC, Africa-Asia Business Forum II. Statistical indicators for inter-regional trade and investment potential. Working document, July 2000.

6. ITC, "Market opportunities in South Africa as a result of the SADC Trade Protocol". Sub-regional trade expansion in Southern Africa. Working document, Projects No. RAF/61/71 and INT/W2/04, January 2001.

7. ITC, Southern African Customs Union-India: Identifying export potential and study of the automotive assembly and components industry. Working document, Project SAF/47/70, 30 November 2001.

8. ITC, Statistical indicators for identifying export potential between SACU and Mercosur. Working document. Project SAF/47/70 – INT/W2/04, 31 July 2001.

9. Most gracious speech to both Houses of Parliament by His Excellency The Governor-General on Friday, the ninth of January, 2004.

10. "Jamaica's approach to the development of non-tourism services exports". ITC, Executive Forum: Small States in Transition – From Vulnerability to Competitiveness, Port of Spain, Trinidad & Tobago, January 2004.

11. "The National strategic export plan. A country paper contributed by the Peruvian Strategy Team". ITC Executive Forum: Competitiveness through Public-Private Partnership: Successes and Lessons Learned, Montreux, September 2004.

12. Tripartite Committee (ECLAC, IDB, OAS), "National strategy to strengthen trade-related capacity. Antigua and Barbuda". Free Trade Area of the Americas. Hemispheric Cooperation Programme, October 8, 2003 (FTAA.sme/inf/158/Rev.1, May 27, 2004)

13. "Medium term export strategy 2002-2007". Ministry of Commerce and Industry, Government of India, New Delhi, January 2002 (http://commerce.nic.in/medium_term/cover.htm)

14. "Pakistan Export Strategy", Export Promotion Bureau (EPB) Pakistan, Karachi, Pakistan, (www.epb.gov.pk/epb/jsp/export_vision.jsp)

15. Rodolfo P. Ang and Jesse C. Teo, Philippine export promotion policies and their responsiveness to European market conditions. A case study of Philippine handicraft exports to Belgium and Germany. ASEAN Business Case Studies No. 3, Centre for ASEAN Studies and Centre for International Management and Development Antwerp, September 1995

16. "A Trade perspective. A country paper contributed by the Cambodian Strategy Team". ITC, Executive Forum: Competitiveness through Public-Private Partnership: Successes and Lessons Learned, Montreux, September 2004.

17. ITC, Statistical indicators for identifying trade potential in ASEAN, selected SAARC countries and China. Working Document Project INT/W2/04, South-South Trade Promotion Programme, March 2001.

18. Margret Will & Dr. Antila Tanku, Promoting exports from Albania. Recommendation for an Albanian export promotion strategy. GTZ Office Tirana, 2002.

19. "The essential elements of a successful national export strategy. A country paper contributed by the Kyrgyz Strategy Team". ITC Executive Forum: Competitiveness through Public-Private Partnership: Successes and Lessons Learned, Montreux, September 2004.

20. ITC, Identifying export potential among selected Central Asian CIS member countries. Working Document Project No. INT/W2/04, South-South Trade Promotion Unit. Division of Technical Cooperation Coordination, May 2002.

Annex 7.A6

Trends in NTB Cases Filed by Developing Countries

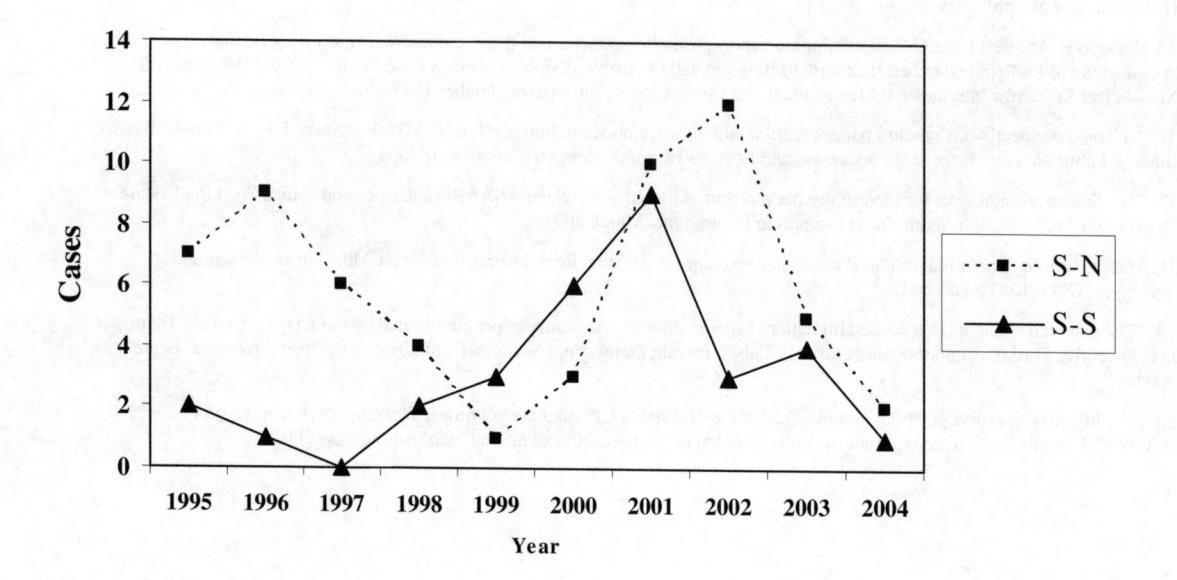

S-N: South North dispute settlement cases. S-S: South-South dispute settlement cases.

Source: OECD, compiled from records of WTO Dispute Settlement Understanding, as of 31 October 2004.

Annex 7.A7
Private sector perceptions on NTBs faced by developing countries:
A. Highlights from existing business surveys: concerns about NTBs in principal OECD and global markets

Survey	India (2004 and 2001 combined)					India (2004)
Export market	United States	EU	Japan	Australia	Mexico	Turkey	Global (mainly United States, Japan, EU)
Data set	Unspecified number of Indian firms exporting a wide range of products						10 pharmaceutical firms
	Tariff quotas	Non-harmonisation of standards	Authorisation requirements	Holding up of samples for SPS	Certification	Quantitative restrictions	Company and product registration
	Customs clearance	Labelling rules and regulations	Import quotas	Quarantine and inspection process	Strict customs laws	Import licences	Product registration
	Excessive fees for customs & harbour	Stringent SPS measures	Quarantine procedures	Pesticide residues	Customs fees	Anti-dumping duties	WHO-GMP certification
	Import prohibitions	Pesticide residues measures	Administrative procedures	Prohibitions	Rules of origin		Packaging and labelling
	Embargo	Health and hygiene conditions	Standards and specifications	SPS standards	Standards/ technical requirements		Import bans
	Strict certification	Testing and certification	Labelling	Import restrictions	Testing procedures		Anti-dumping duties
	Labelling requirements	Restrictions on market access	Strict certification	Health inspection			Discriminatory bilateral agreements
	Strict SPS requirements	Bans on certain imports	Food sanitation law	Non refund of VAT			Pre-shipment inspection
	Differences in state rules & regulations	Subsidies	Large Scale Retail Store Law				Environmental issues
	Extraterritorial application of law		Standards				

B. Highlights from existing business surveys: concerns about NTBs in principal OECD and global markets

Survey	Balkans (2004)	China (2001)		Chile (2000)	Argentina (1999)	
Export market	EU	Japan	Korea	EU, United States, Asia, Latin America	NAFTA	EU
Data set	2 166 Western Balkan companies	115 Chinese firms (of 2 500 approached)		220 firms (goods & services)	224 Argentine firms (out of 2 391 approached)	
	Technical standards and certification	Lack of information (3.47 out of 5.0)	Lack of information (3.45 out of 5.0)	Import policies (34% of firms)	SPS measures	SPS measures
	Quality control and consumer protection	Protectionism (3.38)	Absence of policy (3.42)	Technical measures (30%)	Import policies	Import policies
	Customs procedures	Absence of policy (3.17)	Cultural differences (3.37)	Restrictions on services (8%)	Technical measures	Environmental measures
	Access to final end-users	Language differences (3.08)	Protectionism (3.32)	Subsidies (6%)	Environmental measures	Technical measures
	Bureaucratic company registration	Complex customs & administration (3.05)	SPS measures (3.30)	Trade remedies (6%)	Discriminatory public policies	
		SPS measures (3.05)	Differences in business custom (3.24)	Additional charges (4%)		
		Complex government structure (3.03)	Language differences (3.18)	Intellectual property rights (4%)		
		Restrictions and quotas (3.03)	Restrictions and quotas (3.16)			
		Technical barriers to trade (3.03)	Technical barriers to trade (3.09)			
		Slow administrative measures (2.97)	Unfairness and corruption (3.05)			
		Differences in business custom (2.89)	Complex government structure (2.94)			
		Exclusive culture (2.88)	Licences (2.85)			
		Cultural difference (2.82)	Complex customs & administration (2.83)			

C. Highlights from business surveys: concerns about NTBs in trade among developing countries in Asia and the Pacific

Survey	India (2004)	Vietnam (1999)	Thailand (2001)	ASEAN (unspecified date)
Export market	Africa, Asia, Latin America, Baltic countries	ASEAN countries	Asia and Pacific	ASEAN countries
Data set	Unspecified number of firms	31 Vietnamese enterprises	Unspecified number of SMEs	331 companies (of 2 000 approached)
	Legalisation of documents	Customs surcharges ("stronger" since 1996)	Increased competition from other APEC nations (9.3 out of 10)	Monopolistic practices
	Registration of imports	Special consumption tax, internal taxes (stronger)	Lack of advanced technological production processes (9.0)	Trade documentation and customs procedures
	Government monopoly	Restrictive foreign exchange (stronger)	Lack of investment (8.0)	Other levies and charges
	Packaging and labelling requirements	Foreign exchange surrender requirement (stronger)	International trade regulations (7.7)	Import restrictions
	Certification and testing (delays, discrimination)	Quotas and prohibitions (stronger)	Little knowledge of foreign market characteristics (7.5)	Import licensing/permits
	Customs delays and fees	Special customs formalities (stronger)	Difficulty of obtaining government support (6.6)	Standards and other technical requirements
	Inspection	Minimum price lists ('much the same' since 1996)	Lack of financial resources to market products overseas (6.5)	Customs classification and valuation
	Import restrictions	Trade licensing ("weaker" since 1996)	Language barrier (5.6)	
	Heavy fines	Monopolistic measures (weaker)	Ineffective/unclear government export promotion policy (6.3)	
	Health rules	Lack of clarity and frequent changes of trade policy	Complicated export and shipping documentation (5.4)	
	Regional trading agreements		Improper packaging (5.2)	

D. Highlights from existing business surveys: concerns about NTBs in trade among developing countries in South America

Survey	Mercosur (2001-2000)		ALADI (2001)	Argentina (2002)
Export market	Mercosur countries	Mercosur countries	ALADI countries	Brazil
Data set	82 Argentine firms (of 174 firms approached)	412 Brazilian firms (of 4 683 firms approached)	33 Uruguayan firms (of 52 firms approached)	30 SMEs (of 220 approached)	1 firm exporting rice/milk products
	Quantity control measures	Freight and insurance cost (49% of firms)	Transport costs (esp. rail transport)	Product standards: lack of information (17 notifications)	Import licences
	Differences in internal taxes	Customs clearance fees and charges (48%)	Customs fees	Customs and bureaucratic procedures (12)	Product requirements
	Product registration problems	Labelling requirements (48%)	Pre-shipment inspection	Finance and payment mechanisms (11)	Labelling requirements
	SPS requirements not commonly applied	Excessive customs procedures (35%)	Labelling requirements	Non-tariff barriers – not specified (9)	Pre-shipment inspection
	Collection of payments/cashing problems	Pre-shipment inspection (32%)	Import licensing	Competition in costs and production (9)	Customs procedures
	Price control measures	Inspection and testing requirements (31%)	Customs procedures	Transportation: costs, frequency, insecurity (9)	Public procurement
	Financing restrictions	Import licensing (23%)	Product and company registration	Lack of information-regulations and regional agreements (7)	Administrative barriers
	Customs delays	Product registration (21%)	Rules of origin	SPS and heterogeneous technical measures (5)	Technical regulations
	Labelling requirements	Technical certification (19%)	Internal taxes	Asymmetrical physical and technological infrastructure (5)	Rules of origin
	Monopolistic measures	Indirect taxes (17%)		Political and economic instability (1)	Anti-dumping investigations
	Inspection	Exporters' registration requirements 916%)		Product standards: lack of information (17)	
	Rules of origin	Transportation regulations (15%)		Customs and bureaucratic procedures (12)	

E. Highlights from business surveys: concerns about NTBs in trade among developing countries in Central America and the Caribbean

Survey	Central America (1999)	Andean Community (2000)	Association of Caribbean States (2003)	CARICOM (2002)
Export market	Countries of the Central American Common Market	6 member states of the Andean Community (AC)	70% to the Caribbean, Central America, Colombia, Venezuela	Caribbean Community countries
Data set	45 Guatemalan industrial firms	118 AC firms	22 ACS firms (of 518 firms approached)	Broad consultation of private sector and other actors
	Customs problems	Not specified (29% of respondents)	Limited knowledge of market (59% rated as poor/very poor)	Para-tariff measures (customs charges, internal taxes, others)
	Theft	Administrative barriers (18%)	Quality and cost of local transportation (45%)	Price control measures (administrative price fixing)
	Legal differences and other requirements	Technical regulations (16%)	Cost of international maritime transport (41%)	Finance measures
	Limitations to licences	Customs procedures (11%)	Damage to goods during removal from storage (36%)	Import licensing measures (automatic and non-automatic)
	Local problems in other countries (such as strikes)	Application of AC's regulations (7%)	Frequency of vessels (32%)	Quantity control measures (quotas and prohibitions)
	Conditions of the road	Differences in tax systems (5%)	Cost of international air transport (32%)	Monopolistic measures (single channel for imports)
	Requirement for special bills of import by some countries	Financial restrictions (5%)	Brokerage costs (32%)	Technical measures
	Unexpected changes in customer demand – low demand	Regulations of transport of goods (5%)	Documentation requirements (28%)	Countervailing duties
	Lack of professionalism by transport companies	Government restrictions for public procurement (5%)	Cost of international land transport (28%)	
	Excessive formalities		Mobilisation of international land transport (28%)	
	Competition from other countries		Sanitary requirements (23%)	

F. Highlights from business surveys: concerns about NTBs in trade among developing countries in Africa and the Middle East

Survey	SADC (2003)	COMESA (1999)	Morocco (2001)	MENA (2000)
Export market	SADC countries	COMESA countries	Members of the Organization on the Islamic Conference	9 markets in the Middle East and North Africa (MENA)
Data set	238 South African firms (of 2040 firms approached)	Studies conducted involving consultation with private sector	3 associations and 29 firms	250 firms (manufacturing and services)
	Credit risk (average percentage 75%)	Difficulties in issuing passport or visa	Administrative regulations (12 countries	Customs duties (average score = 3.0)
	Corruption (74%)	Cumbersome and bureaucratic customs clearance, i.e. centralised clearing process for licences	Customs valuation (10)	Domestic taxes (6.0)
	Bureaucracy (70%)	Non-standardisation of customs documentation	Customs clearance procedures (9)	Customs clearance (2.5)
	Labour - training & productivity (65% and 64%, respectively)	Pre-shipment inspection	Pre-shipment inspection (5)	Public sector corruption (2.4)
	Financing, administration and cost (64 and 62%, respectively)	Insecurity of transit traffic and high charges related to transit and air cargo	Subsidies and government assistance (4)	Inspection, conformity certification (2.2)
	Interest rate (63%)	Inadequate physical and communication infrastructure	Additional charges for registration of products (4)	Trans-shipment regulatory measures (2.1)
	Customs and excise (61%)	Unjustified import bans	Exchange rate problems (4)	Entry visa restrictions for business (1.8)
	Exchange rate- volatility and control (61%)	Unharmonised axle load limitations	Import licensing and prior import declaration (3)	
	Border regulations & border taxes, import quotas (60% each)	Inconsistent application of standards	SPS measures (3)	
	State intervention & socio-political instability (57% each)	Non-acceptance of certificates of origin	Conformity assessment procedures (3)	
	Export incentives (44%)	Inconsistent application of SPS requirements	Country risk (3)	
	Government procurement –domestic content requirements (44%)	Foreign exchange restrictions	Requirements for additional documentation (3)	
	Health and safety regulations (36%)	Linguistic barriers	Problems with customs procedures (3)	

G. Highlights from business surveys: concerns about NTBs in trade among developing countries in South-East Europe

Survey		European Commission Survey in South East Europe (2004)				
Export market	Western Balkan countries	Western Balkan countries	Western Balkan countries	Western Balkan countries	Western Balkan countries	Western Balkan countries
Respondent	Albania	Bosnia and Herzegovina	Bulgaria	Croatia	Macedonia	Republic of Serbia and Montenegro	UNMIK/Kosovo
	Quotas	Customs classification	Transport requirements	Import licensing	Customs procedures	Customs procedures and formalities	Determination of origin
	Conformity assessment	Testing procedures (unclear, long)	Tariff rate quotas	Customs valuation and classification	State protection of domestic production	Public procurement	Quotas and tariff rate quotas
	Import licensing	SPS requirements	Environmental tax	Customs clearance formalities	Import licensing procedures	Certificate of origin	Transit taxes
	Standards (labelling)	Rules of origin	Verifying origin of goods	Lack of coordination customs authorities	Health examination of products	Regime for transport	Import licensing
		Transit charges & licences	Testing procedures and laboratories	SPS certification	Public procurement	Transit taxes and other import charges	Customs procedures
		Import licensing	Surcharges on imports	Non-application of EU standards	Arbitrary allocation of import quotas	SPS inspections	
		Charges levied for sanitary inspection	Non-recognition of certification	Registration	Parking taxes and transit taxes	Import licensing	
		Discriminatory excise tax rates	State monopoly	Rules of origin		Export duties	
		Transport licences		Import bans		High fees for financial transactions	
		Fraudulent certification		Road tolls		Transport costs	
		Discriminatory toll rates		Restrictions on transport routes		Domestic content requirements	
				Conformity testing of trucks		State trade monopoly	
						Import prohibitions	

Note: The information collected above derives from questionnaires completed by firms in addition to broad consultation with general trade stakeholders. The table above is a synthesis of measures cited in these sources.

Bibliography

Literature review

Bora, B. and S. Laird (2002), "Quantification of Non-Tariff Measures", *Policy Issues in International Trade and Commodities,* Study Series No. 18, UNCTAD, Geneva.

Deardorff, A. (2000), "Market Access for Developing Countries", Research Seminar in International Economics, Discussion Paper No. 461, University of Michigan, Ann Arbor.

Department of Foreign Affairs and Trade of the Australian Government (2004), *South-South Trade: Winning from Liberalisation.*

Fontagné, L., F. von Kirchbach and M. Mimonu (2003), "An Assessment of Environment-related SPS and TBT", Second IDB/CEPII Conference on Economic Implications of thr Doha Development Agenda for Latin America and the Caribbean, CEPII and IDB, Washington, D.C.

Francois, J. (2001), "The Next WTO Round: North-South Stakes in New Market Access Negotiations", Center for International Economic Studies, Adelaide.

Guerrieri, P and I. Falautino (2000), "A Birds-Eye View of the Agenda: The Developing Countries and the Millennium Round", Working Paper 2010.

Hertel, T and W. Martin (1999), *Developing Country Interests in Liberalizing Manufactures Trade*, Purdue University and World Bank.

Laird, S. (1999), "Millennium Round Market Access Negotiations in Goods and Services", Paper prepared for a meeting of the International Economics Study Group, Birmingham, 14-16 September.

Laird, S. (1999b), "Patterns of Protection and Approaches to Liberalization", paper presented to CEPR Workshop on "New Issues in the World Trading System", Centre for Economic Research, London.

Laird, S. (2002), "Millennium Round Market Access Negotiations in Goods and Services" in C. Milner and R. Read (eds.) *Trade Liberalisation, Competition and the WTO*. Edward Elgar, Cheltenham.

Martin, W., "Developing Countries' Changing Participation in World Trade", *The World Bank Observer*, Vol. 28, No. 2, pp. 187-203.

Michalopoulos, C. (1999), *Trade Policy and Market Access Issues for Developing Countries: Implications for the Millennium Round,* World Bank, Washington, DC.

Miranda, J., R. Torres and M. Ruiz (1998), "The International Use of Antidumping: 1987-1997", *Journal of World Trade*, Vol. 32 No. 5 (October), pp. 5-71.

Neven, D. (2000), "Evaluating the Effects of Non-tariff Barriers: The Economic Analysis of Protection in WTO Disputes", University of Lausanne and CEPR.

OECD (2002), "Analysis of Non-Tariff Measures: The Case of Non-Automatic Import Licensing", TD/TC/WP(2002)39/FINAL, Paris.

OECD (2002), "Overview of Non-tariff Barriers: Findings from Existing Business Surveys", TD/TC/WP(2002)38/FINAL, Paris

OECD (1997), "Market Access for the Least Developed Countries: Where are the Obstacles?", OCDE/E/GD(97)174, Paris.

Otsuki, T., J. Wilson and M. Sewadeh (2001), "Saving Two in a Billion: Quantifying the Trade Effects of European Food Safety Standards on African Exports", *Food Policy 26*, The World Bank, Washington, DC.

UNCTAD (2003), *Market Access Issues in the Doha Agenda: The Trade and Development Linkage*, United Nations, New York and Geneva.

Zanardi, M. (2004), *Anti-dumping: What are the Numbers to Discuss at Doha?*, Blackwell Publishing, Oxford.

Zarrilli, S. and I. Musselli (2004), "The Sanitary and Phytosanitary Agreement, Food Safety Policies, and Product Attributes", in D. Merlinda and J. Nash (eds.) *Agriculture in the WTO: Creating a Trading System for Development*, World Bank and Oxford University Press, Washington, DC.

Region-by-region analysis

Asia Pacific

Asia-Pacific Economic Cooperation (2004), *Tariffs and Non-Tariff Measures: 2003 Collective Action Plan (CAP)*.

Association of Southeast Asian Nations (ASEAN) (undated). *Non-Tariff Barriers*.

Bhattacharyya, B. (1999), "Non-Tariff Measures on India's Exports: An Assessment", Occasional Paper No. 16, Indian Institute of Foreign Trade, New Delhi.

Bhattacharyya, B. and S.Mukhopadyaha (2002a), *Non-Tariff Measures on South Asia's Exports: An Assessment*, August 2002, South Asian Association for Regional Cooperation (SAARC).

Bhattacharyya, B. and S. Mukhopadyaha (2002b), "Barricading Trade through Non-Tariff Measures – through the Indian Eyes", in A. Dasgupta and B. Debroy (eds.), *Salvaging the WTO's Future Doha and Beyond*, Konark New Delhi.

Center for International Trade, Economics and Environment (CITEE) (1997), *Non-Tariff Barriers or Disguised Protectionism*, Briefing Paper No. 2, Jaipur, India.

Center for International Trade, Economics and Environment (CITEE) (1998), "Trade Liberalisation, Market Access and Non-Tariff Barriers", Briefing Paper No. 4, Jaipur, India.

Chaturvedi, S. and G. Nagpal (1999), *WTO and Product Related Environmental Standards: Emerging Issues and Policy Options before India*, RIS, New Delhi.

Commonwealth Secretariat (2001), "Non-Tariff Measures on India's Exports: Case Studies of Pharmaceuticals, Engineering, Leather Products, Marine Products, and Mangoes", Commonwealth Secretariat, mimeo, London.

Day, M., M. Khan and M. Oshikawa (2001), "Tariff and Non-Tariff Barriers to Trade and Economic Development in Bangladesh", *Journal of World Trade* (35) 2, pp. 253-273.

Harilal, K. and P. Beena (2003), "The WTO Agreement on Rules of Origin: Implications for South Asia", Working Paper 353, December, Center for Development Studies, India.

McGuire, G., R. Scollay and S. Stephenson (2002), "APEC and Non-Tariff Measures", draft.

Mohanty, S. K.. and T.R Manoharan, (2002), *Analysis of Environment related Non-Tariff Measures in the European Union. Implications for South Asian Exporters*, RIS-DP No. 38/2002, RIS, New Delhi, India.

Pacific Economic Cooperation Council (PEEC) (1995), "Milestones in APEC Liberalisation: A Map of Market Opening Measures by APEC Economies", PEEC Secretariat, Singapore.

Riedel, J. (1999), "Trade Policy Reform Issues in Vietnam", Report to the Ministry of Trade, Government of the Socialist Republic of Vietnam, James Riedel Associates, Washington, DC.

Stephenson, S. (1999), "Non-tariff Barriers within APEC", paper prepared for the Pacific Economic Cooperation Council (PECC) and presented on behalf of the PECC to the meeting of the APEC Market Access Group on 3 February, Wellington, New Zealand.

United Nations Economic and Social Commission for Asia and the Pacific (UNESCAP) (2000), *Non-Tariff Measures with Potentially Restrictive Market Access Implications Emerging in a Post-Uruguay Round Context*, Studies in Trade and Investment 40, United Nations, New York.

Wiig, A. (2001), "Non-tariff Barriers to Trade and Development: The Case of the Garment Industry in Bangladesh", in O. Koht (ed.), *Bangladesh Faces the Future*, University Press Limited, Dhaka.

Latin America and the Caribbean

Association of Caribbean States (ACS) (1999), *Study of Trade Obstacles of the Association of Caribbean States*, ACS Secretariat, Trinidad and Tobago.

Berlinski, J., with R. Soifer (2000), *Evaluación de Restricciones al Comercio Interno del MERCOSUR: Su Perspectiva desde Argentina, Brasil y Uruguay*. Instituto Di Tella, Buenos Aires, Argentina.

Bureau, J.C., S. Drogué and P. Ramos (2003), *Economic Implications of the Doha Development Agenda for Latin America and the Caribbean: Non-Tariff Measures.* Paper presented at Second IDB/CEPII Conference on Economic Implications of the Doha Development Agenda for Latin America and the Caribbean, Washington, DC, October.

Caribbean Export Development Agency (2002), *Inventory on Non-Tariff, Trade Restricting Measures Applied by Member States*, CARICOM Secretariat, Georgetown, Guyana.

Centurión L. A. (2002), "Restricciones no arancelarias en el MERCOSUR," Paper presented at *Foro de Politica 'Los Nuevos Desafios para la Integracion Regional."* BID-INTAL and CEI, Buenos Aires, Argentina, October.

Economic Commission for Latin America and the Caribbean (ECLAC) (2001), *Barriers to Latin American and Caribbean Exports in the U.S. Market 2000-2001*, ECLAC, Washington, DC.

Economic Commission for Latin America and the Caribbean (ECLAC) (2003), *Access of Latin American and Caribbean Exports to the U.S. Market 2002-2003*, ECLAC, Washington, DC.

Estevadeordal, A. and R. Devlin (eds.) (2001), *Las Americas sin barreras*, Inter-American Development Bank, Washington, DC.

Comisión Nacional de Comercio Exterior (CINCE) (1999) Informe de barreras a las exportaciones argentinas en el NAFTA (1999), Buenos Aires, Argentina

Comisión Nacional de Comercio Exterior (CINCE) (1999) Informe de barreras a las exportaciones argentinas en la UE, 1999, Buenos Aires, Argentina.

Inter-American Development Bank (2002*), Market Access in the Americas: An Unfinished Agenda,* IDB, Washington, DC.

Laird, S. (1992), "Non-tariff Measures in Hemispheric Free Trade Area Negotiations", IDB-ECLAC Working Papers on Trade in the Western Hemisphere, WP-TWH-18.

Scandizzo, S. (2002) *Latin American Merchandise Trade and U.S. Trade Barriers,* Andean Development Corporation (CAF), Carcas, Venezuela.

SIECA (2004), *Medidas Contrarias al Libre Comercio Intrarregional* SIECA Secretariat, Guatemala.

Africa

African Bank of Development (AFDB) (1997), "Export Barriers in CBI Countries" Cross Border Initiative Synthesis Paper, www.afdb.org/cbi.

Amjadi, A., U. Reincke and A.J. Yeats (1996), "Did External Barriers Cause the Marginalization of Sub-Saharan Africa in World Trade?", The World Bank, Washington, DC.

Arnjadi, A. and A. J. Yeats (1995), "Non-tariff Barriers Faced in Africa. What did the Uruguay Round Accomplish and What Remains to Be Done?", Policy Research Working Paper, World Bank, Washington, DC.

Burmann, Alexandra von (2004), "Regionaler Handel in Africa: Umfang und Bestimmungsgrunde", prepared on behalf of the Deutsche Welrhungerhilfe, June.

COMESA (2003), "Market Access and SPS Issues", *COMESA Newsletter*, Vol. 1, Issue 2, July.

Coulibaly S. and L. Fontagne (2003), "South-South Trade: Geography Matters", Working Paper 2004-08, CEPII, Paris.

Erzan, R. and P. Svedberg (1991), "Protection facing Exports from Sub-Saharan Africa in the EC, Japan and the US", in A. Frimpog, R. Kanbur and P. Svedberg (eds.), *Trade and Development in Sub-Saharan Africa*, Manchester University Press, Manchester.

Koerber, E. von (2003), "Overcoming Barriers to Trade and Investment in the Middle East and North Africa", Annual Conference of the Club of Rome 2003, Amman.

Otsuki, T., J. Wilson and M. Sewadeh (2001), "Saving Two in a Billion: Quantifying the Trade Effects of European Food Safety Standards on African Exports", *Food Policy 26*, The World Bank, Washington, DC.

Private Sector Foundation (n.d.), *The Impact of Non-tariff Barriers on Regional Trade: Most Prevalent NTBs in the East African Community (EAC)*, Uganda, www.psfuganda.org/about_us.php

Sandrey, R. (2003), "Non-Tariff Measures: The Bigger Picture for South and Southern Africa", TIPS Trade and Industry Monitor No. 28: *Unlocking the Benefits of Trade Policy*, Pretoria, South Africa, December.

Stern, J. and M. Gugerty (1996), "Structural Barriers to Trade in Africa", Development Discussion Paper No. 561, Harvard Institute for International Development, Cambridge, Massachusetts.

Eastern and South-eastern Europe

Bodenstein, T., T. Plumber and G. Schneider (2003), "Two Sides of Economic Openness: Non-tariff Barriers to Trade and Capital Controls in Transition Countries, 1993-2000", *Communist and Post-Communist Studies* 36, pp. 231-243.

Daly, M. and H. Kuwahara (1999), "Tariffs and Non-Tariff Barriers to Trade in Hungary. The Impact of the Uruguay Round and EU Accession", *Economics of Transition*, Vol. 7 (3), pp. 717-739.

Hanspeter, T. and L. Wiedmer (2001), "Non-Tariff Barriers to Trade in the Core Countries of the Stability Pact for South Eastern Europe", Bureau Arthur Dunkel, Geneva.

OECD (1994), *Barriers to Trade with the Economies in Transition*, OECD, Paris.

Legal analysis

Bown, C. (2004), "Developing Countries as Plaintiffs and Defendants in GATT/WTO Trade Disputes", Blackwell Publishing Ltd, Oxford.

Neven, D. (2000), "Evaluating the Effects of Non Tariff Barriers: The Economic Analysis of Protection in WTO Disputes", University of Lausanne and CEPR.

Spinanger, D. (2002), "Misinterpreted Governance: The Case of Antidumping Measures", paper prepared for the EU-LDC Network Conference, Chiang-Mai, Thailand, 8-10 December.

Zanardi, M. (2004), *Antidumping: What are the Numbers to Discuss at Doha?*, Blackwell Publishing Ltd, Oxford.

Business surveys

ALADI (2001), *Informe sobre los requerimientos de las PYMES para impulsar el comercio intraregional que podría desarrollar la ALADI*. Montevideo, Uruguay.

Andean Community Secretariat (2000), *Encuesta de opinión realizada entre los empresarions asistenetes al tercer foro empresarial andino* Andean Community Secretariat, Lima.

Association of Caribbean States (2003), "Trade Barriers at the Business Level and Business Facilitation in Member States of the Association of Caribbean States (ACS)", ACS, Trinidad & Tobago.

Association Marocain des Exportateurs (2001), "Les exportateurs marocains face aux barriers non-tarifaires dans le cadre inter-islamique", Casablanca, June.

Berlinski, J. (2002), *El efecto en el comercio y bienestar de las restricciones no arancelarias en el Mercosur: El caso de las exportaciones argentinas de arroz y productos lácteos al Brasil.*

Berlinski, J (2000), *Evaluación de Restricciones al Comercio Interno del Mercosur : Su perspectiva desde Argentina, Brasil y Uruguay.* Buenos Aires, Argentina

EUROCHAMBERS (2004), *Competitiveness of Western Balkan Countries*, Brussels.

European Commission and HTSPE Limited (2005), *Helping to Tackle Non-tariff Barriers in the Western Balkans*, The European Union's CARDS Programme for the Western Balkans.

Fisher, R. (2003), *Effects of Protectionism on Chilean Exporters: An Exploratory Survey. Paper presented at the* "APEC Capacity-Building Workshop on Quantitative Methods for Assessing Non-tariff Measures and Trade Facilitation", Bangkok, October 8-10, 2003.

Henson , H. *et al.* (2000), *Impact of Sanitary and Phytosanitary Measures on Developing Countries*, The University of Reading.

Kume, H., P. Anderson and M. Oliveira (2001), "Identificacao das barreiras ao comercio no Mercosul, A percepcao das empresas exportadoras brasileiras", , IPEA Discussion Paper No. 789, Rio de Janeiro.

McCarty, A. (1999), *Vietnam's Integration with ASEAN: Survey of Non-Tariff Measures Affecting Trade*, United Nations Development Project, Hanoi.

Ministry of Commerce and Industry (2001), *Non-tariff Barriers Faced by India and Policy Measures,* new Delhi.

Ministry of Commerce and Industry (2004), "Highlights of the Latest NTBs Study" in *India's Foreign Trade*, New Delhi.

Nixson, F and G. Wignaraja (2004), "Non-Tariff Measures, Technological Capability Building and Exports in India's Pharmaceutical Firms", United Nations University, Institute for New Technologies UNU/INTECH,

PROCOMER (2001), *Capacidad Exportadora en Costa Rica: Principales Resultados,* San José. Costa Rica

ProEra Group (2004), *Cost of Doing Business Survey: Republic of Moldova.* Chisinau, Moldova.

Roda, P. (2000), "Central America: Towards Open Regionalism or Towards an Opening without Regionalism?", Asociación de Investigaciones y Estudios Sociales, Guatemala.

Soontiens, W. (2003a) "The Relevance of Non-Tariff Barriers to Regional Trade: Experiences of South African Exporters", *Global Business Review*, 2003, Vol. 4, No. 1, pp. 1-14, Elsevier Science B.V., Amsterdam.

Soontiens, W. (2003b) "Export Management: Identifying and Clustering Non-Tariff Barriers in the Southern African Region." *Journal of International Marketing and Exporting* Vol. 8, No. 1, pp. 50-67.

Tekere, M. (1995), *Performance and Constraints to Zimbabwe's manufacturing sector in intra-COMESA trade*. Report available through COMESA's electronic Regional Integration Research Project. (www.comesa.int/finance/tekere.htm).

Other

Ang, R.P. and J.C. Teo (1995), "Philippine Export Promotion Policies and Their Responsiveness to European Market Conditions. A Case Study of Philippine Handicraft Exports to Belgium and Germany", ASEAN Business Case Studies No. 3, Centre for ASEAN Studies and Centre for International Management and Development Antwerp.

Clark, D.P. (1993), "Non-tariff Measures and Developing Country Exports", *The Journal of Developing Areas,* 27, January, pp. 163-172.

Economic and Social Commission for Asia and Pacific (ECLAC) (2000), *Non-tariff Measures with Potentially Restrictive Market Access Implications Emerging in a Post-Uruguay Round Context*, Studies in Trade and Investment No. 40, United Nations, New York.

Export Promotion Bureau Pakistan (2004), Pakistan Export Strategy, Karachi, Pakistan, (www.epb.gov.pk/epb/jsp/export_vision.jsp).

Gupta, A. (2001), "Kingdom of Saudi Arabia: A vision for export promotion", February 27, mimeo.

Hertel, T.W. and W. Martin (1999), "Would Developing Countries Gain from Inclusion of Manufactures in the WTO Negotiations?", paper for the WTO/World Bank Conference on Developing Countries' in a Millennium Round, WTO, Geneva, 20-21 September.

International Trade Centre (ITC) (2000a), "Economic Community of West African States (ECOWAS) Statistical Indicators for Subregional Trade Potential", working document, Geneva.

ITC (2000b), "Africa-Asia Business Forum II. Statistical indicators for inter-regional trade and investment potential", working document, Geneva.

ITC (2001a), "Market Opportunities in South Africa as a Result of the SADC Trade Protocol. Subregional Trade Expansion in Southern Africa", working document, Projects No. RAF/61/71 and INT/W2/04, Geneva.

ITC (2001b), "Southern African Customs Union-India: Identifying Export Potential and Study of the Automotive Assembly and Components Industry", working document, Project SAF/47/70, Geneva.

ITC (2001c), "Statistical Indicators for Identifying Export Potential between SACU and MERCOSUR", working document, Project SAF/47/70 – INT/W2/04, Geneva.

ITC (2001d), "Statistical Indicators for Identifying Trade Potential in ASEAN, Selected SAARC Countries and China", working document, Project INT/W2/04, South-South Trade Promotion Programme, Geneva.

ITC (2002), "Identifying Export Potential among Selected Central Asian CIS Member Countries", working document, Project No. INT/W2/04, South-South Trade Promotion Unit, Division of Technical Cooperation Coordination, Geneva.

ITC (2004a), "Namibia – National Export Strategy: Scope, Focus and Process. ITC Executive Forum: Small States in Transition – From Vulnerability to Competitiveness", Port of Spain, Trinidad & Tobago, January.

ITC (2004b), "Jamaica's approach to the development of non-tourism services exports", ITC Executive Forum: Small States in Transition – From Vulnerability to Competitiveness, Port of Spain, Trinidad & Tobago.

ITC (2004c), "A Trade Perspective. A Country Paper Contributed by the Cambodian Strategy Team", ITC Executive Forum: Competitiveness through Public-Private Partnership: Successes and Lessons Learned, Montreux, September.

ITC (2004d), "The Essential Elements of a Successful National Export Strategy. A Country Paper Contributed by the Kyrgyz Strategy Team", ITC Executive Forum: Competitiveness through Public-Private Partnership: Successes and Lessons Learned, Montreux, September.

ITC (2004e), "The Essential Elements of a Successful National Export Strategy. A Country Paper Contributed by the Jordanian Strategy Team", ITC Executive Forum: Competitiveness through Public-Private Partnership: Successes and Lessons Learned, Montreux, September.

ITC (2004f), "The National Strategic Export Plan. A Country Paper Contributed by the Peruvian Strategy Team", ITC Executive Forum: Competitiveness through Public-Private Partnership: Successes and Lessons Learned, Montreux September.

Ministry of Commerce and Industry, Government of India (2002), Medium-term Export Strategy 2002-2007. New Delhi, http://commerce.nic.in/medium_term/cover.htm.

Ng, Francis and Alexander Yeats (2002), "What Can Africa Expect From Its Traditional Exports?", Africa Region Working Paper Series No. 26, February, The World Bank, Washington, DC.

OECD (2001), *The Development Dimensions of Trade*. OECD, Paris.

The Governor-General His Excellency Sir Daniel Williams, GCMG, QC, Throne Speech, Delivered on the occasion of the Ceremonial State Opening of the First Session of the Seventh Parliament on 9 January 2004, Grenada.

Tripartite Committee (ECLAC, IDB, OAS) (2003), "National strategy to strengthen trade-related capacity. Antigua and Barbuda", Free Trade Area of the Americas, Hemispheric Cooperation Programme, 8 October (FTAA.sme/inf/158/Rev.1, 27 May 2004).

UNCTAD (2003), *Back to Basics: Market Access Issues in the Doha Agenda*, United Nations, New York.

Will, M. and A. Tanku (2002), "Promoting Exports from Albania. Recommendation for an Albanian Export Promotion Strategy", GTZ Office, Tirana.

WTO, Sub-Committee on Least-Developed Countries (1998), "Market Access for Exports of Goods and Services of the Least-Developed Countries: Barriers and Constraints", WT/COMTD/LDC/W/11/Rev1, 14 December, WTO, Geneva.

OECD PUBLICATIONS, 2, rue André-Pascal, 75775 PARIS CEDEX 16
PRINTED IN FRANCE
(22 2006 01 1 P) ISBN 92-64-01460-8– No. 54493 2005